MW00527932

Currency Trading

4th Edition

by Paul Mladjenovic, Kathleen Brooks, and Brian Dolan

for
dummies®
A Wiley Brand

Currency Trading For Dummies®, 4th Edition

Published by: **John Wiley & Sons, Inc.**, 111 River Street, Hoboken, NJ 07030-5774, www.wiley.com

Copyright © 2022 by John Wiley & Sons, Inc., Hoboken, New Jersey

Published simultaneously in Canada

No part of this publication may be reproduced, stored in a retrieval system or transmitted in any form or by any means, electronic, mechanical, photocopying, recording, scanning or otherwise, except as permitted under Sections 107 or 108 of the 1976 United States Copyright Act, without the prior written permission of the Publisher. Requests to the Publisher for permission should be addressed to the Permissions Department, John Wiley & Sons, Inc., 111 River Street, Hoboken, NJ 07030, (201) 748-6011, fax (201) 748-6008, or online at http://www.wiley.com/go/permissions.

Trademarks: Wiley, For Dummies, the Dummies Man logo, Dummies.com, Making Everything Easier, and related trade dress are trademarks or registered trademarks of John Wiley & Sons, Inc., and may not be used without written permission. All other trademarks are the property of their respective owners. John Wiley & Sons, Inc., is not associated with any product or vendor mentioned in this book.

LIMIT OF LIABILITY/DISCLAIMER OF WARRANTY: WHILE THE PUBLISHER AND AUTHORS HAVE USED THEIR BEST EFFORTS IN PREPARING THIS WORK, THEY MAKE NO REPRESENTATIONS OR WARRANTIES WITH RESPECT TO THE ACCURACY OR COMPLETENESS OF THE CONTENTS OF THIS WORK AND SPECIFICALLY DISCLAIM ALL WARRANTIES, INCLUDING WITHOUT LIMITATION ANY IMPLIED WARRANTIES OF MERCHANTABILITY OR FITNESS FOR A PARTICULAR PURPOSE. NO WARRANTY MAY BE CREATED OR EXTENDED BY SALES REPRESENTATIVES, WRITTEN SALES MATERIALS OR PROMOTIONAL STATEMENTS FOR THIS WORK. THE FACT THAT AN ORGANIZATION, WEBSITE, OR PRODUCT IS REFERRED TO IN THIS WORK AS A CITATION AND/OR POTENTIAL SOURCE OF FURTHER INFORMATION DOES NOT MEAN THAT THE PUBLISHER AND AUTHORS ENDORSE THE INFORMATION OR SERVICES THE ORGANIZATION, WEBSITE, OR PRODUCT MAY PROVIDE OR RECOMMENDATIONS IT MAY MAKE. THIS WORK IS SOLD WITH THE UNDERSTANDING THAT THE PUBLISHER IS NOT ENGAGED IN RENDERING PROFESSIONAL SERVICES. THE ADVICE AND STRATEGIES CONTAINED HEREIN MAY NOT BE SUITABLE FOR YOUR SITUATION. YOU SHOULD CONSULT WITH A SPECIALIST WHERE APPROPRIATE. FURTHER, READERS SHOULD BE AWARE THAT WEBSITES LISTED IN THIS WORK MAY HAVE CHANGED OR DISAPPEARED BETWEEN WHEN THIS WORK WAS WRITTEN AND WHEN IT IS READ. NEITHER THE PUBLISHER NOR AUTHORS SHALL BE LIABLE FOR ANY LOSS OF PROFIT OR ANY OTHER COMMERCIAL DAMAGES, INCLUDING BUT NOT LIMITED TO SPECIAL, INCIDENTAL, CONSEQUENTIAL, OR OTHER DAMAGES.

For general information on our other products and services, please contact our Customer Care Department within the U.S. at 877-762-2974, outside the U.S. at 317-572-3993, or fax 317-572-4002. For technical support, please visit https://hub.wiley.com/community/support/dummies.

Wiley publishes in a variety of print and electronic formats and by print-on-demand. Some material included with standard print versions of this book may not be included in e-books or in print-on-demand. If this book refers to media such as a CD or DVD that is not included in the version you purchased, you may download this material at http://booksupport.wiley.com. For more information about Wiley products, visit www.wiley.com.

Library of Congress Control Number: 2021948878

ISBN 978-1-119-82472-5 (pbk); ISBN 978-1-119-82473-2 (ebk); ISBN 978-1-119-82474-9 (ebk)

SKY10031205_110421

Contents at a Glance

Table of Contents

Introduction

Today, millions of individual traders and investors all over the world are discovering the excitement and challenges of trading in the forex (short for "foreign exchange") market. You don't even have to be at your desk to trade — these days, you can trade on the go using a smartphone or other handheld device.

No question about it, the forex market can be one of the fastest and most volatile financial markets to trade. Money can be made or lost in a matter of seconds or minutes. At the same time, currencies can display significant trends lasting several days to weeks and even years. Most important, forex markets are always moving, providing an accessible and target-rich trading environment.

In contrast to stock markets, which are more familiar and relatively intuitive to most investors, the forex market somehow remains more elusive and seemingly complicated to newcomers.

In this book, we show you how the forex market really works, what moves it, and how you can actively trade it. We also provide you with the tools you need to develop a structured game plan for trading in the forex market without losing your shirt.

About This Book

If you're an active trader looking for alternatives to trading stocks or commodity futures, the forex market is hard to beat due to its sheer size (more than $6 trillion turnover per day at last count) and the depth of the market.

But as an individual trader, gaining access to the forex market is only the beginning. Just because you've got the keys to a Formula One race car doesn't mean you're ready to compete in a Grand Prix. First, you have to understand how the car works. Then you have to figure out some of the tactics and strategies the pros use. And *then* you have to get behind the wheel and practice, developing your skills, instincts, and tactics as you go.

To succeed in the forex market, you have to do the same. This book gives you the no-nonsense information you need, with the perspective, experience, and insight of forex market veterans. In this book, we cover the following:

- ≫ Getting a handle on the forces that drive currency movements
- ≫ Understanding forex market trading conventions and strategies
- ≫ Interpreting economic data and official statements
- ≫ Finding sources of data and market intelligence
- ≫ Gauging market psychology, sentiment, and positioning
- ≫ Identifying key traits of individual currency pairs
- ≫ Utilizing technical analysis to spot trade opportunities
- ≫ Developing a regimented and disciplined approach to trading currencies
- ≫ Focusing on risk management to minimize losses and keep more of your gains

Whether you're an experienced trader in other markets looking to expand into currencies, or a total newcomer to trading looking to start out in currencies, this book has what you need. Best of all, it's presented in the easy-to-use *For Dummies* format. Divided into easy-to-follow parts, this book can serve as both your reference and troubleshooting guide.

Note: Trading foreign currencies is a challenging and potentially profitable opportunity for educated and experienced investors. However, before deciding to participate in the forex market, you should carefully consider your investment objectives, level of experience, and risk appetite. Most important, don't invest money you can't afford to lose. The leveraged nature of forex trading means that any market movement will have an equally proportional effect on your deposited funds; this may work against you as well as for you. (To manage exposure, employ risk-reducing strategies such as stop-loss or limit orders.) Any off-exchange foreign exchange transaction involves considerable exposure to risk, including, but not limited to, leverage, creditworthiness, limited regulatory protection, and market volatility that may substantially affect the price or liquidity of a currency or currency pair. Using the internet to trade also involves its own risks, including, but not limited to, the failure of hardware, software, and internet connection.

I (coauthor Paul) certainly can't do better on guiding you through the exciting and challenging world of forex than coauthors Kathleen and Brian. Since the third edition of this book, there have been exciting changes in the currency world that I think readers should be aware of. Here is a brief list of new content in this fourth edition to help you succeed in the world of currency trading:

- >> Currency exchange-traded funds (ETFs) are a hot opportunity and a great vehicle for currency beginners.

- >> Currency futures contracts offer speculators great opportunities.

- >> Call and put options can add firepower to your currency trading pursuits.

- >> The world of cryptocurrencies has exploded on the scene in recent years and is included.

- >> You discover how to keep more of your currency trading profits with a chapter on taxes.

One last note: This book is a reference. You don't have to read it from beginning to end, in order; instead, you can use the table of contents and index to find the information you need right now. *Sidebars* (text in gray boxes) and anything marked with the Technical Stuff icon are skippable — they're interesting but not essential to your understanding of currency trading. Also, within this book, you may note that some web addresses break across two lines of text. If you're reading this book in print and you want to visit one of these web pages, simply key in the web address exactly as it's noted in the text, pretending as though the line break doesn't exist. If you're reading this as an e-book, you've got it easy — just click the web address to be taken directly to the web page.

Foolish Assumptions

Making assumptions is always a risky business, but knowing where we're coming from may help put you at ease. Obviously, not all these assumptions will apply to you, but at least we'll have it all out in the open. In writing this book, we assume the following:

- >> You've heard about currency trading, and you're looking to find out more about what's involved before you try it.

- >> You're intrigued by the international dimensions of the forex market, and you want to find out how to profit from currency movements.

- >> You're seeking to diversify your trading activities or hedge your investments.

- >> You want to discover more about technical analysis and how it can be used to improve trading results.

- >> You understand that trading currencies carries the risk of losses.

- >> You're prepared to devote the time and resources necessary to understand what's involved in currency trading.

>> You have the financial resources to pursue margin trading, meaning that you'll never risk more than you can afford to lose without affecting your lifestyle.

>> You aren't gullible enough to believe the infomercials that promise easy money by trading currencies.

>> You understand that there is a big difference between gambling and speculating.

These assumptions should serve as a healthy reality check for you before you decide to jump into currency trading actively. A lot of it is similar to being a weekend golfer and being disappointed when your play doesn't reach pro-level scores. But when you think about it, why should it? The pros are out there practicing and playing all day, every day — it's their full-time job. Most people can only hope to get in a round on the weekend or get to the driving range for a few hours a week. Keep your perspective about what's realistic for you, and you'll be in a much better position to profit from actively trading.

Icons Used in This Book

Throughout this book, you see icons in the margins, highlighting certain paragraphs. Here are the icons we use and what they mean.

TIP

Theories are fine, but anything marked with a Tip icon tells you what currency traders *really* think and respond to. These are the tricks of the trade.

REMEMBER

Paragraphs marked with the Remember icon contain the key takeaways from this book and the essence of each subject's coverage.

WARNING

Achtung, baby! The Warning icon highlights potential errors and misconceptions that can cost you money, your sanity, or both.

TECHNICAL
STUFF

You can skip anything marked by the Technical Stuff icon without missing out on the main message, but you may find the information useful for a deeper understanding of the subject.

Beyond the Book

In addition to the material in the print or e-book you're reading right now, this product also comes with some access-anywhere goodies on the web. Check out the free Cheat Sheet for tips on choosing a broker for currency trading, the fundamentals of currency rates, and more. To get this Cheat Sheet, simply go to www.dummies.com and search for "*Currency Trading For Dummies* Cheat Sheet" in the Search box.

Where to Go from Here

This book is set up so you can jump right into the topics that are of greatest interest to you. If you're an absolute newcomer to trading in general and currencies in particular, we recommend reading Parts 1 and 2 to build a foundation for the other topics. If you have more experience with trading, use the table of contents and index to find the subject you have questions about right now. This book is a reference — keep it by your computer and turn to it whenever you have a question. We wish you a successful journey in the world of currency trading.

1

Getting Started with Currency Trading

» Getting a sense of what moves currencies

» Developing trading strategies to exploit opportunities

» Implementing the trading plan

Chapter **1**

Currency Trading 101

The forex (foreign exchange) market has exploded onto the scene and is the hot new financial market. It's been around for years, but advances in electronic trading have now made it available to individual traders on a scale unimaginable just a few years ago.

We've spent our professional careers in the forex market, and we can't think of a better traders' market. In our opinion, nothing quite compares to the speed and exhilaration of the forex market or the intellectual and psychological challenges of trading in it. We've always looked at our work as essentially doing the same thing every day, but no two days are ever the same in the forex market. Not many people can say that about their day jobs, and we wouldn't trade it for the world, no pun intended.

What Is Currency Trading?

At its heart, currency trading is about speculating on the value of one currency versus another. The key words in that last sentence are *speculating* and *currency*. We think that looking at currency trading from those two angles — or two dimensions, if you allow us to get a little philosophical — is essential.

REMEMBER

On the one hand, it's speculation, pure and simple, just like buying an individual stock or any other financial security, in the hope that it will make a profitable return. On the other hand, the securities you're speculating with are the currencies of various countries. Viewed separately, that means that currency trading is about both the dynamics of market speculation, or trading, and the factors that affect the value of currencies. Put them together and you've got the largest, most dynamic, and most exciting financial market in the world.

Throughout this book, we approach currency trading from those two perspectives, looking at them separately and blending them together to give you the information you need to trade in the forex market.

Speculating as an enterprise

Speculating is all about taking on financial risk in the hope of making a profit. But it's not gambling, and it's not investing. Gambling is about playing with money even when you know the odds are stacked against you. Investing is about minimizing risk and maximizing return, usually over a long time period. Speculating, or active trading, is about taking calculated financial risks to attempt to realize a profitable return, usually over a very short time horizon.

To be a successful trader in any market requires

>> Dedication (in terms of both time and energy)

>> Resources (technological and financial)

>> Discipline (emotional and financial)

>> Decisiveness

>> Perseverance

>> Knowledge

REMEMBER

But even if you have all those traits, there's no substitute for developing a comprehensive trading plan (see Chapters 6, 10, and 11). You wouldn't open up a business enterprise without first developing a business plan (at least we hope not!). So you shouldn't expect any success in trading if you don't develop a realistic trading plan and stick to it. Think of trading as if it were your own business, and approach it as you would a business enterprise, because that's what it is.

TIP

Above all, try not to take your trading results too personally. Financial markets are prone to seemingly irrational movements on a regular basis, and the market doesn't know or care who you are and what your trade idea is.

Currencies as the trading vehicle

If you've heard anything at all about the forex market, it's probably that it's the largest financial market in the world, at least in terms of daily trading volumes. To be sure, the forex market is unique in many respects. The volumes are, indeed, huge, which means that liquidity is ever present. It also operates around the clock six days a week, giving traders access to the market almost any time they need it. (In Chapter 2, we give you a sense of the scale of the forex market and how it operates on a daily basis. In Chapter 3, we look at who the major forex players are.)

Few trading restrictions exist — no daily trading limits up or down, no restrictions on position sizes, and no requirements on selling a currency pair short. (We cover all the mechanics and conventions of currency trading in Chapter 4.)

REMEMBER

Selling a currency pair short means you're expecting the price to decline. Because of the way currencies are quoted and because currency rates move up and down all the time, going short is as common as going long.

Most of the action takes place in the major currency pairs, which pit the U.S. dollar (USD) against the currencies of the *Eurozone* (the European countries that have adopted the euro as their currency), Japan, Great Britain, and Switzerland. There are also plenty of trading opportunities in the minor pairs, which see the U.S. dollar traded against the Canadian, Australian, and New Zealand dollars. On top of that, there's cross-currency trading, which directly pits two non-USD currencies against each other, such as the Swiss franc against the Japanese yen. Altogether, there are anywhere from 15 to 20 different major currency pairs, depending on which forex brokerage you deal with. (See Chapters 5 and 7 for a look at the fundamental and market factors that affect the most widely traded currency pairs.)

Most individual traders trade currencies via the internet — on a desktop, tablet, or even smartphone — through a brokerage firm. Online currency trading is typically done on a margin basis, which allows individual traders to trade in larger amounts by leveraging the amount of margin on deposit.

One of the key features of the forex market is trading with leverage. The *leverage*, or margin trading ratios, can be very high, sometimes as much as 200:1 or greater, meaning a margin deposit of $1,000 could control a position size of $200,000. (*Note:* Margin rules can vary by country.) Trading on margin is the backdrop against which all your trading will take place. It has benefits, but it carries its own rules and requirements as well. Leverage is a two-edged sword, amplifying gains and losses equally, which makes risk management the key to any successful trading strategy.

WARNING

Before you ever start trading in any market, make sure you're only risking money that you can afford to lose, what's commonly called *risk capital.* Risk management is the key to any successful trading plan. Without a risk-aware strategy, margin trading can be an extremely short-lived endeavor. With a proper risk plan in place, you stand a much better chance of surviving losing trades and making winning ones. (We incorporate risk management throughout this book, but especially in Chapters 11 and 18.)

REMEMBER

Downturns don't affect the forex market as they do other financial markets. Selling a currency pair is normal in the forex market. This is different from other markets — for example, stock markets, where retail investors rarely sell physical stocks due to the financial risks involved. Because selling is so common in the forex market, the forex market is fairly immune to downturns. You trade one currency against another, so something is always going up, even in times of financial crisis. (We talk more about risk on and risk off and what this means for currencies in Chapter 2.)

What Affects Currency Rates?

In a word, information is what affects currency rates. Information is what drives every financial market, but the forex market has its own unique roster of information inputs. Many different cross-currents are at play in the currency market at any given moment. After all, the forex market is setting the value of one currency relative to another, so at the minimum, you're looking at the themes affecting two major international economies. Add in half a dozen or more other national economies, and you've got a serious amount of information flowing through the market.

Fundamentals drive the currency market

Fundamentals are the broad grouping of news and information that reflects the macroeconomic and political fortunes of the countries whose currencies are traded. (We look at those inputs in depth in Chapters 7, 8, and 9.) Most of the time, when you hear people talking about the fundamentals of a currency, they're referring to the economic fundamentals. Economic fundamentals are based on

>> Economic data reports

>> Interest rate levels

>> Monetary policy

>> International trade flows

>> International investment flows

There are also political and geopolitical fundamentals (see Chapter 7). An essential element of any currency's value is the faith or confidence that the market places in the value of the currency. If political events, such as an election, a war, or a scandal, are seen to be undermining the confidence in a nation's leadership, the value of the country's currency may be negatively affected.

REMEMBER

Gathering and interpreting all this information is just part of a currency trader's daily routine, which is one reason why we put dedication at the top of our list of successful trader attributes (see the earlier section "Speculating as an enterprise").

But sometimes it's the technicals that are driving the currency market

The term *technicals* refers to *technical analysis,* a form of market analysis most commonly involving chart analysis, trend-line analysis, and mathematical studies of price behavior, such as momentum or moving averages, to mention just a couple.

We don't know of too many currency traders who don't follow some form of technical analysis in their trading. Even the stereotypical seat-of-the-pants, trade-your-gut traders are likely to at least be aware of technical price levels identified by others. If you've been an active trader in other financial markets, chances are that you've engaged in some technical analysis or at least heard of it.

REMEMBER

If you're not aware of technical analysis but you want to trade actively, we strongly recommend that you familiarize yourself with some of its basics (see Chapter 6). Don't be scared off by the name. Technical analysis is just a tool, like an electric saw — you don't need to know the circuitry of the saw to know how to use it. But you do need to know how to use it properly to avoid injury.

Technical analysis is especially important in the forex market because of the amount of fundamental information hitting the market at any given time. Currency traders regularly apply various forms of technical analysis to define and refine their trading strategies, with many people trading based on technical indicators alone.

Or something else may be a driving force

We're not trying to be funny here. Honest. What we are trying to do is get across the idea of the many cross-currents that are at play in the forex market at any given time. Earlier in this chapter, we note that currency trading is just one form of market speculation, and that speculative trading involves an inherent market dynamic (see the section "What Is Currency Trading?" earlier in this chapter).

REMEMBER

Call it what you like — trader's instinct, market psychology, sentiment, position adjustment, or more buyers than sellers. The reality is that the forex market is made up of hundreds of thousands of different traders, each with a different view of the market and each expressing their view by buying or selling different currencies at various times and price levels.

That means that in addition to understanding the currency-specific fundamentals and familiarizing yourself with technical analysis, you also need to have an appreciation of the market dynamic (see Chapter 8). And that's where trading with a plan comes in (see the following section).

Developing a Trading Plan

If your email inbox is anything like ours, you probably get inundated with random penny-stock tips or the next great Chinese stock initial public offering (IPO). (If you're not, please send us your spam filter.)

Those are about the only times you're going to get a message telling you how to trade. The rest of the time you're going to be on your own. But isn't that what speculative trading is all about, anyway?

Don't get us wrong; we're not trying to scare you off. We're just trying to make it clear that you're the only one who knows your risk appetite and your own trading style. And very likely, you may not have even settled on a trading style yet.

Finding your trading style

Before you can develop a trading plan, settling on a trading style is essential. Different trading approaches generally call for variations on trading plans, though there are plenty of overarching trading rules that apply to all styles. (See the Appendix for more on trading strategies.)

REMEMBER

What do we mean by a *trading style?* Basically, it boils down to how you approach currency trading in terms of

>> **Trade time frame:** How long will you hold a position? Are you looking at short-term trade opportunities (day trading), trying to capture more-significant shifts in currency prices over days or weeks, or something in between?

>> **Currency pair selection:** Are you interested in trading in all the different currency pairs, or are you inclined to specialize in only one or two?

>> **Trade rationale:** Are you fundamentally or technically inclined? Are you considering creating a systematic trading model? What strategy will you follow? Are you a trend follower or a breakout trader?

>> **Risk appetite:** How much are you prepared to risk and what are your return expectations?

TIP

We don't expect you to have answers to any or all of those questions, and that's exactly the point. As you read this book, we hope you'll be thinking about what trading style you'd like to pursue. Feel free to experiment with different styles and strategies — that's what *practice accounts,* or demo accounts, are for. (See Chapter 2 for the best way to utilize practice accounts.)

At the end of the day, though, zeroing in on a trading style that you feel comfortable with and that you can pursue on a consistent basis helps. Your own individual circumstances (including work, family, free time, finances, temperament, and discipline) will be the key variables, and you're the only one who knows what they are.

Planning the trade

Whatever trading style you ultimately choose to follow, you won't get very far if you don't establish a concrete trading plan and stick to it. Trading plans are what keep small bad trades from becoming big bad trades, and they can turn small winners into bigger winners. More than anything, though, they're your road map, helping you to navigate the market after the adrenaline and emotions start pumping, no matter what the market throws your way.

REMEMBER

We're not telling you that currency trading is any easier than any other financial market speculation. But we can tell you that trading with a plan will greatly improve your chances of being successful in the forex market over time. Most important, we want to caution you that trading without a plan is a surefire recipe for disaster. You may survive a few close calls, but a day of reckoning comes for any trader without a plan — it's just what happens in markets.

The starting point of any trading plan is to identify a trading opportunity. No one is going to give you a call or shoot you an email telling you what and when to trade. You have to devote the effort and gray cells to spotting viable trading opportunities yourself.

Throughout this book, we offer our own observations on how the forex market behaves in various market conditions. We think there are plenty of kernels for spotting trade opportunities in those observations. Above all, be patient and wait for the market to show its hand, which it always does, one way or the other.

Executing the Trading Plan from Start to Finish

The start of any trade comes when you step into the market and open up a position. How you enter your position, how you execute the first step of your trading plan, can be as important as the trade opportunity itself (see Chapter 10). After all, if you never enter the position, the trade opportunity will never be exploited. And probably nothing is more frustrating as a trader than having pinpointed a trade opportunity, having it go the way you expected, but having nothing to show for it because you never put the trade on.

The effort and resources you invest in researching, monitoring, and analyzing the market come to a concrete result when you open a trade. This process is made easier by formulating a personal trading system, with trigger points and setups to help you enter the trade. Placing the trade is just the beginning.

Just because you have a trading plan doesn't mean the market is necessarily going to play ball. You need to be actively engaged in managing your position to make the most of it if it's a winner and to minimize the damage if the market isn't going in your favor.

REMEMBER

Active trade management is also critical to keeping more of what you make in a trade. In our experience, making money in the forex market is not necessarily the hard part. More often than not, keeping what you've made is the *really* hard part.

You need to stay on your toes, and keep thinking about and monitoring the market while your trade is still active. The market will always be moving, sometimes faster than at other times, and new information will still be coming into the market. In Chapter 11, we look at several different ways you can monitor the market while your trade is open, as well as how and when you should adjust your trade strategy depending on events and time.

Exiting each trade is the culmination of the entire process, and you're either going to be pleased with a profit or disappointed with a loss. Every trade ends in either a profit or a loss (unless you get out at the entry price); it's just the way the market works. While your trade is still active, however, you're still in control and you can choose to exit the trade at any time.

Even after you've exited the position, your work is not done. If you're serious about currency trading as an enterprise, you need to review your prior trade for what it tells you about your overall trading style and trade execution. Keeping a record of your trading history is how you stay focused, learn from your mistakes, and avoid lapses in discipline that could hurt you on your next trade. Only then is it time to move on to the next trading opportunity. (And don't forget the last step regarding your trades: the potential tax bite. Find out more in Chapter 12.)

TIP

By the way, there is more than one way to make a buck in the world of currencies; currency trading isn't the only game in town. For some, it's too complicated a game anyway. But fear not! I (coauthor Paul) invite you to peruse Part 4, which could open up a new world of currency opportunities. I personally like currency exchange-traded funds (ETFs) and options on them for some uncomplicated trading opportunities. Currency ETFs are in Chapter 13, while options are covered in Chapter 15. Don't forget currency futures (see Chapter 14) and the popular new kid on the block, cryptocurrencies — they are in Chapter 16.

Chapter **2**

What Is the Forex Market?

We like to think of forex as the Big Kahuna of financial markets. The foreign exchange market — most often called the *forex* market, or simply the FX market — is the largest and most liquid of all international financial markets. (See the later section "Getting liquid without getting soaked" for our discussion of liquidity.)

The forex market is the crossroads for international capital, the intersection through which global commercial and investment flows have to move. International trade flows, such as when a Swiss electronics company purchases Japanese-made components, were the original basis for the development of the forex markets.

Today, however, global financial and investment flows dominate trade as the primary nonspeculative source of forex market volume. Whether it's an Australian pension fund investing in U.S. Treasury bonds, a British insurer allocating assets to the Japanese equity market, or a German conglomerate purchasing a Canadian manufacturing facility, each cross-border transaction passes through the forex market at some stage.

The forex market is the ultimate traders' market. It's a market that's open around the clock six days a week, enabling traders to act on news and events as they happen. It's a market where half-billion-dollar trades can be executed in a matter of seconds and may not even move prices noticeably. That is what's unique about forex — try buying or selling a half-billion of anything in another market and see how prices react.

Firms such as FOREX.com, Saxo Bank, Oanda, CMC Markets, and IG Group have made the forex market accessible to individual traders and investors. You can now trade the same forex market as the big banks and hedge funds.

SOME EYE-OPENING STATS ON TRADERS

"Ninety-five perfect of all traders fail." How often have you heard that? If I (coauthor Paul) had a dollar for every time I heard that, I would've gotten back my money from my first failed trade! That is closer to the truth than you may realize, however. The folks at Tradeciety (www.tradeciety.com) posted the eye-opening results from a recent study that studied broker data about trading. Now I can't attest to the veracity of these findings, but my gut and experience tell me this rings true. Here are some of the findings:

- Eighty percent of day traders quit within two years.

- Forty percent of traders quit after one month of activity.

- Only 7 percent remain in their trading activity after five years.

- Day traders with a strong past performance tend to continue doing well into the future. But only about 1 percent of all day traders are predictably profitable after factoring in fees and commissions.

- Lower-income individuals tend to spend a greater portion of their income on lottery tickets, and they tend to increase lottery purchases as their income declines.

The study lists 24 findings, which can be found at https://tradeciety.com/24-statistics-why-most-traders-lose-money/. The big takeaway from this study is that traders (and speculators) are more apt to succeed when they approach trading as a disciplined activity coupled with ongoing education and sticking to proven and tested trading action plans. The biggest reasons cited for unsuccessful trading were that folks came in with big dreams of success but traded on emotion and guesswork. But I bet you guessed that.

Getting Inside the Numbers

Average daily currency trading volumes exceed $6.6 trillion per day (as of 2019). That's a mind-boggling number, isn't it? $6,600,000,000,000 — that's a lot of zeros, no matter how you slice it. To give you some perspective on that size, it's about 10 to 15 times the size of daily trading volume on all the world's stock markets *combined.*

That $6-trillion-a-day number, which you may have seen in the financial press or other books on currency trading, actually overstates the size of what the forex market is all about — spot currency trading.

Trading for spot

REMEMBER

Spot refers to the price at which you can buy or sell currencies *now,* as in "on the spot." If you're familiar with stock trading, the price you can trade at is essentially a spot price. The term is primarily meant to differentiate spot, or cash, trading from futures trading, or trading for some future delivery date. The spot currency market is normally traded for settlement in two business days. Unless otherwise specified, the spot price is most likely to be what you buy and sell at with your currency broker.

Speculating in the currency market

While commercial and financial transactions in the currency markets represent huge nominal sums, they still pale in comparison to amounts based on speculation. By far the vast majority of currency trading volume is based on speculation — traders buying and selling for short-term gains based on minute-to-minute, hour-to-hour, and day-to-day price fluctuations.

Estimates are that upwards of 90 percent of daily trading volume is derived from speculation (meaning commercial or investment-based FX trades account for less than 10 percent of daily global volume). The depth and breadth of the speculative market means that the liquidity of the overall forex market is unparalleled among global financial markets.

The bulk of spot currency trading, about 75 percent by volume, takes place in the so-called "major currencies," which represent the world's largest and most developed economies (see Chapter 8 for details). Trading in the major currencies is largely free from government regulation and takes place outside the authority of any national or international body or exchange.

Additionally, activity in the forex market frequently functions on a regional "currency bloc" basis, where the bulk of trading takes place between the USD bloc, JPY bloc, and EUR bloc, representing the three largest global economic regions.

Trading in the currencies of smaller, less-developed economies, such as Thailand or Chile, is often referred to as *emerging market* or *exotic* currency trading. Although trading in emerging markets has grown significantly in recent years, in terms of volume it remains some way behind the developed currencies. Due to some internal factors (such as local restrictions on currency transactions by foreigners) and some external factors (such as geopolitical crises and the financial market crash, which can make emerging market currencies tricky to trade), the emerging-market forex space can be illiquid, which can be a turnoff for a small investor.

Getting liquid without getting soaked

Liquidity refers to the level of *market interest* — the level of buying and selling volume — available at any given moment for a particular asset or security. The higher the liquidity, or the *deeper* the market, the faster and easier it is to buy or sell a security.

REMEMBER

From a trading perspective, liquidity is a critical consideration because it determines how quickly prices move between trades and over time. A highly liquid market like forex can see large trading volumes transacted with relatively minor price changes. An illiquid, or *thin,* market tends to see prices move more rapidly on relatively lower trading volumes. A market that only trades during certain hours (futures contracts, for example) also represents a less liquid, thinner market.

TIP

We refer to liquidity, liquidity considerations, and market interest throughout this book because they're among the most important factors affecting how prices move, or *price action.*

REMEMBER

It's important to understand that, although the forex market offers exceptionally high liquidity on an overall basis, liquidity levels vary throughout the trading day and across various currency pairs. For individual traders, though, variations in liquidity are more of a strategic consideration rather than a tactical issue. For example, if a large hedge fund needs to make a trade worth several hundred million dollars, it needs to be concerned about the tactical levels of liquidity, such as how much its trade is likely to move market prices depending on when the trade is executed. For individuals, who generally trade in smaller sizes, the amounts aren't an issue, but the strategic levels of liquidity are an important factor in the timing of when and how prices are likely to move.

In the next section, we examine how liquidity and market interest changes throughout the global trading day with an eye to what it means for trading in particular currency pairs. (We look at individual currency pairs in greater detail in Chapters 8 and 9.)

Around the World in a Trading Day

The forex market is open and active 24 hours a day from the start of business hours on Monday morning in the Asia-Pacific time zone straight through to the Friday close of business hours in New York. At any given moment, depending on the time zone, dozens of global financial centers — such as Sydney, Tokyo, or London — are open, and currency trading desks in those financial centers are active in the market.

In addition to the major global financial centers, many financial institutions operate 24-hour-a-day currency trading desks, providing an ever-present source of market interest.

TIP

Currency trading doesn't even stop for holidays when other financial markets, like stocks or futures exchanges, may be closed. Even though it's a holiday in Japan, for example, Sydney, Singapore, and Hong Kong may still be open. It may be the Fourth of July in the United States, but if it's a business day, Tokyo, London, Toronto, and other financial centers will still be trading currencies. About the only holiday in common around the world is New Year's Day, and even that depends on what day of the week it falls on.

The opening of the trading week

There is no officially designated starting time to the trading day or week, but for all intents the market action kicks off when Wellington, New Zealand, the first financial center west of the international dateline, opens on Monday morning local time. Depending on whether daylight saving time is in effect in your own time zone, it roughly corresponds to early Sunday afternoon in North America, Sunday evening in Europe, and very early Monday morning in Asia.

REMEMBER

The Sunday open represents the starting point where currency markets resume trading after the Friday close of trading in North America (5 p.m. eastern time [ET]). This is the first chance for the forex market to react to news and events that may have happened over the weekend. Prices may have closed New York trading at one level, but depending on the circumstances, they may start trading at different levels at the Sunday open. The risk that currency prices open at different levels on Sunday versus their close on Friday is referred to as the *weekend gap risk* or the *Sunday open gap risk.* A *gap* is a change in price levels where no prices are tradable in between.

WARNING

As a strategic trading consideration, individual traders need to be aware of the weekend gap risk and know what events are scheduled over the weekend. There's no fixed set of potential events, and there's never any way of ruling out what may transpire, such as a terror attack, a geopolitical conflict, or a natural disaster. You just need to be aware that the risk exists and factor it into your trading strategy.

Of typical scheduled weekend events, the most common are quarterly Group of Twenty (G20) meetings (see Chapter 3 for more on the G20) and national elections or referenda. Just be sure you're aware of any major events that are scheduled. During the height of the Eurozone sovereign debt crisis, a lot of last-minute bailout decisions were made over the course of a weekend, which had major implications for the markets when they opened.

On most Sunday opens, prices generally pick up where they left off on Friday afternoon. The opening price spreads in the interbank market are much wider than normal, because only Wellington and 24-hour trading desks are active at the time. Opening price spreads of 10 to 30 points in the major currency pairs are not uncommon in the initial hours of trading. When banks in Sydney, Australia, and early Asian centers enter the market over the next few hours, liquidity begins to improve and price spreads begin to narrow to more normal levels.

REMEMBER

Because of the wider price spreads in the initial hours of the Sunday open, most online trading platforms do not begin trading until 5 p.m. ET on Sundays, when sufficient liquidity enables the platforms to offer their normal price quotes. Make sure you're aware of your broker's trading policies with regard to the Sunday open, especially in terms of order executions.

Trading in the Asia-Pacific session

Currency trading volumes in the Asia-Pacific session account for about 20 percent of total daily global volume, according to the 2019 triennial BIS survey. (BIS, by the way, is the Bank for International Settlements, and the survey can be found at www. bis.org.) The principal financial trading centers are Wellington, New Zealand; Sydney, Australia; Tokyo, Japan; Hong Kong; and Singapore. (A *session* is a trading period, or trading hours, for a given global region. There are three sessions, or sets of trading periods/hours: Asia-Pacific, European, and North American.)

News and data reports from New Zealand, Australia, and Japan hit the market during this session. New Zealand and Australian data reports are typically released in the early morning local time, which corresponds to early evening hours in North America. Japanese data is typically released just before 9 a.m. Tokyo time, which equates to roughly 7 or 8 p.m. ET. Some Japanese data reports and events also take place in the Tokyo afternoon, which equates to roughly midnight to 4 a.m. ET.

The overall trading direction for the NZD, AUD, and JPY can be set for the entire session depending on what news and data reports are released and what they indicate.

In addition, news from China, such as economic data, interest rate changes, and official comments or currency policy adjustments, may also be released. Occasionally as well, late speakers from the United States, such as Federal Reserve officials speaking on the West Coast of the United States, may offer remarks on the U.S. economy or the direction of U.S. interest rates that affect the value of the U.S. dollar against other major currencies.

TIP

Because of the size of the Japanese market and the importance of Japanese data to the market, much of the action during the Asia-Pacific session is focused on the Japanese yen currency pairs, such as USD/JPY and the JPY crosses, like EUR/JPY and AUD/JPY. Of course, Japanese financial institutions are also most active during this session, so you can frequently get a sense of what the Japanese market is doing based on price movements.

For individual traders, overall liquidity in the major currency pairs is more than sufficient, with generally orderly price movements. In some less liquid, non-regional currencies, like GBP/USD or USD/CAD, price movements may be more erratic or nonexistent, depending on the environment. With no Canadian news out for the next 12 hours, for example, there may be little reason or interest to move that pair. But if a large market participant needs to make a transaction in that pair, the price movement may be larger than normal.

Trading in the European/London session

About midway through the Asian trading day, European financial centers begin to open up and the market gets into its full swing. European financial centers and London account for over 51 percent of total daily global trading volume, with London alone accounting for about one-third of total daily global volume, according to the 2019 BIS triennial survey.

TIP

The European session overlaps with half of the Asian trading day and half of the North American trading session, which means that market interest and liquidity are at their absolute peak during this session.

News and data events from the Eurozone (and individual countries like Germany and France), Switzerland, and the United Kingdom are typically released in the early-morning hours of the European session. As a result, some of the biggest moves and most active trading take place in the European currencies (EUR, GBP, and CHF, or Swiss franc) and the euro cross-currency pairs (EUR/CHF and EUR/GBP).

Asian trading centers begin to wind down in the late-morning hours of the European session, and North American financial centers come in a few hours later, around 7 a.m. ET.

Trading in the North American session

Because of the overlap between North American and European trading sessions, the trading volumes are much more significant. Some of the biggest and most meaningful directional price movements take place during this crossover period. On its own, however, the North American trading session accounts for roughly 28 percent of global trading volume.

The North American morning is when key U.S. economic data is released and the forex market makes many of its most significant decisions on the value of the U.S. dollar. Most U.S. data reports are released at 8:30 a.m. ET, with others coming out later (between 9 and 10 a.m. ET). Canadian data reports are also released in the morning, usually between 7 and 9 a.m. ET. There are also a few U.S. economic reports that variously come out at noon or 2 p.m. ET, livening up the New York afternoon market. (See Chapter 9 for more details on individual economic data reports.)

London and the European financial centers begin to wind down their daily trading operations around noon ET each day. The London or European close, as it's known, can frequently generate volatile flurries of activity. A directional move that occurred earlier in European trading or the New York session may be reversed if enough traders decide to *take profit* (selling out or exiting long positions) or *cover shorts* (buying back short positions). Or the directional move may extend farther, as more traders jump onboard before the end of the trading day. There's no set recipe for how the European close plays out, but significant flurries of activity frequently occur around this time.

REMEMBER

On most days, market liquidity and interest fall off significantly in the New York afternoon, which can make for challenging trading conditions. On quiet days, the generally lower market interest typically leads to stagnating price action. On more active days, where prices may have moved more significantly, the lower liquidity can spark additional outsized price movements, as fewer traders scramble to get similarly fewer prices and liquidity. Just as with the London close, there's never a set way in which a New York afternoon market move will play out, so traders just need to be aware that lower liquidity conditions tend to prevail, and adapt accordingly.

WARNING

Lower liquidity and the potential for increased volatility is most evident in the least-liquid major-currency pairs, especially USD/CHF and GBP/USD.

North American trading interest and volume generally continue to wind down as the trading day moves toward the 5 p.m. New York close, which also sees the change in value dates take place. (See Chapter 4 for more on rollovers and value dates.) But during the late New York afternoon, Wellington and Sydney have reopened and a new trading day has begun.

TIP

As you can see, in terms of volume, London is the center of the forex world, but plenty of opportunities exist during the New York and Asia-Pacific sessions. As a general rule, if you trade during the Asian session and no major data releases or events have taken place, the themes from the U.S. session the day before tend to prevail. When the European session comes around, there are usually a few meaty events to move the markets and create new themes — likewise during the U.S. trading session.

Key daily times and events

In addition to the ebb and flow of liquidity and market interest during the global currency trading day (covered earlier in this chapter), you need to be aware of the following daily events, which tend to occur around the same times each day.

Expiring options

Currency options are typically set to expire either at the Tokyo expiry (3 p.m. Tokyo time) or the New York expiry (10 a.m. ET). The New York option expiry is the more significant one because it tends to capture both European and North American option market interest. When an option expires, the underlying option ceases to exist. Any hedging in the spot market that was done based on the option being alive suddenly needs to be unwound, which can trigger significant price changes in the hours leading up to and just after the option expiry time.

REMEMBER

The amount and variety of currency option interest is just too large to suggest any single way that spot prices will always react around the expiry (there may not even be any significant option interest expiring on many days), but if you do notice some volatility around 10 a.m. ET, it may be due to the expiry of some currency options.

Setting the rate at currency fixings

There are several daily currency fixings in various financial centers, but the two most important are the 8:55 a.m. Tokyo time and the 4 p.m. London time fixings. A *currency fixing* is a set time each day when the prices of currencies for commercial transactions are set, or fixed. (See Chapter 3 for more on fixings.)

From a trading standpoint, these fixings may see a flurry of trading in a particular currency pair in the run-up (generally 15 to 30 minutes) to the fixing time that abruptly ends exactly at the fixing time. A sharp rally in a specific currency pair on fixing-related buying, for example, may suddenly come to an end at the fixing time and see the price quickly drop back to where it was before.

Squaring up on the currency futures markets

The Chicago Mercantile Exchange (CME), one of the largest futures markets in the world, offers currency futures through its International Monetary Market (IMM) subsidiary exchange. A currency futures contract specifies the price at which a currency can be bought or sold at a future date. Daily currency futures trading closes each day on the IMM at 2 p.m. central time (CT), which is 3 p.m. ET. Many futures traders like to square up or close any open positions at the end of each trading session to limit their overnight exposure, or for margin requirements. Currency futures are covered in Chapter 14.

REMEMBER

The 30 to 45 minutes leading up to the IMM closing occasionally generate a flurry of activity that spills over into the spot market. Because the amount of liquidity in the spot currency market is at its lowest in the New York afternoon, sharp movements in the futures markets can trigger volatility in the spot market around this time. There's no reliable way to tell if or how the IMM close will trigger a move in the New York afternoon spot market, so you just need to be aware of it and know that it can distort prices in the short term.

The U.S. dollar index

The U.S. dollar index is traded on the Intercontinental Exchange (ICE). The dollar index is an average of the value of the U.S. dollar against a basket of six other major currencies, but it's heavily weighted toward European currencies.

TECHNICAL STUFF

The exact weightings of other currencies in the U.S. dollar index are

>> **Euro:** 57.6 percent

>> **Japanese yen:** 13.6 percent

>> **British pound:** 11.9 percent

>> **Canadian dollar:** 9.1 percent

>> **Swedish krona:** 4.2 percent

>> **Swiss franc:** 3.6 percent

The European currency share of the basket — Eurozone, United Kingdom, Sweden, and Switzerland — totals 77.3 percent. From time to time, the currency weightings may be adjusted.

THE RISE OF THE CHINESE RENMINBI

China has been climbing the global economic ranks. At the time of writing, it was the world's second-largest economy, but the same is not true for the Chinese currency, the renminbi (also known as the yuan). Although the role of the renminbi in global forex trading has surged, according to the 2019 BIS Triennial Central Bank Survey, the renminbi was the eighth most-traded currency in the world, with a share of 4.3 percent in global forex volumes. However, most of this trading activity is for trade purposes only.

The renminbi is a managed currency, which means that the Chinese government controls its value. This makes it very difficult to trade for speculative purposes. Either the currency doesn't move very much (because it can move only within a controlled band, which means there are few trading opportunities), or the government intervenes out of the blue, creating a wave of volatility that can take you out of your position before you know it.

Most currency brokers allow you to trade the renminbi, but why would you want to? Some people believe that the Chinese government will eventually loosen its control over the renminbi and allow it to trade freely. Due to the importance of the Chinese economy, if the currency could trade freely, the renminbi might become a currency that would be liquid enough to rival the U.S. dollar. For now, though, it doesn't look like Beijing will embark on a liberal currency regime any time soon.

Warning: A managed currency like the renminbi can be fairly illiquid, so it can experience large price moves if the government suddenly chooses to intervene. Due to this, trading the renminbi is considered risky.

The U.S. dollar is the most important global currency, with the bulk of forex trading usually involving the dollar on one side of the transaction. Commodities are priced in dollars, and a vast amount of global currency reserves held by central banks is in dollars. This makes the dollar (also affectionately referred to as the "greenback" or the "buck") the most liquid currency in the world. As a trader, you need to know whether the dollar is strong or weak. The U.S. dollar index helps you do this because it gives you a broad-based view of how the dollar is performing in the G10 forex space. As a currency trader, be sure to follow the U.S. dollar index, especially its technical developments.

TIP

The easiest way to trade the U.S. dollar index is through a futures account (see Chapter 14) using call and put options, which are covered in Chapter 15.

Looking at Currencies and Other Financial Markets

As much as we like to think of the forex market as the be-all and end-all of financial trading markets, it doesn't exist in a vacuum. You may even have heard of some of these other markets: gold, oil, stocks, and bonds.

There's a fair amount of noise and misinformation about the supposed interrelationship among these markets and currencies or individual currency pairs. To be sure, you can always find a correlation between two different markets over some period of time, even if it's only zero (meaning the two markets aren't correlated at all).

WARNING

Be very careful about getting caught up in the supposed correlations between the forex market and other financial markets. Even when a high degree of correlation is found (meaning the two markets move in tandem or inversely to each other), it's probably over the long term (months or years) and offers little information about how the two markets will correlate in the short term (minutes, hours, and days). The other point to consider is that even if two markets have been correlated in the period, you have no guarantee that the correlation will continue to exist now or into the future. For example, depending on when you survey gold and the U.S. dollar, which supposedly have a strong negative correlation, you may find a correlation coefficient of as much as −0.8 (a solidly negative correlation) or as low as −0.2 (very close to a zero correlation, meaning that the two are virtually noncorrelated).

REMEMBER

Always keep in mind that all the various financial markets are markets in their own right and function according to their own internal dynamics based on data, news, positioning, and sentiment. Will markets occasionally overlap and display varying degrees of correlation? Of course, and it's always important to be aware of what's going on in other financial markets. But it's also essential to view each market in its own perspective and to trade each market individually.

With that rather lengthy disclaimer in mind, the following sections look at some of the other key financial markets and show what conclusions we can draw for currency trading.

Gold

Gold is commonly viewed as a hedge against inflation, an alternative to the U.S. dollar, and a store of value in times of economic or political uncertainty. Over the long term, the relationship is mostly inverse, with a weaker USD generally accompanying a higher gold price, and a stronger USD coming with a lower gold price. However, in the short run, each market has its own dynamics and liquidity, which makes short-term trading relationships generally tenuous.

REMEMBER

Overall, the gold market is significantly smaller than the forex market, so if we were gold traders, we'd sooner keep an eye on what's happening to the dollar, rather than the other way around. With that noted, extreme movements in gold prices tend to attract currency traders' attention and usually influence the dollar in a mostly inverse fashion.

Oil

A lot of misinformation exists on the internet about the supposed relationship between oil and the USD or other currencies, such as CAD, NOK (Norwegian krone), or JPY. The idea is that, because some countries are oil producers, their currencies are positively (or negatively) affected by increases (or decreases) in the price of oil. If the country is an importer of oil, the theory goes, its currency will be hurt (or helped) by higher (or lower) oil prices.

Correlation studies show no appreciable relationships to that effect, especially in the short run, which is where most currency trading is focused. When there is a long-term relationship, it's as evident against the USD as much as, or more than, any individual currency, whether an importer or exporter of black gold.

REMEMBER

The best way to look at oil is as an inflation input and as a limiting factor on overall economic growth. The higher the price of oil, the higher inflation is likely to be and the slower an economy is likely to grow. The lower the price of oil, the lower inflationary pressures are likely (but not necessarily) to be. Because the United States is a heavily energy-dependent economy and also intensely consumer-driven, the United States typically stands to lose the most from higher oil prices and to gain the most from lower oil prices. We like to factor changes in the price of oil into our inflation and growth expectations, and then draw conclusions about the course of the USD from them (see Chapter 7). Above all, oil is just one input among many.

Stocks

Stocks are microeconomic securities, rising and falling in response to individual corporate results and prospects, while currencies are essentially macroeconomic securities, fluctuating in response to wider-ranging economic and political developments. As such, there is little intuitive reason that stock markets should be related to currencies. Long-term correlation studies bear this out, with correlation coefficients of essentially zero between the major USD pairs and U.S. equity markets over the last five years.

The two markets occasionally intersect, though this is usually only at the extremes and for very short periods. For example, when equity market volatility reaches extraordinary levels (say, the Standard & Poor's [S&P] loses 2+ percent in a day), the USD may experience more pressure than it otherwise would — but there's no guarantee of that. The U.S. stock market may have dropped on an unexpected hike in U.S. interest rates, while the USD may rally on the surprise move.

In another example, the Japanese stock market is more likely to be influenced by the value of the JPY, due to the importance of the export sector in the Japanese economy. A rapid rise in the value of the JPY, which would make Japanese exports more expensive and lower the value of foreign sales, may translate to a negative stock-market reaction on the expectation of lower corporate sales and profitability.

TIP

In the world of currencies, the investing and speculative choices for participating have expanded greatly since the last edition of this book. I (coauthor Paul) think that currency exchange-traded funds (ETFs) are a fantastic way to speculate in the currency markets without all the head-scratching complexity of forex and currency futures (check out ETFs in Chapter 13). Another currency-related vehicle that has grown tremendously in terms of popularity and acceptance in recent years has been cryptocurrencies. Find out more in Chapter 16.

RISK ON/RISK OFF: WAX ON, WAX OFF

One of the first things new clients ask is what *risk on/risk off* means. This is a piece of financial market jargon that all traders should know, because it can determine the direction of a currency. *Risk on/risk off* refers to changes in investment behavior in response to global economic conditions. For example, when risk is perceived as being low, risk on/risk off states that investors tend to engage in higher-risk activities; in contrast, when the risks are perceived as high, investors tend to move toward lower-risk investments.

Risky currencies include emerging markets and some of the less liquid G10 currencies, such as the Scandis (the Norwegian krone and Swedish krona), CAD, AUD, and NZD. Interestingly, most of the higher-risk currencies are also the currencies of commodity producers. According to risk on/risk off, these currencies should fall when risk is perceived as being high.

In contrast, the JPY, the CHF, and, occasionally, the USD are considered safe havens and tend to be bought during periods when risk aversion is high. The JPY is probably the most-famous safe haven; it can rally when the risk is centered in Japan. For example, after the 2011 Japanese tsunami, the yen surged.

Bonds

Fixed income and bond markets have a more intuitive connection to the forex market because they're both heavily influenced by interest rate expectations. However, short-term market dynamics of supply and demand interrupt most attempts to establish a viable link between the two markets on a short-term basis. Sometimes the forex market reacts first and fastest depending on shifts in interest rate expectations. At other times, the bond market more accurately reflects changes in interest rate expectations, with the forex market later playing catch-up (because it takes longer to turn a bigger ship around).

TIP

Overall, as currency traders, you definitely need to keep an eye on the yields of the benchmark government bonds of the major-currency countries to better monitor the expectations of the interest rate market. Changes in relative interest rates exert a major influence on forex markets. (See Chapter 7 for more on interest rates and currencies.)

Getting Started with a Practice Account

For newcomers to currency trading, the best way to get a handle on what currency trading is all about is to open a *practice account* at any of the online forex brokers. Most online forex brokers offer practice accounts to allow you to experience the real-life price action of the forex market. Practice accounts are funded with "virtual" money, so you're able to make trades with no real money at stake and gain experience in how margin trading works.

Practice accounts give you a great chance to experience the minute-to-minute price movements of the forex market. You'll be able to see how prices change at different times of the day, as well as how various currency pairs may differ from each other. Be sure to check out the action when major news and economic data is released, so you can get a sense of how the forex market reacts to new information.

In addition to witnessing how the forex market really moves, you can

>> Start trading in real market conditions without any fear of losing money.

>> Experiment with different trading strategies to see how they work.

>> Gain experience using different orders and managing open positions.

>> Improve your understanding of how margin trading and leverage work.

>> Start analyzing charts and following technical indicators.

TIP

We think using a practice account while you read this book is a great way to experience many of the ideas and concepts we introduce. If a picture is worth a thousand words, then a real-time currency trading platform with constantly changing prices, market updates, and charting tools has to be worth a book. We'd like to think we're pretty good at explaining how currency trading works, but nothing beats being able to see it for yourself.

TIP

We recommend that you open practice accounts with a few different forex brokers, because each trading platform has varying capabilities and functionalities. In addition, different brokers have different trading policies, charting packages, and research offerings. Also, try to get a feel for the level of customer support you'll receive as a client. (You can find more information on choosing a forex broker on the Cheat Sheet. Visit www.dummies.com and type "Currency Trading For Dummies Cheat Sheet" in the search box.)

INTERPRETING YOUR RESULTS REALISTICALLY

Trading in a practice account is the 21st-century form of paper trading. *Paper trading* is writing down trades on paper based on real-time market prices but not having any real money at risk. Practice accounts are a souped-up version of paper trading — you only have to click and deal, and the trading platform does all the recording for you.

Whether you're trading in an online forex practice account or paper trading on stock quotes from the morning newspaper, be sure to keep in mind that your results aren't real because you never had any real money at stake.

Think of it this way: If you make a handshake bet with a friend on a sports game, you're probably not going to be too concerned with whether you win or lose. You may not even watch the game. But if you bet $50 or $100 on the game, you're probably going to watch the whole game and cheer and yell while you do. The difference: Your emotions come alive when real money is on the line.

Practice accounts are a great way to experience the forex market up close and personal. They're also an excellent way to test-drive all the features and functionality of a broker's platform. However, the one thing you can't simulate is the emotions of trading with real money. To get the most out of your practice-account experience, you have to treat your practice account as if it were real money as much as you can.

Chapter **3**

Who Trades Currencies? Meet the Players

The forex market is regularly referred to as the largest financial market in the world based on trading volumes. But this massive market was unknown and unavailable to most individual traders and investors until the early 2000s.

That leaves a lot of people in the dark when it comes to exactly what the currency market is: how it's organized, who's trading it, and why. In this chapter, we take a look at how the FX market is structured and who the major players are. Along the way, we clue you in to how they go about their business and what it means for the market overall.

If you believe that information is the lifeblood of financial market trading, which we certainly do, we think you'll appreciate this guide to the movers and shakers of the currency market. When you have a better understanding of who's active in the FX market, you'll be able to make better sense of what you see and hear in the market.

The Interbank Market Is "the Market"

When people talk about the "currency market," they're referring to the *interbank market*, whether they realize it or not. The interbank market is where the really big money changes hands. Minimum trade sizes are one million of the base currency, such as €1 million of EUR/USD or $1 million of USD/JPY. Much larger trades (in the hundreds of millions) are routine and can go through the market in a matter of seconds. Even larger trades and orders are a regular feature of the market.

For the individual trading FX online, the prices you see on your trading platform are based on the prices being traded in the interbank market.

The sheer size of the interbank market is what helps make it such a great trading market, because investors of every size are able to act in the market, usually without significantly affecting prices. It's one market where we would say size really doesn't matter. We've seen spot traders be right with million-dollar bets, and sophisticated hedge funds be wrong with half-billion-dollar bets.

REMEMBER

Daily trading volumes are enormous by any measure, dwarfing global stock trading volumes many times over. The most recent Bank of International Settlement (BIS) report, released in 2019, estimated daily FX trading volumes of over $6.6 trillion. Find out more at www.bis.org.

Getting inside the interbank market

So what is the interbank market and where did it come from? The forex market originally evolved to facilitate trade and commerce between nations. The leading international commercial banks, which financed international trade through letters of credit and bankers' acceptances, were the natural financial institutions to act as the currency exchange intermediary. They also had the foreign branch network on the ground in each country to facilitate the currency transfers needed to settle FX transactions.

REMEMBER

The result over a number of years was the development of an informal interbank market for currency trading. As the prefix suggests, the *interbank* market is "between banks," with each trade representing an agreement between the banks to exchange the agreed amounts of currency at the specified rate on a fixed date. The interbank market is alternately referred to as the *cash market* or the *spot market* to differentiate it from the currency futures market, which is the only other organized market for currency trading.

Currency futures markets operate alongside the interbank market, but they are definitely the tail being wagged by the dog of the spot market. As a market, currency futures are generally limited by exchange-based trading hours and lower liquidity than is available in the spot market. (See Chapter 14 for more about currency futures.)

The interbank market developed without any significant governmental oversight, and it remains largely unregulated to this day. In most cases, there is no regulatory authority for spot currency trading apart from local or national banking regulations. Interbank trading essentially evolved based on credit lines between international banks and trading conventions that developed over time.

The big commercial banks used to rule the roost when it came to currency trading, as investment banks remained focused more on stocks and bonds. But the financial industry has undergone a tremendous consolidation over the last 25 to 30 years, as bank merger after bank merger has seen famous names subsumed into massive financial conglomerates. Just 20 years ago, there were over 200 banks with FX trading desks in New York City alone. Today that number is well below a hundred. But overall trading volumes have steadily increased, a testament to the power of electronic trading.

Currency trading today is largely concentrated in the hands of about a dozen major global financial firms, such as UBS, Deutsche Bank, Citibank, JPMorgan Chase, Barclays, and Goldman Sachs, to name just a few. Hundreds of other international banks and financial institutions trade alongside the top banks, and all contribute liquidity and market interest.

Bank to bank and beyond

The interbank market is a network of international banks operating in financial centers around the world. The banks maintain trading operations to facilitate speculation for their own accounts, called *proprietary trading* or just *prop trading* for short, and to provide currency trading services for their customers. Banks' customers can range from corporations and government agencies to hedge funds and wealthy private individuals.

Trading in the interbank market

REMEMBER

The interbank market is an over-the-counter (OTC) market, which means that each trade is an agreement between the two counterparties to the trade. There are no exchanges or guarantors for the trades, just each bank's balance sheet and the promise to make payment.

The bulk of spot trading in the interbank market is transacted through electronic matching services, such as EBS and Reuters Dealing. Electronic matching services allow traders to enter their bids and offers into the market, *hit bids* (sell at the market), and *pay offers* (buy at the market). Price spreads vary by currency pair and change throughout the day depending on market interest and volatility.

The matching systems have prescreened credit limits, and a bank will only see prices available to it from approved counterparties. Pricing is anonymous before a deal, meaning you can't tell which bank is offering or bidding, but the counterparties' names are made known immediately after a deal goes through.

The rest of interbank trading is done through currency brokers, referred to as *voice brokers* to differentiate them from the electronic ones. Traders can place bids and offers with these brokers the same as they do with the electronic matching services. Prior to the electronic matching services, voice brokers were the primary market intermediaries between the banks.

Stepping onto a currency trading floor

Although trading rooms in the large banks have shrunk since the 2008–2009 financial crisis, interbank trading rooms can still be lively and are staffed by a variety of different market professionals, each of whom has a different role to play. The typical currency trading room has

>> **Flow traders:** Sometimes called *execution traders,* these are the market-makers, showing two-way prices at which to buy and sell, for the bank's customers. If the customer makes a trade, the execution trader then has to cover the resulting deal in the interbank market, hopefully at a profit. These traders are also responsible for watching and executing customer orders in the market. These are the traders who are generating most of the electronic prices and price action.

>> **Proprietary traders:** These traders are focused on speculative trading for the bank's own account. Their strategies can run the gamut from short-term day trading to longer-term macroeconomic bets. In the wake of the 2008–2009 financial crisis and changes to regulation such as the Volcker Rule, there has been a sharp decline in banks' trading for their own accounts, and many proprietary trading desks have closed down or moved to hedge funds.

>> **Forward traders:** Forward traders are active in the *forward* currency market, which refers to trades made beyond the normal spot value date. The forward market is essentially an interest rate differential market, where the interest rates of the various currencies are traded. These traders provide the bank's customers with pricing for non-spot deals or currency swap agreements. They also manage the bank's interest rate exposure in the various currencies.

>> **Options traders:** Options traders manage the bank's portfolio, or book, of outstanding currency options. They hedge the portfolio in the spot market, speculate for the bank's own account with option strategies, and provide pricing to the bank's customers on requested option strategies. (Flip to Chapter 15 for more about currency options.)

>> **Sales staff:** The sales staff acts as the intermediary between the trading desk and the bank's customers. They advise the bank's customers on market flow, as well as who's buying and selling; recommend spot and option trading strategies; and execute trades between the bank and its customers.

Hedgers and Financial Investors

The forex market sits at the crossroads of global trade and international finance and investing. Whether it's a U.S. conglomerate managing its foreign affiliates' balance sheets or a German mutual fund launching an international stock fund, they all have to go through the forex market at some point.

REMEMBER

Participants in the forex market generally fall into one of two categories: financial transactors and speculators. *Financial transactors* are active in the forex market as part of their overall business but not necessarily for currency reasons. *Speculators* are in it purely for the money.

The lion's share of forex market turnover comes from speculators. Market estimates suggest that upwards of 90 percent of daily FX trading volume is based solely on speculation. We look at the types and roles of speculators later in this chapter, but here we want to introduce the players who are active in the forex markets for nonspeculative reasons.

Financial transactors are important to the forex market for several reasons:

>> Their transactions can be extremely sizeable, typically hundreds of million or billions.

>> Their deals are frequently one-time events.

>> They are generally not price sensitive or profit maximizing.

REMEMBER

Add up those reasons and you're looking at potentially very large, one-off trading flows that are not really concerned with where the current market is trading or which way it's headed. They enter the market to do their deal and then they're gone, which can introduce an element of market inefficiency that can allow traders to take advantage of counter-trend movements.

Hedging your bets

Hedgers come in all shapes and sizes, but don't confuse them with *hedge funds.* (Despite the name, a hedge fund is typically 100 percent speculative in its investments.)

Hedging is about eliminating or reducing risk. In financial markets, hedging refers to a transaction designed to insure against an adverse price move in some underlying asset. In the forex market, hedgers are looking to insure themselves against an adverse price movement in a specific currency rate.

Hedging for international trade purposes

One of the more traditional reasons for hedging in the forex market is to facilitate international trade. Say you're a widget maker in Germany and you just won a large order from a UK-based manufacturer to supply it with a large quantity of widgets. To make your bid more attractive, you agreed to be paid in British pounds (GBP).

But because your production cost base is denominated in euros (EUR), you face the exchange rate risk that GBP will weaken against the EUR. That would make the amount of GBP in the contract worth fewer EUR back home, reducing or even eliminating your profit margin on the deal. To insure, or *hedge,* against that possibility, you would seek to sell GBP against EUR in the forex market. If the pound weakened against the euro, the value of your market hedge would rise, compensating you for the lower value of the GBP you'll receive. If the pound strengthens against the euro, your loss on the hedge is offset by gains in the currency conversions. (Each pound would be worth more euros.)

Trade hedgers follow a variety of hedging strategies and can utilize several different currency hedging instruments. Currency *options* can be used to eliminate downside currency risk and sometimes allow the hedger to participate in advantageous price movements. Currency *forward* transactions essentially lock in a currency price for a future date, based on the current spot rate and the interest rate differentials between the two currencies.

Trade-related hedging regularly comes into the spot market in two main forms:

>> **At several of the daily currency fixings:** The largest is the London afternoon fixing, which takes place each day at 4 p.m. local time, which corresponds to 11 a.m. eastern time (ET). The Tokyo fixing takes place each day at 8:55 a.m. Tokyo time, which corresponds to 6:55 p.m. eastern time (ET). A *fixing* is a process where commercial hedgers submit orders to buy or sell currencies in advance. The orders are then filled at the prevailing spot rate (the rate is fixed) at the time of the fixing.

REMEMBER

The difference between the amount of buying and selling orders typically results in a net amount that needs to be bought or sold in the market prior to the fixing time. On some days, this can see large amounts (several billion dollars or more) being bought or sold in the hour or so leading up to the fixing time. After the fix, that market interest has been satisfied and disappears. Month-end and quarter-end fixings typically see the largest amounts of volume.

TIP

Short-term traders need to closely follow live market commentaries to see when there is a substantial buying or selling interest for a fixing. (See Chapter 2 for more on potential future changes to the fixing process.)

>> **Mostly in USD/JPY, where Japanese exporters typically have large amounts of USD/JPY to sell:** Japanese exporters receive dollars for their exports, which must then be converted into JPY (sell USD/buy JPY). The Japanese export community tends to be closely knit and their orders are likely to appear together in large amounts at similar levels. Again, real-time market commentaries are the most likely source for individual traders to hear about Japanese exporter selling interest.

Hedging for currency options

The currency option market is a massive counterpart to the spot market and can heavily influence day-to-day spot trading. Currency option traders are typically trading a portfolio of option positions. To maximize their returns, options traders regularly engage in delta hedging and gamma trading. Without getting into a major options discussion here (we cover currency call and put options in Chapter 15), option portfolios generate a synthetic, or hypothetical, spot position based on spot price movements.

To maximize the return on their options portfolios, they regularly trade the synthetic spot position as though it were a real spot position. Trading the synthetic positions generated by options is called *delta hedging* or *gamma trading.*

TIP

Option hedgers are frequently found selling at technical resistance levels or buying on support levels. When a currency pair stays in a range, it can do quite nicely. But when range breakouts occur, options traders frequently need to rush to cover those range bets, adding to the force of the directional breakout. Keep an eye out for reports of option-related buying and selling as technical levels are tested. (See Chapter 6 for more about technical analysis.)

REMEMBER

Another daily feature of the spot market is the 10 a.m. ET option expiry, when options due to expire that day that finish out of the money cease to exist. Any related hedging that was done for the option then needs to be unwound, though this is likely to have been done prior to the expiry if the option is well out of the money. Traders need to follow market commentaries to see whether large option interest is set to expire on any given day and generally anticipate a flurry of option-related buying/selling that may suddenly reverse course after the 10 a.m. expiry.

Global investment flows

REMEMBER

One of the reasons forex markets remain as lightly regulated as they are is that no developed nation wants to impose restrictions on the flow of global capital. International capital is the lifeblood of the developed economies and the principal factor behind the rapid rise of the BRIC economies (Brazil, Russia, India, and China). The forex market is central to the smooth functioning of international debt and equity markets, allowing investors to easily obtain the currency of the nation they want to invest in.

Financial investors are the other main group of nonspeculative players in the forex market. As far as the forex market is concerned, financial investors are mostly just passing through on their way to another investment. More often than not, financial investors look at currencies as an afterthought, because they're more focused on the ultimate investment target, be it Japanese equities, German government bonds, or French real estate.

Mergers and acquisitions (M&A) activity is often international and shows no sign of abating. International firms are now involved in a global race to gain and expand market share, and cross-border acquisitions are frequently the easiest and fastest way to do that.

REMEMBER

When a company seeks to buy a foreign business, there can be a substantial foreign exchange implication from the trade. When large M&A deals are announced, note the answers to the following two questions:

>> **Which countries and which currencies are involved?** If a French electrical utility buys an Austrian power company, there are no currency implications because both countries use the euro (EUR). But if a Swiss pharmaceutical company announces a takeover of a Dutch chemical firm, the Swiss company may need to buy EUR and sell Swiss francs (CHF) to pay for the deal.

>> **How much of the transaction will be in cash?** Again, if it's an all stock deal, then there are no forex market implications. But if the cash portion is large, forex markets will take note and begin to speculate on the currency pair involved.

Speculators: Running the Forex Show

Speculators are market participants who are involved in the market for one reason only: to make money. In contrast to hedgers, who have some form of existing currency market risk, speculators have no currency risk until they enter the market. Hedgers enter the market to neutralize or reduce risk. Speculators embrace risk taking as a means of profiting from long-term or short-term price movements.

Speculators (*specs* for short) are what really make a market efficient. They add liquidity to the market by bringing their views and, most important, their capital into the market. That liquidity is what smooths out price movements, keeps trading spreads narrow, and allows a market to expand.

In the forex market, speculators are running the show. Conventional market estimates are that upwards of 90 percent of daily trading volume is speculative in nature. If you're trading currencies for your own account, welcome to the club. If you're trading currencies to hedge a financial risk, you can thank the specs for giving you a liquid market and reducing your transaction costs.

Speculators come in all types and sizes and pursue all different manner of trading strategies. In this section, we take a look at some of the main types of speculators to give you an idea of who they are and how they go about their business. Along the way, you may pick up some ideas to improve your own approach to the market. At the minimum, we hope this information will allow you to better understand market commentaries about who's buying and who's selling.

Hedge funds

Hedge funds are a type of *leveraged fund,* which refers to any number of different forms of speculative asset management funds that borrow money for speculation based on real assets under management. For instance, a hedge fund with $100 million under management can *leverage* those assets (through margin agreements with their trading counterparties) to give them trading limits of anywhere from $500 million to $2 billion. Hedge funds are subject to the same type of margin requirements as you or we are, just with a whole lot more zeroes involved.

The other main type of leveraged fund is known as a Commodity Trading Advisor (CTA). A CTA is principally active in the futures markets. But because the forex market operates around the clock, CTAs frequently trade spot FX as well.

The major difference between the two types of leveraged funds comes down to regulation and oversight. CTAs are regulated by the Commodity Futures Trading Commission (CFTC), the same governmental body that regulates retail FX firms.

As a result, CTAs are subject to a raft of regulatory and reporting requirements. Hedge funds, on the other hand, remain largely unregulated. What's important is that they all pursue similarly aggressive trading strategies in the forex market, treating currencies as a separate asset class, like stock or commodities.

TIP

In the forex market, leveraged funds can hold positions anywhere from a few hours to days or weeks. When you hear that leveraged names are buying or selling, it's an indication of short-term speculative interest that can provide clues as to where prices are going in the near future.

Speculating with black boxes, models, and systems

Many leveraged funds have opted for a *quantitative* approach to trading financial markets. A quantitative approach is one that uses mathematical formulas and models to come up with buy and sell decisions. The *black box* refers to the proprietary quantitative formula used to generate the trading decisions. Data goes in, trading signals come out, and what's inside the black box, no one knows. Black box funds are also referred to as *models* or *system-based funds.*

Some models are based on complex statistical relationships between various currencies, commodities, and fixed income securities. Others are based on macroeconomic data, such as relative growth rates, inflation rates, and geopolitical risks. Still others are based on technical indicators and price studies of the underlying currency pair. These are frequently referred to as *rules-based trading systems,* because the system employs defined rules to enter and exit trades.

TIP

If you're technically or statistically inclined, you can create your own model or rules-based trading system. Many online trading platforms offer application programming interface (API) access to their trading platforms, allowing you to draw price data from the platform, filter it through your trading system, and generate trading signals. Some even allow for automated trade execution without any further user action. Check with your online currency brokerage firm to see whether it has an API and supports automated trade executions.

These days there are also ready-made automated trading systems available, called expert advisors (EAs). Most currency brokers offer these to retail clients. If you're happy to let someone else create a trading program, this could make your life easier, but all automated programs come with their own level of risk that you should be aware of.

Trading with discretion

The opposite of a black box trading system is a *discretionary* trading fund. The discretion, in this case, refers to the fund manager's judgment and overall market view. The fund manager may follow a technical or system-based approach but prefer to have a human make the final decision on whether a trade is initiated. A more refined version of this approach accepts the trade signals but leaves the execution up to the discretionary fund manager's trading staff, which tries to maximize position entry/exit based on short-term market dynamics.

Still another variation of discretionary funds is those that base their trading strategies on macroeconomic and political analysis, known as *global-macro funds.* This type of discretionary fund manager is typically playing with a longer time horizon in mind. The fund may be betting on a peak in the interest rate cycle or the prospect that an economy will slip into recession. Shorter-term variations on this theme may take positions based on a specific event risk, such as the outcome of the next central bank meeting or national election.

HIGH-FREQUENCY TRADING

High-frequency trading (HFT) is a type of algorithmic or black-box trading that has grown in significance in the last 20 years. It's a rapid way to trade currencies and other asset classes. High-frequency traders move in and out of short-term positions in seconds or even fractions of seconds, sometimes aiming to capture a fraction of a cent of profit on every trade.

HFT has exploded onto the scene and has grown rapidly since 2000. However, it isn't without its critics. Some people believe that HFT causes excessive market volatility — it was found to contribute to the 2010 "flash crash."

Today HFT is mostly centered in the institutional and hedge-fund space. Most retail brokers don't offer HFT and actively stop clients from using it for a couple of reasons:

- **Cost:** HFT execution happens in just a fraction of a second, so it requires top-notch internet connections and hardware, which retail traders may not have. Any latency in your trading (for example, if there is a delay between placing your trade and execution because of a slow internet connection) could leave you exposed to losses.

- **Regulation:** On balance, reputable retail brokers apply high standards to how they trade, and the reputational issues that currently surround HFT have thus far been a turnoff.

Day traders, big and small

REMEMBER

This is where you and we fit into the big picture of the forex market. If the vast majority of currency trading volume is speculative in nature, then most of that speculation is short-term in nature. Short-term can be minute-to-minute or hour-to-hour, but rarely is it longer than a day or two. From the interbank traders who are scalping EUR/USD (high frequency in-and-out trading for few pips) to the online trader looking for the next move in USD/JPY, short-term day traders are the backbone of the market.

Intraday trading was always the primary source of interbank market liquidity, providing fluid prices and an outlet for any institutional flows that hit the market. Day traders tend to be focused on the next 20 to 30 pips in the market, which makes them the source of most short-term price fluctuations.

When you're looking at the market, look in the mirror and imagine several thousand similar faces looking back, all trying to capture the same currency trading gains that you're shooting for. It helps to imagine this so you know you're not alone and also so you know who you're up against.

The rise of online currency trading has thrust individual retail traders into the mainstream of the forex market. Online currency brokerage firms are referred to as *retail aggregators* by the institutional interbank market, because brokerage firms typically aggregate the net positions of their clients for hedging purposes. The online brokerages then transact with the interbank market to manage their market exposure.

Governments and Central Banks

National governments are routinely active in the forex market, but not for purposes of attempting to realign or shift the values of the major currencies. (We discuss those currency policies in greater depth in Chapter 7.)

Instead, national governments are active in the forex market for routine funding of government operations, making transfer payments, and managing foreign currency reserves. The first two functions have generally little impact on the day-to-day forex market, so we won't bore you with the details. But the last one has taken on increased prominence in recent years, and all indications are that it will continue to play a major role in the years ahead.

Currency reserve management

Currency reserve management refers to how national governments develop and invest their foreign currency reserves. Foreign currency reserves are accumulated through international trade. Countries with large trade surpluses will accumulate reserves of foreign currency over time. Trade surpluses arise when a nation exports more than it imports. Because it is receiving more foreign currency for its exports than it is spending to buy imports, foreign currency balances accumulate. China, one of the world's largest exporters, has many trillions of dollars as reserves.

The USD has historically been the primary currency for international reserve holdings of most countries. International Monetary Fund (IMF) data from December 2020 showed that the USD accounted for just over 59 percent of global currency reserve holdings, with EUR (20 percent) and remaining currencies (such as the Japanese yen, British pound, and so on) all under 10 percent. You can see more currency data at the IMF's site at `https://data.imf.org`.

In recent years, however, the United States has run up massive trade and current account deficits with the rest of the world. The flip side has been the accumulation of large trade surpluses in other countries, most clearly in Asia. The U.S. deficits essentially amount to the United States borrowing money from the countries with trade surpluses, while those other countries (think China) buy IOUs in the form of U.S. Treasury debt securities.

The problem is one of perception and also of prudent portfolio management:

>> **The perception problem stems from the continuing growth of U.S. deficits, which equates to your continually borrowing money from a bank.** At a certain point, no matter how good your credit is, the bank will stop lending you money because you've already borrowed so much in the first place. In the case of the United States, no one is sure exactly where that point is, but let's just say we don't want to find out. In recent years, the U.S. Congress has had to raise its debt ceiling to accommodate its growing need to borrow. At the time of writing, the U.S. debt ceiling stood at more than $28.5 trillion.

>> **The portfolio-management problem arises from the need to diversify assets in the name of prudence.** Due to the high proportion of U.S. dollars in global forex reserves, forex reserve managers need to be cognizant of the risks they face if there is a sharp drop in the U.S. dollar's value. This was particularly relevant after the financial crisis when the U.S. dollar started to weaken.

The result has been an effort by many national governments to begin to diversify their reserves away from the USD and into other major currencies. The euro, the Japanese yen, the British pound, and to a lesser extent the Australian dollar have been the principal beneficiaries of this shift. But before you think the sky is falling, the USD remains the primary reserve currency globally.

In terms of daily forex market trading, national governments (or their operatives) have become regular market participants over the last few years. Generally speaking, they appear to be engaging in active currency reserve management, selling USD on rallies, and buying EUR on weakness. But they're also not averse to then selling EUR on subsequent strength and buying USD back on weakness.

REMEMBER

Currency reserve management has taken on a market prominence in recent years that never existed before. Market talk of central bank buying or selling for reserve management purposes has become almost a daily occurrence. The impact of this in the market varies, but it can frequently lead to multiday highs and lows being maintained in the face of an otherwise compelling trend.

TIP

Traders need to closely follow real-time market commentaries for signs of central bank involvement.

The Bank for International Settlements

The Bank for International Settlements (BIS) is the central bank for central banks. Located in Basel, Switzerland, the BIS also acts as the quasi-governmental regulator of the international banking system. It was the BIS that established the capital adequacy requirements for banks that today underpin the international banking system.

As the bank to national governments and central banks, the BIS frequently acts as the market intermediary of those nations seeking to diversify their currency reserves. By going through the BIS, those countries can remain relatively anonymous and prevent speculation from driving the market against them.

TIP

Market talk of the BIS being active in the market is frequently interpreted as significant reserve interest to buy or sell. Keep an eye out for market rumors of the BIS, but also keep in mind that the BIS performs more routine and smaller trade execution on behalf of its clients.

The Group of Twenty

The Group of Twenty, or G20, is a forum for the governments and central bank governors of the world's 20 largest economies. Members include the developed markets and the larger emerging markets, including Mexico, Brazil, China, and South Korea, along with Saudi Arabia. The G20 superseded the G7 and the G8 as the global leaders' summit to keep an eye on. G20 summits take place each year; depending on the circumstances, currency values may be on the agenda for these meetings, and the *communiqué,* the official statement issued at the end of each gathering, may contain an explicit indication for a desired shift among the major currencies. If currencies are not a hot-button topic, the G20 will include a standard boilerplate statement that currencies should reflect economic fundamentals and that excessive currency volatility is undesirable.

TIP

Forex markets closely follow the preparations leading up to the meetings for several weeks in advance. Traders are looking first to see whether currencies will even be discussed, and then to see which currency or currencies will be on the agenda. The market will generally have a sense of whether currencies are an issue, and the general feeling of what the G20 would like to see done, well in advance. Still, comments from ministers and their deputies holding the preparatory consultations set the stage for the market's expectations and can provoke market reactions even before the G20 meets, although this can be rare.

Chapter **4**

The Mechanics of Currency Trading

The currency market has its own set of market trading conventions and related lingo, just like any other financial market. If you're new to currency trading, the mechanics and terminology may take some getting used to. But at the end of the day, you'll see that most currency trade conventions are pretty straightforward.

Buying and Selling Simultaneously

The biggest mental hurdle facing newcomers to currencies, especially traders familiar with other markets, is getting their head around the idea that each currency trade consists of a simultaneous purchase and sale. In the stock market, for instance, if you buy 100 shares of Google, it's pretty clear that you now own 100 shares and hope to see the price go up. When you want to exit that position, you simply sell what you bought earlier. Easy, right?

REMEMBER

But in currencies, the purchase of one currency involves the simultaneous sale of another currency. This is the *exchange* in *foreign exchange.* To put it another way, if you're looking for the dollar to go higher, the question is "Higher against what?" The answer has to be another currency. In relative terms, if the dollar goes up against another currency, it also means that the other currency has gone down against the dollar. To think of it in stock-market terms, when you buy a stock, you're selling cash, and when you sell a stock, you're buying cash.

Currencies come in pairs

To make matters easier, forex markets refer to trading currencies by pairs, with names that combine the two different currencies being traded against each other, or exchanged for one another. Additionally, forex markets have given most currency pairs nicknames or abbreviations, which reference the pair and not necessarily the individual currencies involved.

REMEMBER

The U.S. dollar is the central currency against which other currencies are traded. In its most recent triennial survey of the global foreign exchange market in 2019, the Bank for International Settlements (BIS) found that the U.S. dollar was on one side of 88 percent of all reported forex market transactions, and the dollar's position as the world's dominant currency has remained virtually unchallenged for decades. Keep watching, though, as Russia, China, and other global currency players have indicated that they aim to challenge the U.S. dollar's dominance by boosting their currency transactions with their trading partners and excluding the dollar.

The U.S. dollar's central role in the forex markets stems from a few basic factors:

» The U.S. economy is the largest national economy in the world.

» The U.S. dollar is the primary international reserve currency.

» The U.S. dollar is the medium of exchange for many cross-border transactions. For example, oil is priced in U.S. dollars. So even if you're a Japanese oil importer buying crude from Saudi Arabia, you're going to pay in U.S. dollars.

» The United States has the largest and most liquid financial markets in the world.

» The United States is a global military superpower, with a stable political system, even if we have seen a dysfunctional Congress in recent years!

Major currency pairs

REMEMBER

The major currency pairs all involve the U.S. dollar on one side of the deal. The designations of the major currencies are expressed using International Standardization Organization (ISO) codes for each currency. Table 4-1 lists the most frequently traded currency pairs, what they're called in conventional terms, and what nicknames the market has given them.

TABLE 4-1 **The Major U.S. Dollar Currency Pairs**

ISO Currency Pair	Countries	Long Name	Nickname
EUR/USD	Eurozone*/United States	Euro-dollar	N/A
USD/JPY	United States/Japan	Dollar-yen	N/A
GBP/USD	United Kingdom/United States	Pound-dollar	Sterling or Cable
USD/CHF	United States/Switzerland	Dollar-Swiss	Swissy
USD/CAD	United States/Canada	Dollar-Canada	Loonie
AUD/USD	Australia/United States	Australian-dollar	Aussie or Oz
NZD/USD	New Zealand/United States	New Zealand-dollar	Kiwi

The Eurozone is made up of all the countries in the European Union that have adopted the euro as their currency. As of this printing, the Eurozone countries are Austria, Belgium, Cyprus, Estonia, Finland, France, Germany, Greece, Ireland, Italy, Latvia, Lithuania, Luxembourg, Malta, the Netherlands, Portugal, Slovakia, Slovenia, and Spain.

TIP

Currency names and nicknames can be confusing when you're following the forex market or reading commentary and research. Be sure you understand whether the writer or analyst is referring to the individual currency or the currency pair:

» If a bank or a brokerage is putting out research suggesting that the Swiss franc will weaken in the future, the comment refers to the *individual* currency, in this case CHF, suggesting that USD/CHF will move *higher* (USD stronger/ CHF weaker).

» If the comment suggests that Swissy is likely to weaken going forward, it's referring to the currency *pair* and amounts to a forecast that USD/CHF will move *lower* (USD weaker/CHF stronger).

Major cross-currency pairs

Although the vast majority of currency trading takes place in the dollar pairs, cross-currency pairs serve as an alternative to always trading the U.S. dollar. A cross-currency pair, or *cross* or *crosses* for short, is any currency pair that does not include the U.S. dollar. Cross rates are derived from the respective USD pairs but are quoted independently and usually with a narrower spread than you could get by trading in the dollar pairs directly. (The *spread* refers to the difference between the bid and offer, or the price at which you can sell and buy, and spreads are applied in most financial markets.)

REMEMBER

Crosses enable traders to more directly target trades to specific individual currencies to take advantage of news or events. For example, your analysis may suggest that the Japanese yen has the worst prospects of all the major currencies going forward, based on interest rates or the economic outlook. To take advantage of this, you'd be looking to sell JPY, but against which other currency? You consider the USD, potentially buying USD/JPY (buying USD/selling JPY), but then you conclude that the USD's prospects are not much better than the JPY's. Further research on your part may point to another currency that has a much better outlook (such as high or rising interest rates or signs of a strengthening economy), say the Australian dollar (AUD). In this example, you would then be looking to buy the AUD/JPY cross (buying AUD/selling JPY) to target your view that AUD has the best prospects among major currencies and the JPY the worst.

TIP

Cross trades can be especially effective when major cross-border mergers and acquisitions (M&A) are announced. If a UK conglomerate is buying a Canadian utility company, the UK company is going to need to sell GBP and buy CAD to fund the purchase. The key to trading on M&A activity is to note the cash portion of the deal. If the deal is all stock, then you don't need to exchange currencies to come up with the foreign cash.

The most actively traded crosses focus on the three major non-USD currencies (namely EUR, JPY, and GBP) and are referred to as euro crosses, yen crosses, and sterling crosses. The remaining currencies (CHF, AUD, CAD, and NZD) are also traded in cross pairs. Tables 4-2, 4-3, and 4-4 highlight the key cross pairs in the euro, yen, and sterling groupings, respectively, along with their market names. Table 4-5 lists other cross-currency pairs.

TABLE 4-2

Euro Crosses

ISO Currency Pair	Countries	Market Name
EUR/CHF	Eurozone/Switzerland	Euro-Swiss
EUR/GBP	Eurozone/United Kingdom	Euro-sterling
EUR/CAD	Eurozone/Canada	Euro-Canada
EUR/AUD	Eurozone/Australia	Euro-Aussie
EUR/NZD	Eurozone/New Zealand	Euro-Kiwi

TABLE 4-3

Yen Crosses

ISO Currency Pair	Countries	Market Name
EUR/JPY	Eurozone/Japan	Euro-yen
GBP/JPY	United Kingdom/Japan	Sterling-yen
CHF/JPY	Switzerland/Japan	Swiss-yen
AUD/JPY	Australia/Japan	Aussie-yen
NZD/JPY	New Zealand/Japan	Kiwi-yen
CAD/JPY	Canada/Japan	Canada-yen

TABLE 4-4

Sterling Crosses

ISO Currency Pair	Countries	Market Name
GBP/CHF	United Kingdom/Switzerland	Sterling-Swiss
GBP/CAD	United Kingdom/Canada	Sterling-Canadian
GBP/AUD	United Kingdom/Australia	Sterling-Aussie
GBP/NZD	United Kingdom/New Zealand	Sterling-Kiwi

TABLE 4-5

Other Crosses

ISO Currency Pair	Countries	Market Name
AUD/CHF	Australia/Switzerland	Aussie-Swiss
AUD/CAD	Australia/Canada	Aussie-Canada
AUD/NZD	Australia/New Zealand	Aussie-Kiwi
CAD/CHF	Canada/Switzerland	Canada-Swiss

The long and the short of it

Forex markets use the same terms to express market positioning as most other financial markets do. But because currency trading involves simultaneous buying and selling, being clear on the terms helps — especially if you're totally new to financial market trading.

BASE CURRENCIES AND COUNTER CURRENCIES

When you look at currency pairs, you may notice that the currencies are combined in a seemingly strange order. For instance, if sterling-yen (GBP/JPY) is a yen cross, then why isn't it referred to as "yen-sterling" and written "JPY/GBP"? The answer is that these quoting conventions evolved over the years to reflect traditionally strong currencies versus traditionally weak currencies, with the strong currency coming first.

It also reflects the market quoting convention where the first currency in the pair is known as the *base currency*. The base currency is what you're buying or selling when you buy or sell the pair. It's also the *notional*, or *face*, amount of the trade. So if you buy 100,000 EUR/JPY, you've just bought 100,000 euros and sold the equivalent amount in Japanese yen. If you sell 100,000 GBP/CHF, you've just sold 100,000 British pounds and bought the equivalent amount of Swiss francs.

The second currency in the pair is called the *counter currency*, or the *secondary currency*. Hey, who said this stuff isn't intuitive? Most important for you as an FX trader, the counter currency is the denomination of the price fluctuations and, ultimately, what your profit and losses will be denominated in. If you buy GBP/JPY, it goes up, and you take a profit, your gains are not in pounds, but in yen. (We run through the math of calculating profit and loss later in this chapter.)

Going long

No, we're not talking about running out deep for a football pass. A *long position*, or simply a *long*, refers to a market position in which you've bought a security. In FX, it refers to having bought a currency pair. When you're long, you're looking for prices to move higher, so you can sell at a higher price than where you bought. When you want to close a long position, you have to sell what you bought. If you're buying at multiple price levels, you're *adding to longs* and *getting longer*.

Getting short

A *short position*, or simply a *short*, refers to a market position in which you've sold a security that you never owned. In the stock market, selling a stock short requires borrowing the stock (and paying a fee to the lending brokerage) so you can sell it. In forex markets, it means you've sold a currency *pair*, meaning you've sold the base currency and bought the counter currency. So you're still making an exchange, just in the opposite order and according to currency–pair quoting terms. When you've sold a currency pair, it's called *going short* or *getting short*, and it means you're looking for the pair's price to move lower so you can buy it back at a profit. If you sell at various price levels, you're *adding to shorts* and *getting shorter*.

TIP

In most other markets, *short selling* either comes with restrictions or is considered too risky for most individual traders. In currency trading, going short is as common as going long. "Selling high and buying low" is a standard currency trading strategy.

REMEMBER

Currency pair rates reflect relative values between two currencies and not an absolute price of a single stock or commodity. Because currencies can fall or rise relative to each other, both in medium and long-term trends and minute-to-minute fluctuations, currency pair prices are as likely to be going down at any moment as they are up. To take advantage of such moves, forex traders routinely use short positions to exploit falling currency prices. Traders from other markets may feel uncomfortable with short selling, but it's just something you have to get your head around.

Squaring up

If you have no position in the market, it's called being *square* or *flat.* If you have an open position and you want to close it, it's called *squaring up.* If you're short, you need to buy to square up. If you're long, you need to sell to go flat. The only time you have no market exposure or financial risk is when you're square.

Looking at Profit and Loss

Profit and loss (P&L) is how traders measure success and failure. You don't want to be looking at the forex market as some academic or thrill-seeking exercise. Real money is made and lost every minute of every day. If you're going to trade currencies actively, you need to get up close and personal with P&L.

A clear understanding of how P&L works is especially critical to online margin trading, where your P&L directly affects the amount of margin you have to work with. (We introduce online margin trading in Chapter 2.) Changes in your margin balance determine how much you can trade and for how long you can trade if prices move against you.

Margin balances and liquidations

As we mention in Chapter 2, one of the benefits of forex trading is that you can use leverage, which allows you to gain a large exposure to a financial market while only tying up a small amount of your capital. The initial capital that you have to post to your account in order to open a trade is called *margin.*

That initial margin deposit becomes your opening *margin balance* and is the basis on which all your subsequent trades are collateralized. Think of this as a bit like the collateral a bank will ask for if you apply for a loan. Unlike futures markets or margin-based equity trading, online forex brokerages do not issue *margin calls* (requests for more collateral to support open positions). Instead, they establish ratios of margin balances to open positions that must be maintained at all times.

If your account's margin balance falls below the required ratio, even for just a few seconds, your broker probably has the right to close out your positions without any notice to you. In most cases, that only happens when an account has losing positions. If your broker liquidates your positions, that usually means your losses are locked in and your margin balance just got smaller.

WARNING

Be sure you completely understand your broker's margin requirements and liquidation policies. Requirements may differ depending on account size and whether you're trading standard lot sizes (100,000 currency units), mini lot sizes (10,000 currency units), or micro lots (1,000 currency units). Some brokers' liquidation policies allow for all positions to be liquidated if you fall below margin requirements. Others close out the biggest losing positions or portions of losing positions until the required ratio is satisfied again. You can find the details in the fine print of the account opening contract that you sign. Always read the fine print to be sure you understand your broker's margin and trading policies.

Unrealized and realized profit and loss

REMEMBER

Most online forex brokers provide real-time mark-to-market calculations showing your margin balance. *Mark-to-market* is the calculation that shows your unrealized P&L based on where you could close your open positions in the market at that instant. Depending on your broker's trading platform, if you're long, the calculation will typically be based on where you could sell at that moment. If you're short, the price used will be where you can buy at that moment. Your margin balance is the sum of your initial margin deposit, your unrealized P&L, and your realized P&L.

Realized P&L is what you get when you close out a trade position or a portion of a trade position. If you close out the full position and go flat, whatever you made or lost leaves the unrealized P&L calculation and goes into your margin balance. If you only close a portion of your open positions, only that part of the trade's P&L is realized and goes into the margin balance. Your unrealized P&L will continue to fluctuate based on the remaining open positions and so will your total margin balance.

If you've got a winning position open, your unrealized P&L will be positive and your margin balance will increase. If the market is moving against your positions, your unrealized P&L will be negative and your margin balance will be reduced. FX prices are constantly changing, so your mark-to-market unrealized P&L and total margin balance will also be constantly changing.

Calculating profit and loss with pips

Profit-and-loss calculations are pretty straightforward in terms of math — it's all based on position size and the number of pips you make or lose. A *pip* is the smallest increment of price fluctuation in currency prices. Pips can also be referred to as *points*; we use the two terms interchangeably.

TECHNICAL STUFF

We're not sure where the term *pip* came from. Some say it's an abbreviation for *percentage in point*, but it could also be the FX answer to bond traders' *bips*, which refers to *bps*, or *basis points* (meaning 1/100 of 1 percent).

Even the venerable pip is in the process of being updated as electronic trading continues to advance. Just a couple of paragraphs earlier, we tell you that the pip is the smallest increment of currency price fluctuations. Not so fast. The online market is rapidly advancing to decimalizing pips (trading in 1/10 pips), and half-pip prices have been the norm in certain currency pairs in the interbank market for many years.

REMEMBER

But for now, to get a handle on P&L calculations, you're better off sticking with pips. Looking at a few currency pairs can help you to get an idea of what a pip is. Most currency pairs are quoted using five digits. The placement of the decimal point depends on whether it's a JPY currency pair — if it is, there are two digits behind the decimal point. For all other currency pairs, there are four digits behind the decimal point. In all cases, that last itty-bitty digit is the pip.

Here are some major currency pairs and crosses, with the pip underlined:

>> **EUR/USD:** 1.353<u>5</u>

>> **USD/CHF:** 0.907<u>4</u>

>> **USD/JPY:** 101.4<u>3</u>

>> **GBP/USD:** 1.614<u>2</u>

>> **EUR/JPY:** 138.0<u>1</u>

Focus on the EUR/USD price first. Looking at EUR/USD, if the price moves from 1.3535 to 1.3555, it's just gone up by 20 pips. If it goes from 1.3535 down to 1.3515, it's just gone down by 20 pips. Pips provide an easy way to calculate the P&L. To turn that pip movement into a P&L calculation, all you need to know is the size of the position. For a 100,000 EUR/USD position, the 20-pip move equates to $200 (EUR 100,000 × 0.0020 = $200).

Whether the amounts are positive or negative depends on whether you were long or short for each move. If you were short for the move higher, that's a − in front of the $200; if you were long, it's a +. EUR/USD is easy to calculate, especially for USD-based traders, because the P&L accrues in dollars.

REMEMBER

If you take USD/CHF, you've got another calculation to make before you can make sense of it. That's because the P&L is going to be denominated in Swiss francs (CHF) because CHF is the counter currency. If USD/CHF drops from 0.9074 to 0.9040 and you're short USD 100,000 for the move lower, you've just caught a 34-pip decline. That's a profit worth CHF 340 (USD 100,000 × 0.0034 = CHF 340). Yeah, but how much is that in real money? To convert it into USD, you need to divide the CHF 340 by the USD/CHF rate. Use the closing rate of the trade (0.9032), because that's where the market was last, and you get USD 376.43.

Factoring profit and loss into margin calculations

The good news is that online FX trading platforms calculate the P&L for you automatically, both unrealized while the trade is open and realized when the trade is closed. So why did we just drag you through the math of calculating P&L using pips? Because online brokerages will only start calculating your P&L for you *after* you enter a trade.

TIP

To structure your trade and manage your risk effectively (How big a position? How much margin to risk?), you're going to need to calculate your P&L outcomes *before* you enter the trade. Understanding the P&L implications of a trade strategy you're considering is critical to maintaining your margin balance and staying in control of your trading. This simple exercise can help prevent you from costly mistakes, like putting on a trade that's too large, or putting *stop-loss orders* beyond prices where your account falls below the margin requirement. At the minimum, you need to calculate the price point at which your position will be liquidated when your margin balance falls below the required ratio. Because every firm can be different regarding margin requirements, check with your forex broker's customer service department.

Understanding Rollovers and Interest Rates

One market convention unique to currencies is *rollovers*. A rollover is a transaction where an open position from one *value date* (settlement date) is rolled over into the next value date. Rollovers represent the intersection of interest-rate markets and forex markets.

Currency is money, after all

Rollover rates are based on the difference in interest rates of the two currencies in the pair you're trading. That's because what you're actually trading is good old-fashioned cash. That's right: Currency is cold, hard cash with a fancy name. When you're long a currency (cash), it's like having a deposit in the bank. If you're short a currency (cash), it's like having borrowed a loan. Just as you would expect to earn interest on a bank deposit or pay interest on a loan, you should expect an interest gain/expense for holding a currency position over the change in value.

The catch in currency trading is that if you carry over an open position from one value date to the next, you have two bank accounts involved. Think of it as one account with a positive balance (the currency you're long) and one with a negative balance (the currency you're short). But because your accounts are in two different currencies, the two interest rates of the different countries will apply.

TIP

The difference between the interest rates in the two countries is called the *interest-rate differential.* The larger the interest-rate differential, the larger the impact from rollovers. The narrower the interest-rate differential, the smaller the effect from rollovers. You can find relevant interest-rate levels of the major currencies from any number of financial-market websites, but www.marketwatch.com and www.fxstreet.com have especially good resources. Look for the base or benchmark lending rates in each country.

How great of an impact rollover rates have on you depends on the size of your position. They have a bigger impact on someone trading in the millions than they do on someone trading in the tens. However, regardless of your size, it's still handy to know how a rollover affects you.

So how do interest rates get turned into currency rates? After all, interest rates are in percentages and currency rates are, well, *not* in percentages. The answer is that deposit rates yield actual cash returns, which are netted, producing a net cash return. That net cash return is then divided by the position size, which gives you the currency pips, which is the rollover rate.

The following calculation illustrates how this works. We've simplified matters by using just one interest rate for each currency. In the real world, each currency would have a slightly different interest rate depending on whether you're borrowing or lending (depositing).

Position: Long EUR/USD 100,000 at 1.3000 (long EUR/short USD 130,000)

EUR interest rate: 3.50 percent per annum → 1 day = $0.035 \times (1 \div 365) = 0.009589$ percent

Euro deposit earns: $100,000 \times 0.00009589 = EUR + 9.59$

USD interest rate: 5.25 percent per annum → 1 day = 0.0525 × (1 ÷ 365) = 0.01438 percent

USD loan costs: 130,000 × 0.0001438 = USD – 18.70

Because EUR/USD pips are denominated in USD, convert the EUR to USD: EUR 9.59 × 1.3000 = USD 12.47

Net the USD amounts 12.47 – 18.70 = USD – 6.23 ÷ 100,000 = 0.0000623

On a long EUR 100,000 position, the rollover costs 0.0000623, or –0.623 pips.

Value dates and trade settlement

When we talk about currency trading, we're implicitly referring to trading the spot forex market. A *spot market* is one that's trading for immediate delivery of whatever security is being traded. But in the real world, *immediate* means a few business days, to allow banks and financial firms time to settle a trade (make payment, deliver/receive a security).

REMEMBER

In forex markets, *spot* refers to trade settlement in *two* business days, which is called the *value date*. That time is needed to allow for trade processing across global time zones and for currency payments to be wired around the world.

The forex market operates on a 24-hour trade date basis beginning at 5 p.m. eastern time (ET) and ending the next day at 5 p.m. ET. So if it's a Monday, spot currencies are trading for value on Wednesday (assuming no holidays). At 5 p.m. ET on Monday, the trade date becomes Tuesday and the value date is shifted to Thursday. If you have an open position on Monday at 5 p.m. ET closing, your position will be rolled over to the next value date, in this case from Wednesday to Thursday, or a *one-day rollover*.

If you close your position the next day (Tuesday) and finish the trade date square, there are no rollovers because you have no position. The same is true if you never carry a position through the daily 5 p.m. ET close.

WARNING

On Wednesday trade dates, spot currencies are normally trading for a Friday value date. At 5 p.m. ET on Wednesday, the value date changes from Friday to Monday, a *weekend rollover*. In rollover calculations, that's a *three-day rollover* (Saturday, Sunday, and Monday), which means the rollover costs/gains are going to be three times as much as any other day.

REMEMBER

The one exception to the two-day spot convention in FX are trades in USD/CAD. And that's because the main financial centers in the United States and Canada share the same time zone, so communications and wire transfers can be made more quickly. USD/CAD trades settle in one business day. The weekend rollover for USD/CAD takes place on Thursday after the 5 p.m. ET close, when the value date shifts from Friday to Monday. This only applies to USD/CAD and not to other pairs involving CAD, such as CAD/JPY or EUR/CAD.

Market holidays and value dates

REMEMBER

Value dates are based on individual currency pairs to account for banking holidays in respective countries. Rollover periods can be longer if there is a banking holiday in one of the countries whose currency is part of the trade. For example, if it's Wednesday and you're trading GBP/USD, the normal spot value date would be Friday. But if there's a banking holiday in the United Kingdom on Friday, UK banks are not open to settle the trade. So the value date is shifted to the next valid banking day common to the United Kingdom and the United States, typically the following Monday. In this case, the weekend rollover would take place at the close on Tuesday at 5 p.m. ET, when the value date would change from Thursday to Monday, skipping Friday's holiday. That's a *four-day rollover* (Friday, Saturday, Sunday, and Monday).

So what happens at the change in value date at Wednesday's 5 p.m. ET close? No rollovers in GBP/USD, that's what. Because the value date for trades made on Wednesday is already Monday, no rollover is needed because trades made on Thursday are also for value on Monday. That's called a *double value date,* meaning two trade dates (Wednesday and Thursday) are settling for the same value date (Monday).

WARNING

A few times each year (mostly around Christmas, New Year's, and Golden Week spring holidays in Japan) when multiple banking holidays in various countries coincide over several days, rollover periods can be as long as seven or eight days. So you may earn or pay rollovers of seven or eight times normal on one day, but then not face any rollovers for the rest of the holiday period.

Applying rollovers

Rollover transactions are usually carried out automatically by your forex broker if you hold an open position past the change in value date.

Rollovers are applied to your open position by two offsetting trades that result in the same open position. Some online forex brokers apply the rollover rates by adjusting the average rate of your open position. Other forex brokers apply rollover rates by applying the rollover credit or debit directly to your margin balance. In terms of the math, it's six of one, half a dozen of the other.

Here's an example of how the rollover of an open position would work under each model:

> *Position:* Long 100,000 AUD/JPY at a rate of 90.15 for a value date of January 10
>
> At 5 p.m. ET, the rollover takes place and the following rollover trades hit your account. (**Remember:** This is done automatically by most online brokers.)
>
> You sell 100,000 AUD/JPY at 90.22 for a value date of January 10. (This trade closes the open position for the same value date.)
>
> You buy 100,000 AUD/JPY at 90.206 for a value date of January 11. (This trade reopens the same position for the new value date.)
>
> The difference in the rates represents the rollover points. (90.22 – 90.206 = 0.014, which is expressed as 1.4 points.)
>
> If the rollover is applied to your average rate on the open position, your new average rate on the position is 90.136. (Here's the math: 90.15 – 0.014 = 90.136.) Because you're now long from a lower average price, you earned money on the rollover.
>
> If the rollover is applied directly to your margin balance, the rollover points are multiplied by the position size (100,000 × 0.014 = JPY 1,400 earned) and converted into USD (JPY 1,400 ÷ 116.00 [the USD/JPY rate] = $12.07) and added to your margin balance.

REMEMBER

Here's what you need to remember about rollovers:

>> Rollovers are applied to open positions after the 5 p.m. ET change in value date, or trade settlement date.

>> Rollovers are not applied if you don't carry a position over the change in value date. So if you're square at the close of each trading day, you'll never have to worry about rollovers.

>> Rollovers reflect the interest rate return or cost of holding an open position.

>> Rollovers represent the difference in interest rates between the two currencies in your open position, but they're applied in currency-rate terms.

>> Rollovers constitute net interest earned or paid by you, depending on the direction of your position.

>> Rollovers can earn you money if you're long the currency with the higher interest rate and short the currency with the lower interest rate.

>> Rollovers will cost you money if you're short the currency with the higher interest rate and long the currency with the lower interest rate.

>> Rollovers can have spreads applied to them by some forex brokers, which can reduce any interest earned by your position.

>> Rollover costs/credits are based on position size — the larger the position, the larger the cost or gain to you.

>> Rollovers should be considered a cost of doing business and rarely influence overall trading decisions.

TIP

If you're going to be trading a relatively large account with an online forex broker (say, over $25,000 in margin deposited), you'll probably be able to negotiate a tighter rollover spread with your broker. This will enable you to capture more of the gains if you're positioned the right way, or to reduce your cost of carry if you're not.

Checking Out Currency Prices

Now we're getting down to the brass tacks of actually making trades in the forex market. Before we get ahead of ourselves, though, it's critical to understand exactly how currency prices work and what they mean to you as a trader. Earlier in this chapter, we show you that *buying* means "buying the *currency pair*" and *selling* means "selling the *currency pair*."

REMEMBER

Here, we look at how online brokerages display currency prices and what they mean for trade and order execution. Keep in mind that different online forex brokers use different formats to display prices on their trading platforms. A thorough picture of what the prices mean will allow you to navigate different brokers' platforms and know what you're looking at.

Bids and offers

REMEMBER

When you're in front of your screen and looking at an online forex broker's trading platform, you'll see two prices for each currency pair. The price on the left-hand side is called the *bid* and the price on the right-hand side is called the *offer* (some call this the *ask*). Some brokers display the prices above and below each other, with the bid on the bottom and the offer on top. The easy way to tell the difference is that the bid price will always be lower than the offer price.

The price quotation of each bid and offer you see will have two components: the big figure and the dealing price. The *big figure* refers to the first three digits of the overall currency rate and is usually shown in a smaller font size or even in shadow. The *dealing price* refers to the last two digits of the overall currency price and is brightly displayed in a larger font size.

For example, in Figure 4-1 the full EUR/USD price quotation is 1.40225/1.40246. The 1.40 is the big figure and is there to show you the full price level (or big figure) that the market is currently trading at. The 225/246 portion of the price is the bid/offer dealing price.

FIGURE 4-1:
A dealing box
from the FOREX.
com trading
platform for
EUR/USD.

Source: FOREX.com

Spreads

A *spread* is the difference between the bid price and the offer price. Most online forex brokers utilize spread-based trading platforms for individual traders. In one sense, you can look at the spread as the commission that the online brokers charge for executing your trades. So even if they *say* they're commission free, they may be earning the difference when one trader sells at the bid price and another trader buys at the offer price. Another way to look at the spread is that it's the compensation the broker receives for being the market-maker and providing a regular two-way market.

TIP

Spreads vary from broker to broker and by currency pairs at each broker as well. Generally, the more liquid the currency pair, the narrower the spread; the less liquid the currency pair, the wider the spread. This is especially the case for some of the less-traded crosses.

Executing a Trade

It's trigger-pulling time, pardner. In this section, we assume you've signed up for a practice account at an online forex broker and you're ready to start executing some practice trades. Getting a feel for executing deals now, before you're ready to commit any real money to a trade, is very helpful. (See Chapters 2 and 6 for more on using a practice account.)

REMEMBER

There are two main ways of executing trades in the FX market: live trades and orders. If you're an adrenaline junkie, don't focus only on the "Trading online or on the phone" section — the "Orders" section gives you plenty of juice to keep you going, too.

Trading online or on the phone

WARNING

Live dealing is how you access the market to buy or sell at current market rates. Knowing exactly what you want to do is important, because when you make a live deal, it's a *done* deal. If you make a mistake, you'll have to make another trade to correct your erroneous trade, and that is very likely going to cost you real money.

There are a few different avenues to get to the market depending on how your broker is set up. In the following sections, we cover all the bases.

Clicking and dealing

Most forex brokers provide live streaming prices that you can deal on with a simple click of your computer mouse. On those platforms, to execute a trade, follow these steps:

1. **Specify the amount of the trade you want to make.**

2. **Click the Buy or Sell button to execute the trade you want.**

   The forex trading platform will respond back, usually within a second or two, to let you know whether the trade went through:

   - If the trade went through, you'll see the trade and your new position appear in your platform's list of trades.

   - If the trade failed because of a price change, you need to start again from the top.

   - If the trade failed because the trade was too large based on your margin, you need to reduce the size of the trade.

   When the trade goes through, you have a position in the market and you'll see your unrealized P&L begin updating according to market price fluctuations.

Click-and-deal platforms usually have a number of shortcuts to enable more rapid trading. Some of these are for more advanced or active traders, so be sure you know what they are before you engage them. Here are the parameters that you can usually set up in advance:

- >> **Preset trade amounts:** These are so you don't have to specify the amount each time you make a deal.

- >> **Automatic stop-loss orders at a predetermined distance from the trade-entry price:** These automatic stop-loss functions can be turned on or off, and you define the number of pips away for the stop loss. These functions are good for providing fail-safe stop-loss protection until you can enter a more detailed order for your trade strategy.

REMEMBER

You never know when a headline will roil the market, and you don't want to get caught with your pants down.

>> **Close buttons:** These will appear next to all open positions. By clicking them, you'll automatically square up (close) the open position you've selected (assuming the position size is within the maximum per-trade deal size).

WARNING

Some online brokers advertise narrower trading spreads as a way to attract traders. If your click-and-deal trade attempts frequently fail, and the platform then asks if you'd like to make the trade at a worse price, you're probably being re-quoted. *Re-quoting* is when brokers offer you a worse price to make your trade, meaning you end up paying a larger spread than you bargained for.

TRADING USING SMARTPHONES

More than 50 percent of FOREX.com's trading volume is now conducted using a smartphone. In the past, people traded using devices that were constantly plugged into a power source (such as your desktop computer) or over the phone. Most major forex trading firms now have a smartphone app to make your trading easier.

The evolution of trading apps that allow individuals to trade on their phones or tablets has many benefits — you can trade when you're in line at a store or at a football game — but this new way of trading comes with new risks. For example, if your phone has an unreliable battery, it could die when you're in the middle of placing a trade, potentially leaving you exposed to losses.

Here are a few tips for trading on a smartphone:

- Make sure your battery is well charged before you attempt to place a new trade or change an existing trade.

- Close other apps while you're trading on your smartphone. You need the best possible internet connection when you're trading to ensure you get constant price updates. Having multiple apps open at once can slow your connection and interfere with your trading.

- Make sure you have an uninterrupted internet signal when you're trading. Don't trade if you're on a train and about to go through a tunnel that will cut your signal. This could also cost you money.

- If your phone is unreliable, don't trade on it. Get a new device or trade on a desktop. Using a high-quality device can save you money and protect your profits.

Phone dealing

Placing live trades over the phone is available from most online forex brokers (although it's probably the least popular form of trading). You need to find out from your broker whether it offers this service and exactly what its procedures are before you can be ready to use it.

REMEMBER

The capability to make trades over the phone is critical if you're frequently trading while you're away from your computer or tablet or in cases of technological disruptions. At the minimum, you need to have the dealing phone number in your contact list and a reliable phone connection in case something goes wrong with your internet connection. If your dog chews through your mouse cable or your kid spills a sippy cup of juice on your tablet, you'll need a fallback plan to protect your market exposure. (We cover risk throughout this book and highlight major points in Chapter 18.)

To place a trade over the phone, you'll need to do the following:

1. **Call the telephone number at your broker for placing a trade.**

2. **When you're connected to a representative, identify yourself by name and give your trading account number.**

   Be ready to provide whatever account password is needed. (Knowing what's required *before* you call to place the trade is a good idea.)

   Know what your position is. If you're not sure, your broker will be able to give you this info, but be prepared for time delays.

3. **Ask what the current price is for the currency pair you're trading.** The broker's representative will quote you a two-way bid/offer price, such as "EUR/USD is trading at 1.3213/15."

4. **If you don't want the price, say, "No, thank you."**

5. **If you want the price, specify *exactly* what trade you would like to make.**

   Don't just say "Close my position" or "Square me up." Note the direction (buy or sell), the amount (don't use lots — use the real amounts), and the currency pair. For example, "I would like to sell 140,000 EUR/USD."

   The broker should then say, "Done" or "That's agreed."

6. **Confirm with your broker exactly what trade you just made.**

   For example, say, "To confirm, I just sold 140,000 EUR/USD at 1.3213."

   Be sure the broker confirms the trade. You can double-check that the trade was correct by asking the broker to input the trade and update your position.

7. **Get the name of the broker's representative you just made the trade with in case you have to call back.**

Orders

REMEMBER

Currency traders use orders to catch market movements when they're not in front of their screens. The forex market is open 24 hours a day. A market move is just as likely to happen while you're asleep or in the shower as it is while you're watching your screen. If you're not a full-time trader, then you've probably got a full-time job that requires your attention when you're at work — at least your boss *hopes* they have your attention. Orders are how you can act in the market without being there.

Experienced currency traders also routinely use orders to

>> Implement a trade strategy from entry to exit

>> Capture sharp, short-term price fluctuations

>> Limit risk in volatile or uncertain markets

>> Preserve trading capital from unwanted losses

>> Maintain trading discipline

>> Protect profits and minimize losses

REMEMBER

We can't stress enough the importance of using orders in currency trading. Forex markets can be notoriously volatile and difficult to predict. Using orders helps you capitalize on short-term market movements, as well as limit the impact of any adverse price moves. A disciplined use of orders can also help you quantify the risk you're taking and, with any luck, give you peace of mind in your trading. *Bottom line:* If you don't use orders, you probably don't have a well-thought-out trading strategy — and that's a recipe for pain.

Types of orders

In this section, we introduce you to all the types of orders available in the forex market. Bear in mind that not all order types are available at all online brokers. So add order types to your list of questions to ask your prospective forex broker. (For more in-depth information on executing and managing the trade, check out Chapters 10 and 11.)

TAKE-PROFIT ORDERS

Don't you just love that name? There's an old market saying that goes, "You can't go broke taking profit." You'll use *take-profit orders* to lock in gains when you have an open position in the market. If you're short USD/JPY at 107.20, your take-profit order will be to buy back the position and be placed somewhere below that price, say at 106.80. If you're long GBP/USD at 1.6640, your take-profit order will be to sell the position somewhere higher, maybe 1.6675.

TIP

Partial take-profit orders are take-profit orders that close only a portion of your open position. Say you bought 200,000 EUR/USD at 1.2950 expecting it to move higher — and it does. But to take some money off the table and lock in some gains, you decide to sell half the position (100,000 EUR/USD) at 1.3000 and to allow the market to see how high it wants to go with the rest. Or you can place two partial take-profit orders to close the whole position at two different levels.

LIMIT ORDERS

Technically speaking, a take-profit order is a type of *limit order.* The key difference is that take-profit orders close or reduce open positions and limit orders open new positions or add to existing positions in the same direction.

REMEMBER

A limit order is any order that triggers a trade at more favorable levels than the *current* market price. Think "Buy low, sell high." If the limit order is to buy, it must be entered at a price below the current market price. If the limit order is to sell, it must be placed at a price higher than the current market price.

STOP-LOSS ORDERS

Boo! Sound's bad doesn't it? Actually, stop-loss orders are critical to trading survival. The traditional *stop-loss order* does just that: It stops losses by closing out an open position that is losing money. You can use stop-loss orders to limit your losses if the market moves against your position. If you don't, you're leaving it up to the market, and that's always a dangerous proposition.

Stop-loss orders are on the other side of the current price from take-profit orders, but in the same direction (in terms of buying or selling). If you're long, your stop-loss order will be to sell, but at a lower price than the current market price. If you're short, your stop-loss order will be to buy, but at a higher price than the current market.

TRAILING STOP-LOSS ORDERS

TIP

A trailing stop is a beautiful little tool, especially when you've got a winning trade going. You may have heard that one of the keys to successful trading is to cut losing positions quickly and let winning positions run. A trailing stop-loss order allows you to do just that. The idea is that when you have a winning trade on, you wait for the market to stage a reversal and take you out, instead of trying to pick the right level to exit on your own.

WHEN STOPS DON'T LOSE, AND TAKE PROFITS DON'T PROFIT

Sometimes the roles of take-profit orders and stop-loss orders reverse. This can happen if you adjust your order levels after you've entered a position and the market has already moved away from your entry price.

With both take-profit orders and stop-loss orders, the important price is not your entry price, but the current market price. For example, you may be short USD/JPY at 108.00 and the market is trading higher at 108.30. You originally had your take-profit order below to buy back at 107.60, but now you're having second thoughts. You decide to raise your take-profit order to 108.15 to try to close the position on a dip. The order is still a take profit because it is below the current market price (108.30), even though it will result in a loss if it's filled.

The same can apply to stop losses. If you bought AUD/USD at 0.7640 and the price has since moved higher to 0.7670, you may decide to raise your stop-loss sell order from its original level (0.7610) to lock in some of the gains. So you raise your stop-loss order to 0.7655. If your stop-loss sell order is triggered, you'll actually be taking profit.

A trailing stop-loss order is a stop-loss order that you set at a fixed number of pips from your entry rate. The trailing stop adjusts the order rate as the market price moves, *but only in the direction of your trade.* For example, if you're long EUR/CHF at 1.2350 and you set the trailing stop at 30 pips, the stop will initially become active at 1.2320 (1.2350 − 30 pips).

If the EUR/CHF price moves higher to 1.2360, the stop adjusts higher, pip for pip, with the price and will then be active at 1.2330. The trailing stop will continue to adjust higher as long as the market continues to move higher. When the market puts in a top, your trailing stop will be 30 pips (or whatever distance you specify) below that top, wherever it may be.

If the market ever goes down by 30 pips, as in this example, your stop will be triggered and your position closed. So in this case, if you're long at 1.2350 and you set a 30-pip trailing stop, it will initially become active at 1.2320. If the market never ticks up and goes straight down, you'll be stopped out at 1.2320. If the price first rises to 1.2375 and then declines by 60 points, your trailing stop will have risen to 1.2345 (1.2375 − 30 pips) and that's where you'll be stopped out.

Pretty cool, huh? The only catch is that not every online trading platform offers trailing stops. If you find a platform you like and it doesn't offer trailing stops, you can mimic a trailing stop by frequently manually changing the rate on your regular stop-loss order. But this is an imperfect solution unless you can monitor your position constantly.

ONE-CANCELS-THE-OTHER ORDERS

TIP

A *one-cancels-the-other order* (more commonly referred to as an OCO order) is a stop-loss order paired with a take-profit order. It's the ultimate insurance policy for any open position. Your position stays open until one of the order levels is reached by the market and closes your position. When one order level is reached and triggered, the other order automatically cancels.

Say you're short USD/JPY at 101.00. You think if it goes up beyond 101.50, it's going to keep going higher, so that's where you decide to place your stop-loss buying order. At the same time, you believe that USD/JPY has downside potential to 100.25, so that's where you set your take-profit buying order. You now have two orders bracketing the market and your risk is clearly defined.

As long as the market trades between 100.26 and 101.49, your position remains open. If 100.25 is reached first, your take profit triggers and you buy back at a profit. If 101.50 is hit first, then your position is stopped out at a loss.

REMEMBER

OCO orders are highly recommended for every open position.

CONTINGENT ORDERS

TIP

A *contingent order* is a fancy term for combining several types of orders to create a complete currency trade strategy. You can use contingent orders to put on a trade while you're asleep, or otherwise indisposed, knowing that your contingent order has all the bases covered and your risks are defined. Contingent orders are also referred to as *if/then orders.* If/then orders require the *If* order to be *done* first, and *then* the second part of the order becomes active, so they're sometimes called *If done/then* orders.

Take a look at a trade idea to see how a contingent order works. Say NZD/USD has been trading in a range between 0.6700 and 0.6800 and is currently sitting in the middle at 0.6750/54. You think it's going to go higher, but you don't want to jump in at the middle of the range and risk watching it go down before it goes up. So you use a contingent order to implement your strategy, even if you're not watching the market.

Because you're ultimately looking to buy on a dip toward 0.6700 to get long, you place an if/then limit order to buy at 0.6710, the *if* part of the order. The contingent, or *then*, part of the order only becomes active if the *if* part is triggered and you enter a position.

The *then* part consists of either a stop-loss order or a take-profit order, or both in the form of an OCO order.

Continuing with this example, your contingent order may be to place a stop-loss order below 0.6700, in case the range breaks and you're wrong. So you may place your stop-loss order at 0.6690 to sell what you bought in the *if* part. This type of contingent order is called an *if/then stop loss.* You may opt for only an *if/then stop-loss order* if you want to limit your downside risk but let your upside gains run.

If you think the upside is limited to the range highs at 0.6800, you may want to add a contingent take-profit order at 0.6790 to sell what you bought at 0.6710, in addition to your stop-loss order. Now if your position is opened at 0.6710, you have an OCO order to stop sell at 0.6690 or take profit at 0.6790. Now you have a complete trade strategy with defined risk parameters.

If the market continues to trade in the range, it may drop from the level you saw (0.6750/55) before you went to bed. If it hits 0.6710, then your long position is established and your OCO orders are activated. If the range holds and the price moves back up to the range highs, your take profit at 0.6790 may be triggered. If the range fails to hold, your stop-loss order limits your losses and closes out your trade for you.

WARNING

Be careful about using if/then orders with only a contingent take-profit order. Not using a stop loss to protect your downside is always very risky. At the minimum, always use an if/then stop loss to limit your risks.

If you use an if/then OCO order and the market behaves as you expect, you may awaken to find that you bought at 0.6710 and took profit (sold) at 0.6790, all while you slumbered through the night. Or you may awaken to find that your if order to buy was done, but the market has not yet hit either your stop-loss or take-profit levels. But at least your open position is protected by the activated OCO order. Worst-case scenario in this example: You wake up and find that your *if* limit order was filled and your stop was triggered on a break through the bottom of the range, giving you a loss. The key is that you effectively managed your risk.

Spreads and orders in online currency trading

Now that we've covered the different order types, we think it's important for you to be aware of how online trading platforms typically handle traders' orders. We spent some time earlier in this chapter discussing forex market spreads and the role of the market-maker. There was a good reason for that: Online forex brokers accept your orders according to their trading policies, which are spelled out in detail in the fine print in the contract you'll have to sign to open an online trading account. Make sure you read that section to be absolutely certain what your broker's order execution policies are.

REMEMBER

The key feature of most brokers' order policies is that your orders will be executed based on the *price spread* of the trading platform. That means that your limit order to buy will be filled only if the trading platform's offer price reaches your buy rate. A limit order to sell will only be triggered if the trading platform's bid price reaches your sell rate.

In practical terms, say you have an order to buy EUR/USD at 1.2855 and the broker's EUR/USD spread is 3 pips. Your buy order will be filled only if the platform's price deals 1.2852/55. If the lowest price is 1.2853/56, no cigar, because the broker's lowest offer of 56 never reached your buying rate of 55. The same thing happens with limit orders to sell.

WARNING

Stop-loss execution policies are slightly different than in equity trading because most online forex brokers guarantee that your stop-loss order will be executed at the order rate. To be able to guarantee that, brokers rely on the spread:

>> Stop-loss orders to sell are triggered if the broker's *bid* price reaches your stop-loss order rate. In concrete terms, if your stop-loss order to sell is at 1.2820 and the broker's lowest price quote is 1.2820/23, your stop will be filled at 1.2820.

>> Stop-loss orders to buy are triggered if the platform's *offer* price reaches your stop-loss rate. If your stop order to buy is at 1.2875 and the broker's high quote is 1.2872/75, your stop will be filled at 1.2875.

The benefit of this practice is that some firms will guarantee against slippage on your stop-loss orders in normal trading conditions. (Rarely, if ever, will a broker guarantee stop losses around the release of economic reports.) The downside is that your order will likely be triggered earlier than stop-loss orders in other markets, so you'll need to add in some extra cushion when placing them on your forex platform.

We explore in more detail the nuances and strategies of trading with orders in Chapters 10 and 11.

2

Data and Details You Can Use to Trade Currencies

» **Monitoring monetary policy and interest rates**

» **Understanding official currency policies and intervention**

» **Gauging risk sentiment and financial stability**

Chapter **5**

Looking at the Big Picture

The forex market is inherently a big-picture market. FX traders focus on

- » Interest rates and monetary policy developments
- » Economic growth and inflation data
- » Political elections and economic policies in major economies
- » Geopolitical risks, trade conflicts, and terror attacks
- » Major movements in other financial markets

On a daily basis, currency traders have to sort through myriad economic reports, interpret the comments of political and financial officials from around the world, take stock of geopolitical developments, and assess movements in other financial markets. They do all this to help determine what direction major currencies are likely to move.

Unfortunately, there is no set recipe for absorbing the daily flow of data and news to produce a clear-cut answer. Even if there were, many different market actors are pursuing their own interests, which may not be profit maximizing (see Chapter 3). Throw in market sentiment and future expectations, and you're looking at market participants interpreting the same data and reaching different conclusions, or maybe reaching the same conclusions but at different times. In this chapter, we lay the foundation for building the framework to make sense of the many policy, data, and news inputs that affect the forex markets every day.

The first step in laying the foundation is to get a handle on interest rates and monetary policy, because they're the final product of most of the other inputs. Unless you're an economist or banker, following monetary policy developments probably isn't one of your favorite hobbies. But if you're going to actively trade in the forex market, you need to get a handle on monetary policy and interest rates. We're not trying to turn you into an economist or an interest-rate analyst — we just want to give you the lowdown on how interest rates affect currencies.

In this chapter, we lay it all out so you can make sense of how it works, what goes into it, and how it's communicated to the market. We get into the key elements of official currency policies and what happens when governments intervene in forex markets. Lastly, we take a look at the Global Financial Crisis of 2008–2009 (GFC) to see what lessons it holds for currency traders.

Currencies and Interest Rates

If the guiding principle in real estate is "location, location, location," in currency trading it's "interest rates, interest rates, interest rates." The most significant overall determinant of a currency's value relative to other currencies is the nature and direction of monetary policy set by a country's central bank. When we say "monetary policy," we mean policy changes by a country's central bank, such as changing the money supply, setting interest rates, and introducing quantitative easing, among other things.

REMEMBER

Perhaps the most important thing that a central bank does in relation to the forex market is set domestic interest rates, which also influence overall economic activity. Lower interest rates typically stimulate borrowing, investment, and consumption, while higher interest rates tend to reduce borrowing and increase saving over consumption.

Interest rates are important to currencies because they influence the direction of global capital flows and serve as benchmarks for what investors expect to earn investing in a particular country. This situation applies most directly to fixed income investing (bonds), which comprise the lion's share of investments, but it also influences equity and other investment flows. All other things being equal, if you could invest in a government-backed bond that yields 6 percent or one that yields 2 percent, which would you choose? The one with the higher yield, of course. And that's exactly what happens with currencies. Currencies with higher yields (higher interest rates) tend to go up, and currencies with lower yields (lower interest rates) tend to weaken.

REMEMBER

Although we stress interest rates as one of the primary drivers of currency rates, interest rates aren't the only determinant of currency values. Plenty of other elements come into play, affecting currency rates both in short-term trading and in long-term trends. To use an analogy, think of the stage in a theater. Now think of interest rates as being the backdrop and the lighting on that stage. Various actors come and go; sets and props are changed between acts; but all the action on the stage takes place against the backdrop and under the lights. Interest rates provide the backdrop and set the lighting for most major currency movements, even if they're not always the center of attention.

UNDERSTANDING THE FEDERAL RESERVE DIRECTLY FROM ITS OWN SITES

When I (coauthor Paul) do research on an important topic (such as the Federal Reserve), I like to see a diverse group of sources . . . and, in this case, from the Federal Reserve (the "Fed") itself. The Fed is the most powerful central bank in the world today. It's the entity that directly manages the money supply, and it has major influence on credit and interest rates, which in turn exert powerful influence on economic growth (or contraction). So it pays to find out about them, their views, and certainly their policies and announcements. Here are some places for you to check out:

- **Federal Reserve Main site** (www.federalreserve.gov): This is where you find the new policy announcements directly from the Fed. It's where the financial world comes to find out what the Fed is up to and what they plan on doing in the near future.

- **Federal Reserve Education site** (www.federalreserveeducation.org): This site is loaded with information on the Fed's policies and initiatives with age-appropriate educational programs ranging from children to college-age and adult. You can go here to get the Fed's direct explanation of monetary policy, quantitative easing, and other issues often covered in the financial media.

- **St Louis Fed** (www.stlouisfed.org): This site has extensive economic and monetary research and data for the public. This is a treasure trove for investors and speculators to help with your investment decisions.

- **The Federal Reserve services site** (www.frbservices.org): This menu-driven site shows all the services provided to businesses and consumers from the "nation's central bank" along with educational resources.

The future is now: Interest rate expectations

REMEMBER

It's not just the current level of interest rates that matter. Markets are always adjusting to changing circumstances and anticipating future developments. When it comes to currencies and interest rates, forex markets are focused more on the direction of future interest rate moves (higher or lower) than they are on the current levels because they're already priced-in by the market. So even though a currency may have a low interest rate, market expectations of higher interest rates in the future frequently will cause the currency to appreciate.

And what drives interest rate expectations? The evolving economic outlook based on incoming data (we look at understanding and interpreting economic data in Chapter 7), economic assessments, and guidance by monetary policymakers (see the later section "Watching the central bankers"), and a host of other economic, fiscal, and political developments (some of which we look at later in this chapter).

TIP

Keep an eye on various interest rate futures markets, such as the Fed Funds futures contract for U.S. rates, to see what expectations markets are pricing in. These can be found on financial websites like Bloomberg (www.bloomberg.com/), Reuters (www.reuters.com/), and MarketWatch (www.marketwatch.com/). The commentary usually notes that markets have priced-in, say, 18 bps (basis points; 100 basis points is equivalent to 1 percent) of tightening by the next FOMC meeting, meaning the market is expecting a 72 percent chance of a 25 bps rate hike (18 bps ÷ 25 bps = 72 percent). The FOMC, by the way, is the Federal Open Market Committee.

The *outlook period,* or the time frame in which markets are expecting interest rates to change, can span several months or quarters into the future. Depending on the economic circumstances and the outlook, markets may price-in interest rate changes a full year in advance, driving short-term yields and currency levels in the process. Subsequent currency and yield fluctuations are based on incoming data and official guidance relative to the expectations markets have priced-in.

Relative interest rates

It's important to remember that currencies always come in pairs. Rather than focusing solely on a particular currency's interest rate level or outlook, forex markets tend to focus on the potential difference between two currencies' prospective interest rate changes. If two major currencies' central banks are both expected to be raising rates by the same amount in the future, there's little reason for one to outperform the other. But if one is expected to raise rates higher or faster, there are grounds for one currency to strengthen relative to the other.

REMEMBER

Forex market volatility sunk to record lows in 2014 after the major global central banks all kept interest rates at close to record low levels. This is a good reminder of the fact that interest rates are one of the key drivers of the forex market.

Interest-rate differentials

REMEMBER

The difference between the interest rates of the two currencies, known as the *interest-rate differential* or *spread*, is the key rate to watch. An increasing or widening interest-rate differential will generally favor the higher-yielding currency, whereas a falling or narrowing interest-rate differential will tend to favor the lower-yielding currency.

TIP

Some of the largest currency swings occur when two countries' interest rate cycles are moving, or are thought to be set to move, in opposite directions. And they don't necessarily have to both be moving — one currency could see expectations of higher/lower rates, whereas the other's rates are set to stay on hold. By focusing on the interest-rate differential, you can detect such changes more readily than by focusing on the rates of any individual currency.

Traders should monitor the interest-rate differentials among the major currencies by looking at the spreads between short-term government debt yields to spot shifts that may not otherwise be evident. Worth noting: The government bond market tends to price-in expected changes to interest rates, so it can give a more up-to-date view of what the market is thinking about rates compared to, say, the actual level of interest rates announced by a central bank.

For example, U.S. 2-year yields may decline by 5 bps (basis points, or a hundredth of 1 percent) — not an unusual daily development. Around the same time, Australian 2-year yields may move 5 bps higher — again, nothing earth shattering there viewed on its own. But add the two together, and you're looking at a 10 bps move between the two, and that's something to pay attention to. If the same thing happens again the following day, now you're looking at a 20 bps change in the differential, which is nearly equivalent to a typical 25 bps interest rate change from a central bank. You can be sure that if the Reserve Bank of Australia (RBA) unexpectedly raised interest rates by ¼ percent, or the Fed surprised everyone by cutting rates by ¼ percent, there would be some sharp swings in AUD/USD. The same holds true for changes in the interest-rate differentials, and they occur on a daily basis rather than the monthly meetings of most central banks.

Nominal and real interest rates

The interest rate to focus on is not always just the *nominal interest rate* (the base interest rate you see, such as the stated yield on a bond). Markets focus on *real interest rates* (inflation-adjusted rates, which is the nominal interest rate minus the rate of inflation [usually the consumer price index]). So even though a bond may carry a nominal yield of, say, 8.5 percent, if the annual rate of inflation in the country is 4.5 percent, the real yield on the bond is closer to 4 percent.

This phenomenon is most evident in emerging market economies facing hyperinflation. Even though nominal interest rates may be 20 percent, if the annual rate of inflation is 25 percent, the real yield is –5 percent. Hyperinflation and negative yields lead to capital flight. The result is extreme weakness in the domestic currency, even though nominal interest rates may be extremely high.

The same can be true with very low interest rates and *deflation* (negative inflation), such as what happened in Japan from 2000 to 2013. With interest rates at very low levels, eventually zero, and facing deflation, real Japanese yields were significantly higher than the nominal zero rates on offer. (*Note:* If you subtract a negative number, it's the same as adding that positive number.) As a result, the JPY experienced overall appreciation in this period despite very low nominal rates and abysmal economic prospects.

In the rest of this chapter, we introduce the key objectives of monetary policy, take you through the tool kits of monetary policymakers, and show you how to stay on top of the evolving interest-rate picture.

Monetary Policy 101

Monetary policy is the set of policy actions that central banks use to achieve their legal mandates. Most central banks function under legislative mandates that focus on two basic objectives:

>> Promoting price stability (also known as restraining inflation)

>> Promoting sustainable economic growth, sometimes with an explicit goal of promoting maximum employment

WARNING

Although it's a no-brainer that promoting economic growth is more important to those of us who work for a living, central bankers like to focus primarily on inflation. Low inflation fosters stable business and investment environments, so central bankers see it as the best way to promote long-run economic growth. Low inflation is also an end in itself because high inflation erodes asset values and undermines capital accumulation. Some central banks, like the U.S. Federal Reserve, have a joint mandate of price stability and promoting maximum employment. Other central banks, such as the European Central Bank (ECB), have only one mandate — to ensure price stability — with other policy objectives (growth and employment) explicitly relegated to secondary status. Still other central banks — the Swiss National Bank, for example — have a mandate to ensure a stable currency, though most countries have delegated that responsibility to the national finance ministry/treasury department.

Looking at benchmark interest rates

The primary lever of monetary policy is changes to benchmark interest rates, such as the federal funds rate in the United States or the refinance rate in the Eurozone. Changes in interest rates effectively amount to changes in the cost of money, where higher interest rates increase the cost of borrowing and lower interest rates reduce the cost of borrowing. The benchmark rates set by central banks apply to the nation's banking system and determine the cost of borrowing between banks. Banks in turn adjust the interest rates they charge to firms and individual borrowers based on these benchmark rates, affecting domestic retail borrowing costs.

Other tools in the monetary policy tool kit used by central bankers are

>> **Quantitative easing (QE):** An unconventional monetary policy used by central banks, where they buy financial assets from commercial banks and private institutions to raise the price of assets and lower their yields, while simultaneously increasing the monetary base. In the aftermath of the financial crisis, major central banks embarked on programs of QE to try to boost their economies. This included buying government and some corporate bonds to lower bond yields and try to boost lending.

>> **Reserve requirements:** The amount of capital required to be set aside by the banking system; money that cannot be used for lending.

Easy money, tight money

The main thrust (or *bias*, as markets call it) of monetary policy generally falls into two categories: expansionary or restrictive. An expansionary monetary policy aims to expand or stimulate economic growth, while a restrictive bias aims to slow economic growth, usually to fight off inflation.

Expansionary monetary policy

Expansionary monetary policy (also known as accommodative or stimulative monetary policy) is typically achieved through lowering interest rates (that is, reducing the costs of borrowing in the hope of spurring investment and consumer spending). Cutting interest rates is also known as *easing* interest rates and is frequently summed up in the term *easy monetary policy.* Central banks can also increase the money supply — the overall quantity of money in the economy — which also works to lower borrowing costs. A reduction in the reserve requirement of banks frees up capital for lending, adding to the money supply and reducing borrowing costs as well.

An expansionary monetary policy is typically employed when economic growth is low, stagnant, or contracting, and unemployment is rising. Central banks of the major economies reacted to the fallout from the GFC and the global recession by slashing interest rates to historically low levels, near zero in the case of the United States, Switzerland, and Japan.

Restrictive monetary policy

Restrictive monetary policy (also known as contractionary or tighter monetary policy) is achieved by raising, or "tightening," interest rates. Higher interest rates increase the cost of borrowing, and work to reduce spending and investment with the aim of slowing economic growth and lowering inflation.

Central banks typically employ a tighter monetary policy when an economy is believed to be expanding too rapidly. The fear from the central banker's perspective is that heightened demand coupled with the low cost of borrowing may lead to inflation beyond levels considered acceptable to the long-run health of an economy. With too much money chasing the same or too few goods, prices begin to rise, and inflation rears its ugly head. Rapid wage gains, for example, may lead to increased personal consumption, driving up the cost of all manner of retail products.

Changing rates incrementally

TIP

Changes in monetary policy usually involve many small shifts in interest rates, because central bankers are generally reluctant to shock an economy by adjusting interest rates too drastically. Even the *potential* for large interest rate changes could contribute to uncertainty among investors and businesses, potentially disrupting or delaying well-laid business plans, thereby harming the overall economy in the process and potentially boosting unemployment. Typical interest rate changes among the major central banks center on 1/4 percent or 25 basis points (a basis point is 1/100th of 1 percent, or 0.01 percent), with 50 bps (or 1/2 percent) as the next most frequent rate adjustment.

The GFC and the accompanying global recession caused key central banks to slash rates rapidly, with cuts of 75 to 100 bps coming in rapid succession in some cases. Having cut benchmark rates to near zero, several major central banks felt compelled to undertake additional *unconventional easing* measures, such as QE, to support their economies.

Unconventional easing

Central banks can only directly influence the level of short-term interest rates. Longer-term interest rates, the ones used by markets to set business and consumer lending rates, are determined by bond investors and are based on their views of growth, inflation, and creditworthiness. For example, the 10-year U.S. Treasury rate is the benchmark for U.S. mortgage rates.

When central banks cut their benchmark rates to near-zero levels, they were faced with the zero lower bound of interest rates. To further support their economies, they sought to drive down longer-term lending rates through unconventional means, typically large-scale asset purchase programs where the central bank buys longer-term government bonds. (Remember, bond prices move inversely to bond yields — it's just bond math. Buying longer-maturity bonds theoretically pushes bond prices higher and yields lower, hopefully sending consumer and business lending rates down in the process.)

Such large-scale asset purchase programs are frequently referred to as quantitative easing (QE) because the central bank is increasing the money supply, the quantity, by creating money to buy the bonds. In the United States, the Federal Reserve initiated two rounds of quantitative easing, while in the United Kingdom and Japan, the Bank of England and the Bank of Japan also undertook large-scale asset purchase programs. (Japan had also pursued QE repeatedly in the prior decade, well before the GFC.)

Currencies of countries pursuing such unconventional easing typically tend to weaken because such measures may drive down interest rates relative to other countries' rates, at least while the program is in place. Some investors also view an increasing money supply as a currency negative (the greater the supply, the lower the value). But that doesn't always hold true, especially if the extra money seeps out of the economy and into other markets, as it did in the United States in 2009.

A good example of this is when the U.S. Federal Reserve indicated in August 2010 it was considering undertaking a second round of QE, known as QE2. Initially, the USD weakened as the Fed was seen to be trying to lower rates further. But when the actual program was announced, the USD began to strengthen and U.S. yields moved higher. It may look like a case of "sell the rumor, buy the fact," but it was more in response to U.S. data and the immediate outlook: The Fed was looking at QE2 in response to a slowdown in the summer of 2010, but by the time QE2 started in November 2010, U.S. data and the outlook had rebounded. And all that money the Fed was supposedly printing? It mostly ended up back at the Fed in the form of excess reserves held by the banking system, meaning it never entered the real economy.

Watching the central bankers

If you've read this chapter from the beginning, you've probably gotten the impression that determining monetary policy is mostly an exercise in shades of gray rather than a simple black-and-white equation — and you'd be exactly right. But given the significance of monetary policy to currencies, currency traders devote a great deal of attention to trying to divine the intentions of central bankers. This has not always been an easy task, but recent trends among central banks to improve the openness of communications with markets, frequently referred to as *transparency*, have made the process less of a guessing game.

Central bankers communicate with the markets in a number of ways, and their comments can provoke market reactions similar to major economic data releases — by that, we mean sharp initial price movements followed by continued volatility or a potential change in direction:

>> **Rate decisions:** Interest-rate setting committees of central banks meet at regularly scheduled times. At the conclusion of a meeting, they issue a formal announcement of the policy decisions made at the meeting. They can raise, lower, or hold interest rates steady. They can also make changes to reserve requirements or liquidity operations.

>> **Policy statements or guidance:** Along with the interest rate decision, central banks frequently issue an accompanying statement that explains the basis for their policy action. These statements are also used to provide guidance to markets on the future course of monetary policy. The statements are carefully parsed by markets intent on discovering what the central bank is thinking, which way it's leaning, and what the timing may be for future changes. In recent years, rate announcements are often preceded by a press conference by the head of the central bank. The Federal Reserve and the European Central Bank both hold press conferences after some of their meetings. Rate announcements and accompanying policy statements are included on economic data/event calendars.

>> **Public speeches:** Central bankers frequently appear before community and business groups, and address subjects ranging from trends in the financial industry (such as the rise of hedge funds or the use of derivatives) to relatively mundane governance issues (such as financial reporting requirements). But when a central banker gives a speech that assesses the economic outlook or the future course of monetary policy, forex markets are all ears.

TIP

Appearances by central bank officials typically are included on most economic event/data calendars, and you need to be aware of them to avoid being taken by surprise. Sometimes, the topic of the speech is given in advance; other times, it's not. The most important speeches are those that focus on the economic outlook or the current monetary policy assessment.

In most cases, a prepared text is released by financial newswires at the scheduled start time of the speech. Accredited news agencies receive copies of speeches in advance to allow their reporters to prepare stories and headlines, but the release of the information is embargoed until the designated time. The remarks are then encapsulated into a series of headlines that capture the main points of the speech; this is the news that markets receive at the appointed time. When these headlines hit traders' screens, market prices start to react. If a question-and-answer session follows, the central banker's comments will be posted by the newswires as they're delivered live. This setup can make for some exciting headline-driven trading.

REMEMBER

Currency traders need to be aware of and constantly follow the current market thinking on the direction of interest rates because of the strong relationship between interest rates and currency values. The best way to do this is to follow market commentaries in print and online news media, always keeping in mind that such outlets (especially print) are usually one step behind the current market. This makes online news commentaries that much more relevant. Some of the best sites for timely insights and market reporting are Bloomberg (www.bloomberg.com/), Reuters (www.reuters.com/), and MarketWatch (www.marketwatch.com/). Twitter is a great resource for getting the latest central bank headlines. Best of all, for now, most of these sites are free.

TIP

Look for currency brokers that offer real-time market analysis and news updates.

In the next section, we delve a bit deeper into how monetary policy is presented to financial markets by central bank officials. We also look at currency-specific policies and rhetoric. Sometimes, how a message is delivered or who delivers it is more important than the message itself. This is certainly true of monetary or currency policy comments from central bank or government finance officials.

Interpreting monetary policy communications

In the preceding section, we cover the various ways in which central bankers communicate their thinking to market participants. But the process is far more nuanced and evolved than relying simply on official policy statements or speeches before the Rotary Club of Indianapolis. Central bankers are keenly aware that their comments have the ability to move, and potentially disrupt, financial markets all over the world. So they choose their words very carefully, leaving traders to act as interpreters. Before you start interpreting monetary policy statements and commentary, it'll help to know the following.

Not all central bankers are created equal

The interest-rate-setting committees of central banks, frequently known as Monetary Policy Committees (MPCs) — the Fed's Federal Open Market Committee (FOMC) is one of these — typically operate under a one-member/one-vote rule. But when it comes to delivering a message to the markets, the chairman or president of the central bank and its deputies hold far more sway than any other individual member. This is partly in deference to the central bank chief's role as first among equals, but also because that person is frequently viewed as expressing the thinking of the entire committee. Central bankers strive for consensus in reaching their decisions, and who better to represent and present this view than the chairman or president?

TIP

When the head of the central bank gives an update on the economy or the outlook for interest rates, listen up. A scheduled speech by the chair of the Fed, for instance, is likely to be preceded by market speculation similar to that of a major economic data report. And the reaction to his comments can be equally sharp.

In the case of the Fed, the FOMC is composed of 12 voting members consisting of the board of governors and a *rotating* slate of regional Federal Reserve Bank presidents each year. So when a Federal Reserve Bank president is set to speak, make sure you know whether that person is a voting member in the current year before acting on their comments.

WARNING

Remarks by nonvoting FOMC members are frequently discounted or ignored by traders because the speaker isn't going to be casting a vote at the next meeting. But this is a bit of an oversimplification and can be risky. Before downplaying a nonvoter's comments, you need to consider the speaker's comments in the context of the FOMC consensus. Do those comments express that person's own views or elaborate on a shift in consensus thinking?

Birds of a feather: Hawks and doves

Central bank officials are frequently a known commodity to market analysts and traders, either from past policy statements or from their academic or policy writings prior to becoming central bankers. Markets typically refer to central bankers in terms of being hawks or doves. A *hawk* is someone who generally favors an aggressive approach to fighting inflation and is not averse to raising rates even if it will hurt economic growth. A *dove,* on the other hand, is a central banker who tends to favor pro-growth and employment monetary policy, and is generally reluctant to tighten rates if it will hurt the economy. In short, hawks tend to be fixated on fighting inflation, and doves tend to stress growth and employment.

Don't get us wrong: There are plenty of central bankers in the middle who can wear both hats (or feathers, in this instance). In those cases, the middle-of-the-roaders tend to reveal their hawkish or dovish leanings only at the extremes of the policy cycles.

REMEMBER

So if a hawk is slated to speak on the outlook for monetary policy, and that person cites the risks from inflation or the need to prevent any increase in inflationary pressures, guess what? You're not going to see much of a reaction from the markets because that person is a known quantity speaking true to form. You get a much sharper reaction when a hawk downplays the threats from inflation or suggests that inflationary pressures may be starting to recede. Markets will jump all over dovish comments coming from a hawk, and vice versa with hawkish comments made by a dove.

A BIRD'S-EYE VIEW OF THE FED: DOVES VERSUS HAWKS

One thing that financial analysts and "Fed watchers" keep on the lookout for are "doves" and "hawks" that are at the helm of the Fed (on their Federal Open Market Committee).

A "dove" is a Fed official who has a bias toward an expansionary money supply and lower interest rates while a "hawk" has a bias toward a tighter money supply and higher interest rates. Both are divergent views, and their policy impact can be varied and ultimately result in widely different economic outcomes. Additionally, the Fed can be more dovish or hawkish given the economic realities of that time. In the late 1970s inflation was raging, and in 1981 the Fed took a hawkish stance by raising interest rates. This in turn tamed inflation and the dollar strengthened, so those currency traders who took a bullish stance on the door at that time were profitable.

In the wake of the COVID-19 pandemic, the Fed (and the U.S. Treasury) greatly expanded the money supply (from late 2020 to mid-2021) and kept interest rates very low. Given that, the U.S. dollar declined. Those speculators who made bearish bets on the U.S. dollar were profitable.

For those seriously interested in bullish and/or bearish scenarios for the U.S. dollar, it's very important to understand the positions of doves and hawks because they are frequently an "early warning" system for traders who want to keep a step ahead of currency movements and increase the chances for a profitable trade.

Official Currency Policies and Rhetoric

Another major influence on currency values is government policies or official stances regarding the value of individual currencies. Some of the largest changes in currency values in recent decades have been brought on by official policies and multilateral agreements among the major industrialized economies. For instance, the Plaza Accord of 1985 stands out as a watershed in forex market history, ultimately resulting in a roughly 50 percent *devaluation* of the U.S. dollar over the course of the next two years.

National governments have a great deal at stake when it comes to the value of their currencies. After all, in a sense, a nation's currency is the front door to its economy and financial markets. If the currency is viewed as unstable or too volatile, it's tantamount to slamming the front door shut. And no major economy can afford to do that today.

In this section, we look at the major objectives of national currency policies, who sets them, and how they're implemented.

Currency policy or currency stance?

Referring to official government thinking on currencies as a *currency policy* may be a mischaracterization. Instead, you may do better to think of it as a *stance* on particular currency values at a particular point in time.

Daily trading volumes in the forex market dwarf most national central bank currency reserve holdings. (*Currency reserves* are the accumulated stocks of international currencies held by central banks for use in market interventions and overall central bank reserve management.) Japan and China together have more than $2 trillion in central bank currency reserves. That may seem like a lot, but average currency trading volume in the global forex market is over $5 trillion *per day*. This means that even if national governments *wanted* to routinely manage the value of their national currency, they would be hard-pressed to overcome market forces if they were at odds with the official policy.

To summarize why governments are generally reluctant to get involved in trying to influence currency values, it comes down to the following:

>> **They can't because they're too small.** Forex markets are much bigger than any one nation's foreign currency reserves.

>> **They can't because of market structure.** Forex markets operate outside national jurisdictions.

>> **They can't agree on what to do.** Currencies always have another country or countries on the other side of the pair. You may want your currency to weaken, but do others want their currencies to strengthen? Not everyone can have a weak currency.

>> **They don't want to meddle in the free market.** Tampering with international capital flows is a recipe for economic disaster and, in some cases, diplomatic discontent.

REMEMBER

Generally speaking, then, governments prefer to refrain from getting involved in setting currency rates or trying to influence overall currency direction. They recognize that their power is extremely limited and that it must be used sparingly, usually only when extreme circumstances demand action from the national government or collective action from several governments. Moreover, the global economic superpowers are believers in the power of free markets to best allocate capital and maximize long-run economic potential. It simply would not do for them to openly reject free-market policies by regularly seeking to influence currency rates. You have to practice what you preach, or you start losing your following. For governments, that translates to credibility — and that's a trait most governments seek to cultivate and protect.

WARNING

But — and this is a big *but* — governments *do* seek to influence currency rates from time to time. And when they do, it's usually a key long-term turning point in currency values.

In the next section, we look at the principal actors in each country or currency zone and what their recent actions on currencies suggest for their currency policy goals.

Calling the shots on currencies

In the preceding section, we list a number of reasons why national governments are reluctant to get involved in trying to influence the value of their currencies. Chief among these are the size and extent of the global forex market and the need for nations to reach agreement on whether adjustments are even needed. The Group of Seven (G7) used to be the main body that handled currency issues, but globalization has brought more economies to the table in the form of the Group of Twenty (G20; see Chapter 3). With an even larger collection of competing national interests in the bigger G20, collective action on currencies seems less likely.

If governments had their way, they would probably prefer to see fixed exchange rates replace floating rates and avoid the subject entirely, but that's not a realistic option for the foreseeable future. Confronted with the realities of forex markets, most government currency officials go to great lengths to avoid discussing currency values out of fear that their comments will be misinterpreted and lead to sharp exchange rate shifts. That fear was born out of experience, and today's top currency officials are much more discreet than their predecessors just a few decades ago.

Responsibility for currency matters typically falls to the finance ministry or the central bank in the nations of the most heavily traded currencies. In the following sections, we take a look at who has responsibility for setting and implementing currency policies in the five major currencies and what their major motivations are.

The United States

The Department of the Treasury has the legal mandate for all currency matters, from printing the notes and minting the coins to ensuring the soundness of the U.S. dollar in international markets. The secretary of the Treasury is the primary spokesman for the U.S. dollar. The deputy Treasury secretary for international affairs is the hands-on Treasury official responsible for day-to-day currency matters.

TIP

When the U.S. Treasury secretary speaks on the value of the dollar, or any other currency for that matter, FX markets listen.

The Eurozone

The European Central Bank (ECB) is responsible for both monetary policy and currency matters under the agreement that created the single-currency Eurozone in 1999. The ECB's governing council is the primary decision-making body; it's composed of the presidents of the central banks of the participating nations, with the ECB president as the group's chief policy maker and spokesman.

When the ECB needs to intervene in the market, it can do so by itself, along with the central banks of the member states on their behalf. In the EUR's early years, global central banks intervened to prop up the newly formed currency; however, in recent years, there has been no official intervention in the EUR.

REMEMBER

However, individual European countries continue to exert influence over currency policy through their finance ministers, who had responsibility for currencies prior to the introduction of the euro and the creation of the ECB. The Eurozone finance ministers meet regularly as a group and frequently weigh in on forex market developments. There still appears to be great consideration given to the member states' governments by markets with regard to currency values, with the two largest European economies — Germany and France — wielding the greatest influence. But consensus appears to be the key element in deciding if the euro is too strong or too weak, and a clear majority of member states needs to be on board in opposing market movements before the market will pay attention.

The ECB is primarily concerned with fighting inflation and seeks to achieve currency stability as a means of fostering long-term economic growth. Although Europe remains heavily export oriented, so extreme euro strength is a risk factor for the Eurozone economy, the ECB has been reluctant to intervene in the forex market so far.

Japan

The Ministry of Finance (MOF) is responsible for currency matters in Japan. The MOF is the most powerful government ministry in Japan and can wield more influence over economic affairs than even the Bank of Japan (BOJ), the central bank. The MOF devotes a great deal of attention to the value of the JPY. The primary day-to-day currency spokesman for the MOF is the vice minister for international affairs, but during periods of volatility, the finance minister will frequently issue statements. It is not at all uncommon for the MOF to issue daily comments on the forex markets, particularly when JPY volatility increases. The MOF last ordered an intervention in September 2010 as the JPY was strengthening and USD/JPY was threatening to drop under the key 80.00 level as the Fed geared up for a second round of quantitative easing. The Japanese authorities, along with the major global central banks, also intervened in the JPY in the aftermath of the 2011 tsunami. The yen surged on the back of safe-haven flows, but the intervention was necessary to limit JPY strength and help rebuild the Japanese economy on the back of this tragic event. (We discuss currency market intervention later in this chapter.)

REMEMBER

Japan's economy remains highly export oriented, so the value of the JPY is important to export competitiveness and corporate profitability. Excessive JPY strength, which makes exports more expensive abroad and lowers the profit from foreign sales, is usually the trigger point for the MOF to express concern and possibly take action in the market.

The United Kingdom

The Chancellor of the Exchequer (treasury secretary or finance minister) is the individual responsible for the British pound's fate. The governor of the Bank of England (BOE) also shares responsibility for the pound in a bit of a holdover arrangement from when the BOE became independent from the government in 1997.

The chancellor/BOE generally stays out of currency matters and appears most concerned with the pound's exchange rate versus the euro, because the bulk of UK trade is conducted with the Eurozone.

The United Kingdom is closely aligned with European economies and would be a candidate to join the Eurozone single currency, but nationalism runs deep when it comes to getting rid of the pound. The standing government line is that no decision on joining the euro would be made without conducting a national referendum.

Switzerland

The Swiss National Bank (SNB) is charged with responsibility for the Swiss franc along with setting monetary policy. The SNB is most concerned with the Swiss franc's exchange rate versus the euro, because nearly 80 percent of Swiss trade is conducted with Eurozone nations. The SNB has been known to speak up in opposition to CHF strength or weakness whenever the EUR/CHF exchange rate approaches extreme levels. During the Eurozone debt crisis in late 2009–2010, EUR weakened sharply against the CHF and prompted the SNB to intervene repeatedly to stem CHF strength, but without any success.

However, in 2011, the SNB took the unusual step of imposing a 1.20 peg (a move that acts like an anchor tying one currency to the other) on the EUR/CHF rate. Whenever the EUR/CHF rate approached 1.20, the SNB was ready to intervene to stop it from falling below this level and limit CHF strength. The market took the SNB at its word, and there were only a handful of occasions when the EUR/CHF rate fell below 1.20. This was an unusual situation — usually, intervention occurs only for a temporary period or in response to an economic crisis or national disaster. As of 2015, the SNB got rid of the peg and the Swiss franc soared 20 percent, causing havoc for those who had some financial transactions tied to it, such as mortgages in Swiss francs.

Taking a closer look at currency market intervention

In every big-bank currency trading room in major financial centers, there is a direct line to the open market trading desk of the central bank. When that line lights up, the whole dealing room erupts. That line is reserved for open market intervention by the central bank, and when it rings, it usually means only one thing: The central bank is intervening in the market.

Intervention refers to central banks buying or selling currencies in the open market to drive currency rates in a desired direction. Direct intervention in the market is usually taken only as a last resort. It also may be a stopgap measure to stabilize markets upset by extreme events, such as a stock market collapse or a natural disaster. When it's not necessitated by emergency circumstances, markets are generally aware of the increasing risks of intervention.

TIP

Open market intervention is usually preceded by several less-blunt forms of official intervention. The idea from the government's point of view is to get as much bang for the buck as possible before committing real money. *Note:* Central banks have limited firepower in relation to the overall market, so they have to pick their spots well. Sometimes, the government's objective is simply to slow a market move to restore financial market stability, and less drastic forms of intervention are not yet necessary. Some of the more subtle forms of intervention are

>> **Verbal intervention or jawboning:** These are efforts by finance ministry or central bank officials to publicly suggest that current market directions are undesirable. Basically, it amounts to trying to talk up or talk down a particular currency's value. For example, if the Japanese MOF is intent on preventing further JPY strength to protect its export sector, but the USD/JPY rate keeps moving lower, senior MOF officials may indicate that "excessive exchange rate movements are undesirable." This message is a warning for currency traders to reduce their USD selling/JPY buying or risk the potential consequences. If the market ignores the warning, the MOF may take it up a notch and indicate that it is "closely monitoring exchange rates," which is language typically used before actual open market intervention.

>> **Checking rates:** This is the central bank's open market desk ringing in on the direct line to major currency banks' trading desks. The traders don't know if it's going to be a real intervention or not, but they still react instinctively based on previously indicated preferences. Even rumors of a central bank checking rates are enough to trigger a significant market reaction.

In terms of actual open market intervention, there are several different forms it can take, all depending on which and how many central banks are participating. The more the merrier; better still, there's strength in numbers:

>> **Unilateral intervention:** This is intervention by a single central bank to buy or sell its own currency, such as the SNB. Unilateral intervention is generally the least effective form of intervention because the government is perceived (usually correctly) to be acting alone and without the support of other major governments. Markets will typically revert to the earlier direction after the intervention has run its course to test the central bank's resolve and to see if it's intent on stopping the move or simply slowing it. The MOF/BOJ intervention in fall 2010 was a unilateral intervention and had little success stemming the tide of JPY strength. However, the Swiss authorities were successful at pegging the EUR/CHF rate at 1.20. There is always an exception to every rule.

>> **Joint intervention:** This is when two central banks intervene together to shift the direction of their shared currency pair. For example, if the ECB and the Federal Reserve are concerned about EUR strength versus the USD, they may decide to intervene jointly to sell EUR/USD. This is a clear sign to markets that

the two governments are prepared to work together to alter the direction of that pair's exchange rate. Joint intervention is very rare, and this example is, so far, only hypothetical.

>> **Concerted or multilateral intervention:** This is when multiple central banks join together to intervene in the market simultaneously, also referred to as *coordinated intervention.* This is the most powerful and effective type of intervention because it suggests unity of purpose by multiple governments. Concerted intervention isn't done lightly by major central banks — and markets don't take it lightly either. It's the equivalent of a sledgehammer to the head. Concerted intervention frequently results in major long-term trend changes. This is considered a last resort, and it's typically used only in response to natural disasters such as the 2011 tsunami in Japan.

REMEMBER

In terms of the impact of intervention, different governments are given different degrees of respect by the market. Due to the frequency of past interventions and constant threats of it, the Japanese tend to get the least respect. The BOE, the SNB, and the ECB are treated with considerably more respect by markets, with the ECB being the linchpin of credibility for the Eurozone. Finally, when the U.S. Treasury (via the Fed) formally intervenes, which is a rare occurrence, it's considered a major event, and the market usually respects the intervention.

WARNING

There is a difference between a central bank intervening for its own account and a central bank intervening on behalf of another foreign central bank. For example, during the MOF/BOJ intervention campaign in 2003 and 2004, there were several instances where the U.S. Fed bought USD/JPY during the New York trading day. The first reaction was that the U.S. Treasury was joining in and supporting the intervention by the MOF/BOJ, and this amplified the effect of the intervention. But the U.S. Treasury later denied that it had ordered the intervention. What happened was that the BOJ asked the New York Fed to intervene on its behalf during the New York trading session. Central banks have standing agreements to act as each other's representatives in their local markets. So even though the New York Fed bought dollars, it bought them for the BOJ.

REMEMBER

Does intervention work? That is a question that frequently comes up when central banks get involved. The simple answer is an unequivocal "Yes, but. . . ." Intervention is most effective when it's backed by monetary policy moving in the same direction, such as expected higher interest rates to support a weak currency or easier monetary policy to weaken a strong one. Even then, interest rate changes are no guarantee that the intervention will be successful.

In the short run, the intervention may seem fruitless and counterproductive. This is especially the case with unilateral intervention. The market typically rejects the unilateral intervention and reverts to pushing the market in the direction opposed by the intervention. This situation can go on for weeks and months or — in the

SNB's case in 2010 — years, which can lead central banks to take even more dramatic action, such as imposing a currency peg. When it's a joint or concerted intervention, the results are usually more immediate and successful.

Financial stability

The Global Financial Crisis of 2008–2009 triggered a massive global recession, the likes of which had not been seen since the Great Depression of the 1930s. As a result, major governments' finances were thrown into disarray, as tax revenues plunged and spending was maintained or increased through fiscal stimulus. Suddenly, the creditworthiness and financial stability of major national governments were being questioned by global markets.

REMEMBER

A currency's perceived value is intrinsically linked to the faith investors have in the financial stability of the nation(s) standing behind it. If investors fear a *sovereign debt default,* meaning government bonds won't be paid back, they're likely to sell both those bonds and the country's currency. The result can be a market frenzy in which government bond prices crash, sending yields soaring and increasing the government's borrowing costs, effectively forcing the government out of global capital markets and leading to a default.

The Eurozone debt crisis of 2009–2013 is the most obvious recent example, where bond investors fled Greek, Irish, Portuguese, and Cypriot government debt, raising borrowing costs to unaffordable levels and forcing those governments to seek a bailout from wealthier Eurozone members. From the start of the Greek debt crisis in November 2009 until a temporary bailout mechanism was established in May 2010, the euro weakened against the USD by more than 20 percent and fell even more against other currencies.

And the fallout from the GFC is not confined to government debt. Major global banks lost trillions in the crisis, and some didn't survive. In the aftermath of the financial crisis and the Eurozone debt crisis, some global banks remain extremely fragile and on government life support. In the case of European banks in particular, they hold around half of outstanding Eurozone government debt, meaning sovereign defaults or *restructurings* (a euphemism meaning investors don't get back the full amount or payments are delayed) have the potential to cause additional massive losses to the banking sector, imperiling the Eurozone economy even further.

Debts, deficits, and growth

In the aftermath of the GFC, highly indebted European countries are certainly not alone in having investors question their financial stability. Debt levels in the

United Kingdom, United States, and Japan are routinely cited as potential negatives, weighing on sentiment for those currencies from time to time. The USD's standing as the global reserve currency of choice is increasingly being called into question. And then there are the outliers, like Hungary, Iceland, and Dubai, small economies overall, but credit fears over their financial stability have a way of reverberating throughout global markets and sending risk sentiment (which we discuss later in this chapter) into a tailspin.

As part of your analysis of individual currencies, you need to be aware of the financial stability of the key currency countries. The metrics to keep in mind are

>> **Debt-to-GDP ratio:** A measure of the total amount of government debt relative to the size of the economy. Debt-to-GDP ratios over 90 percent of GDP tend to put countries under the credit-risk microscope.

>> **Deficits as a percent of GDP:** Current and projected deficits add to the total amount of government debt, which can increase the debt/GDP ratio, potentially destabilizing a country's credit outlook. As a general rule, anything over 6 percent is usually considered danger level, and a deficit in the region of 3 percent is considered stable.

>> **Growth rates (GDP):** Low or negative growth can undermine a nation's GDP relative to its debt service obligations, increasing the burdens of debt service and raising the risk of default. The imposition of *austerity measures* (budget cuts and tax increases) in the most beleaguered Eurozone countries during the sovereign debt crisis threatened to lock those countries into a cycle of underperformance, which weighed heavily on their debt loads.

TIP

For the economics novice, this may all seem overwhelming. Don't worry if you couldn't imagine finding out a debt-to-GDP level on your own. Read the business pages in the paper or on the web — they usually flag countries with debt problems well in advance.

Gauging credit risk

Just as with monetary policy and interest rate developments, financial stability evolves over a long time period. But there are day-to-day developments that impact the markets' views of individual countries' financial stability.

TIP

How can you monitor the current state of the markets' views of a nation's creditworthiness? Keep an eye on the following credit risk measures through markets' news reports and economic commentaries:

>> **Credit ratings:** Although often late to the game in the GFC, the sovereign debt ratings issued by Moody's, Standard & Poor's (S&P), and Fitch still carry a lot of weight. A ratings downgrade can make government debt issues ineligible for certain institutional investors, forcing them to sell those government bonds. Prior to a ratings change (they can be upgrades as well as downgrades), the credit rating agencies will typically issue an announcement that a country's debt ratings are under review and offer a bias to that review, such as "Portugal sovereign debt placed on review; outlook negative." Such announcements can have a significant impact on the currency involved.

>> **Yield spreads:** These are the difference between the yields (interest rates) of one government's bonds relative to an ostensibly safer country's bonds. In the Eurozone debt crisis of 2009–2013, for example, markets fixated on the spread between yields of peripheral countries like Greece and Portugal and those of stalwart Germany. A widening spread indicates increasing credit concerns, as the bonds of the weak country are sold, sending yields higher, and bonds of the safe country are bought, sending those yields lower, widening the spread. Yield spreads fluctuate on a daily and intra-day basis, with widening spreads indicating deteriorating credit risk and narrowing spreads indicating greater relief.

>> **Credit default swaps (CDS):** These derivatives are basically an insurance policy in the event of a default, where the buyer pays a premium and the seller is obligated to make good on the bond in the event of a default. CDS are an active speculative counterpart to the underlying bonds themselves, and they may often lead bond market moves. Rising CDS indicate increasing credit risk, and falling CDS rates, expressed in basis points (bps), signal lesser concern.

>> **Debt auction results:** Governments borrow money through regularly scheduled auctions or *issuances,* where the government offers its debt for sale to global investors. The extent of demand and the price investors are willing pay (the yield) are the key measures here. Demand is gauged according to the *bid/cover ratio,* meaning how much is bid, or sought, relative to the amount being offered. The higher the bid/cover ratio, the greater the demand and supposed security. A *failed auction,* one where the government is not able to sell, or borrow, the full amount it seeks is "not a good thing," as Martha Stewart might say. But some investors are usually willing to buy anything if the price is right, and that's where the yield comes in. If investors demand a higher yield (bid a lower price) relative to current rates, it's an indication of concern.

For U.S. Treasury debt, there's yet another indicator, supposedly attesting to the international appetite for U.S. debt, with implications for the value of the USD. The amount bought by *indirect bidders* is viewed as a proxy for foreign central bank and reserve managers' demand. A low turnout by indirect bidders can be interpreted as a vote of no confidence for U.S. debt and/or the USD by other major governments. The bid/cover ratio, yield results, and amount of indirect bids measures are all interpreted relative to prior auction results for similar issuances.

Geopolitical Risks and Events

Geopolitics is nothing more than a fancy word used to describe what's going on in the world at large. As it's applied to the currency markets, geopolitics tends to focus on political, military/security, or natural disruptions to the global economy or individual regions or nations. Because currency markets are the conduits for international capital flows, they're usually the first to react to international events, as global investors shift assets in response to geopolitical developments.

REMEMBER

Currency markets have no national or patriotic allegiances when it comes to favoring one currency over another. The forex market simply calculates the likely economic fallout from an international event and its ultimate currency impact. One example is the popular uprisings in the Middle East and North Africa in early 2011. Egypt is a relatively small economy, meaning that the turmoil there did not threaten the global economic outlook, and forex and other financial markets were not seriously affected. But as the unrest spread to Libya, a major oil producer, oil prices spiked on supply disruptions, and concerns grew that other oil producers could be affected. Stock markets started to wobble, and the USD weakened as oil and gold soared. Likewise, geopolitical tensions between the Ukraine and Russia in 2014 had very little influence on markets because the Ukraine economy is fairly small and the market took the view that the tensions wouldn't escalate or threaten European oil and gas supplies from Russia. You have to interpret each international event dispassionately, with an eye on the short- and long-term economic impact to determine its significance for individual currencies.

The United States tends to wield more influence on the world's stage because it's the largest national economy and the primary military superpower. In addition, the U.S. dollar is the largest global reserve currency and the de facto currency in many developing economies. Finally, with increasing globalization of trade and markets, the U.S. dollar frequently functions as a global risk barometer. For these reasons, the U.S. dollar tends to experience the greatest reaction in times of global turmoil or uncertainty, and the market tends to think in USD-positive and

USD-negative terms, viewing all other currencies in contrast to the U.S. dollar. When geopolitical events are looking problematic, the USD tends to suffer, especially against safe havens like the yen. If the risks or tensions come down, the dollar may go up.

Elections in individual countries, including by-elections and legislative referenda, also fall under the geopolitical risk umbrella, especially when the outcome may lead to a change in government or economic policies. *By-elections* (ad hoc elections to fill individual legislative seats made vacant by death or resignation, for example) are typically seen as interim votes of confidence on the governing party. Depending on how near the next general election is, and on other economic factors, by-elections may have a greater effect on political sentiment.

REMEMBER

As important as geopolitical issues are to the market's overall assessment of a currency's value, they tend to have relatively short-run implications and must be interpreted in light of other prevailing economic fundamentals. For instance, if the USD is weakening based on a weak economic outlook, for example, and there's a disruption to oil supplies from political unrest or a natural disaster, sending oil prices higher, it's just another reason to sell USD. In contrast, if the USD is strengthening based on a more positive economic trajectory and higher rate expectations, a spike in oil prices may see the usual inverse relationship break down, and both oil and the USD move higher.

Gauging risk sentiment

In recent years, the concept of *risk sentiment* has taken hold as a way of expressing overall conditions across financial markets, including forex. Risk sentiment refers to investor behavior and whether investors are actively seeking returns by embracing riskier assets *(risk seeking* or *risk appetite)*, or whether they're seeking the safety of supposedly more secure assets *(risk averse* or *risk aversion)*. These two behavioral modes are frequently referred to as *risk-on* and *risk-off,* or *risk-positive* and *risk-negative.*

For currency traders, the risk environment can be a critical factor in driving currency rate movements. Part of the reason has to do with the interest rates of various major currencies. Hedge funds, commodity trading advisors (CTAs), and other leveraged speculators (see Chapter 3 for more on these guys) borrow funds (the leverage) on a short-term basis at the lowest cost available, meaning currencies with the lowest interest rates are used as *funding currencies.* In a risk-on environment, they then sell those currencies and use the proceeds to buy risk assets with greater price appreciation potential. In a risk-off environment, they're compelled to sell their risk assets and buy back those funding currencies that they previously sold.

Risk on or risk off?

REMEMBER

So what determines whether risk is on or off? In a word, volatility. *Volatility* refers to the size and speed of price movements over a short time frame, meaning hours or days. But volatility is the symptom and not the cause of those price changes. News and events are what dictate market reactions:

>> In the simplest sense, when news and economic data are positive and everyone's feeling good about the outlook, risk is on and risk assets tend to appreciate.

>> When the news or data turns negative or outright catastrophic in the case of the GFC, investors turn more cautious and may exit risk trades, potentially triggering widespread selling that may force prices lower and force other investors to bail out as well, amplifying the sell-off.

We have little doubt that much of the increase in the risk-on/risk-off trading dynamic in recent years is the result of algorithmic, or model-based, trading, which has taken on increased prominence in all markets. If the computer is told that an X percent change in one asset or indicator means it should exit an existing position, it will literally not "think" twice about selling out.

Gauges of risk sentiment

To follow the evolution of risk sentiment, it helps to have a good handle on the current state of market affairs and expectations. For more empirical indications of risk sentiment, pay attention to the following:

>> **VIX index:** This is the options volatility on the S&P 500 U.S. stock index, frequently referred to as the *fear index.* A rising VIX indicates increased risk aversion (stocks are being sold), and a falling VIX signals the outlook is calming.

>> **Government bond yields:** Major government bonds, such as U.S. Treasuries, German bunds, UK Gilts, or Japanese JGBs, are considered safe assets (for now at least). Rising yields typically mean those bonds are being sold and investors are embracing risk. But sometimes those bonds are being sold on credit concerns, which is risk-negative. Falling yields suggest risk aversion, as investors are fleeing risk assets and buying the safety of government bonds.

>> **Emerging-market stock performance:** Investors have become increasingly international in their perspective and buying shares in Shanghai or Rio is no longer considered exotic. Such emerging-market economies have led the way out of the GFC, and their stock markets can be the canary in the coal mine — prices down, risk off; prices up, risk on.

Risky versus safe assets

REMEMBER

The low interest rate environment of recent years has forced investors and speculators alike to chase returns by investing in so-called *risk assets* that offer higher potential returns. The clearest example of risk assets are stocks and commodities: A more positive outlook (risk on) may see stocks gain as corporate profits increase, and commodities may benefit on stronger demand for raw materials and natural resources, like oil. In forex, the risk-on currencies are those linked to commodities (AUD, CAD, and NZD, in particular) and major alternatives to the USD, like EUR and GBP. A risk-on environment may also see carry trades bought, where higher-yielding currencies such as those just mentioned are bought and lower-yielding currencies like the JPY, USD and CHF are sold (funding currencies). For example, a positive risk environment may see AUD/JPY move higher.

On the other side of the risk equation (risk off) are the supposedly safe assets, such as U.S. Treasury bonds, the USD, CHF, and JPY. When bad news and events hit markets (think the Global Financial Crisis or Eurozone debt bailouts), investors typically flee risk assets, selling stocks and commodities and buying the safety of government bonds and safer currencies like CHF, JPY, and the USD. Price moves in a risk-off environment can be extremely volatile because it's a one-two punch where traders exit (sell) risk-on positions and also buy safer, risk-off assets.

TIP

Pay attention to the news when potentially disruptive events threaten the economic outlook, and be aware of the risk-on/risk-off dynamic. Depending on the nature of events, especially whether they're short-term like a natural disaster, or more enduring like a debt crisis in Europe, they can offer potential opportunities to reenter a longer-term trend from lower price levels.

REMEMBER

Sometimes there is no such unifying theme such as risk on/risk off and individual currencies tend to walk to the beat of their own drums. As major global central banks take steps to unwind enormous stimulus programs and normalize monetary policy in the coming months and years, risk on/risk off could be replaced with a greater focus on the economic fundamentals.

» Identifying support and resistance

» Spotting important chart patterns

» Using momentum the right way

Chapter **6**

Cutting the Fog with Technical Analysis

S aying that there is a lot of information to absorb in the forex market is an understatement of major proportions. To help make sense of all the information, a lot of which can be just noise — the fog of the market — professional traders focus on the one piece of information that is not subject to dispute or opinion: price.

TIP

The field of technical analysis is huge, and there's no way we can cover it in its entirety in this single chapter. Literally hundreds of books have been written on technical analysis in general, as well as on specific approaches (such as the Elliott wave principle or candlestick analysis). In Chapter 19, we suggest several of our favorite books on technical analysis as additional reading. We strongly urge you to supplement the material in this chapter with further in-depth study.

In this chapter, we give you as rich a slice of the technical cake as possible, covering the main elements of technical analysis as they apply to the forex market. What's more, we approach it from a trader's perspective, focusing on the technical tools and approaches that we've found most useful in our own currency trading, as well as what it means for trade strategies and spotting trade setups. That approach may get us in trouble with some technical purists out there, but hey, that's what makes a market — a difference of opinion.

The Philosophy of Technical Analysis

Calling technical analysis a philosophy is probably a bit of a stretch, but plenty of technical traders are almost cultish in their devotion to it. More than anything, technical analysis is a subjective approach aimed at bringing a sense of order to seemingly random price movements. Traders use technical analysis to identify trade opportunities, refine their trading strategies (entry and exit levels), and manage their market risk.

TIP

Personally, we like to use fundamentals to guide our overall view of market direction (see Chapter 7), and refine that with technical analysis to identify entry and exit points for specific trades. But not infrequently, technical analysis will suggest a trade opportunity all by itself, even though it may be counter to our fundamental outlook (see the later section "Candlestick patterns" for more).

What is technical analysis?

In a nutshell, *technical analysis* is the study of historical price movements to predict future price movements. You're probably familiar with the standard disclaimer that "past performance is no guarantee of future results," a statement that tends to call into question the validity of using past price data to forecast future price developments.

REMEMBER

But technical analysis is able to get *beyond* those concerns based on two main considerations:

>> **Markets are made up of humans.** Human psychology and investing behavior haven't changed very much over the years, whether it's the Dutch tulip frenzy of the 1600s, the dot-com bubble of the 1990s, or the real estate bubbles of the 21st century. The emotional forces that dictate buying and selling decisions are reflected in historical price patterns that appear over and over in all manner of financial markets. As long as humans are still making the decisions (or are writing the programs for the computers that make the decisions), you'll be able to look at past behavior as a guide to what is likely to happen in the future.

>> **Technical analysis is widely practiced in all markets.** This is the self-fulfilling-prophecy aspect of technical analysis. The greater the number of traders who focus on technical analysis, the more likely their actions will reflect the interpretations of technical analysis, reinforcing the impact of that analysis. Believe us when we say that professional currency traders who don't practice some form of technical analysis are a rarity.

What technical analysis is not

WARNING

Despite its name, technical analysis is not some engineer-designed, surefire, guaranteed method of market analysis. There are no such methods, period. Technical analysis involves a high degree of subjectivity where individual interpretations can vary significantly. Two technical traders looking at the same currency chart could reach opposite conclusions about the course of future prices. What's more, they could both be right, depending on their timing and specific strategies.

Technical analysis requires a great deal of patience, practice, and experimentation based on individual preferences and circumstances. Short-term traders focusing on the next few minutes and hours find certain tools and approaches more helpful than long-term traders do. Longer-term traders looking at multiday or multiweek trades use other tools and indicators entirely. Certain technical approaches work better in some currency pairs than others. Overall market conditions of volatility and liquidity also influence which technical approach works best. The key is to develop your own approach based on your particular circumstances — time frame, risk appetite, and discipline.

TIP

No single, magical technical indicator or approach always works. Be careful about becoming too reliant on any single indicator. A particular indicator may yield excellent signals in certain market environments but fail when market conditions begin to change. We suggest becoming familiar with several different approaches and indicators, using them to cross-check each other depending on market conditions. (We look at this idea in the later section "Waiting for confirmation.")

Forms of technical analysis

Technical analysis can be broken down into three main approaches:

>> **Chart analysis:** Entails visual inspection of price charts to identify price trends, ranges, support, and resistance levels. (We look at chart analysis in the later section "The Art of Technical Analysis.")

>> **Pattern recognition:** Identifies chart formations or patterns that provide specific predictive signals, such as a reversal or a breakout. (We show you some of the most common traditional chart patterns and candlestick formations in the later section "Recognizing chart formations.")

>> **Momentum and trend analysis:** Looks at the rate of change of prices for indications of market sentiment regarding the price movement. Trend indicators seek to determine the presence of a trend and its strength. (We look at these indicators in the later section "The Science of Technical Analysis.")

Finding support and resistance

REMEMBER

One of the basic building blocks of technical analysis is the concept of *support and resistance*:

>> **Support:** A price level where buying interest overwhelms selling interest, causing a price decline to stop, bottom out, or pause. Think of support as a floor for prices in a downmove.

>> **Resistance:** The opposite of support. Resistance is where selling interest materializes and slows or overpowers buying interest, causing prices to peak, stall, or pause in a price rally. Think of resistance as the ceiling in a price advance.

Support and resistance levels are identified based on prior price action, such as highs and lows and short-term (minutes to hours) *consolidation* or *congestion zones* (where prices get all stopped up and can't move one way or the other for a period of time). Support and resistance can also be determined by drawing trend lines. Still other forms of support and resistance come from Fibonacci retracement levels, Ichimoku lines, and moving averages, which we save for later in this chapter. Figure 6-1 shows some basic support and resistance levels from sloping and horizontal trend lines drawn off key highs and lows.

Sloping trend line support from key highs and lows

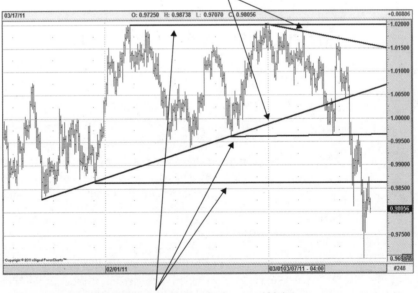

FIGURE 6-1:
Trend lines drawn off key highs and lows can be used to identify important support and resistance levels as well as illuminate unfolding pattern formations.

Horizontal support and resistance from prior lows and highs

Source: eSignal (www.esignal.com)

REMEMBER

One of the key concepts of support and resistance is that after a support or resistance level is broken, it shifts direction. In other words, after a support level is broken in a move to the downside, it becomes resistance in subsequent price attempts to rally. After a resistance level is broken to the upside, it may later act as support for further price gains.

Not all support and resistance are created equal

Support and resistance come in all shapes and sizes. Some support or resistance levels are stronger or weaker than others, and technical analysts typically refer to support as either minor or major. But those terms are subjective and difficult to quantify with any precision.

REMEMBER

The best way to get a handle on the relative strength of a support or resistance level is to view it in the context of time and price significance:

>> **The longer the time frame of the price point, the greater its significance.** A weekly high/low is more important than a daily high/low, which is more important than an hourly high/low, and so on down the time scale.

>> **Trend-line strength is also a function of time frame and durability.** A trend line based on daily charts tends to be stronger than a trend line based on hourly prices. A trend line that dates back six months has greater significance than one that's only a week or two old. Also, the more often a trend line is tested (meaning that prices touch the trend line but do not break through it, or break through it only very briefly and by small amounts), the more valid it is.

>> **The strength of support or resistance levels during a retracement depends on the strength of the support or resistance during the prior directional move.** A retracement refers to a price movement in the opposite direction of a previous price advance or decline. The distance that prices reverse, or retrace, is called a *retracement.* For example, trend lines that were support in a downmove will act as resistance in any retracement higher. The strength of the trend-line support on the way down, such as how many attempts were needed to break below it, will give a good indication of its likely strength as resistance in the retracement.

Support and resistance are made to be broken

REMEMBER

We don't want to leave you with the impression that support and resistance levels are immutable forces in the market that are never challenged or broken. Just the opposite: Forex markets spend much of the time testing support or resistance levels, looking for the weak side in which to push prices.

Different trading styles focus on different types of support and resistance:

» **Tests and breaks of short-term support or resistance levels are the meat and potatoes of intraday trading.** Short-term traders focus on the nearest support or resistance levels (for example, 5- or 15-minute or hourly highs/lows and trend lines) as guides to the immediate direction of prices.

» **Tests and breaks of longer-term support and resistance levels are the fuel that fires longer-term trends or defines medium-term ranges.** Medium- to longer-term traders typically focus on longer-term support or resistance levels, such as daily/weekly highs/lows, and trend lines drawn off them, to guide their trading.

TIP

One of the keys to assessing the significance of a break of support or resistance levels is the strength of follow-through that occurs after the level is broken. *Follow-through* is the price action that takes place after technical support or resistance is broken. After resistance is broken, for example, prices should accelerate higher as shorts who sold in front of the resistance buy back their positions and new buyers enter the market because resistance has been surpassed. The amount of follow-through buying or selling that materializes, or fails to materialize, after the break of a technical support or resistance level is an important indication of the strength of the underlying move.

Waiting for confirmation

We were tempted to title this section "Looking for confirmation," but we thought that sounded too proactive in the sense that if you go looking for something on a chart, odds are you can find it and rationalize it as confirmation. The more disciplined approach involves *waiting* for confirmation, letting market prices provide you with unambiguous signs of a change in direction or break of a chart pattern.

Confirmation refers to price movements that verify, or confirm, a technical observation that suggests a particular outcome. For example, certain chart patterns are useful predictors of a potential reversal in price direction. But note that the starting point in this case is that prices are moving in a trend or steady direction. Blindly following a pattern that suggests that a trend is about to end is very risky. After all, the trend is your friend, so why would you take the risk of going against the trend?

TIP

If you're patient and wait for price action to provide you with confirmation that a directional move or trend is indeed reversing, essentially confirming that the observed chart pattern is playing out as you expected, you're reducing the risks of being wrong-sided or premature in your trade. The trade-off is that you may sacrifice a better entry level for a higher degree of certainty in the overall trade setup.

Looked at the other way around, you're reducing the risks of getting into a trade setup too soon and being wrong if the setup doesn't play out as you expected. The difference is not making as much money as possible or losing money outright. Which would you prefer?

REMEMBER

Technical-based observations provide you with a heads-up alert that a price shift may soon take place — for example, prices may be stalling in a move higher, potentially setting up a reversal lower. Confirmation comes when prices break an established trend line, prior high or low, or other key technical levels of support or resistance. Be careful about looking for confirmation from multiple technical indicators, because they may be measuring the same thing, just in slightly different formats. *Price* is the key element of confirmation.

The Art of Technical Analysis

Chart analysis is at the heart of technical analysis. Don't become reliant on all the fancy indicators and technical studies on your charting system. The most powerful technical indicators you have are your eyes and what's behind them.

In this section, we show you the basics of drawing trend lines and look at some of the most common, yet significant, price patterns you'll encounter over and over again in your trading.

Bar charts and candlestick charts

In this section, we introduce the two main types of charts you'll likely be using as you pursue your own technical analysis: bar charts and candlestick charts.

Measuring markets with price bars

Most charting systems are set to default to show *bar charts,* probably the most widely used form of charting among Western traders. Bar charts are composed of price bars, which encompass the key points of each trading *period* — namely, the open, high, low, and close. A period is the time interval you've selected to analyze, such as 5 or 15 minutes or 1 or 4 hours daily for short-term traders, or weekly for longer-term traders (though short-term traders need to be aware of the longer periods, too). Each bar is displayed as a vertical line with a tick mark on each side of the bar. The tick mark on the left side of the price bar represents the open of the period; the tick mark on the right side is the close of the period; and the upper and lower levels of the bar are the period's highs and lows. For example, Figure 6-1 is a bar chart.

You can use bar charts to draw trend lines, measure retracement levels, and gauge overall price volatility. Each bar represents the trading range for the period; the larger the bar, the greater the range and the higher the volatility (and vice versa for smaller bars). Bar charts are best suited to relatively basic analysis, such as getting a handle on an overall trend.

Lighting the way with candlesticks

We put our favoritism right out front for everyone to see: We love using candlestick charts to spot trade setups, especially impending price reversals. We think candlesticks are among the more powerful predictive tools in the trader's arsenal, and we strongly recommend that you study them further. In particular, we highly recommend reading Steve Nison's *Japanese Candlestick Charting Techniques*, 2nd Edition (see Chapter 19 for more on Nison's book). Another great guide for beginners is *Candlestick Charting For Dummies* by Russell Rhoads (published by Wiley).

Candlestick charts are among the earliest known forms of technical analysis, dating back to trading in the Japanese rice markets in the 18th century. Candlestick charts, or just *candles* for short, provide a more visually intuitive representation of price action than you get from simple bar charts. They do this through the use of color and by more clearly breaking out the key price points of each trading day — open, close, high, and low.

REMEMBER

Figure 6-2 shows the components of two candlesticks. Immediately, you can see that one candle is light, and the other is dark. What does that mean? Think of yin and yang, good and bad, up and down. The light candlestick indicates that the close was higher than the open — it was an up day. The dark candle indicates that the close was lower than the open — a down day.

The light/dark portion in the middle of the candle is called the *real body* or just *body*; it displays the difference between the open and the close. The lines above and below the body are called *tails* (the term we use going forward), *shadows*, or *wicks*; these lines represent the high and low of the period. (We look more at candlesticks in the later section "Candlestick patterns.")

TIP

Candlestick charts are best analyzed using daily or weekly periods rather than intraday periods like 1 hour or 30 minutes. The philosophy behind candlestick analysis is that a full day or week of trading is needed before the market has rendered a verdict, potentially offering signals about future direction.

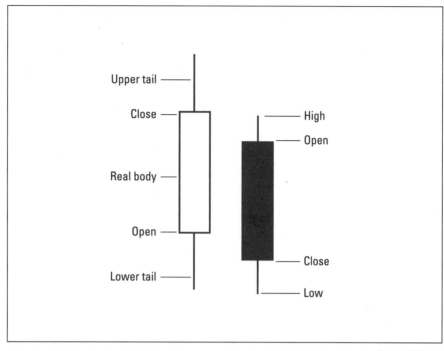

Source: FOREX.com

FIGURE 6-2:
The anatomy of a
candlestick.
Candlesticks
provide a highly
intuitive visual
representation of
price movements.

Drawing trend lines

Probably no exercise in technical analysis is more individualistic than identifying and drawing trend lines. Very often, it comes down to a matter of beauty being in the eye of the beholder. But in the case of chart analysis, beauty is order, and the trend lines you draw are the outlines of that order. Ultimately, drawing trend lines isn't that complicated — with a bit of practice, you'll get the hang of it pretty quickly.

What is a trend line? Basically, a *trend line* is a line that connects significant price points over a defined time period on a price chart. The significant price points are usually the highs and lows of bars or candles, though in the case of candles you can also use the open or close levels of the candle's real body.

Connecting the dots

The starting point in drawing trend lines is looking at the overall price chart in front of you. What do you see? If it's your first time looking at a price chart, it probably looks like a jumble of meaningless bars or candles. The key is to turn that jumble into a meaningful visualization of what's happening to prices.

Scan the chart from left to right, starting in the past and looking into the present. What are prices doing? Are they moving up, down, or a little of both? (If you're looking at a currency chart, you can bet they're doing a little bit of both.) Draw your first trend lines to connect the highest highs (you need only two points to form a line) and the lowest lows, to capture the overall range in the observed period. Always use the extreme points of the price bars or candles when connecting price points (lows with lows, highs with highs).

Look at what's happening between those two trend lines. You'll invariably see a number of smaller, distinct price movements making up the whole. You can draw trend lines to connect the highs of price moves down and the lows of price moves up. Be sure to extend your trend lines all the way to the right edge of the chart, regardless of other bars or candles that later break it. Look for evenness, whether it's horizontal, sloping down, shooting steeply higher, or anything in between. Eventually, that evenness will be broken by price moves that break through the trend lines.

REMEMBER

Your ultimate focus will be on the prices on the right side of the chart because that's the most recent price action, and beyond that lies future price developments. The idea is to winnow out trend lines from the past that appear to have little relevance (they're frequently broken), and keep the trend lines that have the most relevance (prices reverse course when they're hit, and they're largely unbroken) and extend them into the future. Those trend lines are going to act as support and resistance just as they did in the past and provide you with guidance going forward.

Looking for symmetry

When you're drawing trend lines, be alert for symmetrical patterns, such as parallel channels, sloping up or down, or simply horizontal. Look for horizontal tops and bottoms to be made where prior highs and lows were reached. Note that a rising trend line may be heading for a falling trend line, forming a triangle. The two lines are set to intersect at some point in the future, and one of them will be broken, sparking a price reaction.

TIP

Charting systems usually have a trend-line function that allows you to draw a line parallel to another line, or copy an existing line and move it to a parallel position. Experiment with that tool, and you'll be surprised how frequently price points match up to it.

Recognizing chart formations

Pattern recognition, or the identification of chart formations, is another form of technical analysis that helps traders get a handle on what's happening in the market. In the following sections, we cover some of the most widely observed chart formations and what they mean from a trading standpoint. While you're looking through them, keep in mind that the formations can occur in different charting time frames (for example, 15 minutes, hourly, or daily).

REMEMBER

The key to trading on chart formations is to recognize the time period in which they're apparent and to factor that into your trade strategy. A reversal pattern that occurs on an hourly chart, for example, may constitute a reversal that lasts for only a few hours or a day and retrace a relatively smaller pip distance. A reversal pattern on a daily chart, in contrast, can signal a significant multiweek reversal spanning several hundred pips. Keep the formations you observe in the proper time-frame perspective.

Basic chart formations

Chart formations are part and parcel of trends. They're generally grouped into categories that reflect what they mean in the context of a trend. The two most common types of chart patterns are

>> **Reversal patterns:** A reversal pattern indicates that the prior directional price movement is coming to an end. It does not necessarily mean that prices will actually begin to move in the opposite direction, though in many cases they will.

>> **Consolidation and continuation patterns:** Consolidation and continuation patterns represent pauses in directional price moves, where prices undergo a period of back-and-forth consolidation before the overall trend continues.

DOUBLE TOPS AND DOUBLE BOTTOMS

Double tops and *double bottoms* are typically considered among the most powerful chart formations, indicating a reversal in the direction of an overall trend. Double tops form in an uptrend, and double bottoms form in a downtrend. Figure 6-3 shows a double-bottom pattern on a daily AUD/USD chart, and Figure 6-1 shows a double top on a four-hour AUD/USD chart (the double top isn't labeled, but you can see the two highs).

In terms of market dynamics, the idea behind both is that a directional move (up or down) will make a high or low at some point. After a period of consolidation, the market will frequently test the prior high or low for the trend. If the trend is still intact, the market should be able to make a new high or low beyond the prior one. But if the market is unable to surpass the prior high or low, it's taken as a signal that the trend is over, and trend followers begin to exit, generating the reversal.

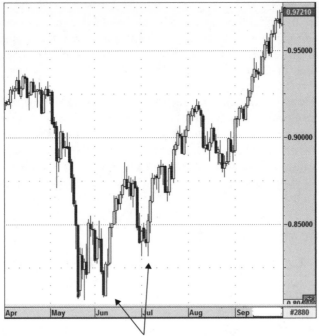

Source: eSignal (www.esignal.com)

FIGURE 6-3:
A double-bottom
formation
suggests that the
prior trend down
may reverse.

Double bottoms signal end of declines

As with most chart formations, double tops and bottoms rarely form perfectly. The second high or low may come up short of the prior high/low; that inability even to retest the prior high/low can create a more rapid and volatile reversal. Other times, the first low may be surpassed by a brief amount and for a brief time (possibly due to stops at the prior low being triggered), only to be rejected, leading to the reversal.

HEAD AND SHOULDERS AND INVERTED HEAD AND SHOULDERS

Head-and-shoulders (H&S) formations are another form of reversal pattern, sometimes referred to as a *triple top.* The H&S top formation develops after an uptrend, and an *inverted H&S* comes after a downtrend. Figure 6-4 shows a classic example of an inverted H&S formation, signaling the end of the EUR's decline after the Eurozone debt crisis. In the case of an uptrend, a high is made at some stage followed by a pullback lower, creating the left shoulder. A subsequent new high is made, generating the head, followed by yet another correction lower. A third attempt to move higher fails to reach the second or highest high and may surpass, equal, or fall short of the left shoulder. Failure to reach the prior high typically triggers selling, and confirmation of a reversal is received when prices fall below the *neckline,* which is formed by connecting the lows seen after each pullback from the shoulder and the head.

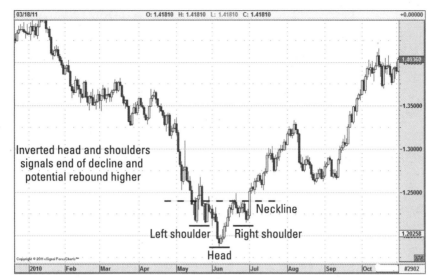

03/18/11 | O: 1.41810 H: 1.41810 L: 1.41810 C: 1.41810 | +0.00000

1.40360

1.35000

Inverted head and shoulders signals end of decline and potential rebound higher

1.30000

1.25000

Neckline

Left shoulder   Right shoulder

1.20258

Head

Copyright © 2011 eSignal ForexCharts™

2010 | Feb | Mar | Apr | May | Jun | Jul | Aug | Sep | Oct | #2902

FIGURE 6-4:
An inverted head-and-shoulders formation in EUR/USD signals that the euro's declines may be ending after the worst of the Eurozone debt crisis.

Source: eSignal (www.esignal.com)

TIP

The standard *measured move objective* (the price move suggested by a chart pattern) in an H&S pattern is the distance from the top of the head to the neckline. When the neckline is broken, prices should subsequently move that distance.

FLAGS

Flags are consolidation patterns that typically form in a counter-trend direction. For example, if prices have moved higher (the trend is up) and run into resistance above, for a flag to form, prices will begin to consolidate in a downward (counter-trend) channel. The formation suggests that the flag consolidation channel will eventually break out in the direction of the prior trend, and the directional move will resume. Perhaps somewhat confusingly, a *bull flag* actually slopes downward, but it's called a bull flag because after it breaks, the bullish trend resumes. A *bear flag* slopes upward, but after it breaks to the downside, the bearish trend resumes.

WARNING

If the opposite side of the flag channel is broken (the lower end of a bull flag/upper end of a bear flag), the pattern is invalidated and it may signal a larger reversal.

Flags have a measured move objective based on the *flagpole,* or the distance of the prior move that ultimately stalled, resulting in the formation of the flag. When the flag is broken, the price target is usually equal to the length of the flagpole projected from the flag break, as shown in Figure 6-5.

CHAPTER 6 **Cutting the Fog with Technical Analysis** 121

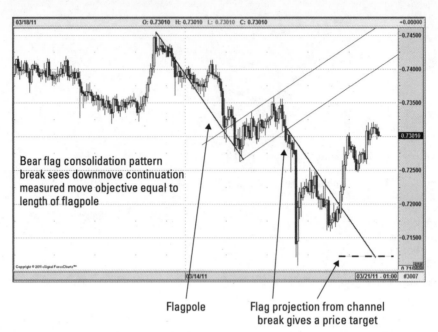

Bear flag consolidation pattern break sees downmove continuation measured move objective equal to length of flagpole

Source: eSignal (www.esignal.com)

FIGURE 6-5:
A break of a bear flag consolidation pattern on an hourly chart of NZD/USD signals that the move down is resuming.

Flagpole

Flag projection from channel break gives a price target

TRIANGLES

Triangles are another type of consolidation pattern, and they come in a few different forms:

>> **Symmetrical triangles:** These formations have downward-sloping upper edges and upward-sloping lower edges, resulting in a triangle pointing horizontally. Symmetrical triangles are mostly neutral for the direction of the ultimate breakout, but they have a slightly greater tendency to break out in the direction in which they entered the triangle consolidation, meaning the trend is resuming.

>> **Ascending triangles:** These formations have a flat or horizontal top and an upward-sloping lower edge (see Figure 6-6). Ascending triangles typically break out to the upside after resistance on the top is overcome. The rising lower edge signifies that buyers keep coming back at ever-higher levels to push through the horizontal top. The minimum measured move objective on a breakout is equal to the distance between the rising bottom and where the flat top is first reached.

>> **Descending triangles:** These formations are the inverse of ascending triangles, where the horizontal edge and the expected direction of the breakout are to the downside.

Source: eSignal (www.esignal.com)

FIGURE 6-6:
The break of the
flat top in an
ascending-
triangle
formation signals
an upside
breakout. Note
that the top of
the triangle
subsequently
acted as support.

Ascending triangle signals upmove
is resuming when flat top is broken

Candlestick patterns

Candlestick patterns are some of the most powerful predictors of future price direction. Candlesticks have little predictive capacity when it comes to the size of future price movements, so you need to look at other forms of technical analysis to gauge the extent of subsequent price moves. But if you can get the direction right, you're more than halfway there.

Candlestick formations come in two main forms:

» **Reversal patterns:** Where a preceding directional move stops and changes direction

» **Continuation patterns:** Where a prior directional move resumes its course after a period of consolidation

We like to look at candlestick patterns primarily for reversal signals because they're among the most reliable of the candlestick patterns.

REMEMBER

The key to interpreting a candle formation as a reversal indicator is that there has to be an identifiable directional move in the preceding days. The directional price move may be part of an extended uptrend or downtrend, or simply a day or two of a clear directional move higher or lower, as shown by relatively large real bodies.

Literally dozens of different candlestick reversal patterns exist, but we focus on the most common patterns in the following sections. Keep in mind that some candle reversal formations consist of a single candle, whereas others depend on two or three candles to constitute the pattern. Look closely, and you'll see that many of them are variations on the same theme (namely that a directional move is losing force, increasing the potential for a price reversal). A good source of candlestick reference can be found for free at www.candlesticker.com.

TIP

Hopefully you notice that many of the candlestick patterns in the following sections have two things in common — long tails and small bodies. As part of your technical analysis routine, we strongly suggest reviewing daily candle charts after each day's close (5 p.m. ET), and on the weekends for weekly candles, to see whether any patterns are evident. They can be powerful signals about where prices are heading in the next trading day or week.

DOJI

Doji are among the most significant of the candlestick patterns because their basic shape forms the basis for many other candlestick patterns. A doji occurs when the close is the same as the open, generating a candlestick with no real body — simply a vertical line with a cross on it.

TIP

On days when the close is only a few points apart from the open, generating a candle with an extremely small real body, you can take some artistic license and consider it a potential doji depending on the preceding candles. If the prior days' candles were composed of long real bodies, that increases the likelihood that the very small real body should be viewed as a doji (or a spinning top, which we cover later in this section). Figure 6-7 is a good example of this — the open and close were only 5 pips apart. Whenever you spot a doji after a daily close, you should note it and consider that the preceding directional move may be ending or set for a reversal.

Doji are significant because they represent indecision and uncertainty. When viewing a doji, think of buyers and sellers fighting to a draw. In the case of a preceding decline lower, for example, it signals that sellers are losing power and buyers have emerged. Figure 6-7 shows a classic doji, where the open and close are the same and about in the middle of the day's trading range. The longer the upper and lower tails are in a doji, the greater the sense of uncertainty displayed by the market and the more likely the prior trend is to be ending.

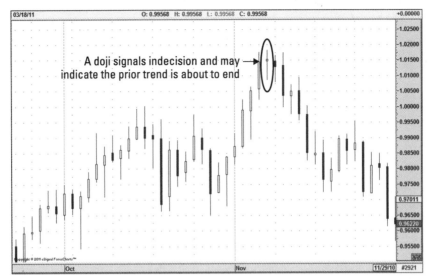

03/18/11   O: 0.99568 H: 0.99568 L: 0.99568 C: 0.99568   +0.00000

A doji signals indecision and may → indicate the prior trend is about to end

FIGURE 6-7:
After a move higher in AUD/USD, a doji signals the gains may be about to reverse.

Source: eSignal (www.esignal.com)

A double doji occurs when two doji appear in successive periods. The increased uncertainty associated with a double doji tends to signal that the subsequent price move will be more significant after the market's indecision is resolved. A long-legged doji, one with larger tails, is another indication that the market's uncertainty may resolve with a more pronounced move.

WARNING

On its own, a doji is considered neutral. You need to wait for subsequent price action, such as a trend-line break, to confirm that the doji is signaling a reversal.

HAMMERS AND SHOOTING STARS

Hammers and *shooting stars* are single-candle formations that indicate a reversal may be in store. Hammers appear after a decline and are notable for a long lower tail (at least twice the height of the real body) and a small real body at the upper end of the candle (akin to a doji or spinning top). A shooting star is the mirror image after a move higher — a long upper tail and a small real body at the bottom of the day's range. The color of the candle can be either light or dark. In both cases the market dynamic is the same: After a price rise, in the case of a shooting star, buyers attempted to extend the advance, but by the end of the day were beaten back by sellers, and vice versa with hammers.

The size of the tails is an important indication of the strength of the signal — the larger the tail, the greater the opposing force to the prior move and the more likely prices are to reverse course. Figure 6-8 shows a shooting star signaling recent gains may be set to reverse. (See Figure 6-10 for a hammer as part of another candle pattern.)

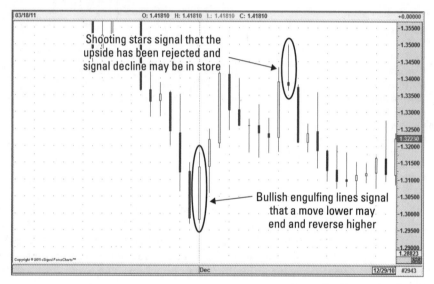

FIGURE 6-8:
A shooting star signals a price peak and potential for a downside reversal. The bullish engulfing line suggests a decline is over and a rebound may follow. Note the white candle's body completely engulfs the prior candle's body.

Source: eSignal (www.esignal.com)

TIP

Hammers and shooting stars are one of our major alerts for price reversals. They're a signal to exit or at least reduce positions in the direction of the prior trend, and a good basis to establish a position in the opposite direction. If the high of a shooting star or the low of a hammer is exceeded, then the signal is negated and you have to get out.

SPINNING TOPS

A *spinning top* (see Figure 6-9) is a single-candle formation that has a small real body and typically a short tail, sort of like a fatter version of a doji, but with a larger tail. (Larger tails may signify a greater potential price move; however, the size of the tails is secondary.) The formation gets its name because it resembles a child's toy top. A spinning top frequently appears in pairs, similar to a double doji. The significance of a spinning top is that it has a small real body, which represents a drop in directional momentum after a series of up or down candles, which may signal a directional move is stalling and is ripe for a correction. Spinning tops require confirmation by subsequent candles, but be on alert for potential reversals if you spot a spinning top.

126 PART 2 **Data and Details You Can Use to Trade Currencies**

Source: eSignal (www.esignal.com)

FIGURE 6-9: Spinning tops are similar to doji both in shape and in that they suggest uncertainty and a potential reversal of the prior directional move.

ENGULFING LINES

Engulfing lines are two-candlestick patterns that can be either bullish or bearish, depending on whether they come after a downmove or an upmove:

» **Bullish engulfing line:** The first candle is dark, followed by a large light candle, the body of which completely engulfs the body of the dark candle, seen in Figure 6-8. The smaller the body of the first candle (think spinning top — see the preceding section), the more significant the reversal signals.

» **Bearish engulfing line:** The first candle is light, followed by a long dark-colored candle that engulfs the body of the first candle, as shown in Figure 6-10 as part of another candle pattern.

TIP

Engulfing lines also rank among our favorite candlestick patterns and are a sufficient basis to establish a position in the opposite direction of the preceding price move. If the high/low of the candle preceding the engulfing candle is exceeded, the pattern is negated and you need to exit.

TWEEZER TOPS AND TWEEZER BOTTOMS

Tweezer formations are two-candlestick patterns that get their name because they resemble the pincer end of a pair of tweezers. Tweezer tops and bottoms (shown in Figure 6-10) correspond to double tops and bottoms in traditional chart analysis, and they mean the same thing — a reversal after failing to make new highs or lows. Tweezer tops and bottoms are characterized by long tails on the bottom after a move down, similar to a hammer, and long tails above after a move higher, like shooting stars. The extremes of the tails should ideally be equal, but if the tails are sufficiently long, we take notice.

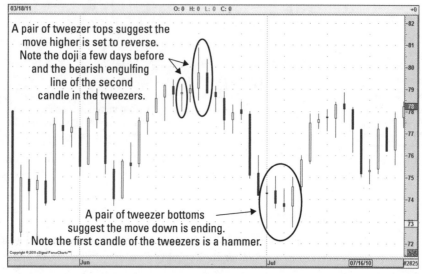

Source: eSignal (www.esignal.com)

FIGURE 6-10: A tweezer top and bottom formation signals that an upmove is set to reverse and that a decline may be ending. Note the doji in the days prior to the tweezer top suggesting that upside sentiment was already uncertain.

Fibonacci retracements

A *retracement* is a price movement in the opposite direction of the preceding price move. For instance, if EUR/USD rises by 150 pips over the course of two days and declines by 75 pips on the third day, prices are said to have retraced half the move higher, or made a 50 percent retracement of the move up. (Fifty percent is not technically a Fibonacci retracement, but we include it here because many traders watch it, too, due to its clean, halfway demarcation.)

Fibonacci retracements come from the ratios between the numbers in the Fibonacci sequence, a nearly magical numerical series that appears in the natural world and mathematics with regularity. The most important Fibonacci retracement percentages are 38.2 percent and 61.8 percent, with 76.4 percent as a secondary, but still important, level.

TIP

Most charting systems contain an automatic Fibonacci retracement drawing tool. All you need to do is click the starting point of a directional price move (the low for an upmove; the high for a downmove) and drag the cursor to the finishing point of the movement. The charting system will then display lines that correspond to 38.2 percent, 50 percent, 61.8 percent, 76.4 percent, and 100 percent.

Currency traders routinely calculate Fibonacci retracement levels to determine support and resistance levels, and Fibonacci retracement levels are strong examples of self-fulfilling prophecies in technical analysis. Figure 6-11 provides a good illustration of how Fibonacci retracement levels can act as resistance in a correction higher following a price decline. You can see the 38.2 percent retracement level put up a pretty good fight for a while, but after it broke above, prices blew right past the 50 percent point and quickly moved to the 61.8 percent level, even exceeding it briefly before a pullback. That pullback was nicely contained by the 38.2 percent level. Prices went on to surpass the 61.8 percent level and then tested 76.4 percent, which also held for a time before sending prices back to the 61.8 percent point. From there they rallied higher and finally broke the 76.4 percent level, setting up potential for a 100 percent retracement of the prior decline.

FIGURE 6-11:
You can identify future support and resistance levels by drawing Fibonacci retracements of prior directional price moves on your charting system.

Source: eSignal (www.esignal.com)

The Science of Technical Analysis

Relax. Nothing is especially artful, scientific, or particularly complicated about technical analysis. Many in the market use the term *science* to describe the mechanics of various technical tools, but in our opinion technical analysis is far more art than science.

Each tool in technical analysis has a number of concrete elements that we need to outline before you can start interpreting what they mean. Unless you're developing your own systematic trading model, you don't need to get too caught up in the math or the calculations behind various indicators. Far more important is understanding what the indicators are measuring and what their signals mean and don't mean.

Momentum oscillators and studies

Momentum refers to the speed at which prices are moving, either up or down. Momentum is an important technical measurement of the strength of the buying or selling interest behind a movement in prices. The higher the momentum in a downmove, for example, the greater the selling interest is thought to be. The slower the momentum, the weaker the selling interest.

REMEMBER

Currency traders use momentum indicators to gauge whether a price movement will be sustained, potentially developing into a trend, or whether a directional move has run its course and is now more likely to reverse direction. If momentum is positive and rising, it means prices are advancing, suggesting that active buying is taking place. If momentum begins to slow, it means prices are advancing more slowly, suggesting that buying interest is beginning to weaken. If buying interest is drying up, selling interest may increase.

Momentum takes on added significance in currencies because there's no viable way of assessing trading volume on a real-time basis. In stock and futures markets, volume data is an important indicator of the significance of a price move. For example, a sharp price movement on high volume is considered legitimate and likely to be sustained, while a similarly sharp move on low volume is discounted and viewed as more likely to reverse.

Momentum indicators fall into a group of technical studies known as *oscillators,* because the mathematical representations of momentum are plotted on a scale that sees momentum rise and fall, or oscillate, depending on the relative speed of the price movements. A variety of different momentum oscillators exist, each calculated by various formulas, but they're all based on the relationship of the current price to preceding prices over a defined period of time.

TIP

Momentum oscillators are typically displayed in a small window at the bottom of charting systems, with the price chart displayed above, so you can readily compare the price action with its underlying momentum.

Overbought and oversold

Momentum oscillators have extreme levels at the upper and lower ends of the oscillator's scale, where the upper level is referred to as *overbought* and the lower level is referred *oversold.* No hard definitions of *overbought* and *oversold* exist, because they're relative terms describing how fast prices have changed relative to prior price changes. The best way to think of overbought and oversold is that prices have gone up or down too fast relative to prior periods.

Many momentum indicators suggest trading rules based on the indicator reaching overbought or oversold levels. For example, if a momentum study enters overbought or oversold territory, and subsequently turns down or up and moves out of the overbought or oversold zone, it may be considered a sell or buy signal.

REMEMBER

Just because a momentum indicator has reached an overbought or oversold level does not mean that prices have to reverse direction. After all, the essence of a trend is a sustained directional price movement, which could see momentum remain in overbought or oversold territory for a long period of time as prices continue to advance or decline in the trend. Breaking news or data may be behind the price move, lending a fundamental urgency to price adjustments that defy momentum analysis. Momentum is only an indicator. The key is to wait for confirmation from prices that the prior direction or trend has, in fact, changed.

Divergences between price and momentum

Another useful way to interpret momentum indicators is by comparing them to corresponding price changes. In most cases, momentum studies and price changes should move in the same direction. If prices are rising, for example, you would expect to see momentum indicators rising as well. By the same token, if momentum begins to stall and eventually turn down, you would expect to see prices turn lower, too. But relatively frequently, especially in shorter, intraday time frames (15 minutes, 1 hour, or 4 hours), prices *diverge* from momentum (meaning, prices may continue to rise even though momentum has started to move lower).

When prices move in the opposite direction of momentum, it's called a *divergence.* Divergences are relatively easy to spot — new price highs are not matched by new highs in the momentum indicator, or new price lows are not matched by new lows in the momentum study. When a new price high or low is made and momentum fails to make a similar new high or low, the price action is not confirmed by the momentum, suggesting that the price move is false and will not be sustained. The expectation, then, is that the price will change direction and eventually follow the momentum.

When prices make new highs and momentum is falling or not making new highs, it's called a *bearish divergence* (meaning that prices are expected to shift lower — move bearishly — in line with the underlying momentum). When prices are making new lows but momentum is rising or not making new lows, it's called a *bullish divergence* (meaning that prices are expected to turn higher — bullish — in line with momentum).

TIP

Divergences are great alerts that something may be out of kilter between prices and the underlying strength or momentum of the price move. Whenever you spot a divergence between price and momentum, you should start looking more closely at what's happening to prices. Are stop-loss levels being run in thin liquidity conditions? Or has some important news just come out that has sent prices moving sharply, such that momentum will eventually catch up?

REMEMBER

In a trending environment, prices may continue to move in the direction of the trend (that's what a trend is), but at a slower pace, causing momentum to diverge. To know for certain, you need to wait for confirmation from prices before you enter a trade based on a divergence.

Using momentum in ranges and trends

Momentum indicators work best in range environments, where price movements are relatively constrained and no trend is evident or has moved into consolidation. As buying drives prices toward the upper end of a range, for example, selling interest comes in, slowing the price advance and turning momentum lower. As the buyers turn around, the selling interest increases and momentum begins to accelerate lower, confirming the change in direction. At the bottom of the range, the same thing happens but in the opposite direction.

WARNING

Momentum studies frequently give off incorrect signals during breakouts and trending markets. This is especially the case when using shorter time frames, such as hourly and shorter periods. The key to understanding why this happens is to recognize that momentum studies are backward-looking indicators. All they can do is quantify the change in current prices relative to what has come before. They have little predictive capacity, which is why you always need to wait for confirmation from prices before trading based on a momentum signal.

TIP

Some of the most extreme price moves typically occur when momentum readings are in overbought or oversold territory. Divergences in shorter time frames also appear frequently, especially during breakouts, where rapid price moves are not reflected quickly enough in momentum studies. By the time the momentum indicator has caught up with the price breakout, prices may already have peaked or bottomed, again causing momentum to signal a divergence. Just because momentum is overbought or oversold doesn't mean prices can't continue to move higher or lower.

Here are the main momentum oscillators used by currency traders:

>> **Relative Strength Index (RSI):** A single-line oscillator plotted on a scale from 0 to 100, based on closing prices over a user-defined period. Common RSI periods are 9, 14, and 21. RSI compares the strength of up periods to the weakness of down periods — hence, the label *relative strength.* RSI readings over 75 are considered overbought; readings below 25 are considered oversold. RSI signals are given when the indicator leaves overbought or oversold territory and on divergences with price.

>> **Stochastic:** A two-line oscillator plotted on a scale of 0 to 100. The two lines are known as *%K* (fast stochastic) and *%D* (slow stochastic). Stochastics are also based on closing prices of prior periods. The basic theory behind stochastics is that the strength of a directional move can be measured by how near the close is to the extreme of a period. In an uptrend, a close near the highs for the period signifies strong momentum; a close in the middle or below signals that momentum is weakening. In a downtrend, the close of a period should be nearer to the lows for momentum to strengthen. As momentum shifts, the %K line will cross over the slower-moving %D line. Crossovers in overbought or oversold territory are considered sell or buy signals. Overbought is above 80, and oversold is below 20.

>> **Moving Average Convergence/Divergence (MACD):** Not really a momentum oscillator, but a complex series of moving averages. (It functions similarly to momentum studies, so we include it here.) MACD fluctuates on either side of a zero line and has no fixed scale, so overbought or oversold are judged relative to prior extremes. MACD also consists of two lines: the MACD line (based on two moving averages) and the signal line (a moving average of the MACD line). Trading signals are generated if the MACD line crosses up over the signal line while below the zero line (buy) or crosses down below the signal line while above the zero line (sell). MACD tends to generate signals more slowly than RSI or stochastics due to the longer periods typically used and the slower nature of moving averages. The result is that it takes longer for MACD to cross over, generally preventing fewer false signals.

Trend-identifying indicators

One of the market's favorite sayings is "The trend is your friend." The idea is that if you trade in the direction of the prevailing trend, you're more likely to experience success than if you trade against the trend. Now, how can you argue with logic like that?

The hard part for us mortals is to determine whether there's a trend in the first place. The question becomes more complex when you look at multiple time frames, because trends can exist in any time frame. On a daily time frame, the market may be largely range bound. But in a shorter time frame, such as hourly or 30 minutes, there may be a trending movement that presents an opportunity for short-term traders.

REMEMBER

Determining whether a trend is in place is also important when it comes to deciding whether to follow the signals given by momentum indicators. Momentum studies are great in relatively range-bound markets, but they tend to give off bad signals during trends and breakouts. The key is to determine whether a trend is in place.

In the following sections, we look at a few technical studies you can use to identify whether a trend is in place and how strong it may be.

Directional Movement Indicator system

The Directional Movement Indicator (DMI) system is a set of quantitative tools designed to determine whether a market is trending. The DMI is based on the idea that when a market is trending, each period's price extremes should exceed the prior price extremes in the direction of the trend. For example, in an uptrend, each successive high should be higher than the prior period's high. In a downtrend, the opposite is the case: Each new low should be lower than the prior period's low. That's the essence of a trend.

The DMI system is comprised of the ADX line (the average directional movement index) and the DI+ and DI– lines (which refer to the directional indicators for up periods [+] and down periods [–]). The ADX is used to determine whether a market is trending (regardless of whether it's up or down), with a reading over 25 indicating a trending market and a reading below indicating no trend. The ADX is also a measure of the strength of a trend — the higher the ADX, the stronger the trend. Using the ADX, traders can determine whether a trend is operative and decide whether to use a trend-following system or to rely on momentum oscillator signals.

As its name would suggest, the DMI system is best employed using both components. The DI+ and DI– lines are used as trade-entry signals. A buy signal is generated when the DI+ line crosses up through the DI– line; a sell signal is generated when the DI– line crosses up through the DI+ line. The *extreme-point rule* states that when the DI+/DI– lines cross, you should note the extreme point for that period in the direction of the crossover (the high if DI+ crosses up over DI–; the low if DI– crosses up over DI+). If that extreme point is exceeded in the next period, the DI+/DI– crossover is considered a valid trade signal. If the extreme point is not surpassed, the signal is not confirmed.

TIP

The ADX can also be used as an early indicator of the end or a pause in a trend. When the ADX begins to move lower from its highest level, the trend is either pausing or ending, signaling that it's time to exit the current position and wait for a fresh signal from the DI+/DI– crossover.

Moving averages

One of the more basic and widely used indicators in technical analysis, moving averages can verify existing trends, identify emerging trends, and generate trading signals. Moving averages are simply an average of prior prices over a user-defined time period displayed as a line overlaid on a price chart. There are two main types of moving averages:

>> **Simple moving average:** Gives equal weight to each historical price point over the specified period

>> **Exponential moving average:** Gives greater weight to more recent price data, with the aim of capturing directional price changes more quickly than the simple moving average

In terms of defining a trend, when prices are above the moving average, an uptrend is in place; when prices are below the moving average, a downtrend is in place.

Traders like to experiment with different periods for moving averages, but a few are more commonly used in the market than others, and they're worth keeping an eye on. The main moving average periods to focus on are 21, 55, 100, and 200. Shorter-term traders may consider looking at the 9- and 14-period moving averages.

TIP

Another way moving averages are used is by combining two or more moving averages and using the crossovers of the moving averages as buy or sell signals based on the direction of the crossover. For example, using a 9- and 21-period moving average, you would buy when the faster-moving 9-period average crosses up over the slower-moving 21-period average, and vice versa for a crossover to the downside.

Trading with clouds: Ichimoku charts

Ichimoku Kinko Hyo, or "one-glance equilibrium," charts are another technical analysis approach imported from Japan that is gaining widespread popularity in forex (and other financial) markets. Often referred to as *cloud charts* because of the central feature of the system (the cloud, or *kumo* in Japanese), Ichimoku is basically a trend-following system. But Ichimoku lines can also define significant support and resistance levels not identified by more traditional technical approaches.

The key components of Ichimoku charts are five lines shown in Figure 6-12:

>> **Tenkan line:** The faster moving average based on the average of the high and low of the prior nine days.

>> **Kijun line:** The slower moving average based on the average of the high and low from the prior 26 days.

>> **Senkou span A (leading span A):** The average of the Tenkan and Kijun lines from the prior 26 days, projected 26 days into the future.

>> **Senkou span B (leading span B):** The average of the high and low of the prior 52 days projected 26 days into the future. The cloud is the space between the two leading spans.

>> **Chikou span (lagging span):** Today's closing price reflected 26 days into the past.

REMEMBER

A few points to note here: Ichimoku is a daily-based chart approach (weekly views can also be used), making it a tool for longer-term traders. Most importantly, intraday breaks of Ichimoku lines are relatively common, but it's only the daily close that matters, reinforcing it as a medium/longer-term trading tool.

FIGURE 6-12: Ichimoku charts provide a quick way to identify trend direction and also offer support and resistance levels not found elsewhere.

Source: FOREX.com

Ichimoku trading signals are based on the position of the current price relative to the lines as well as crossovers of the lines themselves. In the simplest form, the trend is up when prices are above the cloud and down when prices are below. Buying and selling signals also come from crossovers of the Tenkan and Kijun lines, but the strength of the signal depends on the position of price relative to the cloud. A crossover of the Tenkan below the Kijun line (bearish crossover) with price above the cloud is a weak sell signal. If price is inside the cloud, it's a medium-strength sell signal. If prices are below the cloud, it's a strong sell signal. The same applies in bullish crossovers, but in reverse. The Chikou span is also used to gauge the validity of the trade signals, based on where current prices are relative to prior periods. The idea is that if an uptrend is in place, for example, current price should be above those of prior periods, as seen by the lagging span.

TIP

Earlier we indicate that intraday breaks of Ichimoku lines are common, but they have an uncanny way of acting as formidable support and resistance, too. In particular, the slower moving Kijun line can be used as a level to reenter a prevailing trend, buying a downside retracement in an uptrend or selling rebounds higher in a downtrend. We always make a point of noting the Ichimoku levels as part of our daily technical analysis routine.

Chapter **7**

Getting Down and Dirty with Fundamental Data

Fundamental economic data reports are among the most significant information inputs because policy makers and market participants alike use them to gauge the state of the economy, set monetary policy, and make investment decisions. From a trader's perspective, data reports are the routine catalysts that stir up markets and get things moving.

We run through a lot of economic information in this chapter, but you don't need to understand it like an economist — you're mainly interested in what it means for the market reaction. (If you're interested in understanding data like an economist, we recommend reading *The Secrets of Economic Indicators: Hidden Clues to Future Economic Trends and Investment Opportunities,* 3rd Edition, by Bernard Baumohl, published by FT Press.)

REMEMBER

The significance of individual reports varies depending on the economic environment, the market's current focus, and a host of other factors. Always keep in mind that markets interpret incoming data based on what it means for the big picture outlook. If a country's economic outlook is generally viewed as promising, data pointing to stronger growth will reinforce that view, while data that disappoints may suggest a more negative reaction. Most important, the market's reaction to data is more significant than the data itself.

In the first half of this chapter, we look at how to absorb the various data reports and factor them into a broader view of the economic outlook for each particular country, with its attendant implications for interest rates and currency values. In the second half of this chapter, we run through the major data reports to give you an idea of what they cover and how the market interprets them.

Finding the Data

Before you can start processing all the economic data, you need to know where to find it. Here are primary sources that provide the data in greater detail:

>> Bureau of Economic Analysis (www.bea.gov)

>> Commerce Department's economic data and statistics site (www.commerce. gov/data-and-reports)

>> Bureau of Labor Statistics (www.bls.gov)

TIP

The starting point is the economic calendars typically provided by online forex brokerages. Be aware that some calendars are not as comprehensive as others, so be sure to look for calendars that show events and speakers and not just data. Also, look for a broker that provides data and event previews as well as real-time data and market analysis; this type of commentary will help you get a sense of what the market is expecting, how it may be positioned for the news, and how it's likely to react.

Cable TV business channels such as Bloomberg TV, CNBC, and Fox Business News typically carry U.S. data releases live on air. In our opinion, Bloomberg TV does the best job of covering non-U.S. data releases, and CNBC World is another option. But your best bet for seeing U.S. and global data releases immediately can be Twitter.

In addition, Bloomberg (www.bloomberg.com), MarketWatch (www.marketwatch. com), and Reuters (www.reuters.com) provide excellent data coverage, both before and after it's released, along with event calendars. Read the economic data news stories on these sites to get the inside story of the data reports, such as any sub-component readings or significant revisions.

Also, many calendars may include some designations of market significance for each data series, like some are *high impact* or *low impact*. Keep in mind that it's the big picture that counts and even a so-called low-impact report could have a big impact if it's a big enough surprise.

In the next section, we sketch out a model for understanding where the types of data fit into the big picture. It should help you determine which categories of data are most significant, depending on the particular economic environment at any given time.

Economics 101 for Currency Traders: Making Sense of Economic Data

If you're like most people, you probably have a decent idea of what certain economic reports mean, like the unemployment rate or the consumer price index (CPI) which are found at the Bureau of Labor Statistics site (www.bls.gov). But like lots of people, you probably don't have a strong idea of how to put the data together to make sense of it all. Having a fundamental model to put the data in perspective is critical to understanding what the data means and how the market is likely to react to the data. The sooner you're able to make sense of what a specific report means and factor it into the bigger picture, the sooner you'll be able to react in the market.

In the next few sections, we suggest a basic model to interpret the deluge of economic indicators you'll encounter in the forex market. By no means is this model the be-all and end-all of economic theory, but we do think it's a solid framework on which to hang the economic indicators and see how they fit together.

The labor market

REMEMBER

We place the employment picture first for the simple reason that jobs and job creation are the keys to the medium- and long-term economic outlook for any country or economic bloc. No matter what else is going on, always have a picture of the labor market in the back of your mind.

If jobs are being created, more wages are being paid, consumers are consuming more, and economic activity expands. If job growth is stagnant or weak, long-run economic growth will typically be constrained. Signs of broader economic growth will be seen as tentative or suspect unless job growth is also present. Both scenarios have major implications for interest-rate moves and investment themes, which are key currency drivers.

From the currency-market point of view, labor-market strength is typically seen as a currency positive, because it indicates positive growth prospects going forward, along with the potential for higher interest rates based on stronger growth or wage-driven inflation. Needless to say, labor-market weakness is typically viewed as a currency negative.

TIP

The employment indicator that gets the most attention is the monthly U.S. non-farm payrolls (NFP) report. The NFP report triggers loads of attention and speculation for a few days before and after it's released, but then the market seems to stop talking about jobs. Keep an eye on the job-specific reports outlined in the later sidebar "Other labor-market indicators."

To illustrate the importance that markets place on jobs, Figure 7-1 shows changes in U.S. private payrolls overlaid with the S&P 500 stock index. As you can see, major turning points in the stock market (but not necessarily the economy) are closely associated with peaks and troughs in job markets.

FIGURE 7-1:
Job market trends coincide very closely with stock market performance, which reflects the economic outlook (but not necessarily the current state of the economy), as seen in U.S. private payroll changes and the S&P 500.

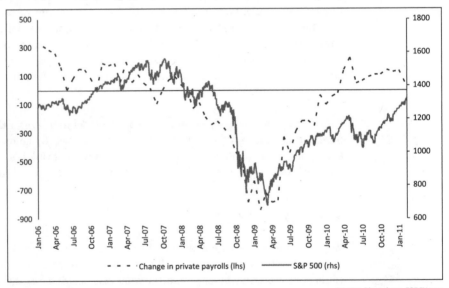

Source: Bloomberg, FOREX.com

The consumer

If it weren't for the overarching importance of jobs to long-run economic growth, the consumer would certainly rank first in any model seeking to understand economic data. The economies of the major currencies are driven overwhelmingly by personal consumption, accounting for 60 to 70 percent or more of overall economic activity in developed economies.

REMEMBER

Personal consumption (also known as *private consumption, personal spending,* and similar impersonal terms) refers to how people spend their money. In a nutshell, are they spending more, or are they spending less? Also, what's the outlook for their spending — to increase, decrease, or stay the same? If you want to gauge the short-run outlook of an economy, look no further than how the individual consumer is faring.

The business sector

Businesses and firms make up the other third of overall economic activity after personal spending. (We're leaving government out of our model to simplify matters.) Firms contribute directly to economic activity through *capital expenditures* (for example, building factories, stores, and offices; buying software and telecommunications equipment) and indirectly through growth (by hiring, meaning there are jobs again), expanding production, and producing investment opportunities.

Look at the data reports coming from the corporate sector for what they suggest about overall sentiment, capital spending, hiring, inventory management, and production going forward.

REMEMBER

Keep in mind that the manufacturing and export sectors are more significant in many non-U.S. economies than they are in the United States. For instance, manufacturing activity in the United States accounts for only about 10 to 15 percent of overall activity versus shares of 30 to 40 percent and higher in other major-currency economies, such as Japan or Germany. So Japanese industrial production data tends to have a bigger impact on the yen than U.S. industrial production has on the dollar.

The structural

Structural indicators are data reports that cover the overall economic environment. Structural indicators frequently form the basis for currency trends and tend to be most important to medium- and long-term traders. The main structural reports focus on

>> **Inflation:** Whether prices are rising or falling, and how fast. Inflation readings can be an important indicator for the direction of interest rates, which is a key determinant of currency values.

>> **Growth:** Indicators of growth and overall economic activity, typically in the form of gross domestic product (GDP) reports. Structural growth reports tell you whether the economy is expanding or contracting, and how fast, which is another key input to monetary policy and the interest rate outlook. Growth

REMEMBER

forecasts from economists are important benchmarks for evaluating subsequent economic data on growth.

» **Trade balance:** Whether a country is importing more or less than it exports. The currency of a country with a *trade deficit* (the country imports more than it exports; the country loses from trade) tends to weaken because more of its currency is being sold to buy foreign goods (imports). A currency with a *trade surplus* (the country exports more than it imports; the country gains from trade) tends to appreciate because more of it is being bought to purchase that country's exports. This is just a rule of thumb — it doesn't always hold true. For example, between 2013 and 2014, the British pound appreciated by more than 11 percent, yet the United Kingdom's trade balance continued to deteriorate.

» **Fiscal balance:** The overall level of government borrowing and the market's perception of financial stability. Countries with high debt levels run the risk of a weakening currency if economic conditions take a turn for the worse and markets fear financial instability. Debts and deficits became a major theme for currency markets in the wake of the Global Financial Crisis of 2008–2009 (GFC), the Eurozone debt crisis of 2009–2013, and the pandemic crisis of 2020, but they were always in the background.

Assessing Economic Data Reports from a Trading Perspective

The data that you find in economic textbooks is very neat and clean — but the data as it actually arrives in the market can be anything *but* neat and clean. We're talking here not only about the imperfections of economic data gathering, but also about how markets interpret individual data reports.

In the following sections, we look at important data-reporting conventions and how they can also affect market reactions. When currencies don't react to the headlines of a data report as you would expect, odds are that one of the following elements is responsible, and you need to look more closely at the report to get the true picture.

Understanding and revising data history

Economic data reports don't originate in a vacuum — they have a history. Another popular market adage expressing this thought is "One report does not make a trend." However, that saying is mostly directed at data reports that come in far out of line with market estimates or vastly different from recent readings in the data series. To be sure, the market will react strongly when data comes in surprisingly better or worse than expected, but the sustainability of the reaction will vary greatly depending on the circumstances. If retail sales are generally increasing, for instance, does a one-month drop in retail sales indicate that the trend is over, or was it a one-off decline due to bad weather keeping shoppers at home?

TIP

When you're looking at upcoming economic data events, not only do you need to be aware of what's expected, but it also helps to know what, if any, trends are evident in the data series. The more pronounced or lengthy the trend is, the more likely the reactions to out-of-line economic reports will prove short lived. The more uneven the recent data has been, the more likely the reaction to the new data will be sustained.

WARNING

The other important element to keep in mind when interpreting incoming economic data is to see whether the data from the prior period has been revised. Unfortunately, there is no rule preventing earlier economic data from being changed. It's just one of those odd facts of life in financial markets that what the market thought it knew one day (and actually traded for several weeks based on that understanding) can be substantially changed later.

When prior-period data is revised, the market will tend to net out the older, revised report with the newly released data, essentially looking at the two reports together for what they suggest about the data trend. For example, if a current report comes out worse than expected, and the prior report is revised lower as well, the two together are likely to be interpreted as more disappointing. If a current report comes out better than expected, but the prior period's revision is negative, the positive reaction to the current report will tend to be restrained by the downgrade to the earlier data.

REMEMBER

As you can imagine, there are many different ways and degrees in which current/revised data scenarios can play out. A general rule is that the larger the revision to the prior report, the more significance it will carry into the interpretation of the current release. The key is to first be aware of prior-period revisions and to then view them relative to the incoming data. In general, current data reports tend to receive a higher weighting by the market if only because the data is the freshest available, and markets are always looking ahead.

Getting to the core

A number of important economic indicators are issued on a headline basis and a core basis. The *headline* reading is the complete result of the indicator, while the *core* reading is the headline reading minus certain categories or excluding certain items. Most inflation reports and measures of consumer spending use this convention.

In the case of inflation reports, many reporting agencies strip out or exclude highly volatile components, such as food and energy. In the United States, for instance, the consumer price index (CPI) is reported on a core basis excluding food and energy, commonly cited as *CPI ex-F&E*. (Whenever you see a data report "ex-something," it's short for "excluding" that something.) The rationale for ignoring those items is that they're prone to market, seasonal, or weather-related disruptions. For example, food prices may change rapidly due to drought, floods, or unseasonably hot or cold weather. By excluding those items, the core reading is believed to paint a more accurate picture of structural, long-term price pressures, which is what concerns monetary policy makers the most.

Looking at consumer spending reports, the retail sales report in the United States is reported on a core basis excluding autos (retail sales ex-autos), which are heavily influenced by seasonal discounting and sales promotions, as well as being relatively large-ticket items in relation to other retail expenditures. The durable goods report is also issued on a core basis excluding transportation (durable goods ex-transportation), which mostly reflects aircraft sales, which are also highly variable on a month-to-month basis as well as extremely big-ticket items that can distort the overall data picture.

REMEMBER

Markets tend to focus on the core reading over the headline reading in most cases, especially where a known preference for the core reading exists on the part of monetary-policy makers. The result can be large discrepancies between headline data and the core readings, such as headline retail sales falling 1 percent on a month-to-month basis but rising 0.5 percent on a core ex-autos basis. Needless to say, market reactions will be similarly disjointed, with an initial reaction based on the headline reading frequently followed by a different reaction to the core.

Market-Moving Economic Data Reports from the United States

In this section, we get down to the nitty-gritty data. Here, we run through the major economic data reports that come out of the United States. (We list the data reports according to the model we outline earlier in this chapter.) Our intention here is not necessarily to magnify the importance of U.S. economic data, even though the United States is the world's largest national economy and the U.S. dollar is on one side of 80 percent of currency trades.

Nope, our aim here is to kill two birds with one stone:

» Introduce you to the major economic reports issued by every major currency country, using U.S. data as the example

>> Let you in on the finer points of how the market views the important data reports

At the end of this chapter, we take you through a country-by-country look at major non-U.S. data reports that don't fall into the main report categories or are too important to be ignored.

Labor-market reports

We put the job market at the top of our economic model because job creation/ destruction is the single-most important driver of overall economic growth. Every major economy issues updates on its labor market by reporting the number of jobs added/lost, the unemployment rate, or some variation of those. United States employment data holds special significance because it reflects on the world's largest economy and the primary global reserve currency. The following are the key U.S. employment reports.

U.S. monthly employment report

Typically released on the first Friday of each month and covering the prior month, the U.S. jobs report is considered among the timeliest of economic indicators. But it's also subject to large revisions to prior periods and significant statistical volatility. The main components of the report include

>> **Change in non-farm payrolls (NFP):** Measures the number of jobs gained or lost in the prior month. This is the big number everyone focuses on. The NFP change is derived from the *establishment survey* (because it's based on responses from companies). The going wisdom among economists is that the United States needs to add around 200,000 jobs each month just to offset population growth and keep the unemployment rate steady. The market's initial reaction is based on the difference between the actual and the forecast change in NFP. The prior two months' NFP changes are also revised, and those revisions will color the market's interpretation of the current report.

>> **Unemployment rate:** Measures unemployed individuals seeking work as a percentage of the civilian labor force. The unemployment rate is derived from a separate survey (the *household survey* because it surveys real households), which also includes a jobs change number that may be at odds with the change in NFP. Increases in the unemployment rate are typically interpreted as a sign of weakness in the labor market and the economy overall, while declines in the rate are considered a positive sign for the job market and the overall economy.

- >> **Change in manufacturing payrolls:** Measures the number of jobs added or lost in manufacturing industries and is looked at as a gauge of near-term production activity.

- >> **Average hourly earnings:** Measures the change in employee wages and is looked at as an indicator of whether incomes are rising or falling and the implications for consumer spending.

- >> **Average weekly hours:** Measures the average number of hours worked each week and is looked at as a rough gauge of the demand for labor, with increasing weekly hours seen as a positive for the labor market.

ADP national employment report

The ADP national employment report is put together by the payroll processing company of the same name (www.adp.com) and works in close collaboration with Moody's Analytics. It comes out on Wednesdays at 8:15 a.m. eastern time (ET), two days before the government's NFP report (see the preceding section).

WARNING

ADP measures only private jobs and excludes government hiring. The ADP report is intended to serve as an alternative measurement of the labor market, but it's got a spotty track record of predicting the NFP with any accuracy. Because of that uncertainty, market reaction to the ADP is typically minor and short-lived, but economists may adjust their forecasts for the NFP depending on what the ADP indicates.

Weekly initial unemployment claims

Initial jobless claims are reported every Thursday at 8:30 a.m. ET for the week ending the prior Saturday and represent first-time filings for unemployment insurance. Initial claims are looked at as interim updates on the overall labor market between monthly NFP reports. The changes in initial claims can be volatile on a week-to-week basis — there are a fair number of hiccups caused by weather, strikes, and seasonal labor patterns — so analysts look at a four-week moving average of initial claims to factor out one-off events. Still, sharp increases or declines in initial claims data will get the market's attention, producing a market reaction on their own, as well as causing estimates of upcoming monthly NFP reports to be downgraded or upgraded.

A second part of the weekly claims report is *continuing claims,* which is a measure of the total number of people receiving unemployment benefits, excluding first-time filers. The market looks at continuing claims as another gauge of labor-market conditions. Increases in continuing claims typically suggest deterioration in the job market, because unemployed individuals are finding it difficult to get work and staying on unemployment insurance longer. Declines in continuing claims, on the other hand, are viewed as an improvement in the job market, because workers are presumably finding jobs more easily.

OTHER LABOR-MARKET INDICATORS

On top of the reports listed in the "Labor-market reports" section of this chapter, a number of other employment indicators come out inside other economic reports. These employment measures don't trigger market reactions in their own right, but they're used to update the overall understanding of the employment outlook. These include

- **Consumer confidence index (CCI):** Within the monthly consumer confidence report by the Conference Board (www.conference-board.org), respondents are asked whether "jobs are hard to get" and also whether "jobs are plentiful." The difference between the two is known as the *labor differential* and serves as another barometer of conditions in labor markets.

- **Institute for Supply Management (ISM) employment indices:** The national ISM purchasing manager indices contain a subcategory asking managers to rate the employment situation at their companies, with responses over 50 indicating plans to hire and expand, and readings below 50 indicating contraction.

- **Regional Federal Reserve indices:** Surveys of manufacturing businesses, like the Philadelphia Fed survey, also include questions on the outlook for hiring. Readings above zero indicate plans to add employees; levels below zero suggest layoffs ahead.

Consumer-level data reports

Personal consumption accounts for two-thirds or more of most developed nations' economies, so how consumers are doing has a big impact on the economic outlook and the direction of interest rates, which are both key drivers of forex rates. Here are the main U.S. data reports focusing on personal consumption.

Consumer sentiment

REMEMBER

Consumer psychology is at the heart of the market's attempts to interpret future consumer activity and, with it, the overall direction of the economy. The theory is that if you feel good, you'll spend more, and if you feel uncertain, you'll cut back spending. The market likes to pay attention to consumer confidence indicators even though there is little correlation between how consumers tell you they feel and how they'll actually go on to spend.

In fact, consumer sentiment is frequently the result of changes in gasoline prices, how the stock market is faring, or what recent employment indicators suggested. More reliable indicators of consumer spending are money-in-the-pocket gauges like average weekly earnings, personal income and spending, and retail sales reports. Still, the market likes to react to the main sentiment gauges, if only in the short run, with improving sentiment generally supporting the domestic currency and softer sentiment hurting it. The key confidence gauges are

>> **Consumer confidence index:** A monthly report issued by the Conference Board comprised of the expectations index (looking six months ahead) and the present-situation index. The surveys ask households about their outlooks for overall economic conditions, employment, and incomes.

>> **University of Michigan consumer sentiment index:** Comes out twice a month: a preliminary reading in the middle of the month and a final reading at the start of the next month.

>> **ABC Consumer Confidence:** A weekly consumer-sentiment report issued each Tuesday evening. The weekly ABC confidence report can be used to update your expectations of upcoming monthly consumer confidence and University of Michigan reports.

TIP

If market forecasts envision an increase in the Michigan or Conference Board's consumer confidence index, for example, but the prior two or three weeks of the ABC survey suggest confidence is waning, you've got a pretty good indication that the monthly surveys may disappoint.

Personal income and personal spending

These two monthly reports always come out together and provide as close an indication as we can get of how much money is going into and out of consumers' pockets. The market looks at these reports to get an update on the health of the U.S. consumer and the outlook for personal consumption going forward. *Personal income* includes all wages and salaries, along with transfer payments (such as Social Security or unemployment insurance) and dividends. *Personal spending* is based on personal consumption expenditures for all types of individual outlays.

Personal income is watched as a leading indicator of personal spending on the basis that future spending is highly correlated with income. The greater the increases in personal income, the more optimistic the consumption outlook will be, and vice versa. But it's important to note that inflation-adjusted incomes are the key. If incomes are just keeping pace with inflation, the outlook for spending is less positive.

Retail sales

REMEMBER

The monthly advance retail sales report is the primary indicator of personal spending in the United States, covering most every purchase Americans make, from gas-station fill-ups to dinner and a movie. Retail sales are reported on a headline basis as well as on a core basis (which excludes automobile purchases;

see the earlier section "Getting to the core" for details). The market focuses mainly on the core number to get a handle on how the consumer is behaving, but substantial strength or weakness in the auto industry doesn't go unnoticed. The advance retail sales report is a preliminary estimate based on survey samples and can be revised substantially based on later data.

Retail sales reports are subject to a variety of distorting effects, most commonly from weather. Stretches of bad weather, such as major storms or bouts of unseasonable cold or heat, can impair consumer mobility or alter shopping patterns, reducing retail sales in the affected period. Sharp swings in gasoline prices can also create illusory effects, such as price spikes leading to an apparent increase in retail sales due to the higher per-gallon price, while overall non-gas retail sales are reduced or displaced by the higher outlays at the pump.

Durable goods orders

Durable goods orders are another major monthly indicator of consumption, both by individuals and businesses. Durable goods measure the amount of orders received by manufacturers that produce items made to last at least three years. As a data series, durable goods is one of the most volatile of them all, with multiple percentage swings (as opposed to 0.1 percent or 0.3 percent changes) between months a norm rather than an exception. Durable goods are reported on a headline basis and on a core basis, excluding transportation, or ex-transportation (mostly aircraft).

TIP

Durables are generally bigger-ticket purchases, such as washing machines and furniture, so they're also looked at as a leading indicator of overall consumer spending. If consumers are feeling flush with cash and confidence, big-ticket spending is more common. If consumers are uncertain or times are tight, high-cost purchases are the first to be postponed. Also, businesses tend to concentrate their spending in the final month of each quarter, which can distort prior months and exaggerate the last.

Housing-market indicators

The real estate or housing market is a major factor behind consumer spending since homes typically represent the largest asset on a household's balance sheet. Rising home prices are seen to support consumption through the *wealth effect* (the richer you feel, the more likely you are to spend), whereas falling house prices can be a major drag on personal spending. The U.S. real estate bubble burst in 2006–2007 and triggered the GFC and recession of 2008–2009, turning U.S. housing data into a major drag on U.S consumption. One of the hangovers from the financial crisis is that the markets continue to look closely at the U.S. housing market as a gauge of economic strength. If you see a weak housing market, it can send a chill through the U.S. dollar market and the U.S. stock markets.

There's a raft of monthly housing market reports to monitor the sector, based on whether the homes are new or existing:

>> **Existing-home sales** data is reported by the National Association of Realtors (NAR). Sales of preexisting homes (condos included) account for the lion's share of residential real-estate activity — about 88 percent of total home sales. Existing-home sales are reported on an annualized rate, and the market looks at the monthly change in that rate. Median home prices and the inventory of unsold homes are important clues to how the housing market is evolving. Existing-home sales are counted after a closing. Pending home sales are a separate report viewed as a leading indicator of existing-home sales. Pending home sales are counted when a contract is signed to buy an existing home.

>> **New-home sales** are just that: brand-new homes and condos built for sale, reported on an annualized basis. New-home sales account for about 12 percent of residential home sales, but the sector was the fastest growing during the recent real-estate boom and has since seen activity decline steeply. New-home sales are counted when a contract is signed to purchase the new home, which means that contract cancellations (not reported) may result in lower actual sales than originally reported.

>> **Housing starts** measure the number of new-home construction starts that took place in each month, reported as an annualized rate. Housing starts are considered a leading indicator of new-home sales but more recently have been looked at as an indication of home builder sentiment, as builders try to reduce inventories of unsold new homes.

>> **Building permits** are the starting point of the whole new-housing cycle and are reported alongside housing starts each month. Building permits are required before construction can begin on new homes, so they're viewed as another leading indicator of housing starts and new-home sales.

Business-level data reports

Getting a handle on how businesses are faring is an important clue to the strength of the economy, which in turn drives the outlook for interest rates and the overall investment environment. The following series of data reports offer insights into how companies are responding at the enterprise level.

Institute for Supply Management and Purchasing Managers Index

The Institute for Supply Management (ISM) calculates several regional and national indices of current business conditions and future outlooks based on surveys of purchasing managers. ISM readings are based on a boom/bust scale, with 50 as the tipping point — a reading above 50 indicates expansion, whereas a reading below 50 signals contraction.

The main ISM reports to keep an eye on are

>> **Chicago Purchasing Managers Index (PMI):** The Chicago PMI remains the key regional manufacturing activity index because the Chicago area and the Midwest region are still significant hubs of manufacturing activity in the United States. The Chicago PMI is also the first of the national PMIs to be reported, and the market frequently views it as a leading indicator of the larger national ISM manufacturing report, which is typically released a day after the Chicago PMI.

>> **ISM manufacturing report:** The ISM manufacturing report is the monthly national survey of manufacturing activity and is one of the key indicators of the overall manufacturing sector. The ISM manufacturing report also includes a prices-paid index, which is viewed as an interim inflation reading, along with other key subsector measurements, like the employment situation. The market tends to react pretty strongly to sharp changes in the report or if the ISM is moving above or below 50, but keep in mind that the manufacturing sector accounts for a relatively small portion of overall U.S. economic activity, so the importance of the ISM manufacturing gauge tends to be exaggerated.

TIP

>> **ISM nonmanufacturing report:** The ISM nonmanufacturing report is the monthly ISM report that covers the other 80 percent of the U.S. economy, namely the service sector. The ISM manufacturing report may get more attention, but the ISM non-manufacturing report is the one to focus on.

The equivalent of the ISM reports in Europe and China are the PMI reports that are put together by a data collection company called Markit. Since 2011, Markit has produced an index for the United States, which is released at the end of each month. Although not as popular as the ISM survey, the fact that it's released before the ISM survey has seen its popularity start to rise, although it has some way to go before it overtakes the ISM as the business survey of choice for the markets.

Regional Federal Reserve indices

A number of the Federal Reserve district banks issue monthly surveys of business sentiment in their regions, usually concentrated on the manufacturing sector. The regional Fed indices are looked at on their own as well as for what they suggest about subsequent national sentiment surveys, like the ISM index (see the previous section). The main index reading is a subjective response on general business conditions, with responses above zero indicating that conditions are improving and readings below zero indicating deterioration. The main regional Fed indices to watch are

>> **Philadelphia Fed index:** Usually the first of the major Fed indices to be reported each month, covering the manufacturing sector in Pennsylvania, New Jersey, and Delaware. The Philly Fed index includes subindices focusing on new orders, employment, inventories, and prices, among others.

>> **New York Empire State index:** Assesses New York state manufacturers' current and six-month outlooks.

>> **Richmond Fed manufacturing index:** A composite index based on new orders, production, and employment, covering the Middle Atlantic states.

Industrial production and capacity utilization

Industrial production measures the amount of output generated by the nation's factories, mines, and utilities on a monthly basis and is viewed as an indication of changes in the broader economy. The manufacturing sector is still viewed as a leading indicator for overall business cycles, so changes here could signal a larger swing in the economic outlook.

The capacity utilization report measures actual output versus a theoretical maximum capacity and is looked at for what it suggests about inflationary pressures. High levels of capacity utilization, above 75 percent, may indicate price pressures are building and send a warning sign to policy makers. Lower levels of capacity utilization (below 75 percent) may signal the absence of inflationary pressures and allow monetary policy makers to keep interest rates lower. According to the Corporate Finance Institute (www.corporatefinanceinstitute.com), 85 percent or higher is the optimal rate for most companies.

The Fed's Beige Book

The Beige Book, named for the color of its cover, is a compilation of regional economic assessments from the Fed's 12 district banks, issued about two weeks before every Federal Open Market Committee (FOMC) policy-setting meeting. The regional Fed banks develop their summaries based on surveys and anecdotal reporting of local business leaders and economists, and the report is then summarized by one of the Fed district banks, all of which take turns issuing the report. The Beige Book is designed to serve as the basis of economic discussions at the upcoming FOMC meeting.

Markets look at the Beige Book's main findings to get a handle on how the economy is developing as well as what issues the FOMC may focus on. A typical Beige Book report may include generalized observations along the following lines:

>> Most districts reported retail sales activity that was steady or moderately expanding.

>> A few districts reported declines in manufacturing activity.

>> Some districts noted increased labor-market tightness and rising wage demands.

>> All districts noted a sharp slowing in real estate activity.

REMEMBER

The key for the market is to assess the main themes of the report, such as the following:

>> Is the economy expanding or contracting? How fast, and how widespread?

>> Which sectors are strongest, and which sectors are weakest?

>> Are there any signs of inflation?

>> How does the labor market look?

TIP

The Beige Book is released in the afternoon (New York time), when liquidity is thinner, so it can generate a larger-than-normal response if its tone or conclusions are significantly different from what markets had been expecting.

Structural data reports

Structural data reports are the big-picture, macroeconomic data that depict the longer-term economic outlook. What is the structure of the economy? Is it growing or contracting? If so, how fast? Is inflation under control or are prices rising too fast? Is the economy gaining or losing from trade? These reports can be some of the most significant drivers of central bank monetary policy.

Inflation gauges

Inflation reports are used to monitor overall changes in price levels of goods and services and as key inputs into setting interest rate expectations. Increases in inflation are likely to be met with higher interest rates by central-bank policy makers seeking to stamp out inflation, while moderating or declining inflation readings suggest generally lower interest-rate expectations.

There are a number of different inflation reports, with each focused on a different source of inflation or stage of the economy where the price changes are appearing. In the United States and other countries, inflation reports come out on a headline (total) basis and a core basis (which excludes food and energy to minimize distortions from these volatile inputs). Inflation indexes report changes on a month-to-month basis (abbreviated MoM, for month-over-month) to monitor short-term changes, as well as changes over the prior year's levels (YoY, for year-over-year) to gauge the longer-term rate of inflation. The main inflation reports to keep an eye on are

>> **Consumer price index (CPI):** The CPI is what most people are familiar with when they think of inflation. The CPI measures the cost of a basket of goods and services at the consumer or retail level — the prices that we're paying. The CPI is looked at as the final stage of inflation.

>> **Producer price index (PPI):** The PPI measures the change in prices at the producer or wholesale level, or what firms are charging one another for goods and services. The PPI looks at upstream inflation by stage of processing and may serve as a leading indicator of overall inflation.

TIP

>> **Personal consumption expenditure (PCE):** The PCE is roughly equivalent to the CPI in that it measures the changes in price of a basket of goods and services at the consumer level. But the PCE has the distinction of being preferred by the Federal Reserve as its main inflation gauge because the composition of items in the PCE basket changes more frequently than in the CPI, reflecting evolving consumer tastes and behavior. If the Fed thinks the more-dynamic basket is the one to watch, who are we to disagree? When the Fed refers to an inflation target or tolerable level of inflation, it's typically referring to core PCE readings.

>> **Institute for Supply Management (ISM) prices paid index:** The national and regional purchasing managers indices have subcategories reporting on the level of prices paid and the level of prices received by firms. The prices-paid component usually gets the most attention as another producer-level indication of price pressures, likely to be mirrored by the PPI.

Gross domestic product

Gross domestic product (GDP) measures the total amount of economic activity in an economy over a specified period, usually quarterly and adjusted for inflation. The percentage change in GDP from one period to the next is looked at as the primary growth rate of an economy. If GDP in the first quarter of a year is reported as +0.5 percent, it means the economy expanded by 0.5 percent in the first quarter relative to the prior fourth quarter's output. GDP is frequently calculated on a quarterly basis but reported in *annualized* terms. That means a 0.5 percent quarterly GDP increase would be reported as a 2 percent annualized rate of growth for the quarter (0.5 percent × 4 quarters = 2 percent). The use of annualized rates is helpful for comparing relative growth among economies.

REMEMBER

In most countries, GDP is reported on a quarterly basis, so it's taken as a big-picture reality check on overall economic growth. The market's economic outlook will be heavily influenced by what the GDP reports indicate. Better-than-expected growth may spur talk of the need for higher interest rates, while steady or slower GDP growth may suggest easier monetary policy ahead. At the same time, though, GDP reports cover a relatively distant economic past — a quarter's GDP report typically comes out almost midway through the next quarter and is looking back at economic activity three to four months ago. As a result, market expectations continue to evolve based on incoming data reports, so don't get too caught up in GDP for too long after its initial release.

Trade and current account balances

Two of the most important reports for the forex markets, because there are direct and potentially long-term currency implications, are trade and current account balances:

» **Trade balance** measures the difference between a nation's exports and its imports. If a nation imports more than it exports, it's said to have a *trade deficit;* if a nation exports more than it imports, it's said to have a *trade surplus.* Trade balances are reported on a monthly basis; prior periods are subject to revision.

» **Current account balance** is a broader measure of international trade, and includes financial transfers as well as trade in goods and services. Current accounts are also either in deficit or surplus, reflecting whether a country is a net borrower or lender to the rest of the world. Nations with current account deficits are net borrowers from the rest of the world, and those with current account surpluses are net lenders to the world. Current account reports are issued quarterly, and because the monthly trade balance comprises the bulk of the current account balance, markets tend to have a good handle on what to expect in current account data.

REMEMBER

Countries with persistently large trade or current account deficits tend to see their currencies weaken relative to other currencies, whereas currencies of countries running trade surpluses tend to appreciate. The basic idea is that the currency of a deficit nation is in less demand (it's being sold to buy more foreign goods) than the currency of a surplus nation (it's being bought to pay for domestically produced goods).

For example, the U.S. dollar was under pressure for several years before the GFC, owing to its widening (increasing) trade and current account deficits. In late 2006, however, the size of the deficit stopped increasing, which removed some of the pressure on the dollar. But because the deficit remains high in absolute and historical terms, the U.S. trade deficit is still a major U.S. dollar negative, although the U.S.'s increased oil production in recent years could cause the trade deficit to shrink sharply in the future and could be a dollar positive in the future.

Government debt and budget deficits

The aftermath of the GFC exposed high debt and deficit levels in many major economies, especially in the United States, Europe, the United Kingdom, and Japan. Fears of a debt *restructuring* (where terms of a bond are altered) or default can seriously undermine confidence in a national currency, leading to an extended bout of weakness, as was seen with the euro in the 2010 European debt crisis.

TIP

There's no single data release that adequately covers the debt situations in major economies, though most national governments typically release a monthly budget statement. Instead, monitoring the debt/deficit picture of key countries depends on a series of news and data flows:

>> **Budget and deficit forecasts:** Issued by individual governments and the IMF, these are the best way to stay on top of evolving fiscal changes.

>> **Government bond yields, spreads, and CDS (credit default swaps):** As investors' fears increase over the creditworthiness of governments, they sell those countries' bonds, driving yields higher. *Yield spreads* are another measure of risk, noting the difference between the yields of an embattled nation and a safer alternative. Credit default swaps are a form of insurance that pays investors in the event of a default — the higher they are, the greater the perceived risk.

>> **Government debt auctions:** When governments seek to borrow in capital markets, lack of demand or too high a price can shut them out and possibly trigger a default. Watch for indicators of demand, like the *bid/cover ratio,* which measures the amount of bids submitted relative to the issuance amount (the higher the better) and pricing (the higher the yield demanded, the greater the risk).

>> **Sovereign credit ratings:** Major credit rating agencies, like Moody's, S&P, and Fitch, may announce periodic credit reviews of sovereign debt, possibly suggesting a downgrade. Actual credit rating downgrades can send investors fleeing, driving up a country's borrowing costs and increasing the risks of default.

Major International Data Reports

In the preceding sections, we cover the main economic reports using U.S. data as the basis for explaining what each report measures and how the market views it. The main data reports of other major national economies essentially mirror the U.S. data reports, but with some minor differences in calculation methods or reporting. In other words, the CPI report out of the United Kingdom is looked at the same way as the CPI report is viewed in the United States — as a measure of consumer-level inflation.

But plenty of national data reports don't have an equivalent in the United States, and others are followed more closely in local markets and require extra attention. In the next few sections, we highlight the main data reports of other national economies beyond what we cover earlier.

Eurozone

The main data reports out of the Eurozone are remarkably similar to those of the United States. The key difference is that individual European countries report national economic data, which comes out alongside Eurozone-wide reports from Eurostat or the European Central Bank (ECB; www.ecb.europa.eu/home/html/index.en.html).

REMEMBER

Because the Eurozone has a common currency and central bank, the forex market focuses primarily on indicators that cover the entire region, such as Eurozone industrial production and CPI, for example. Among individual national reports, the market concentrates on data from the largest Eurozone economies, mainly Germany and France. Keep an eye on all the major reports coming out of those countries. They can generate sizeable reactions based on the idea that they're leading indicators of Eurozone-wide data. If German industrial production slumps, for instance, it may suggest that overall Eurozone industrial production is set to decline, too. Since the Eurozone sovereign debt crisis, the market has also tended to concentrate on how countries that received bailouts (Greece, Ireland, and Portugal) are faring. Believe it or not, a Greek unemployment report has been known to move the market!

The only European reports that may escape your attention due to unusual names are the principal European confidence indicators. These reports can generate sizeable reactions depending on how they compare to forecasts:

>> **ZEW survey:** This survey measures growth expectations over the next six months by institutional investors and analysts. The survey is done for Germany and the whole Eurozone.

>> **IFO and GfK surveys:** IFO is a corporate sentiment survey that queries businesses across Germany on current sentiment and how business is expected to develop over the next six months. The GfK survey is a monthly measure of consumer confidence.

>> **Purchasing Manager Indexes (PMIs):** A data firm called Markit produces monthly PMIs for the manufacturing and service sectors for Germany, France, and the whole Eurozone, similar to the Chicago PMI in the United States. The reports come out on a preliminary and final basis.

>> **Eurozone Confidence:** The European Commission (EC) produces monthly confidence surveys for a variety of sectors: consumer, services, industrial, and overall economic sentiment.

Japan

TIP

When looking at Japanese data, keep in mind that the Japanese economy is still heavily export oriented. In addition to following all the usual reports, pay special attention to industrial production and manufacturing data because of their large role in the economy. Since 2012, the Bank of Japan has tried to fight off the threat of deflation, which means that CPI reports have also taken on a special significance in recent years. Outside the standard reports to watch, keep an eye on the following:

>> **Tankan index:** The Tankan survey is a quarterly survey of business outlooks produced by the Bank of Japan (BOJ). The survey produces four readings — current conditions and future outlook from both large manufacturers and large non-manufacturers. The large all-industry capital expenditures survey is an important gauge of capital spending and is often the focus of the entire Tankan survey.

>> **Trade balance:** Japan's monthly trade balance is nearly always in surplus. The size of that surplus carries indications for the health of the export sector as well as potential political repercussions against excessive JPY weakness when the trade surplus is seen to be too large.

>> **All-industry and tertiary industry (services) indices:** Monthly sentiment gauges of industrial and service-sector firms.

United Kingdom

In addition to the usual major government–issued data reports, be alert for the following reports that can frequently trigger sharp reactions in GBP:

>> **Bank of England (BOE) Minutes:** Released two weeks after each Monetary Policy Committee (MPC) meeting, they show the voting results for the most recent decision. Market expectations and GBP are frequently upended when the policy discussion or vote shows a split leaning in the direction of an interest rate change.

>> **BOE Quarterly Inflation Report:** Although it only comes out quarterly, the BOE's forecasts for growth and inflation over the next two years can have a significant impact on the interest rate outlook and GBP. It also includes a press conference, which is watched closely by the markets.

>> **Purchasing Manager Indexes (PMIs):** A data firm called Markit produces monthly PMIs for the manufacturing, construction, and service sectors.

>> **GfK consumer confidence and Nationwide consumer confidence:** Two separate, monthly, consumer-sentiment gauges put out by GfK, a UK/ European marketing agency, and the Nationwide Building Society, a UK mortgage lender.

>> **CBI distributive trades survey and industrial trends survey:** Two monthly reports put out by the Confederation of British Industry, a private trade group. The distributive trades survey is a measure of retail and wholesale sales, and the industrial trends survey is a survey of manufacturers' current and future outlook.

>> **British Retail Consortium (BRC) retail sales monitor and shop price index:** Two monthly reports put out by the British Retail Consortium, a private trade organization. The retail sales monitor is another measure of retail sales, and the shop price index measures inflation at the retail level.

Canada

Canadian data mirrors U.S. data in many respects, but here are a few other important Canadian indicators to watch:

>> **International securities transactions:** Roughly the equivalent of the U.S. Treasury's TIC report (see the earlier section "Trade and current account balances"), showing net investment flows into and out of Canada on a monthly basis. High inflows typically support the CAD, and outflows tend to hurt it.

>> **Ivey Purchasing Manager index:** A key monthly gauge of Canadian business outlooks issued by the Richard Ivey School of Business. The report covers purchases, employment, inventories, deliveries, and prices.

Australia

Australian data reports exert a strong influence on Aussie, similar in many respects to how UK data affects the pound. In particular, keep an eye on

>> **RBA rate decisions and RBA Minutes:** The Reserve Bank of Australia's statement following a rate decision, and the subsequent release of the minutes two weeks later, can drive interest rate expectations and AUD big time.

>> **Westpac consumer confidence and National Australia Bank (NAB) business confidence:** Two separate monthly sentiment gauges put out by two of Australia's leading banks.

New Zealand

New Zealand data is similarly provocative for the Kiwi. In addition to the main data reports and Reserve Bank of New Zealand (RBNZ) statements, keep an eye on the following Kiwi-specific data:

>> **NZ Card Spending:** This monthly report covers purchases using credit, debit, and store cards, and gives another view of retail sales.

>> **ANZ Consumer Confidence:** This monthly survey of consumer sentiment is conducted by ANZ Bank.

China

In early 2011, China surpassed Japan as the world's second largest national economy after the United States. Chinese growth over the last decade has been nothing short of astronomical and played a major role in supporting the global recovery after the GFC. Data out of China has taken on increased prominence as a result, with global markets frequently reeling on weaker China data or surging on stronger reports.

The Chinese growth outlook affects global markets through a number of different channels. Stronger Chinese growth is good for global trade and tends to positively influence stock markets around the world. Chinese demand for commodities is also influenced by its growth trajectory, with consequent implications for individual commodity markets (China also recently surpassed the U.S. as the largest oil consumer) and commodity producing countries such as Australia and South Africa. As a result, financial markets around the world are increasingly driven by Chinese growth prospects.

In terms of economic reports, Chinese data that reflects growth are the most significant, and we highlight the trade surplus, industrial production, manufacturing PMIs, and quarterly GDP as the key data releases to watch. Chinese consumers are also increasingly seen to be key to developed nations' economic outlooks, and signs of rising imports and gains in retail sales are viewed as supportive of global growth.

REMEMBER

The Chinese still manage their currency, and it's not accessible to individual traders. But Chinese data can have an impact far beyond its borders due to its newfound prominence in the global economy. This is especially relevant for the Aussie dollar, because China is Australia's main trading partner.

Chapter **8**

Getting to Know the Major Currency Pairs

The vast majority of trading volume takes place in the *major* currency pairs: EUR/USD, USD/JPY, GBP/USD, and USD/CHF. These currency pairs account for about two-thirds of daily trading volume in the market and are the most watched barometers of the overall forex market. When you hear about the dollar rising or falling, it's usually referring to the dollar against these other currencies.

Even though these four pairs are routinely grouped together as the major currency pairs, each currency pair represents an individual economic and political relationship. In this chapter, we look at the fundamental drivers of each currency pair to see what moves them. We also look at the market's quoting conventions and what they mean for margin-based trading.

Although it's important to understand *why* a currency rate moves, we think it's also essential to have an understanding of *how* different pairs' rates move. Most currency trading is very short-term in nature, typically from a few minutes to a few days. This makes understanding a currency pair's *price action* (how a currency pair's price moves in the very short term) a key component of any trading strategy.

REMEMBER

When you're reading this chapter, keep in mind that our observations are not hard-and-fast rules. As far as we know, there are no hard-and-fast rules in any market, anywhere, any time. Think of them as rules of thumb that apply more often than not. When it comes to applying our insights into real-life trading, you'll have to evaluate the overall circumstances each time to see whether our insights make sense. The idea is that with a baseline of currency pair behavior, you'll be in a better position to anticipate, interpret, and react to market developments.

The flip side of this coin is that there is information content when our insights don't hold water. If the market usually reacts to certain events in a regular fashion, but it's not doing so this time, it's a clue that something else is at work (usually bigger). And that can be even more valuable trading information.

The Big Dollar: EUR/USD

EUR/USD is by far the most actively traded currency pair in the global forex market. Everyone and his brother, sister, and cousin trades EUR/USD. This will come as no surprise to anyone who has traded in the forex market, because if you have, more likely than not you traded EUR/USD at some point.

The same goes for the big banks. Every major trading desk has at least one, and probably several, EUR/USD traders to deal with the volume in this currency pair. This is in contrast to less liquid currency pairs such as USD/CAD or AUD/USD, for which trading desks may not have a dedicated trader. All those EUR/USD traders add up to vast amounts of market interest, which increases overall trading liquidity.

Trading fundamentals of EUR/USD

EUR/USD is the currency pair that pits the U.S. dollar against the single currency of the Eurozone, the euro. The *Eurozone* refers to a grouping of countries in the European Union (EU) that in 1999 retired their own national currencies and adopted a unified single currency. In one fell swoop, at midnight on January 1, 1999, the Deutsche mark, Italian lira, French franc, and nine other European currencies disappeared and the euro came into being.

The move to a single currency was the culmination of financial unification efforts by the founding members of the European Union. In adopting the single currency, the nations agreed to abide by fiscal policy constraints that limited the ratio of national budget deficits to gross domestic product (GDP), among other requirements. (Some people would say that the 2010 sovereign debt crisis made a mockery of these rules.) The nations also delegated monetary policy (setting interest rates) to the newly founded European Central Bank (ECB).

As of this printing, the countries that use the euro are Austria, Belgium, Cyprus, Estonia, Finland, France, Germany, Greece, Ireland, Italy, Latvia, Lithuania, Luxembourg, Malta, the Netherlands, Portugal, Slovakia, Slovenia, and Spain.

In 2010, the Eurozone underwent its first major challenge, known as the *sovereign debt crisis.* Some states had built up unsustainable debt loads and ended up needing bailouts. Greece was the first member state to topple, with Ireland, Portugal, and Cyprus also requiring financial bailouts in recent years. At the time of writing, the situation had stabilized, although the road to recovery for some of the countries involved is a long one. The sovereign debt crisis has been the defining event of the Eurozone this century.

On a brighter note, even with the sovereign debt crisis, the Eurozone has continued to expand in recent years, boosting the size of the monetary union's population to more than 448 million folks as of early 2020. Although its economy has taken a knock due to the sovereign debt crisis, its total GDP is still about equal to the GDP of the United States.

Trading EUR/USD by the numbers

Standard market convention is to quote EUR/USD in terms of the number of USD per EUR. For example, a EUR/USD rate of 1.3000 means that it takes $1.30 to buy €1.00.

REMEMBER

EUR/USD trades inversely to the overall value of the USD, which means when EUR/USD goes up, the euro is getting stronger and the dollar weaker. When EUR/USD goes down, the euro is getting weaker and the dollar stronger. If you believed the U.S. dollar was going to move higher, you'd be looking to sell EUR/USD. If you thought the dollar was going to weaken, you'd be looking to buy EUR/USD.

EUR/USD has the euro as the base currency and the U.S. dollar as the secondary or counter currency. That means

>> **EUR/USD is traded in amounts denominated in euros.** In online currency trading platforms, standard lot sizes are €100,000, mini lot sizes are €10,000, and micro lots are €1,000.

>> **The pip value, or minimum price fluctuation, is denominated in USD.**

>> **Profit and loss accrue in USD.** For one standard lot position size, each pip is worth $10; for one mini lot position size, each pip is worth $1. For each micro lot, each pip is worth $0.10.

>> **Margin calculations in online trading platforms are typically based in USD.** At a EUR/USD rate of 1.3000, to trade a one-lot position worth €100,000, it takes $1,300 in available margin (based on 100:1 leverage). That calculation changes over time, of course, based on the level of the EUR/USD exchange rate. A higher EUR/USD rate requires more USD in available margin collateral, and a lower EUR/USD rate needs less USD in margin.

Swimming in deep liquidity

Liquidity in EUR/USD is unmatched by other major currency pairs. This is why you tend to get narrower trading spreads in EUR/USD. Normal market spreads for EUR/USD are typically less than 1 pip, although this can vary. Over the years, spreads have narrowed sharply, and you can typically trade most of the major currency pairs for a 1-pip spread or even less.

In terms of concrete numbers, EUR/USD accounted for 32 percent of global daily trading volume, according to the 2019 Bank for International Settlements (BIS) survey of the foreign exchange markets. This has fallen in recent years because the legacy of the sovereign debt crisis has caused some investors to diversify away from the single currency.

Liquidity in EUR/USD is based on a variety of fundamental sources, such as

>> **Global trade and asset allocation:** The Eurozone constitutes the second largest economic bloc after the United States. Not only does this create tremendous commercial trade flows, but it also makes Eurozone financial markets, and the euro, the destination for massive amounts of international investment flows. In April 2007, overall European stock-market valuations surpassed the value of U.S. equity markets for the first time ever.

>> **Central bank credibility:** The ECB has established itself in the eyes of global investors as an effective institution in fighting inflation and maintaining currency stability. It has also been given credit for stabilizing the currency bloc during the sovereign debt crisis, which has enhanced its reputation in recent years.

>> **Enhanced status as a reserve currency:** Central banks around the world hold foreign currency reserves to support their own currencies and improve market stability. The euro is increasing in importance as an alternative global reserve currency to the U.S. dollar, although this has stalled in recent years due to the onset of the sovereign debt crisis.

The euro also serves as the primary foil to the U.S. dollar when it comes to speculating on the overall direction of the U.S. dollar in response to U.S. news or economic data. If weak U.S. economic data is reported, traders are typically going to sell the dollar, which begs the question, "Against what?" The euro is the first choice for many, simply because it's there. It also helps that it's the most liquid alternative, allowing for easy entry and exit.

REMEMBER

This is not to say that EUR/USD only reacts to U.S. economic data or news. On the contrary, Eurozone news, politics, and data can move EUR/USD as much as U.S. data moves the pair and sometimes more so, as during the sovereign debt crisis.

Drivers of the EUR/USD can be cyclical. On any given day, traders respond to European news and data and adjust prices accordingly for several hours until U.S. data is released.

Watching the data reports

Country-specific economic reports, such as Dutch retail sales or Italian industrial production, are increasingly disregarded by the forex market in favor of Eurozone aggregate economic data. However, German and French national economic reports can still register with markets as they represent the two largest Eurozone economies. Here's a list of the major European data reports and events to keep an eye on:

>> **European Central Bank (ECB) interest rate decisions and press conferences after ECB Central Council meetings.** This is when the ECB president explains the ECB's thinking and offers guidance on the future course of interest rates. It includes a press conference by the ECB president.

>> **Speeches by ECB officials and individual European finance ministers.**

>> **EU-harmonized Consumer Price Index (CPI), as well as national CPI and Producer Price Index (PPI) reports.**

>> **EU Commission economic sector confidence indicators.**

>> **Consumer and investor sentiment surveys separately issued by three private economic research firms known by their acronyms: Ifo, ZEW, and GfK.** The Markit sentiment surveys are also closely watched because they give a timely view of confidence across all sectors of the economy.

>> **Industrial production.**

>> **Retail sales.**

>> **Unemployment rate.**

>> **Sovereign debt sales.** These are now closely watched, especially in Europe's smaller, financially fragile states, such as Greece. Although the sovereign debt crisis has calmed down in recent years, a failed bond auction could trigger more sovereign fears and weigh on the EUR.

Trading behavior of EUR/USD

The deep liquidity and tight trading spreads in EUR/USD make the pair ideal for both shorter-term and longer-term traders. The price action behavior in EUR/USD regularly exhibits a number of traits that traders should be aware of.

Trading tick by tick

In normal market conditions, EUR/USD tends to trade tick by tick, as opposed to other currency pairs, which routinely display sharper short-term price movements of several pips. In trading terms, if EUR/USD is trading at 1.2910/13, there are going to be traders looking to sell at 13, 14, and 15 and higher, while buyers are waiting to buy at 9, 8, 7, and lower.

In contrast, other less-liquid currency pairs, like AUD/USD and USD/CAD, typically fluctuate in a far jumpier fashion, which is reflected by the wider price spread in those pairs.

Fewer price jumps and smaller price gaps

The depth of liquidity in EUR/USD also reduces the number of *price jumps* or *price gaps* in short-term trading. A price *jump* refers to a quick movement in prices over a relatively small time frame (roughly 50 pips or more) in the course of normal trading. A price *gap* means prices have instantaneously adjusted over a larger price distance, typically in response to a news event or data release.

REMEMBER

Don't get us wrong; price jumps/gaps do occur in EUR/USD, as anyone who has traded around data reports or other news events can attest. But price jumps/gaps in EUR/USD tend to be generated primarily by news/data releases and breaks of significant technical levels, events that can usually be identified in advance. As a caveat, there were large price gaps during the sovereign debt crisis, as uncertainty about the future of the Eurozone hung in the balance. At the time of writing, trading conditions had mostly returned to normal.

This is in contrast to other major currency pairs where short-term price gaps can develop from a one-off market flow, such as a portfolio manager selling a large amount of AUD/USD or a USD/CAD stop-loss order being triggered. When price gaps do occur in EUR/USD, they tend to be smaller relative to gaps in other pairs.

Backing and filling

When prices move rapidly in one direction, they tend to reach a short-term stopping point when opposite interest enters the market. For instance, say EUR/USD just traded higher from 1.2910/13 to 1.2922/25 in relatively orderly fashion, tick by tick over two minutes, meaning no price gaps. When the price move higher pauses, short-term traders who were long for the quick 12-pip move higher will look to exit and sell.

As selling interest begins to enter the market and prices stop rising, other not-so-fast longs will also start *hitting bids* (selling), pushing prices lower. From the other side, traders who missed the quick run up, or who were not as long as they wanted to be, will enter their buying interest in the market. Other buyers, sensing selling interest, may wait and place their buying interest at slightly lower levels. This back-and-forth consolidation after a short-term price movement is referred to as *backing and filling.* The price *backs up* and *fills* the short-term movement, though it can happen in both up and down price movements.

TIP

When it comes to EUR/USD price action, backing and filling is quite common and tends to be more substantial than in most currency pairs, meaning a greater amount of the directional move is retraced. Look at Figure 8-1 to get a visual idea of what backing and filling looks like. When EUR/USD isn't backing and filling the way you would expect, it means the directional move is stronger and with greater interest behind it.

FIGURE 8-1:
A one-minute EUR/USD chart showing periods of backing and filling price action after short-term directional moves. Backing and filling occurs in price declines, too.

03/22/11   O: 1.42190   H: 1.42500   L: 1.41780   C: 1.42120   -0.00070

Advance

Decline

Copyright © 2011 eSignal ForexCharts™

03:30   04:00   04:30   05:00   05:30   03/15/11 - 06:14   #2130

Source: eSignal (www.esignal.com)

Prolonged tests of technical levels

When it comes to trading around technical support and resistance levels, EUR/USD can try the patience of even the most disciplined traders. We say this because EUR/USD can spend hours (an eternity in forex markets) or even several days undergoing tests of technical levels. (See Chapter 6 for a primer on technical analysis.)

This goes back to the tremendous amount of interest and liquidity that define the EUR/USD market. All those viewpoints come together in the form of market interest (bids and offers) when technical levels come into play. The result is a tremendous amount of market interest that has to be absorbed at technical levels, which can take time.

Looking at GBP/USD and USD/CHF as leading indicators

TIP

Given the tremendous two-way interest in EUR/USD, it can be very difficult to gauge whether a test of a technical level is going to lead to breakout or a rejection. To get an idea of whether a test of a technical level in EUR/USD is going to lead to a break, professional EUR/USD traders always keep an eye on GBP/USD (the British pound versus the U.S. dollar) and USD/CHF (the U.S. dollar versus the Swiss franc), as they tend to be leading indicators for the bigger EUR/USD and dollar moves in general.

If GBP/USD and USD/CHF are aggressively testing (trading at or through the technical level with very little pullback) similar technical levels to EUR/USD (for example, daily highs or equivalent trend-line resistance), then EUR/USD is likely to test that same level. If GBP/USD and USD/CHF break through their technical levels, the chances of EUR/USD following suit increases. By the same token, if GBP/USD and USD/CHF are not aggressively testing the key technical level, EUR/USD is likely to see its similar technical level hold.

GBP/USD and USD/CHF lead times can be anywhere from a few seconds or minutes to several hours or even days. Just make sure you're looking at the equivalent technical levels in each pair.

Tactical trading considerations in EUR/USD

We've looked at the major trading attributes of EUR/USD, and now it's time to look at how those elements translate into real-life trading tactics. After all, that's where the real money is made and lost.

Deciding whether it's a U.S. dollar move or a euro move

Earlier in this chapter, we note that EUR/USD routinely acts as the primary vehicle for forex markets to express their view on the USD. At the same time, we also indicated that EUR/USD will also react to euro-centric news and data. So for traders approaching EUR/USD on any given day, it helps to understand whether the driving force at work is dollar-based or euro-based. Are they bearish on the USD, or are they bullish on the EUR? Or is it some combination of the two?

Having a sense of which currency is driving EUR/USD at any given moment is important so you can better adapt to incoming data and news. If it's a EUR-based move higher, for instance, and surprisingly positive USD news or data is released later in the day, guess what? We've got countertrend information hitting the market, which could spark a reversal lower in EUR/USD (in favor of the dollar). By the same token, if that U.S. data comes out weaker than expected, it's likely to spur further EUR/USD gains, because EUR-buying interest is now combined with USD-selling interest.

Being patient in EUR/USD

Earlier in this chapter, we explore why EUR/USD can spend hours trading in relatively narrow ranges or testing technical levels. The key in such markets is to remain patient based on your directional view and your technical analysis. You should be able to identify short-term support that keeps an upside test alive or resistance that keeps a down-move going. If those levels fail, the move is stalling at the minimum and may even be reversing.

Taking advantage of backing and filling

Because EUR/USD tends to retrace more of its short-term movements, you can usually enter a position in your desired direction by leaving an order to buy or sell at slightly better rates than current market prices may allow. If the post–08:30 ET U.S. data price action sees EUR/USD move lower, and you think getting short is the way to go, you can leave an offer slightly (roughly 5 to 10 pips) above the current market level and use it to get short, instead of reaching out and hitting the bid on a downtick.

If your order is executed, you've got your desired position at a better rate than if you went to market, and you're probably in a better position rhythm-wise with the market (having sold on an uptick). Alternatively, you can take advantage of routine backing and filling at the market by selling on market price upticks and buying on market price downticks.

Allowing for a margin of error on technical levels

TIP

When it comes to determining whether EUR/USD has broken a technical level, we like to use a 10- to 15-pip margin of error. (Shorter-term traders may want to use a smaller margin of error.) Some very short-term traders and technical purists like to pinpoint an exact price level as support or resistance. If the market trades above or below their level, they'll call it a break and that's that. But the spot forex market rarely trades with such respect for technical levels to make such a clear and pinpointed distinction. And given the amount of interest in EUR/USD, it's especially prone to hazy technical lines in the sand.

REMEMBER

The key point to take away from this is that all sorts of interest emerges around technical levels, and it's still going through the market even though the pinpointed level might have been breached. And this is where our margin of error comes in. Again, it's not a hard-and-fast rule, but generally speaking, EUR/USD will have chewed through most of the market interest around a technical level within about 10 to 15 points beyond the level.

East Meets West: USD/JPY

USD/JPY is one of the more challenging currency pairs among the majors, and trading in it requires a higher degree of discipline and patience. Where other currency pairs typically display routine market fluctuations and relatively steady, active trading interest, USD/JPY seems to have an on/off switch. It can spend hours or even days in relatively narrow ranges and then march off on a mission to a new price level.

USD/JPY can offer some of the clearest trade setups among the major pairs. When you're right in USD/JPY, the returns can be astonishingly quick. When you're wrong in USD/JPY, you'll also know it pretty quickly. The key to developing a successful trading game plan in USD/JPY is to understand what drives the pair and how the price action behaves.

Trading fundamentals of USD/JPY

The Japanese yen is the third major international currency after the U.S. dollar and the European single currency, the euro. USD/JPY accounts for 13.2 percent of global trading volume, according to the 2019 BIS survey of foreign exchange markets. Japan stands as the third largest national economy after the United States and China in terms of GDP, and the JPY represents the third major currency group after the USD and the EUR groupings.

Trading USD/JPY by the numbers

Standard market convention is to quote USD/JPY in terms of the number of JPY per USD. For example, a USD/JPY rate of 115.35 means that it takes ¥115.35 to buy $1.

REMEMBER

USD/JPY trades in the same direction as the overall value of the USD, and inversely to the value of the JPY. If the USD is strengthening and the JPY is weakening, the USD/JPY rate will move higher. If the USD is weakening and the JPY is strengthening, the USD/JPY rate will move lower.

USD/JPY has the U.S. dollar as the base currency and the JPY as the secondary or counter currency. This means

>> **USD/JPY is traded in amounts denominated in USD.** In online currency trading platforms, standard lot sizes are $100,000, mini lot sizes are $10,000, and micro lot sizes are $1,000.

>> **The pip value, or minimum price fluctuation, is denominated in JPY.**

>> **Profit and loss accrue in JPY.** For one standard lot position size, each pip is worth ¥1,000; for one mini lot position size, each pip is worth ¥100; and for each micro lot, each pip is worth ¥10. To convert those amounts to USD, divide the JPY amount by the USD/JPY rate. Using 115.00 as the rate, ¥1,000 = $8.70 and ¥100 = $0.87.

>> **Margin calculations are typically calculated in USD.** So it's a straightforward calculation using the leverage rate to see how much margin is required to hold a position in USD/JPY. At 100:1 leverage, $1,000 of available margin is needed to open a standard-size position of 100,000 USD/JPY.

USD/JPY is heavily influenced by U.S. interest rates

If we had to identify the main driver of USD/JPY, it would easily be the movements in U.S. interest rates. The main reason for this is the massive amount of U.S. government debt held by the Japanese government and Japanese investors. As of January 2021, the Bank of Japan (BOJ) is the largest holder of U.S. Treasury debt (at $1.28 trillion). If U.S. interest rates begin to fall, the prices of U.S. government bonds rise, increasing the USD-value of Japan's U.S. debt holdings. To offset, or hedge, their larger USD-long currency exposure, Japanese reserve managers need to sell more USD. This causes USD/JPY to closely track U.S. Treasury yields, as seen in Figure 8-2, which shows the USD/JPY rate and the yield on two-year U.S. Treasury notes on a monthly basis over ten years.

FIGURE 8-2:
USD/JPY
exchange rate
and yields on
two-year
U.S. Treasury
notes over ten
years on a
monthly basis.
USD/JPY closely
follows the track
of U.S. Treasury
yields due to
asset manager
hedging
operations.

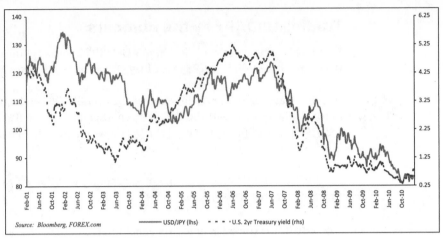

Source: Bloomberg, FOREX.com

TIP

Long-term traders can take advantage of U.S. interest-rate cycles via USD/JPY, buying the pair when U.S. rates are set to rise and selling when rates have peaked and begin to decline.

It's politically sensitive to trade

USD/JPY is the most politically sensitive currency pair among the majors. Japan remains a heavily export-oriented economy, accounting for more than 40 percent of overall economic activity. This means the JPY is a critical policy lever for Japanese officials to stimulate and manage the Japanese economy — and they aren't afraid to get involved in the market to keep the JPY from strengthening beyond desired levels.

REMEMBER

A weak currency makes a nation's exports cheaper to foreigners and, all other things being equal, creates a competitive advantage to gain market share. The flip side of a weak currency is that it makes imports from abroad more expensive, putting foreign exporters at a disadvantage in the domestic market.

In the past, this has led to accusations of currency manipulation by trade partners and efforts to force the JPY to strengthen. But with China's incredible growth in the last decade, Japan and the yen seem to have dropped from the radar screen as the primary target of free-market advocates. But this is more a function of China's vast current and future potential rather than any change to how the Japanese effectively manage the JPY.

The Ministry of Finance is routinely involved in the forex market

Currency intervention is usually a last resort for most major national governments. Instead, the Japanese Ministry of Finance (MOF) engages in routine verbal intervention in not-so-subtle attempts to influence the level of the JPY. The chief spokesman on currencies is, of course, the Minister of Finance, but the Vice Finance Minister for International Affairs is the more frequent commentator on forex market developments. Also watch comments from the Bank of Japan (see Chapter 5).

The Japanese financial press devotes a tremendous amount of attention to the value of the JPY, similar to how the U.S. financial media cover the Dow or S&P 500. Press briefings by MOF officials are routine. During times of forex market volatility, expect near-daily official comments. These statements move USD/JPY on a regular basis.

Beyond such jawboning, known as verbal intervention, the MOF has been known to utilize covert intervention through the use of sizeable market orders by the pension fund of the Japanese Postal Savings Bank, known as Kampo. After the 2011 tsunami, the yen surged in value, as its safe-haven status kicked in. To limit the damage to the Japanese economy, a multilateral effort was made by major global central banks to sell the yen and bring down its value.

In 2012, the prime minister, Shinzo Abe, announced a radical economic program to try to boost the economy. One side effect of this was a weaker yen, which was supported by an extremely loose monetary policy from the Bank of Japan. As you can see, there are many ways that politics can get in the way of the yen.

Japanese asset managers tend to move together

If Americans are the ultimate consumers, then the Japanese are the consummate savers. The Japanese *savings rate* (the percentage of disposable income that's not spent) is above 20 percent as of 2020. (Compare that with the U.S. savings rate at around 9.6 percent.) As a result, Japanese financial institutions control trillions of dollars in assets, many of which find their way to investments outside of Japan. The bulk of assets are invested in fixed income securities, and this means Japanese asset managers are on a continual hunt for the best yielding returns.

This theme has taken on added prominence in recent years due to extremely low domestic yields in Japan. At the time of writing, the Bank of Japan had yields of close to 0 percent, and a massive QE (quantitative easing) program to keep interest rates low for the long term. These low yields tend to weigh on the yen's value, so Japanese investors and asset managers tend to sell the yen and buy higher-yielding currencies that are stronger than the yen. This makes domestic interest-rate yields in Japan a key long-term determinant of the JPY's value.

Japanese financial institutions also tend to pursue a highly collegial approach to investment strategies. The result for forex markets is that Japanese asset managers tend to pursue similar investment strategies at the same time, resulting in tremendous asset flows hitting the market over a relatively short period of time. This situation has important implications for USD/JPY price action (see the next section).

Important Japanese data reports

Keep in mind that politics and government officials' (MOF) comments are quite frequent and can shift market sentiment and direction as much as, or more than, the fundamental data. The key data reports to focus on coming out of Japan are

>> Bank of Japan (BOJ) policy decisions, monthly economic assessments, and Monetary Policy Committee (MPC) member speeches

>> Tankan Report (a quarterly sentiment survey of Japanese firms by the BOJ — the key is often planned capital expenditures)

>> Industrial production

>> Machine orders

>> Trade balance and current account

>> Retail trade

>> Bank lending

>> Domestic Corporate Goods Price Index (CGPI)

>> National CPI and Tokyo-area CPI

>> All-Industry Activity Index and Tertiary Industry (service sector) Activity Index

The CPI data is extremely important these days, because the Bank of Japan has pledged to keep monetary policy low until inflation moves to a 2 percent target. Given that Japan has traditionally been mired in deflation, this is no small feat.

THE ULTIMATE SAFE HAVEN

JPY is considered a safe haven, which means that it tends to rally when there is panic in the markets. For example, in the three months after the collapse of investment bank Lehman Brothers in 2008, the yen rallied more than 20 percent against the U.S. dollar. So, if there are periods of panic in the market, be wary of taking a short position in the yen.

Price action behavior of USD/JPY

Earlier in this chapter, we note that USD/JPY seems to have an on/off switch when compared to the other major currency pairs. Add to that the fact that USD/JPY liquidity can be similarly fickle. Sometimes, hundreds of millions of USD/JPY can be bought or sold without moving the market noticeably; other times, liquidity can be extremely scarce.

This phenomenon is particularly acute in USD/JPY owing to the large presence of Japanese asset managers. As we mention earlier, the Japanese investment community tends to move en masse into and out of positions. Of course, they're not the only ones involved in USD/JPY, but they do tend to play the fox while the rest of the market is busy playing the hounds.

Prone to short-term trends, followed by sideways consolidations

The result of this concentration of Japanese corporate interest is a strong tendency for USD/JPY to display short-term trends (several hours to several days) in price movements, as investors pile in on the prevailing directional move. This tendency is amplified by the use of standing market orders from Japanese asset managers.

For example, if a Japanese pension fund manager is looking to establish a long position in USD/JPY, he's likely to leave orders at several fixed levels below the current market to try to buy dollars on dips. If the current market is at 102.00, he may buy a piece of the total position there, but then leave orders to buy the remaining amounts at staggered levels below, such as 101.75, 101.50, 101.25, and 101.00. If other investors are of the same view, then they'll be bidding below the market as well.

If the market begins to move higher, the asset managers may become nervous that they won't be able to buy on weakness and raise their orders to higher levels, or buy at the market. Either way, buying interest is moving up with the price action, creating a potentially accelerating price movement. Any countertrend move is met by solid buying interest and quickly reversed.

Such price shifts tend to reach their conclusion when everyone is onboard — most of the buyers who wanted to buy are now long. At this point, no more fresh buying is coming into the market, and the directional move begins to stall and move sideways. The early buyers may be capping the market with profit-taking orders to sell above, while laggard buyers are still buying on dips. This leads to the development of a consolidation range, which can be as wide as ¥1 or ¥2, or as narrow as 40 to 50 pips.

Short-term traders can usually find trading opportunities in such consolidation ranges, but medium- and longer-term traders may want to step back and wait for a fresh directional movement. In summer 2014, USD/JPY experienced a prolonged period of sideways movement, which made *volatility* (a measure of variation of price movement over time) fall to its lowest-ever level. During that time, USD/JPY was a yawn to trade.

Technical levels are critical in USD/JPY

TIP

So if you're a regular trader or investor and you don't work at a Japanese bank, how can you know where the orders are? Simple: Focus on the technical levels.

Perhaps no other currency pair is as beholden to technical support and resistance as USD/JPY (see Chapter 6 for an introduction to support and resistance). In large part, this has to do with the prevalence of substantial orders, where the order level is based on technical analysis. USD/JPY displays a number of other important trading characteristics when it comes to technical trading levels:

>> **USD/JPY tends to respect technical levels with far fewer false breaks.** This situation is typically due to the presence of substantial order interest at the technical level. If trend-line analysis or daily price lows indicate major support at 101.20, for example, sizeable buying orders are likely to be located there. The bank traders watching the order may buy in front of it, preventing the level from ever being touched or tested. If the selling interest is not sufficient to fill the buying order, the level will hold. On the other hand, if the technical level is breached, it's a clear indication the selling interest is far greater and is likely to continue.

>> **USD/JPY's price action is usually highly directional (one-way traffic) on breaks of technical support and resistance.** When technical support or resistance is overcome, price movements tend to be sharp and one-sided, with minimal pullbacks or backing and filling (prices coming back to test the breakout level). This situation is the result of strong market interest overcoming any standing orders, as well as likely stop-loss orders beyond the technical level. For example, after USD/JPY broke above 80.00 back in September 2012, USD/JPY went on to rally (the yen lost value) more than 30 percent over the next nine months.

>> **Spike reversals from technical levels are relatively common.** A *spike reversal* is a sharp — 20- to 50-pip — price movement in the opposite direction of the prior move. Spike reversals are evidence of a significant amount of market interest in the opposite direction and frequently define significant highs and lows. They're also evidence that the directional move that was reversed was probably false, which suggests greater potential in the direction of the reversal.

>> **Orders frequently define intraday highs and lows and reversal points.**
Japanese institutional orders also tend to be left at round-number prices, such
as 84.00, 84.25, 84.50, and so on. When you look at charts involving JPY,
always note tops/bottoms close to round-number price levels because there
could be significant orders there.

Tactical trading considerations in USD/JPY

Earlier, we note USD/JPY's tendency to either be active directionally or
consolidating — the on/off switch. As such, we like to approach USD/JPY on a
more strategic, hit-and-run basis — getting in when we think a directional move
is happening and standing aside when we don't. We look for breaks of trend lines,
spike reversals, and candlestick patterns as our primary clues for spotting a pend-
ing directional move (see Chapter 6).

TIP

On the tactical level, USD/JPY is generally a cleaner trading market than most of
the other majors, so we like to approach it with generally tighter trading rules.
The idea is that if we're right, we'll be along for the ride. But if we're wrong, we
jump off the bus at the next stop.

Actively trading trend-line and price-level breakouts

One of our trigger points for jumping into USD/JPY is breaks of trend lines and key
price levels, such as daily or weekly highs/lows. We note earlier that it usually
takes a significant amount of market interest to break key technical levels. We
look at the actual breaks as concrete evidence of sizeable interest, rather than
normal back-and-forth price action.

Jumping on spike reversals

TIP

After USD/JPY has seen a relatively quick (usually within two to three hours) move
of more than 70 to 80 pips in one direction, we're on alert for any sharp reversals
in price. Spike reversals of 30 to 40 pips that occur in very short time frames (5 to
20 minutes) are relatively common in USD/JPY. We look at them as an indication
that the prior move has ended and it's now time to exit. Spike reversals are short-
term phenomena, and if you can't be in front of your trading screen, using a 30-
to 40-point trailing stop-loss order is one way to guard against rapid reversals.
Take a look at Figure 8-3 to see how spike reversals can frequently indicate significant turning points.

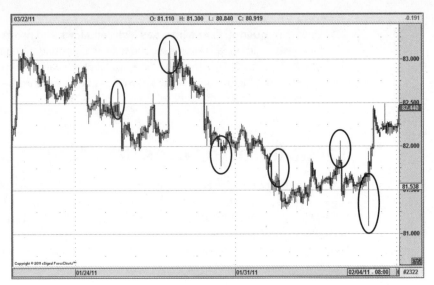

Source: eSignal (www.esignal.com)

FIGURE 8-3:
Hourly USD/JPY
chart highlighting
spike reversals
(circled areas).
Quick 20- to
30-point reversals
can be an
important signal
that a directional
move has ended
and may be
reversing.

Monitoring EUR/JPY and other JPY crosses

TIP

USD/JPY is heavily influenced by cross flows and can frequently take a back seat to them on any given day. In evaluating USD/JPY, we always keep an eye on the JPY crosses and their technical levels as well. A break of important support in GBP/JPY, for instance, could unleash a flood of short-term USD/JPY selling, because GBP/JPY is mostly traded through the dollar pairs.

EUR/JPY is the most actively traded JPY cross and its movements routinely drive USD/JPY on an intraday basis. Be alert for when significant technical levels in the two pairs coincide, such as when both USD/JPY and EUR/JPY are testing a series of recent daily highs or lows. A break by either can easily spill into the other and provoke follow-through buying/selling in both.

The Other Majors: Sterling and Aussie

The other two major currency pairs are GBP/USD (otherwise known as sterling or cable) and AUD/USD. The pound is counted as a major currency pair, but its trading volume and liquidity are significantly less than EUR/USD or USD/JPY. In recent years, there has been a big shift in the most actively traded currencies, with the Aussie and Kiwi dollars overtaking the likes of the Swissy (Swiss franc) and the CAD (Canadian dollar). The Aussie in particular has seen its star rise, which is why we're including it in this section.

The British pound: GBP/USD

Trading in cable presents its own set of challenges, because the pair is prone to sharp price movements and seemingly chaotic price action. But it's exactly this type of price behavior that keeps the speculators coming back — when you're right, you'll know very quickly, and the short-term results can be significant.

Trading fundamentals of GBP/USD

The UK economy is the third largest national economy in Europe, after Germany and France, according to the 2013 GDP data, and the pound is heavily influenced by cross-border trade and mergers and acquisitions (M&A) activity between the United Kingdom and continental Europe. Upwards of two-thirds of UK foreign trade is conducted with EU member states, making the EUR/GBP cross one of the most important trade-driven cross rates.

The 2019 BIS survey of foreign exchange turnover showed that GBP/USD accounted for 13 percent of global daily trading volume, making cable the third most active pairing in the majors. But you may not believe that when you start trading cable, where liquidity seems always to be at a premium. These days, you can trade GBP/USD fairly cheaply and most brokers offer a spread of 1 pip or below.

Trading sterling by the numbers

GBP/USD is quoted in terms of the number of dollars it takes to buy a pound, so a rate of 1.6015 means it costs $1.6015 to buy £1. The GBP is the primary currency in the pair and the USD is the secondary currency. That means

>> **GBP/USD is traded in amounts denominated in GBP.** In online currency trading platforms, standard lot sizes are £100,000, mini lot sizes are £10,000, and micro lots are GBP 1,000.

>> **The pip value, or minimum price fluctuation, is denominated in USD.**

>> **Profit and loss accrue in USD.** For one standard lot position size, each pip is worth $10; for one mini lot position size, each pip is worth $1; and for a micro lot, it is $0.10.

>> **Margin calculations are typically calculated in USD in online trading platforms.** Because of its high relative value to the USD, trading in GBP pairs requires the greatest amount of margin on a per-lot basis. At a GBP/USD rate of 1.9000, to trade a one-lot position worth £100,000, it takes $1,900 in available margin (based on 100:1 leverage). That calculation changes over time, of course, based on the level of the GBP/USD exchange rate. A higher GBP/USD rate requires more USD in available margin collateral, and a lower GBP/USD rate needs less USD in margin.

Trading alongside EUR/USD, but with a lot more zip!

REMEMBER

Cable is similar to the EUR/USD in that it trades inversely to the overall USD. But while EUR/USD frequently gets bogged down in tremendous two-way liquidity, cable exhibits much more abrupt volatility and more extreme overall price movements. If U.S. economic news disappoints, for instance, both sterling and EUR/USD will move higher. But if EUR/USD sees a 60-point rally on the day, cable may see a 100+ point rally.

This goes back to liquidity and a generally lower level of market interest in cable. In terms of daily global trading sessions, cable volume is at its peak during the UK/European trading day, but that level of liquidity shrinks considerably in the New York afternoon and Asian trading sessions. During those off-peak times, cable can see significant short-term price moves simply on the basis of position adjustments (for example, shorts getting squeezed out).

REMEMBER

Another important difference between cable and EUR/USD comes in their different reactions to domestic economic/news developments. Cable tends to display more explosive reactions to unexpected UK news/data than EUR/USD does to similar Eurozone news/data. For example, if better than expected Eurozone data comes out, EUR/USD may only politely acknowledge the data and move marginally higher. But if surprisingly strong UK data is reported, GBP/USD can take off on a moonshot.

Important UK data reports

TIP

Cable tends to react sharply to UK economic reports, especially when the data is in the opposite direction of expectations, or when the data is contrary to current monetary policy speculation. For example, if the market is expecting that the next rate move by the Bank of England (BOE) will be higher, and a monthly inflation report is released indicating a drop in price pressures, then GBP/USD is likely to drop quickly as interest-rate bets are unwound.

Key UK data reports to watch for are

>> BOE Monetary Policy Committed (MPC) rate decisions, as well as speeches by MPC members and the BOE governor, and BOE Inflation Reports, which are released four times a year

>> BOE MPC minutes (released two weeks after each MPC meeting)

>> Inflation gauges, such as CPI, PPI, and the British Retailers Consortium (BRC) shop price index

- Retail sales and the BRC retail sales monitor

- Royal Institution of Chartered Surveyors (RICS) house price balance

- Industrial and manufacturing production

- Trade balance

- GfK (a private market research firm) U.K. consumer confidence survey

The new kid in town: Trading the Aussie

The Aussie dollar (AUD) has overtaken some of the other major currencies in recent years to become the fifth most commonly traded USD pair, according to the 2019 BIS Triennial survey on foreign exchange turnover. This was triggered by a few developments:

- The Australian economy weathered the 2008 financial crisis extremely well, and was the only one of the major economies not to fall into recession.

- The Aussie is often traded as a proxy for China. It has extremely close trade links to China, so its currency often reflects Chinese economic fundamentals.

Trading fundamentals of AUD/USD

TIP

The Aussie is the sixth most widely traded currency in the world, according to the 2019 BIS survey. It can be traded as a proxy for China, so its fortunes are closely linked to the performance of the Chinese economy. So, when you trade the Aussie, you need to be aware of Chinese data releases.

Australia is also one of the world's major commodity producers, which influences the Aussie in two ways:

- **It can be sensitive to changes in commodity prices.** When commodity prices fall, this can be bad news for the Aussie because it reduces the value of Australian exports and can impact the economy. The reverse is also true.

- **Big exports tend to favor a weaker currency to boost the attractiveness of their exports.** This means that the Aussie can be at risk from verbal intervention from its central bank, the Reserve Bank of Australia (RBA), although the RBA rarely intervenes physically in the market, unlike the Bank of Japan or the Swiss National Bank.

Trading Aussie by the numbers

AUD/USD is quoted in terms of the number of U.S. dollars it takes to buy an Aussie dollar, so a rate of 0.9550 means it costs $0.9550 to buy AU$1. The AUD is the primary currency in the pair, and the USD is the secondary currency. That means

>> **AUD/USD is traded in amounts denominated in AUD.** In online currency trading platforms, standard lot sizes are AU$100,000, mini lot sizes are AU$10,000, and micro lots are AU$1,000.

>> **The pip value, or minimum price fluctuation, is denominated in USD.**

>> **Profit and loss accrue in USD.** For one standard lot position size, each pip is worth $10; for one mini lot position size, each pip is worth $1; and for a micro lot, it is $0.10.

>> **Margin calculations are typically calculated in USD in online trading platforms.** At a AUD/USD rate of 0.9000, to trade a one-lot position worth $100,000, it takes $900 in available margin (based on 100:1 leverage). That calculation changes over time, of course, based on the level of the AUD/USD exchange rate. A higher AUD/USD rate requires more USD in available margin collateral, and a lower AUD/USD rate needs less USD in margin.

Important Australian data reports

TIP

The Aussie can be sensitive to interest rates. Australia tends to have higher levels of interest rates than elsewhere. For example, the RBA did not embark on QE or negative interest rates in the aftermath of the financial crisis. This makes it attractive as a carry trade. Changes in interest rates and speeches from the head of the RBA can trigger volatility in the Aussie.

Key Australian data reports to watch for are

>> RBA rate decisions, as well as speeches by RBA members and in particular the RBA governor

>> RBA MPC minutes (released two weeks after each RBA meeting)

>> Inflation gauges, such as CPI and PPI

>> Retail sales

>> House prices

>> Industrial and manufacturing production

>> Trade balance

>> Employment data

>> Chinese data, including manufacturing PMI survey data, trade data, and interest rate changes

Understanding Forex Positioning Data

Forex is not traded on an exchange, so how can you know which currencies people are buying and which ones people are selling? Never fear — there are many sources of forex positioning data. Because the forex market is so big, the best you can hope for is a snapshot of trading activity, based on a certain segment of the market. For example, the Commodities Futures Trading Commission (CFTC) releases data each week (at 3:30 p.m. Eastern time on Friday) that measures the net noncommercial (speculative) futures positions for the major currencies versus the U.S. dollar. This gives you a good idea of whether the market is *long* (buying a currency) or *short* (selling a currency) on a weekly basis.

This data is useful because it can be interpreted as an indicator of current trading activity in the forex market.

How to interpret the data

The data show you the number of open positions in dollar pairs. They can be *positive* (people are buying the dollar pair) or *negative* (people are selling the dollar pair). Often, if a currency is trending higher against the USD, you see CFTC positioning data also moving higher. This data can be used to confirm the strength of a trend. For example, if a large segment of the forex community — the futures community — is buying the pound, then GBP/USD is likely to be in an uptrend. However, it can also be used as a contrarian indicator: If the market has been buying sterling for a while, some traders may use that as a sell signal. Because, by definition, trends don't go on forever, the contrarian trader may look at CFTC data to see whether the market is too stretched to the upside in one currency pair (say, GBP/USD), and if he thinks that it is, he may choose to go short on GBP/USD.

WARNING

Positioning data can be a useful resource, although we don't recommend that you trade only using CFTC positioning data, because it can be a lagging indicator and doesn't reflect news events or economic data that can impact a currency pair on a more frequent basis.

The FX fix

When you read about foreign exchange in the business press or if you go into a forex dealing room, you're likely to hear the term the *FX fix*. So, what is it? The FX fix is essentially a 60-second window at which major exchange rates are set. The forex market isn't controlled by any central exchange, so the fix is used to form benchmark forex rates.

The most popular fix times take place at 4 p.m. and 8 p.m. London time. The 4 p.m. London FX fix is a particularly popular benchmark, primarily because it was the first one introduced by the WM Company (it's now a joint venture with Thomson Reuters). These prices are mostly used by the investment community, which uses these FX rates to compare their portfolios against benchmarks and other portfolios, without concern for changes in exchange rates.

Trading at a fixing time is an example of point-in-time (PIT) trading. This involves buying or selling currencies at particular times each day. But retail traders should be wary of trading any of the major FX pairs during fixing times because it can trigger a spike in volatility. This trading strategy involves trading at times when the currency markets are transitioning from one global region to another. During this time, liquidity can start to fade, which can increase volatility.

Forex and regulation

Despite being the largest market in the world, the forex market has largely escaped official regulation. This means that traders can set prices on their own, without getting an official body involved in the process.

Because there are no formal rules or regulation in the forex market, trust is of the utmost importance. The forex market works because both sides of a transaction trust each other. However, in the aftermath of the 2008 financial crisis, there has been a push for more formal regulation. As we mention earlier, changes are afoot to make the FX fix less susceptible to manipulation.

In the coming years, we expect big changes in the forex regulatory space. There is a push to impose more electronic trading and new codes of conduct. Although retail traders nearly always trade on an electronic platform, codes of conduct could impact how you trade.

At FOREX.com, we believe that any push toward greater transparency is good for the market and good for the retail trader.

REMEMBER

Make sure that your broker is regulated before you start trading with it.

Chapter **9**

Minor Currency Pairs and Cross-Currency Trading

Trading in the major currency pairs (see Chapter 8) accounts for the lion's share of overall currency market volume, but speculative trading opportunities extend well beyond just the four major *dollar pairs* (currency pairs that include the USD). For starters, three other currency pairs — commonly known as the *minor* or *small* dollar pairs — round out the primary trading pairs that include the U.S. dollar. Still more trading options are available in the currencies of Scandinavian nations that haven't adopted the EUR, referred to as the *Scandies.* Then there are the *cross-currency* pairs, or *crosses* for short, which pit two non-USD currencies against each other.

In this chapter, we take a closer look at the minor currency pairs, Scandies, and cross-currency pairs to see how they fit into the overall market and offer an additional array of speculative trading opportunities. Although the USD is frequently the focus of the currency market, you're going to want to know where the opportunities are when the spotlight isn't on the greenback.

Trading the Minor Pairs

The minor dollar pairs are USD/CAD (the U.S. dollar versus the Canadian dollar) and NZD/USD (the New Zealand dollar versus the U.S. dollar). In the past, the AUD/USD (Australian dollar) was a minor currency, but trading volumes in the AUD have surged in recent years, so we include it in Chapter 8. Technically speaking, the Swissy should take the place of the AUD, but it rests somewhere between the majors and minors, so we haven't included it here. Worth noting: The minor currency pairs are also commonly referred to as *commodity currencies*; the Aussie is still a commodity currency because Australia is still a major commodity producer.

TIP

The *commodity currencies* reference stems from the key role that oil, metals, agricultural, and mining industries play in the national economies of Canada, Australia, and New Zealand. See the nearby sidebar "The (not just) commodity currencies" for important qualifications about the commodity relationship. AUD/USD and USD/CAD account for 5.4 percent and 4.4 percent of global daily trading volume, respectively, according to the 2019 Bank for International Settlements (BIS) survey of forex market volumes. NZD/USD accounts for 1.6 percent of spot trading volume. But these three pairs offer more than ample liquidity to be actively traded and can offer significant trading opportunities, both for short-term traders and medium- to longer-term speculators.

Trading fundamentals of USD/CAD

The Canadian dollar (nicknamed the *Loonie* after the local bird pictured on the dollar coins) trades according to the same macroeconomic fundamentals as most other major currencies. That means you'll need to closely follow Bank of Canada (BOC) monetary-policy developments, current economic data, inflation readings, and political goings-on, just as you would any of the majors.

REMEMBER

A key element to keep in mind when looking at USD/CAD is that the trajectory of the Canadian economy is closely linked to the overall direction of the U.S. economy. The United States and Canada are still each other's largest commercial trading partners, and the vast majority of Canadians live within 100 miles of the U.S./Canadian border. Even the BOC regularly refers to the U.S. economic outlook in its own economic outlooks. So we don't think it's an overgeneralization to say that as goes the U.S. economy, so goes the Canadian economy. But it's a long-term dynamic, making for plenty of short-term trading opportunities, especially when U.S. and Canadian outlooks diverge.

THE (NOT JUST) COMMODITY CURRENCIES

We don't want to leave you with the impression that the so-called commodity currencies' trading behavior is strictly a function of what's happening to commodity prices. To be sure, recent years' price movements in those pairs are generally highly correlated to movements in underlying commodities, like gold, silver, and oil. But correlation is not causation. What that means is that just because two assets may move together in a statistically significant relationship, the movement of one is not necessarily causing movement in the other.

More typically, they may both be responding to broader fundamental developments that affect each similarly, such as the strength of global demand as seen in Chinese growth data. China is a tremendous consumer of raw materials, and Australia is a leading exporter of metals, coal, and grains. Market perceptions of strong demand could see prices move higher for such commodities. Gains in commodity prices may improve profitability at Australian mining and agricultural firms, attracting global investors who need AUD to buy such Australian stocks. In this scenario, it would not be surprising to see the AUD gain alongside commodity prices.

But there are also plenty of scenarios that could see such relationships break down, especially in the short run, and see prices diverge. Carrying on with the previously mentioned China/Australia relationship, strong growth and commodity demand could see the Reserve Bank of Australia (RBA), the Australian central bank, indicate that interest rates may need to be raised, reinforcing the positive correlation and tending to support AUD. But if the RBA later postpones raising rates due to unforeseen events, such as happened after massive floods in early 2011, currency market expectations may be disappointed and the AUD could weaken, even as commodity prices maintain gains, but now on production disruptions. We hope you get the idea that correlations between currencies and commodities are not carved in stone.

To give you a more concrete picture, the following tables show the historical correlations (correlation coefficients) between these currencies and individual commodities over a two-year and ten-year period ending in February 2011, respectively, based on weekly data and percentage changes. A correlation coefficient is a statistical measure of how closely two securities values change relative to each other. Coefficients can range from +1.00 to −1.00, with a coefficient of +1.00 meaning the two assets are perfectly positively correlated (meaning that a 1 percent gain in one would see a 1 percent gain in the other). A coefficient of −1.00 would mean the two are perfectly negatively correlated (meaning that a rise of 1 percent in the first would see a decline of 1 percent in the second). A coefficient of zero means there is no statistically identifiable relationship, and the two are said to be non-correlated. As a rough benchmark, a correlation of +0.7/−0.7 or more is considered a pretty strong relationship. But remember, correlations exist

(continued)

(continued)

over time. What's closely correlated today may not be so closely correlated tomorrow or next month. Medium- and longer-term traders may find such correlations more useful than short-term, intraday traders, where individual market news is more likely to cause a breakdown in the observed relationship.

The following tables show quarterly correlations between the commodity currencies and the commodities. CRB stands for the Commodities Research Bureau (CRB) index, which tracks an aggregate of major commodities' prices.

Two-Year Correlations

	CRB	OIL	GOLD	SILVER
AUD/USD	0.60	0.95	0.89	0.60
NZD/USD	0.60	0.96	0.92	0.64
CAD/USD	−0.86	−0.51	−0.62	−0.43

Ten-Year Correlations

	CRB	OIL	GOLD	SILVER
AUD/USD	0.93	0.70	0.77	0.74
NZD/USD	0.87	0.40	0.603	0.80
CAD/USD	−0.83	−0.61	−0.60	−0.91

Note the higher level of correlations over the more recent two-year period compared to the longer ten-year time frame. So instead of thinking of these currencies as strictly commodity-price driven, think of commodity price movements as just one factor affecting these currencies.

TIP

The sharp rise in commodity demand from China and other rapidly developing economies in recent years has heightened the sensitivity of CAD to overall commodity price developments, although as China slowed in 2013–2014 and commodity prices seemed to have peaked, the relationship between CAD and commodities has also declined. However, it's still worth factoring in the global economic outlook when evaluating the Canadian outlook.

TIP

Geography also plays a role when it comes to U.S. and Canadian economic data, because both countries issue economic data reports around the same time each morning or only a few hours apart. At one extreme, the result can be a negative USD report paired with strong Canadian data, leading to a sharp drop in USD/CAD (selling USD and buying CAD). At the other end, strong U.S. data and weak Canadian numbers can see USD/CAD rally sharply. Mixed readings can see a stalemate, but it always depends on the bigger picture.

Trading USD/CAD by the numbers

REMEMBER

The standard market convention is to quote USD/CAD in terms of the number of Canadian dollars per USD. A USD/CAD rate of 1.0200, for instance, means it takes CAD 1.02 to buy USD 1. The market convention means that USD/CAD trades in the same overall direction of the USD, with a higher USD/CAD rate reflecting a stronger USD/weaker CAD and a lower rate showing a weaker USD/stronger CAD.

USD/CAD has the USD as the primary currency and the CAD as the counter currency. This means

>> **USD/CAD is traded in amounts denominated in USD.** For online currency trading platforms, standard lot sizes are USD 100,000, and mini lot sizes are USD 10,000.

>> **The *pip value,* or minimum price fluctuation, is denominated in CAD.**

>> **Profit and loss registers in CAD.** For a standard lot position size, each pip is worth CAD 10, and each pip in a mini lot position is worth CAD 1. Using a USD/CAD rate of 1.0200 (which changes over time, of course), that equates to a pip value of USD 9.80 for each standard lot and USD 0.98 for each mini lot.

>> **Margin calculations are typically based in USD.** So seeing how much margin is required to hold a position in USD/CAD is a simple calculation using the leverage ratio. At 50:1 leverage, for instance, $2,000 of available margin is needed to trade 100,000 USD/CAD, and $200 is needed to trade 10,000 USD/CAD.

REMEMBER

USD/CAD is unique among currency pairs in that it trades for spot settlement only one day beyond the trade date, as opposed to the normal two days for all other currency pairs. The difference is due to the fact that New York and Toronto, the two nations' financial centers, are in the same time zone, allowing for faster trade confirmations and settlement transfers. For spot traders, the difference means that USD/CAD undergoes the extended weekend (three-day) rollover after the close of trading on Thursdays, instead of on Wednesdays like all other pairs, assuming no holidays are involved. However, if you trade spot FX in the short term or with your FX broker, you usually don't even notice these details about settlement dates (although understanding what's going on is handy).

Canadian events and data reports to watch

TIP

On top of following U.S. economic data to maintain an outlook for the larger economy to the south, you'll need to pay close attention to individual Canadian economic data and official commentaries. CAD can react explosively when data or events come in out of line with expectations. In particular, keep an eye on the following Canadian economic events and reports:

» Bank of Canada speakers, rate decisions, and economic forecasts

» Employment report

» Gross domestic product (GDP) reported monthly

» International securities transactions

» International merchandise trade

» Wholesale and retail sales

» Consumer price index (CPI) and BOC CPI

» Manufacturing shipments

» Ivey Purchasing Managers Index

Trading fundamentals of NZD/USD

The New Zealand dollar is nicknamed the *Kiwi*, as are most things New Zealand, after the indigenous bird of the same name; the term *Kiwi* refers to both the NZD and the NZD/USD pair. (What is it with birds and currency nicknames, anyway?) Given the relatively small size of the New Zealand economy, Kiwi is among the most interest-rate sensitive of all currencies.

The New Zealand economy has undergone a major transformation over the past two decades, moving from a mostly agricultural export orientation to a domestically driven service and manufacturing base. The rapid growth has seen disposable incomes soar; with higher disposable incomes have come generally high levels of inflation. As a result, the Reserve Bank of New Zealand (RBNZ), the central bank, has frequently been among the more hawkish central banks.

REMEMBER

We put Kiwi in the commodity currency grouping, but there is an important distinction to note. New Zealand is primarily an agricultural-commodity-producing economy (dairy products and meat in particular), as opposed to the metals and energy commodities of Canada and Australia. As such, Kiwi displays a weaker relationship than CAD and AUD to the prices of gold, silver, and oil, as seen in the two tables in the earlier sidebar "The (not just) commodity currencies."

TIP

In addition to all the standard New Zealand economic data and official pronouncements you'll need to monitor, Kiwi trading is closely tied to Australian data and prospects, due to a strong trade and regional relationship.

No set formula exists to describe the currencies' relationship, but a general rule is that when it's a USD-based move, Aussie and Kiwi tend to trade in the same direction as each other relative to the USD. But when Kiwi or Aussie news comes in, the AUD/NZD (Aussie/Kiwi) cross exerts a larger influence. For example, disappointing Aussie data may see AUD/USD move lower, which tends to drag down NZD/USD as well. But Aussie/Kiwi cross selling (selling AUD/USD on the weaker data and buying NZD/USD for the cross trade) typically reduces the extent of NZD/USD declines relative to AUD/USD losses. A similar effect plays out when New Zealand data or news is the catalyst.

New Zealand events and data reports to watch

TIP

RBNZ commentary and rate decisions are pivotal to the value of Kiwi, given the significance of interest rates to the currency. Finance ministry comments are secondary to the rhetoric of the independent RBNZ but can still upset the Kiwi cart from time to time. Additionally, keep an eye on the following:

>> Consumer prices, housing prices, and food prices

>> Retail sales and electronic-card spending (debit and credit)

>> Westpac and ANZ consumer confidence indices

>> Quarterly GDP and monthly trade balance

>> National Bank of New Zealand (NBNZ) business confidence survey

Trading Aussie and Kiwi by the numbers

You can find out more about AUD in Chapter 8, but it's worth looking at the numbers for AUD and NZD together as AUD/USD and NZD/USD are both quoted in the same way. AUD/USD and NZD/USD rates reflect the number of USD per AUD or NZD. For example, a NZD/USD rate of 0.7000 means it costs USD 0.70 (or 70¢) to buy NZD 1. Aussie and Kiwi trade in the opposite direction of the overall value of the USD, so a weaker USD means a higher Aussie or Kiwi rate, and a lower Aussie or Kiwi rate represents a stronger USD.

AUD and NZD are the primary currencies in the pairs, and the USD is the counter currency, which means

>> **AUD/USD and NZD/USD are traded in position sizes denominated in AUD or NZD.**

>> **The pip values are denominated in USD.**

>> **Profit and loss accrues in USD.** On a 100,000 NZD/USD position, each pip is worth USD 10; on a 10,000 Aussie position size, each pip is worth USD 1.

>> **Margin calculations are typically based in USD on margin trading platforms.** Using an NZD/USD rate of 0.7000 and a leverage ratio of 50:1, a 100,000 Kiwi position requires USD 1,400 in margin, while a 10,000 NZD/USD position would need only USD 140 in margin.

Tactical trading considerations in USD/CAD, AUD/USD, and NZD/USD

We group these three currency pairs together because they share many of the same trading traits and even travel as a pack sometimes — especially Aussie and Kiwi, given their regional proximity and close economic ties. Whether they're being grouped as the commodity currencies or just smaller regional currencies versus the U.S. dollar, they can frequently serve as a leading indicator of overall USD market direction.

Liquidity and market interest are lower

One of the reasons these pairs tend to exhibit leading characteristics is due to the lower relative liquidity of the pairs, which amplifies the speculative effect on them. If sentiment is shifting in favor of the U.S. dollar, for example, the effect of speculative interest — the fast money — is going to be most evident in lower-volume currency pairs.

When a hedge fund or other large speculator turns around a directional bet on the U.S. dollar (for example, from short to long), it's going to start buying U.S. dollars across the board (meaning against most all other currencies). A half-billion EUR/USD selling order (650 million USD equivalent at 1.3000 EUR/USD) is relatively easily absorbed in the high-volume, liquid EUR/USD market and may move it only a few points (say, 10 to 20 pips, depending on the circumstances). However, a proportionately smaller order to sell Aussie, sell Kiwi, or buy USD/CAD (large speculators typically allocate smaller position sizes to less-liquid currency pairs), amounting to only 100 million or 200 million in notional terms, may generate a 20- to 40-pip movement in these currency pairs, depending on the time of day and overall environment.

TIP

In general, you need to be aware that overall liquidity and market interest in these pairs is significantly lower than in the majors, although Aussie has caught up with the majors in recent years and has overtaken the CHF (Swiss franc) as the fifth most traded currency in the world. On a daily basis, liquidity in these pairs is at its peak when the local centers (Toronto, Sydney, and Wellington) are open. London market makers provide a solid liquidity base to bridge the gap outside the local markets, but you can largely forget about USD/CAD during the Asia/Pacific session, and the Aussie and Kiwi markets are problematic after the London/European session close until their financial centers reopen a few hours later. The net result is a concentration of market interest in these currency pairs among the major banks of the currency countries, which has implications of its own (see the later section "Technical levels can be blurry").

Price action is highly event driven

As a result of the overall lower level of liquidity in these currency pairs, in concert with relatively high levels of speculative positioning (at times), you've got the ultimate mix for explosive reactions after currency-specific news or data comes out. A dovish statement from a previously hawkish Bank of Canada governor can trigger a sea change in sentiment against the CAD. If expectations are running high for an NZD interest-rate hike and a key inflation report contradicts that outlook (it's lower than expected), we've got a relatively small market, probably overpositioned in one direction (long NZD/USD), that's all heading for the exit (selling) at the same time.

REMEMBER

The bottom line in these currency pairs is that significant data or news surprises, especially when contrary to expectations and likely market positioning, tends to have an outsized impact on the market. Traders positioning in these currencies need to be especially aware of this and to recognize the greater degree of volatility and risk they're facing if events don't transpire as expected. It's one thing if Eurozone CPI comes in higher than expected, but it's another thing entirely if Australian CPI surprises to the upside.

TIP

A data or event surprise typically leads to a price gap when the news is first announced. If the news is sufficiently at odds with market expectations and positioning, subsequent price action tends to be mostly one-way traffic, as the market reacts to the surprise news and exits earlier positions. If you're caught on the wrong side after unexpected news in these pairs, you're likely better off getting out as soon as possible than waiting for a correction to exit at a better level. The lower liquidity and interest in these currency pairs mean you're probably not alone in being caught wrong-sided, which tends to see steady, one-way interest, punctuated by accelerations when additional stop-loss order levels are hit.

All politics (and economic data) is local

WARNING

Most of our discussion of market drivers centers on economic data and monetary policy, but domestic political developments in these smaller-currency countries can provoke significant movements in the local currencies. National elections, political scandals, and abrupt policy changes can all lead to upheavals in the value of the local currency. The effect tends to be most pronounced on the downside of the currency's value (meaning that bad news tends to hurt a currency more than good news — if there ever is any in politics). Of course, every situation is different, but the spillover effect between politics and currencies is greatest in these pairs, which means you need to be aware of domestic political events if you're trading them.

In terms of economic data, these currency pairs tend to participate in overall directional moves relative to the U.S. dollar until a local news or data event triggers more concentrated interest on the local currency. If the USD is under pressure across the board, for instance, USD/CAD is likely to move lower in concert with other dollar pairs. But if negative Canadian news or data emerges, USD/CAD is likely to pare its losses and may even start to move higher if the news was bad enough. If the Canadian news was CAD-positive (say, a higher CPI reading pointing to a potential rate hike), USD/CAD is likely to accelerate to the downside, because USD selling interest is now amplified by CAD buying interest.

Technical levels can be blurry

WARNING

The relatively lower level of liquidity and market interest in these currency pairs makes for sometimes-difficult technical trading conditions. Trend lines and retracement levels in particular are subject to regular overshoots. Prices may move beyond the technical level — sometimes only 5 to 10 pips, other times for extensive distances or for prolonged periods — only to reverse course and reestablish the technical level later.

The basic reason behind this tendency to overshoot technical levels is that market interest is concentrated in fewer market-makers for these pairs — usually the local banks of the currency country. The result is a concentration of market interest in fewer hands, which can result in order levels being triggered when they may not be otherwise. For example, if you're an interbank market-maker watching a stop-loss order for 5 million AUD/USD, it's not a big deal, because 5 million Aussie is transacted easily. But if you have a stop loss for 50 million or 100 million AUD/USD, you're going to need to be fast (and, likely, preemptive) to fill the order at a reasonable execution rate.

TIP

If the price break of a technical level is quickly reversed, it's a good sign that it was just a position-related movement. If fresh news is out, however, you may be seeing the initial wave of a larger directional move.

It's worth noting that things are changing, however, as the commodities currencies (the AUD and CAD, in particular) gain more of the FX market share of volume. Flip to Chapter 6 for the basics of technical analysis.

Trading the Scandies: SEK, NOK, and DKK

A few of the Scandinavian, or Nordic, countries chose not to join the monetary union that led to the euro — namely Sweden, Norway, and Denmark. Trading volumes in the Scandies are generally light, but sufficient enough to offer additional speculative trading opportunities depending on the circumstances. Most of the trading in the Scandies is done versus EUR, driven by intra-European divergences in either growth or interest-rate outlooks. Generally speaking, trading the USD versus the Scandies tends to mimic EUR/USD, but in mirror image due to quoting conventions.

Swedish krona: "Stocky"

The Swedish krona is affectionately referred to as Stocky after the capital Stockholm, and its currency code is SEK. Trading volumes in USD/SEK (dollar/Stocky) and EUR/SEK (euro/Stocky) amounted to 1.3 percent and 0.5 percent, respectively, of daily global volume, according to the 2019 BIS survey of forex markets. Compared to the 2013 survey, trading volume in the SEK was down in 2019, potentially due to the rising popularity of currencies such as the Chinese renminbi and other currencies such as the Aussie dollar. The Swedish central bank, *Sveriges Riksbank* in Swedish, is independent and is the key actor in setting interest rates and maintaining currency stability.

REMEMBER

In addition to following the economic data coming out of Sweden, pay close attention to comments from the governor and other Riksbank officials. The Riksbank follows an *inflation target,* a desired level of inflation, so CPI reports are also critical inputs to the outlook for interest rates and SEK. The Swedish central bank also has a history of speaking out on the value of the krona itself, especially when it's either too strong or weak relative to EUR, where most of Swedish trade is conducted. EUR/SEK can become especially active when the Riksbank and the European Central Bank (ECB) are seen to be on divergent interest rate paths.

Technically speaking, after joining the European Union in 1995, Sweden is obliged to adopt the euro at some point in the future but has effectively opted out and shows no signs of joining the euro.

Norwegian krone: "Nokkie"

The Norwegian krone (NOK) is nicknamed Nokkie after its currency code and in symphony with Stocky. USD/NOK and EUR/NOK trading volumes were at 1.1 percent and 0.5 respectively, as per the 2019 BIS survey. Still, liquidity in NOK is more than sufficient, especially during European trading hours. Norway's central bank, *Norges Bank,* is independent and pursues a traditional policy of maintaining price stability. Keep an eye out for guidance from the governor and other central bank officials, as Norges Bank policy may frequently diverge from ECB policy.

TIP

Norway is exceptionally wealthy owing to its large energy reserves, mainly North Sea oil, which has given it a large sovereign wealth fund, making it an important global asset manager. More importantly for day-to-day trading, Norway is the world's 15th largest oil producer, and NOK tends to trade as a petro-currency, similar to CAD, strengthening as oil prices rise and vice versa. Norway is not a member of the EU and so is unlikely to ever adopt the euro.

Danish krone: "Copey"

The Danish krone (DKK) is sometimes called Copey in reference to the capital of Copenhagen. Rather than pursuing currency independence like Sweden and Norway, Denmark opted to enter into a cooperative exchange rate agreement with Eurozone members, and the Danish krone is linked to the euro at a fixed exchange rate of 7.4362 +/– 2.25%. Within this arrangement, the Danish central bank (Danmarks Nationalbank) effectively sets interest rates according to ECB decisions. The result is that the USD/DKK pair trades in mirror opposite fashion to EUR/USD and that the EUR/DKK pair trades in a very narrow band, typically about 0.2 percent, around the fixed rate. As such, there is little incentive for trading DKK, as EUR/USD offers better liquidity and EUR/DKK doesn't move.

In the aftermath of the Eurozone sovereign debt crisis, the Danish government has backed away from holding a referendum on Euro membership. However, the government seems happy to stick with the EUR/DKK peg for now.

Checking Out Cross-Currency Pairs

A *cross-currency pair* (or *cross*, for short) is any currency pair that does not have the U.S. dollar as one of the currencies in the pairing. (Turn to Chapter 4 for a list of all the different cross pairs.) But the catch is that cross rates are derived from the prices of the underlying USD pairs. For example, one of the most active crosses is EUR/JPY, pitting the two largest currencies outside the U.S. dollar directly against each other. But the EUR/JPY rate at any given instant is a function (the product) of the current EUR/USD and USD/JPY rates.

The most popular cross pairs involve the most actively traded major currencies, like EUR/JPY and EUR/GBP. (In the past, EUR/CHF would have been in the mix, but since the 2011 peg, EUR/CHF has become less attractive to trade.) According to the 2019 BIS survey of foreign-exchange market activity, direct cross trading accounted for a relatively small percentage of global daily volume — under 7 percent for the major crosses combined.

But that figure significantly understates the amount of interest that is actually flowing through the crosses, because large interbank cross trades are typically executed through the USD pairs instead of directly in the cross markets. If a Japanese corporation needs to buy half a billion EUR/JPY (*half a yard*, in market parlance), for example, the interbank traders executing the order will alternately buy EUR/USD and buy USD/JPY to fill the order. Going directly through the EUR/JPY market would likely tip off too many in the market and drive the rate away from them. (We look at how large cross flows can drive the dollar pairs in the later section "Stretching the legs.")

REMEMBER

For individual traders dealing online, however, the direct cross pairs offer more than ample liquidity and narrower spreads than can be realized by trading through the dollar pairs. Additionally, most online platforms do not net out positions based on overall dollar exposure, so you'd end up using roughly twice the amount of margin to enter a position through the dollar pairs to create the same position you'd have if you'd gone through the direct cross market. The advances in electronic trading technology even make relatively obscure crosses like NZD/JPY and GBP/CHF easily accessible to individual online traders.

Understanding reasons for trading the crosses

Cross pairs represent entirely new sets of routinely fluctuating currency pairs that offer another universe of trading opportunities beyond the primary USD pairs. Developments in the currency market are not always a simple bet on what's happening to the U.S. dollar. Crosses are the other half of the story, and their significance has increased as a result of electronic trading. Years ago, if you wanted a price in a cross pair, a human would have to push the buttons on a calculator to come up with the cross quote. Today's streaming price technology means that cross rates are as fluid as the dollar pairs, making them as accessible and tradable as USD/JPY or EUR/USD.

REMEMBER

In particular, cross trading offers the following advantages:

>> **You can pinpoint trade opportunities based on news or fundamental trends.** If the outlook and data for the United Kingdom is steadily deteriorating, you may be looking to sell GBP. But against what? If the USD is also weakening, buying USD and selling GBP may not yield any results. Selling GBP against another currency with better immediate prospects (such as selling GBP/CAD or GBP/NOK) may yield a more appreciable return.

>> **You can take advantage of interest-rate differentials.** Selling low-yielding currencies against higher-yielding currencies is known as a *carry trade.* Carry trades seek to profit from both interest-rate differentials and spot price appreciation, and can form the basis of significant trends.

>> **You can exploit technical trading opportunities.** The majors may be range bound or showing no actionable technical signals, but a cross rate may be extremely volatile and could provide a nice price breakout. Survey charts of cross rates to spot additional technical trading setups. (See Chapter 6 for more about technical analysis.)

>> **You can expand the horizon of trading opportunities.** Instead of looking at only four to seven dollar pairs, cross rates offer another dozen currency pairs that you can look to for trading opportunities.

>> **You can go with the flow.** Speculative flows are ever-present in the currency market, but they don't always involve the dollar pairs. Today's speculative flow may be focused on the JPY crosses or selling CAD across the board on the back of surprisingly weak CAD data. The more attuned you are to cross-currency pairs, the more likely you are to identify and capitalize on the speculative move du jour.

Stretching the legs

A lot of interbank cross-trading volume doesn't go through the direct cross market, because institutional traders have a vested interest in hiding their operations from the rest of the market. In many cases, too, standing liquidity is simply not available in less-liquid crosses (GBP/JPY or NZD/JPY, for example). So they have to go through the *legs*, as the dollar pairs are called with respect to cross trading, to get the trade done. They also have an interest in maximizing the prices at which they're dealing — to sell as high as possible and to buy as low as possible.

One of the ways they're able to do that is to alternate their trading in the dollar legs. For instance, if you have to sell a large amount of EUR/JPY, you can alternate selling EUR/USD, which may tend to drive down EUR/USD but also push USD/JPY higher (because U.S. dollars overall are being bought). You now (you hope) have a higher rate at which to sell the USD/JPY leg of the order. But selling USD/JPY may push USD/JPY lower or cap its rise, leading EUR/USD to stop declining and recover higher, because U.S. dollars are now being sold. Now you have a slightly better EUR/USD rate to keep selling the EUR/USD leg of the order. By alternating the timing of which U.S. dollar leg you're selling, you have (you hope) executed the order at better rates than you could have directly in the cross and likely managed to obscure your market activity in the more active dollar pairs.

TIP

Of course, it doesn't always work out as neat and clean as what we just described. The net result in the market is a steady directional move in the cross rate, while the USD pairs remain relatively stagnant or within recent ranges. Be alert for such dollar-based movement, and consider that it may be a cross-driven move and a potential trading opportunity.

REMEMBER

Cross-rate movements can also have a pronounced effect on how individual dollar pairs move in an otherwise dollar-based market reaction. Suppose that some very USD-positive news or data has just been released, and the market starts buying USD across the board. (We focus on buying USD/JPY and selling EUR/USD in this example.) If USD/JPY happens to break a key technical resistance level, it may accelerate higher and prompt EUR/JPY to break a similarly significant resistance level, bringing in EUR/JPY buyers. The net effect in this case is that EUR/USD will not fall as much or as rapidly as USD/JPY will rally, because of the EUR/JPY cross buying. If you went short EUR/USD on the positive U.S. news, you may not get as much joy. But the legs also tend to move in phases, and continued EUR/USD selling may eventually break through support, sending EUR/JPY lower and capping USD/JPY in the process.

As you can see, crosses can affect the market in virtually limitless ways, and there's no set way these things play out. Luckily, with the onset of online trading, you don't have to work out cross trading in the same way the guys did in the olden days! However, it's still interesting to find out how it was done and see how the dynamics of the market actually work.

REMEMBER

When the U.S. dollar is not the primary focus of the market's attention, or if major U.S. news is approaching — like a nonfarm payrolls (NFP) report or a Federal Open Market Committee (FOMC) decision in a few days — sending market interest to the sidelines, speculative interest frequently shifts to the crosses. Always consider that the market's focus may be cross-driven rather than centered on the USD or any other single currency. Some days it's a dollar market, and other days it's a cross market. GBP may be weakening across the board on weak UK data, but if the USD is similarly out of favor, the pound's weakness is likely to be most evident on the crosses.

WARNING

When looking at cross-trade opportunities, you may be tempted to translate the cross idea into a USD-based trade. You may think that AUD/JPY is forming a top, for example. If you're right, you may be thinking that one of two moves is likely — USD/JPY will move lower or AUD/USD will move lower — and you may be tempted into selling one of the legs (AUD/USD or USD/JPY) because you don't want to get involved in a cross. But there's another possibility: One leg may go down precipitously while the other moves higher, still sending the cross lower as you expected. But if you went short the wrong leg, you missed the boat.

TIP

When you spot a trade opportunity in a cross, trade the cross. Don't try to outguess the market and pick which component will make the cross move. Trust that if your trade analysis is correct, the cross will move the way you expect. And with the onset of electronic trading, it has never been easier to trade the crosses.

Trading the JPY crosses

The JPY crosses constitute one of the primary cross families and basically pit the JPY against the other major currencies. EUR/JPY is the highest volume of the JPY crosses, but the prominence of the carry trade, where the low-yielding JPY is sold and higher-yielding currencies are bought, has seen significant increases in AUD/JPY and NZD/JPY trading volume. Those currencies offer the highest interest-rate differentials against the JPY.

JPY crosses have their pip values denominated in JPY, meaning profit and loss will accrue in JPY. The margin requirement varies greatly depending on which primary currency is involved, with GBP/JPY requiring the greatest margin and NZD/JPY requiring the least.

WARNING

In terms of JPY-cross fundamentals, risk sentiment (see Chapter 5) and overall volatility tend to have the greatest impact, but as we caution earlier, trying to pin down which leg is going to cause the JPY crosses to move is a risky game. When trading in the JPY crosses, you need to keep an eye on USD/JPY in particular, due to its relatively explosive tendencies and its key place as an outlet for overall carry trade buying or selling. Be alert for similar technical levels between USD/JPY and the JPY crosses, as a break in either could spill over into the other.

Trading the EUR crosses

REMEMBER

Outside of EUR/JPY, EUR cross action tends to be concentrated in EUR/GBP and EUR/CHF, where the cross direction is largely determined by changing outlooks between the Eurozone economy relative to the UK and Swiss economies. Reactions to Eurozone and Swiss news or data are most likely to be felt in the EUR crosses as opposed to EUR/USD or USD/CHF, whereas UK news/data is going to explode all over GBP/USD and EUR/GBP. Trading in EUR/SEK and EUR/NOK offers yet another way to exploit divergent economic or interest-rate trajectories between continental Europe and the Scandinavian countries.

Sharp USD-driven moves also affect these crosses, with the brunt of the USD move being felt in GBP/USD and USD/CHF, frequently biasing those legs to drive their EUR cross in the short run. That means frequently (but not always) a sharp move higher in the USD tends to see a higher EUR/CHF and EUR/GBP, while a rapid USD move lower tends to see lower EUR/CHF and EUR/GBP.

The pip values of these EUR crosses is denominated in either GBP or AUD. (EUR/CHF used to be a popular EUR cross, but since the 2011 peg was introduced by the Swiss National Bank, it has seen a dip in volume to 1.1 percent of daily trading volume, according to the 2019 BIS FX survey, down from 1.8 percent in 2010.) Typical daily ranges in the EUR crosses are relatively small on a pip basis — roughly 20 to 40 pips on average — but they're still substantial on a pip-value basis and roughly equivalent to daily EUR/USD ranges.

3
Executing a Trading Plan

Understand the most common trading styles in the forex market.

Find out how to determine which trading strategy fits you best.

Keep more of your trading profits by understanding taxes.

Chapter **10**

Pulling the Trigger

"Y ou gotta be in it to win it" is a favorite saying that currency traders like to throw around. The "in it" part refers to being "in" the market, having the right directional view expressed with an open position (long/short) in a currency pair.

But there's always a trade-off between having the right position and getting into that position at the most advantageous price. For example, being short AUD/USD may be the correct position to have, but if you enter at the wrong price, you may have to endure some pain before the trade moves your way.

In this chapter, we walk you through some of the different ways of entering trades and establishing the position to fit your overall strategy.

Getting into the Position

You can make trades in the forex market one of two ways:

» You can trade *at the market*, or the current price, using the click-and-deal feature of your broker's platform.

» You can employ orders, such as limit orders and if/then contingent orders. (We discuss order types in Chapter 4.)

But there's a lot more to it than that. Certain trade setups suggest a combination of both methods for entering a position, while others rely strictly on orders to capture rapid or unexpected price movements. Then there's the fine art of timing the market to get in at the best price at the moment.

Buying and selling at the current market

Many traders like the idea of opening a position by trading at the market as opposed to leaving an order that may or may not be executed. They prefer the certainty of knowing that they're in the market. Actively buying and selling is also what makes trading as fun and exhilarating as it is hard work.

REMEMBER

Deciding whether to enter now (at the market) or wait for better price levels (using orders) depends greatly on the nature of your strategy. If you're aiming to trade short term (minutes/hours) on news or economic data reports, for instance, you're going to be trading mostly at the market. If you're looking to position for a larger price adjustment over the next day(s), you're better off using orders to execute your market entry.

For short-term trade entry at the market, you want a good handle on the recent price action, which means knowing where prices have been over the past several hours. Just because you've settled on a strategy to buy USD/CAD doesn't mean you have to close your chart window, open your trading platform, and pay the offer.

Take a step back and look at shorter-term charts, such as 5 or 15 minutes, to get an idea of where prices have been trading recently. Chances are you'll observe a relatively narrow range of price action, typically between 20 and 30 pips. Unless the situation is urgent, a little patience can go a long way toward improving your entry level. Why buy at 1.0550 when you have a viable chance to buy at 1.0535?

TIP

Let the routine price fluctuations work to your advantage by trying to buy on downticks and sell on upticks in line with your overall strategy. Selecting your trade size in advance helps — so when the price gets to your desired level, you need to click only once to execute the trade. You can also use limit orders to buy or sell just a few pips from the current market, letting the broker's platform execute automatically in case the price moves are too quick to click and deal manually.

REMEMBER

As you watch the price action, keep a disciplined entry price in mind, both in your favor and in case prices start to move away from your desired entry level. If the market cooperates and moves to your desired trade entry price, stay with your plan and make the trade. If prices move away from you, have a worst-case entry level in mind and be prepared to pull the trigger so you can still execute your overall strategy. You may not be able to enter at better prices every time, but we think you'll be surprised how often you can.

Averaging into a position

REMEMBER

Medium- and longer-term trade strategies typically benefit from averaging into a position. *Averaging into a position* refers to the practice of buying/selling at successively lower/higher prices to improve the average rate of the desired long/short position. The idea here is to allow larger market swings to unfold and use them to establish a larger position at better prices than current levels in anticipation that the market will eventually reverse course in line with your strategy.

Take a look at a detailed example of averaging into a position to see how it works. Imagine that the USD/JPY is moving lower from 82.20 on a weak U.S. economic release, but you think USD/JPY is unlikely to decline below 81.00, where the 200-day moving average is located.

One possible strategy would be to buy USD/JPY on the current weakness, spacing your buys so that you can buy as low as possible, but above 81.00 where you don't expect it to trade. (The stop-loss exit in this example would be somewhere below 81.00.) Imagine that you buy one lot of USD/JPY at the market, now at 82.00, just so you have some piece of the position in case the market rebounds abruptly. You decide that 81.20 is another good level to buy at because it's a margin of error above the key 81.00 level. If your order to buy at 81.20 is filled, you'll be long two lots at an average price of 81.60 ([82.00 + 81.20] ÷ 2 = 81.60).

Take a look at what just happened there. To begin with, you were long one lot from 82.00. To add to the position at 81.20 means the market was trading lower, which also means you were looking at an unrealized loss of –80 pips on your initial position from 82.00. After you buy the second lot, your unrealized loss has not changed substantially (assuming that the market is still at 81.20 and excluding the spread, you're still out –80 pips, now –40 pips on 2 lots), but your position size has just doubled, which means your risk has also just doubled.

If the market rebounds from 81.20, your unrealized loss will be reduced. But if the market continues to decline, your losses are going to be twice what they were had you not added on to your position. If your strategy plays out and the market reverses higher, you now have a larger position from a better entry price than if you had entered the two lot position earlier at higher levels.

WARNING

We've seen the practice referred to as *pyramiding* in other trading books, and the advice is usually to avoid doing it (as in "Don't pyramid into a losing position"). Sometimes "adding on" to winning positions is acceptable, such as after a technical level breaks in the direction of your trade. The result of adding on to winning positions, however, is a worse average rate for the overall position — a higher average long price or a lower average short price. If the market reverses after you add on, any gains in the overall trade can be quickly erased.

So what's the deal? Should you average into positions or not? As with most questions on trading tactics, the answer is a straightforward "It depends." Before deciding whether to average into positions, consider the following:

>> **Time frame of the trade:** Short-term trades seek to exploit the immediate direction of the market. If you're wrong on the direction in the first place, adding to the position at better rates will likely only compound your losses. For medium- and longer-term trades, averaging into a position can make sense if the trade setup anticipates a market reversal. (We talk about this a bit more in the later section "When averaging into a position makes sense.")

>> **Account size:** Depending on your account size, you may not have the capability to add to positions. You also need to keep in mind that adding to a position will further reduce your available margin, which reduces your cushion against adverse price movements, bringing you closer to liquidation due to insufficient margin. If that means trading smaller position sizes, such as 10,000 mini-lots, go with that.

>> **Volatility:** If the overall market or the currency pair you're trading is experiencing heightened volatility, averaging into trades is probably not a good idea. Increased volatility is usually symptomatic of uncertainty or fresh news hitting the market, both of which are prone to see more extreme directional price moves, in which case averaging is a losing proposition. In contrast, lower volatility conditions tend to favor range-trading environments, where averaging can be successful.

Signs that averaging into a trade is not a good idea

Many trading books recommend avoiding averaging into, or adding on to, a losing position — and with good reason. The tactic can lead to dramatically higher losses on smaller incremental price movements. Also, if you're adding on to a losing position, you're missing out on the current directional move. In other words, not only are you losing money, but you're also not making money, which is the opportunity cost of averaging.

But that still doesn't stop people from averaging into losing trades, even professional traders. Here are some indications that averaging is probably not a good idea:

>> **The market just blew through your stop-loss level.** But you didn't have a stop-loss order in place, so you're still holding onto the losing position. First tactical error: Trading without an active stop-loss order. Second tactical error: Instead of exiting the position in line with your trade plan, you're reluctant to

take the larger loss than you initially reckoned with, so you decide to hold on to the position, hoping it will recover. This is usually the first wipeout on the slippery slope of relinquishing trading discipline. Save yourself some money and don't commit a third tactical error by averaging into an even larger position (which you had already planned to be out of by that point anyway).

>> **The range just broke.** You may have had great success in recent trades playing a range-bound market, and you're in a position again based on that range. But ranges do break, and prices do move to new levels. Remember the basis for your trade — the range is going to hold — and don't hang on, much less add on, to positions beyond your predetermined stop-loss exit level based on the range.

>> **News is out, but the currency pair isn't responding the way it should.** The news or data may be USD-positive, for example, but the dollar is coming under selling pressure anyway. Keep in mind that multiple cross-currents are at work at any given moment in the forex market. Sometimes they're position related (a large hedge fund may be turning around a multibillion-dollar position); other times they're based on news or information that isn't widely known in the market, like a mergers-and-acquisitions (M&A) deal or a rumor.

REMEMBER

The market reaction to a news/data report is more important than the report itself. If you've taken a position based on the news, don't second-guess the market reaction by adding on to the position if the market doesn't respond the way you think the data indicates. Instead, accept that something else is going on and that the news you based your trade on is not it.

When averaging into a position makes sense

Depending on the trade setup, you may be entirely justified in averaging into a position. In fact, with some trade opportunities, you'll be hoping to have the chance to average into the position at better rates, because if the trade setup is correct, you'll want to have as large a position as possible.

REMEMBER

Even though we're suggesting that certain trade opportunities warrant averaging into a position, we want to stress that you still need to identify the ultimate stop-loss exit point in every trade setup. In other words, you can average into a position as much as you want up to a certain point, but after that the trade setup is invalidated, and you need to exit the position.

TIP

The trade setups we're referring to are those where a *reversal* is anticipated. Prices frequently move into *counter-trend consolidation ranges*, where prices move in the opposite direction of the primary trend for a time before the trend resumes. You may see signs of an impending reversal from daily candlestick patterns, such as a shooting star/hammer or a tweezers top/bottom. You may begin to suspect a reversal after a significant intraday spike reversal/rejection from key technical levels. The market may also be nearing important long-term trend-line support or resistance that suggests a medium-term bottom or top is close by. (See Chapter 6 for more about technical analysis.)

What all these setups have in common is a price difference between current market levels and the ideal entry point based on the setup. For example, major daily trend-line resistance dating back six months may lie above 1.2960/70 in EUR/USD. Current market levels are well below at 1.2890, and there has been a spike rejection from an intraday test to 1.2930/35. Adding up these observations, we may justifiably conclude that the current market price is just below an area of major resistance, suggesting a short position as the overall way to proceed.

But we have no accurate way of predicting how much higher the market might trade, or even if it will, before the anticipated reversal lower takes place. The market could start moving directly lower from current levels. It could retest the spike highs seen earlier in the day, or it could make it all the way to test the key trend-line resistance before stalling. So where might we look to get short?

The answer is in that zone of resistance we just identified between current market levels and the daily trend-line resistance. This is where it makes sense to average into a trade to exploit the trade setup.

As an example of our own approach, we may not know how much higher the market will go, so we may be prepared to short a portion of the overall position at current market levels, in case the top has already been seen and prices move directly lower. We may also be prepared to sell remaining portion(s) of the position at successively higher levels, if the market allows it. We'll save our last portion of the position for the trend-line resistance level in case it's reached.

When considering where to leave your limit-entry orders to average into a trade, be aware of what your final average rate will be if all your orders are filled. The difference between that average rate and your stop-loss level multiplied by the total position size will give you the total amount you're risking on the trade.

TIP

Although there are no 100 percent accurate gauges to tell us how much higher the market is likely to trade, we can use short-term momentum studies — such as stochastic models, the Relative Strength Index (RSI), or Moving Average Convergence/Divergence (MACD) — to make an educated guess as to how much more upside potential there may be. (RSI and MACD are covered in Chapter 6.)

If hourly momentum studies have already topped out and crossed over to the downside, for example, the upside potential is likely more limited. This may argue for being more aggressive in establishing a short position, such as making the initial sale at current market levels and placing any additional limit orders to sell above at closer levels. But if hourly momentum studies are still moving higher, we can reasonably wait and look to sell at relatively higher levels using limit sell orders.

WARNING

Averaging into a reversal setup requires that you're able to buy/sell multiple lots over relatively large price zones, sometimes as much as 100 pips or more. Make sure that you have sufficient margin resources available *before* you start averaging into your overall position. Depending on the size of the buy/sell zone and your available margin balance, you may have to space your limit-entry orders farther apart or trade fewer lots overall.

REMEMBER

It's always a trade-off between being in the right position to catch the move and getting in at the best price possible. It's quite frustrating to identify a potentially significant market reversal, leave a single limit-entry order, but then see the reversal take place without your order being filled. Averaging into the position starting at current prices is one way to make sure you're on board for at least some of the move.

If the setup works out, you'll have taken advantage of any favorable price moves the market has made, resulting in a better average rate on your position. If the setup fails, averaging into the position at successively better rates will cost less in the end than entering the whole position at the current market level.

Trading breakouts

REMEMBER

A *breakout* or *break* refers to a price movement that moves beyond, or breaks out of, recent established trading ranges or price patterns captured with trend lines. Breakouts can occur in all time frames, from weeks and days on down to hours and minutes. The longer the time frame, the more significant the breakout in terms of the overall expected price movement that follows.

In the very short term, prices on a 15-minute chart may establish a trading range of 20 to 30 pips over several hours, for example. A breakout on such a short time scale may result in a 30- to 50-pip movement in a matter of minutes/hours. Daily trading ranges of 300 to 400 pips may see a breakout result in an initial 50- to 150-pip movement in subsequent hours, with more to come in following sessions.

There's no real fixed ratio or scale for range breakouts; we've just given the preceding examples to give you an idea of the relative scales involved. To be sure, a breakout of a 15-minute range can lead to the break of an hourly range, which can lead to a breakout of a daily range.

Breakouts are important because they represent a shift in market thinking. Most trading theories start with the premise that the current price reflects all the known information on that market at the moment. But rather than settling on one price and stopping, markets tend to consolidate into a zone of prices, or a range, where relatively minor price fluctuations are simply noise in terms of the grand theories of market price behavior.

For a range to break, then, by definition something must have changed in the market's thinking. And there's only one thing that will change the market's thinking: new information. New information can be anything from news and data to rumors or comments, down to the prices themselves. Many traders rely on price information as their primary source of decision-making information. If prices in USD/CHF have been capped by 1.0500 for the past four weeks, a price move above that level is new information and requires adjustments in the market.

The beauty of breakouts from an individual trader's perspective is that you don't necessarily need to know the reason for the breakout — just that prices have broken out. Of course, being aware of what's going on and what news is driving the market always helps give you a leg up in anticipating and preparing for potential breakouts.

In terms of entering a position, breakouts frequently represent important signals to get in or out of positions. In that sense, they take a lot of the guesswork out of deciding where to enter or exit a position.

Identifying potential breakout levels

The first step in trading on a breakout is to identify where breakouts are likely to occur. Pinpointing likely breakout levels is most easily done by drawing trend lines that capture recent high/low price ranges. In many cases, these ranges will form a sideways or horizontal range of prices, where sellers have repeatedly emerged at the same level on the upside and buyers have regularly stepped in at the lower level. Horizontal ranges are mostly neutral in predicting which direction the break will occur.

Other ranges are going to form price patterns with sloping trend lines on the top and bottom, such as flags, pennants, wedges, and triangles. These patterns have more predictive capacity for the direction of the eventual breakout and even the distance of the breakout. (We review the most common patterns and what they imply in greater detail in Chapter 6.)

The time frame that you're looking at will determine the overall significance of the breakout and go a long way toward determining whether you should make a trade based on it. Very short time frames (less than an hour) are going to have much less significance than a break of a four-hour range or a daily price pattern.

The length of time that a price range or pattern has endured also gives you an idea of its significance. A break of a range that has formed over the past 48 hours is going to have less significance for price movements than the break of a range that has persisted for the past three weeks.

Trading breaks with stop-loss entry orders

After you've identified a likely breakout point, you can use a resting stop-loss entry order placed just beyond the breakout level to get into a position if a break occurs. To get long for a break to the upside, you would leave a stop-loss entry order to buy at a price just above the upper level of the range or pattern. To get short for a break lower, you would leave a stop-loss entry order to sell at a price just below the lower level of the range or pattern. Figure 10-1 is a chart showing EUR/USD and where stop-loss entry orders could be placed to trade breakouts.

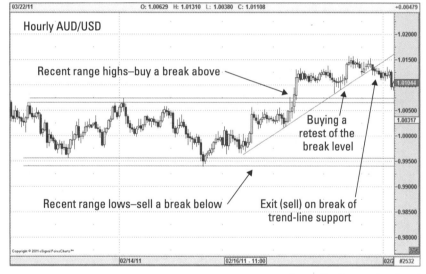

FIGURE 10-1:
Placing stop-loss orders to trade a breakout identified with trend lines.

Source: eSignal (www.esignal.com)

The appeal of using stop-loss entry orders is that you're able to trade the breakout without any further action on your part. Breakouts can occur in the blink of an eye. Just when you thought the upper range level was going to hold and prices started to drift off, for example, they'll come roaring back and blow right through the breakout level.

Price moves like that can leave the most experienced traders caught like deer in the headlights. By the time they react, the break has already seen prices jump well beyond their desired entry level. Worse, by trying to trade at the market in a fast-moving breakout, you may miss your price and have to reenter the trade, by which time prices may have moved even farther in the direction of the break.

WARNING

When placing a stop-loss entry order to trade a breakout level, be aware of any major data or news events that are coming up. If your stop-loss entry order is triggered as a result of a news event, the execution rate on the order could be subject to slippage, which may reduce much of the gains from getting in on the breakout.

Trading the retest of a breakout level

The other way to trade a breakout is after the break has occurred. You may not have noticed the significance of a particular technical level, or you may not have left orders in overnight to exploit a break. You turn on your computer the next morning to discover that prices have jumped higher overnight and feel like you've missed the boat. But you *may* still get a chance to trade the breakout if prices return to retest the breakout level.

A *retest* refers to prices reversing direction after a break and returning to the breakout level to see whether it will hold. In the case of a break to the upside, for example, after the initial wave of buying has run its course, prices may stall and trigger very short-term profit-taking selling. The tendency is for prices to return to the breakout level, which should now act as support and attract buying interest.

TIP

You can use these retests to establish a position in the direction of the breakout, in this case getting long on the pullback. Figure 10-1 shows where you could have bought on the retest of the break higher in AUD/USD. Note that prices did not make it exactly back to the breakout level. When trying to get in on a retest, you may consider allowing for a margin of error in case the exact level is not retested. You can also consider using a strategy of averaging into a position, discussed earlier in this chapter, to establish a position on any pullbacks following a breakout. Here the averaging range would be between current prices and the break level.

REMEMBER

Earlier we say that you *may* get the chance to buy/sell a retest of a breakout level. The reason is that not every breakout sees prices return to retest the break level. Some retests may retrace only a portion of the breakout move, stopping short of retesting the exact break level, which is typically a good sign that the break is for real and will continue. Other breakouts never look back and just keep going.

But to the extent that it's a common-enough phenomenon, you still need to be aware of and anticipate that prices may return to the breakout level. From a technical perspective, if prices do retest the breakout level, and the level holds, it's a strong sign that the breakout is valid because market interest is entering there in the direction of the break.

Guarding against false breaks

Breakouts are relatively common events in currency trading, especially in the very short-term. But not every breakout is sustained. When prices break through key support or resistance levels, but then stop and reverse course and ultimately move back through the break level, it's called a *false break.*

WARNING

There's no way to tell whether any given breakout is going to turn out to be a false break except in hindsight. To protect against false breaks (as well as maintaining trading discipline and sound risk management), you also need to follow up your stop-loss entry with a contingent stop-loss exit order to close out the position if the market reverses course.

Although there's no surefire way to tell whether a breakout is a false break or a valid one that you should trade, here are a few points to keep in mind:

>> **Time frame of the breakout level:** The shorter the time frame you're looking at, the greater the potential for a false break. The break of a price range on an hourly chart may trigger stop losses only from short-term intraday traders. But the break of a daily price range dating back several weeks is likely to spark greater interest from the market, especially systematic models.

>> **Significance of the price level:** The more important the price level that's broken, the more likely it is to provoke a market response and to be sustained. A break of a three-month daily trend line is more likely to trigger a market response than the break of recent hourly highs/lows.

>> **Duration of the break:** The longer the breakout level is held, the more likely the breakout is to be valid. Many false breaks are reversed in a matter of minutes. An hourly closing price beyond the break level increases confidence that it's a valid breakout, and a daily close beyond confirms it.

>> **Currency pair volatility:** Relatively volatile currency pairs, such as GBP/USD and USD/CHF, are more prone to false breaks than others, especially in short-term time frames. Look for confirmation in bigger pairs, like EUR/USD and USD/JPY. If they're pressing against similar price levels, the less-liquid pairs could be leading the way.

>> **Fundamental events and news:** What's the fundamental reason for the breakout? Did someone say something? Have major market expectations on monetary policy, for example, been disappointed or surprised? Sustained breakouts tend to have a fundamental catalyst behind them — a significant piece of news that has altered the market's outlook. If the news is relatively minor or not entirely "new" news, it increases the chances it's a false break.

REMEMBER

Trading breakouts is a relatively aggressive trading strategy and is certainly not without risks. Until you've gained some experience in the forex market, you're probably better off focusing only on breaks of levels identified by trend-line analysis in longer time frames, such as daily charts, or breaks of longer-term price levels, like daily or weekly highs/lows. They may not occur as frequently, but they'll tend to be more reliable.

Making the Trade Correctly

When using an online trading platform, entering a position is as easy as making a few simple mouse clicks. At the same time, the simplicity and speed of online trading platforms make those simple mouse clicks a done deal that puts your trading capital at risk.

REMEMBER

That's why it's important to understand from the get-go that any action you take on a trading platform is your responsibility. You may have meant to click Buy instead of Sell, but no one knows for sure except you.

TIP

If you do make a mistake, correct it as soon as you discover and confirm it. Don't try to trade your way out of it. Don't try to manage it. Don't start rationalizing that it may work out anyway. No trader is error-proof, and you're bound to make a mistake someday. Just cover the error and get your position back to what you want it to be. Covering errors immediately is one of the few hard-and-fast rules we subscribe to in trading any market.

Buying and selling online

We take you through the basic steps of making a trade online in Chapter 4, but here we aim to clue you in to some of the human and technical aspects common to online trading.

Most every online trading brokerage now provides for click-and-deal trade execution. *Click and deal* refers to trading on the current market price by clicking either the Buy button or the Sell button in the trading platform. Before you can click and deal, you have to do the following:

1. **Select the right currency pair.**

   This may sound silly, but make sure you've selected the currency pair that you actually want to make a trade in. When the market gets hectic, and you're switching between your charts and the trading platform, you could easily mistake EUR/USD for EUR/CHF if you're not careful. This can also happen when different currency pairs are trading around similar price levels. If EUR/USD is trading at 30/33 and USD/JPY is trading at 31/34, it's easy to home in on the price and overlook the big figures, which would tell you you're in the wrong pair.

2. **Select the correct trade amount.**

   Make sure you've specified the correct amount you want to trade. Different platforms have different ways of inputting the trade amount. Some use radio buttons, others use scroll-down menus, and others allow you to type the amount manually. When the trading is fast and furious, make sure your selection has been properly registered on the platform. Some trading platforms allow you to customize your default trade sizes in advance, so you're able to simply click and deal on the currency pair of your choice.

3. **Double-check your selections.**

REMEMBER

   This is your money; be certain now or be sorry later. In case you think input errors can't happen to you, think about the equity trader at a New York investment bank who meant to sell 10 million shares of a stock but ended up entering 10 *billion*. By the time the trade was stopped, the system had sold several hundred million shares. Ouch!

4. **Click Buy or Sell.**

   Be sure you know which side of the price you want to deal on. If you want to buy, you'll need to click the higher price — the trading platform's offer. If you want to sell, you'll have to click the lower price — the platform's bid. Most platforms have labeled the sides of the prices from the user's perspective, so the bid side will be labeled Sell, and the offer side will be labeled Buy.

After you've clicked Buy or Sell, the trading platform will confirm whether your trade went through successfully, usually within a second or less. If your trade request went through, you'll receive a confirmation from the platform. Double-check your position, and make sure it's what you want it to be.

If the trading price changed before your request was received, you'll receive a response indicating "trade failed," "rates changed," "price not available," or something along those lines. You then need to repeat the steps to make another trade attempt.

Attempts to trade at the market can sometimes fail in very fast-moving markets when prices are adjusting quickly, like after a data release or break of a key technical level or price point. Part of this stems from the *latency effect* of trading over the internet, which refers to time lags between the platform price reaching your computer and your trade request reaching the platform's server.

TIP

If you're continually getting failed trade responses, it may be due to the speed of your internet connection, which is preventing your trade requests from getting to the brokerage trading platform in a timely way or delaying the incoming prices you're seeing so that they're always behind the real market. For more on how to optimize your trading on your smartphone or tablet, turn to Chapter 4.

REMEMBER

Whatever the outcome of your trade request, you need to be sure you've received a response from the trading platform. If you have not gotten a response back after more than a few seconds, you need to call your broker immediately and confirm the status of the trade request. The deal may have gone through, but confirmations may be delayed due to processor slowness. Or the trade may have never been received by the trading platform because your computer lost its internet connection.

Placing your orders

REMEMBER

Orders are critical trading tools in the forex market. Think of them as trades waiting to happen because that's exactly what they are. If you enter an order, and subsequent price action triggers its execution, you're in the market. So you need to be as careful as you are thorough, if not more so, when placing your orders in the market.

TIP

We go over the different types of orders and how they're used in Chapter 4. Here are some additional important tips to keep in mind when placing and managing your orders:

>> **Input your orders correctly.** Make sure you've correctly specified the currency pair, order type, amount, and price. Most trading platforms are designed to reject an order that is obviously wrong, such as a stop-loss order to buy at a price below the current market, and will prompt you to correct it. But other errors, such as a wrong big figure on the order price, can be accepted and end up being your problem. Double-check your order after it has been accepted by the trading platform. If it's wrong, edit it or cancel it and start again.

>> **Note the expiration of your orders.** Order expirations are typically good-'til-cancelled (GTC), where the order remains active until *you* cancel it, or good until the end of the day (EOD), which means that the order automatically expires at the end of the trading day (5 p.m. Eastern time [ET]). If you had an intraday position with a stop-loss good until EOD, and you later decided to hold the position overnight, you'd need to revise the expiration. GTC orders will expire on some trading platforms after an extended period of time, such as 90 days, so be clear on your broker's policy.

» **Cancel unwanted orders.** Some trading platforms allow orders to be *associated with a position,* meaning that the order will remain valid as long as the position is open. Such *position orders* will also usually adjust the order amount if you increase or reduce the associated position. Other orders are *independent of positions,* so even if you close out your position, the independent orders will remain active. Make sure you understand the difference between the two types, and remember to cancel any independent orders if you close the position they were based on, such as take profits, stop losses, or OCO. (OCO stands for "one order cancels other." This is the act of placing two simultaneous orders, and in the event one order is triggered, the other is automatically cancelled.)

Chapter **11**

Managing the Trade

So, you've pulled the trigger and opened up the position, and now you're in the market. Time to sit back and let the market do its thing, right? Not so fast, amigo. The forex market isn't a roulette wheel where you place your bets, watch the wheel spin, and simply take the results. It's a dynamic, fluid environment where new information and price developments create new opportunities and alter previous expectations. Actively managing a trade when you're in it is just as important as the decision-making that went into establishing the position in the first place.

We hope you'll take to heart our recommendations about always trading with a plan — identifying in advance where to enter and where to exit every trade, on both a stop-loss and take-profit basis. (We go into more detail about trading strategies in Chapter 10 and the Appendix. Don't forget tax considerations in Chapter 12.) Bottom line: You improve your overall chances of trading success and minimize the risks involved by thoroughly planning each trade before getting caught up in the emotions and noise of the market.

REMEMBER

Depending on the style of trading you're pursuing (short-term versus medium- to long-term) and overall market conditions (range-bound versus trending), you'll have either more or less to do when managing an open position:

>> If you're following a medium- to longer-term strategy, with generally wider stop-loss and take-profit parameters, you may prefer to go with the "set it and forget it" trade plan you've developed. But a lot can happen between the time

you open a trade and prices hitting one of your order levels, so staying on top of the market is still a good idea, even for longer-term trades.

» Shorter-term trading styles looking to capture intraday and even smaller price movements will necessarily have more frequent adjustments to overall trade strategies. We say *necessarily* because short-term price movements can be extremely rapid as well as short lived. If your trade strategy is designed to capture only smaller price shifts — say, on the order of 30 to 50 pips — you'll need to be more proactive in guarding against short-term reversals of 15 to 25 pips, which constitute nearly half of your expected upside.

On top of that, short-term price movements are the market noise that makes up larger price movements. There will be a lot more 30- to 50-point moves than 100- to 200-pip moves. If you're going after the more frequent fluctuations, you'll have to be more nimble when it comes to adjusting to incoming news and price developments.

Monitoring the Market While Your Trade Is Active

No matter which trading style you follow, it'll pay to keep up with market news and price developments while your trade is active. Unexpected news that impacts your position may come into the market at any time. News is news; by definition, you couldn't have accounted for it in your trading plan, so fresh news may require making changes to your trading plan.

REMEMBER

The starting point for any trading plan is determining how much you're prepared to risk, which is ultimately the result of the size of the position and the pip distance to the stop-loss point. When we talk about making changes to the trading plan, we're referring only to reducing the overall risk of the trade, by taking profit (full or partial) or moving the stop loss in the direction of the trade. The idea is to be fluid and dynamic in one direction only: taking profit and reducing risk. Keep your ultimate stop-out point where you decided it should go before you entered the trade, when your emotions weren't in play.

Following the market with rate alerts

TIP

One way to follow the market from a distance is to set rate alerts from either your charting system or your trading platform. A *rate alert* is an electronic message that alerts you when a price you've specified is touched by the market in a currency pair you specify. Rate alerts are a great way to keep tabs on the market's progress.

Rate alerts on charting systems usually have the capability of alerting you to price developments only while you're logged on to your computer or using your smartphone or tablet and the charting service. With charting systems, you're able to work on other tasks on your computer and keep the charting system minimized or in the background, which means you can use these at your job. If your requested price level is hit by the market, the chart system will typically start beeping or flashing and send a pop-up message.

Some forex brokers, including FOREX.com, can send rate alerts via email and text message direct to your smartphone. Many brokers now also have a large presence on Twitter and Facebook, so it's worth following your broker on social networks as well.

WARNING

Rate alerts are a convenient way to follow the market remotely, but they don't take the place of live orders and should never be substituted for stop-loss orders. By the time you respond to a rate alert and log on to the trading platform or call your broker's trading desk, prices may have moved well beyond your desired stop-out level, leaving you with a larger loss than you anticipated. Rate alerts are a nice little extra service, but only orders represent obligations on the part of your broker to take an action in the market for your account.

Staying alert for news and data developments

REMEMBER

Every trade strategy needs to take into account upcoming news and data events before the position is opened. Ideally, you should be aware of all data reports and events scheduled to occur during the anticipated time horizon of your trade strategy. You should also have a good understanding of what the market is expecting in terms of event outcomes and anticipate how the market is likely to react.

For instance, if the Fed chair is scheduled to deliver remarks on the economy or the monetary policy outlook, find out what recent comments have been like. Are they currently leaning hawkish or dovish? If it's an economic data release, make sure you understand what the report covers and what it means for the market's current expectations. At the minimum, be sure you know what the consensus expectations are for the report and what the data series has been indicating recently.

TIP

It's often said that the market's reaction to news and data is more important than the news or data itself. But you can't properly interpret the market's reaction if you don't have a grasp on what the news means in the first place. (See Chapter 7 for a detailed look at economic reports and Chapter 5 for major fundamental drivers and how the market interprets them.)

The other reason to stay alert for news while your trade is active is that many trade strategies are based on fundamental data and trends. If your trade rationale is reliant on certain data or event expectations, you need to be especially alert for upcoming reports on those themes.

Part of your determination to go short EUR/USD, for instance, may be based on the view that Eurozone inflation pressures are receding, suggesting lower Eurozone interest rates ahead. If the next day's Eurozone consumer price index (CPI) report confirms your view, the fundamental basis for maintaining the strategy is reinforced. You may then consider whether to increase your take-profit objective depending on the market's reaction. By the same token, if the CPI report comes out unexpectedly high, the fundamental basis for your trade is seriously undermined and serves as a clue to exit the trade earlier than you originally planned. There's no sense hanging on until the bitter end if your trade rationale has already been knocked down. You may even consider reversing your position in light of the new data.

REMEMBER

Speculating based on expected event or data outcomes is perfectly okay. It becomes a problem only if you maintain the trade even after the data/event outcome has come out against your expectations and strategy. Always relate incoming news and data back to the original reason for your trade and be prepared to adapt your trade strategy accordingly.

Keeping an eye on other financial markets

Forex markets function alongside other major financial markets, such as stocks, bonds, and commodities. Although these financial markets have seen higher long-term correlations with forex in recent years, short-term correlations are far less reliable.

But there are still important fundamental and psychological relationships between other markets and currencies, especially the U.S. dollar. In that sense, we look to developments in other financial markets to see whether they confirm or contradict price moves in the dollar pairs. So, even though there may not be a statistically reliable basis on which to trade currencies based on movements in other financial markets, you'll be a step ahead if you keep an eye on the following other markets.

U.S. Treasury yields

U.S. government bond yields are a good indicator of the overall direction of U.S. interest rates and expectations. We focus on the benchmark ten-year Treasury-note yield as the main interest rate to monitor. We also keep an eye on shorter-term rates, like three-month T-bills and two-year notes. Rising yields tend to be dollar positive, and falling yields tend to be negative for the dollar. If yields are rising but the dollar isn't, it suggests that other factors are at work keeping the dollar down and that dollar bulls should be cautious. If yields are falling and the dollar is falling, too, you're getting confirmation from the bond market of a negative U.S. dollar environment — lower interest rates.

TIP

Make sure you understand the reason for the bond yield's movements, because it can suggest different interpretations. If it's based on interest-rate expectations — due to data or Fed comments, for instance — it's more likely to reflect overall dollar direction. If it's due to market uncertainty and a flight to quality — due to European debt concerns, for example — the impact on the U.S. dollar may be more positive. The larger the change in yields, the more important is the message that's coming from the bond market. Yield changes of more than 5 basis points (1/100 of a percent) should get your attention.

Gold and silver prices

Precious metals like gold and silver are typically viewed as hedges against inflation and safe-haven investments in times of financial market uncertainty. In recent years, gold and silver have seen heightened demand as alternatives to the major currencies, most especially the U.S. dollar but also the euro, as the European debt crisis has threatened the single currency. As such, gold and silver prices tend to move in the opposite direction of the U.S. dollar overall (inverse correlation), but the short-term correlations are trickier. Gold and silver are relatively illiquid markets and mostly take their cues from the larger forex market, but the metals are no stranger to their own market-specific gyrations, typically based on breaks of technical levels.

TIP

Look for confirmation of the U.S. dollar direction in gold and silver prices. If the dollar is rallying and the metals are falling, for instance, it's a good sign that the dollar's gains are for real. If the dollar is rallying but gold is holding steady or even rising, the dollar's strength looks more suspect.

Oil

Oil is similar to the precious metals and other commodities in that it has a long-term inverse correlation to the U.S. dollar (dollar down/oil up and vice versa). But the same caveat also holds true — shorter-term correlations are less reliable, and oil is especially vulnerable to oil-specific supply/demand shocks. We would also note an *asymmetric bias* to the relationship between oil and the U.S. dollar. That means oil is likely to experience greater strength on a falling dollar than weakness on a rising dollar, if all else is equal.

We also like to look to oil price developments for what they suggest about interest-rate expectations and relative economic growth. Higher oil prices tend to increase inflation pressures, which may lead to higher interest rates. At the same time, higher oil prices tend to reduce economic growth by undermining personal consumption. Between the two, oil's impact on the growth outlook is more important due to the speed with which consumers react to changes in oil prices. Interest-rate changes take longer. The recent surge in emerging market nations' growth has also heightened global demand for oil, so oil increasingly functions as a barometer for overall global growth.

Stocks

Over the long term, such as over the last decade, there is very little correlation between stock markets and currencies. However, since the Global Financial Crisis of 2008–2009, there has been a stronger relationship between stocks and forex, especially the U.S. dollar. The relationship is best described as risk on/risk off (see Chapter 5 for more on risk sentiment), where stocks are considered risk-seeking assets and the dollar is viewed as the safe-haven asset, as investors buy USD to buy U.S. Treasury debt, the ultimate safe harbor.

In recent years, the risk-on/risk-off scenario has typically played out as follows: When the overall market environment is positive, investors embrace risk and buy stocks, reducing the demand for dollars, usually leading to dollar weakness. When the news turns bad, however, investors have dumped stocks and fled to the safety of U.S. Treasuries and the greenback. As long as financial travails plague the global economy, this relationship seems set. But when economic and financial conditions begin to improve to something resembling normalcy, we would expect the stocks/forex relationship to return to lower historical correlations.

Updating Your Trade Plan as Time Marches On

If you're like most traders, after you enter a position you're keenly aware of every single pip change in prices, at least as long as you're watching the market. Every little price change, and the attendant change in your unrealized profit and loss (P&L), evokes emotions ranging from joy to despair and everything in between. And that's to be expected. After all, at the end of the day, it's the P&L that matters, and pips are how that's measured.

But one element that tends to receive remarkably little attention from traders, at least on a conscious level, is the passage of time. Prices may seem to stand still for extended periods — when a currency pair may be stuck in a range (that is, it keeps trading back and forth over the same ground) — but time is constantly moving forward.

REMEMBER

Staying aware of time and its passing is an important skill for traders to develop. You know where the market price is now, so the real question is this: Where will the market price be in the future? As soon as you think of the future, it becomes a question of time: *When* will it be there? If you consider these questions as you formulate each trade strategy, you'll go a long way toward incorporating time into your overall trade planning. More important, you'll gain an intuitive appreciation of the importance of time in trading, and you'll find yourself asking *when* as often as *why* or *where.*

On the most concrete level, as time progresses, it brings with it routine daily events, such as option expirations and the daily fixings, to name just two. These are specific time periods where traders can reasonably expect a flurry of activity, though it doesn't always materialize. (We run through the series of regular trading-day time events in Chapter 2.)

Time's passing also brings you nearer to scheduled news or data events. The *pricing in* of market expectations for major events occurs in the hours and days ahead of the event or data release. As the release time draws closer, anticipative speculation generally declines, and price movements can become more erratic as traders take to the sidelines ahead of the release. Prices may chop around more but ultimately not go anywhere. All these market reactions are as much the result of time as they are of the event itself.

On a more objective level, as time progresses, it can add significance to, or detract significance from, price movements that have already occurred, frequently providing trading signals as a result. For instance, the failure of prices to make an hourly close below a break of trend-line support suggests that it may be a false break and that prices are likely to rebound higher. But if the break occurred at 10:12 eastern time (ET), for instance, you won't know until the next hourly close in 48 minutes. Potentially more significant trading signals are generated from longer time periods, such as a daily close above long-term trend-line resistance or a prior daily high.

Trend lines move over time

REMEMBER

If you're basing your trading strategies on trend-line analysis, you need to be aware that price levels derived from trend lines will change depending on the slope of the trend line. The *slope* of a trend line refers to the angle of a trend line relative to a horizontal line. The steeper the slope of the trend line, the more the relevant price level will change over time; the shallower the slope, the more gradually the price levels will change with time.

Figure 11-1 gives you a good idea of how short-term price levels based on a 15-minute trend line will shift over the course of just a few hours. Note how steeply the trend line is sloping upward. For prices to continue to move higher in line with this trend line, they must stay above the trend line as it rises over time, suggesting price gains of 10 to 15 pips per hour are needed.

Source: eSignal (www.esignal.com)

FIGURE 11-1:
Trend-line levels can change over time, depending on their slope.

TIP

Using your charting system, you can pinpoint relatively accurately where prices must be in the future for the trend line to remain active as a support/resistance level. To do this, slide the cursor along the trend line, and note the time that appears on the horizontal axis at the bottom of the chart.

The same applies with longer-term charts, but the price shifts are typically less pronounced, meaning an hourly trend line may see levels adjust by 10 to 15 pips every 6 to 12 hours, and daily charts may see levels shift by 10 to 30 pips over a few days. But there are no concrete rules on this; it all depends on the slope of the trend line.

REMEMBER

No matter what time frame you're trading, be sure to factor in the shifting levels of trend lines, if they're part of your trade strategy. You may need to adjust your order levels accordingly. In particular, consider the following:

>> **Short-term and overnight positions:** Consider where trend-line support or resistance will be over the next 6 to 12 hours, when your position is still active but you may not be able to actively follow the market. You may want to use a trailing stop as a proxy for changes in trend-line-based support/resistance levels.

>> **Limit-entry orders:** If your limit buying/selling order is based on a sloping trend line, periodically adjust your order so that it's still in play according to changes in the trend line. You may miss a trade entry if the trend line is eventually touched, but in the meantime, its level has shifted away from where you first placed the order.

>> **Breakouts:** A significant trend line that looks to be a mile away one week may suddenly be within striking distance in the following week or two weeks, substantially altering the market's outlook. Alternatively, the market may be focused on a price high/low as a breakout trigger, when a sloping trend line touching that high/low may actually be the catalyst for a breakout.

Impending events may require trade plan adjustments

REMEMBER

As you develop your trading plan, we strongly recommend that you look ahead to see what data and events are scheduled during the expected life of the trade. If you follow that simple advice, you strongly reduce the chances of having your trade strategy upset by largely predictable events. More important, you'll be able to anticipate likely catalysts for price shifts, which will give you greater insight into subsequent price movements. Forewarned is forearmed.

TIP

If you've entered into a trade strategy based on an upcoming event — an expected weak U.S. data report, for instance — and the market has cooperated and priced in a lower U.S. dollar before the report is released, you may be looking at a profitable position before the data is even released. As the release time draws near, you may consider taking some profit off the table and holding on to the remaining partial position.

Consider the possible outcomes. If the data comes in negative for the U.S. dollar, and the market reacts by selling the U.S. dollar, you're still in the partial position to gain from further dollar weakness. But what if the data comes in stronger than expected? Or what if the data comes in weak as expected, but the market takes profit on short-dollar positions made in advance, in a "sell-the-rumor/buy-the-fact" reaction? You've protected your profit and taken some money out of the market before the event ever transpired. Now, that's called playing the market!

REMEMBER

In the preceding scenario, we intentionally depict a short trade to remind you that being short is as common as being long in currency trading. You may be more familiar with "Buy the rumor, sell the fact." We just want to make sure you know that it works both ways.

Before major data and events, the market also frequently goes into a sideways holding pattern. The event speculators have all put on their positions, and the rest of the market is waiting for the data to decide how to react. These holding patterns can develop hours or days in advance, depending on what event is coming. Especially if you're trading from a short-term perspective, be prepared for these doldrums and consider whether riding through them is worthwhile.

Updating Order Levels as Prices Progress

Just because you've got a well-developed and considered trade plan doesn't mean it has to be carved in stone. Well, at least the ultimate stop-loss exit should be carved in stone. But when you're in a position, and the market is moving in your favor, it's important to be flexible in adjusting take-profit targets and amending stop-loss orders to protect your profits.

TIP

The key to being flexible in this regard is also being prudent — don't adjust your take-profit targets without also adjusting your stop-loss order in the same direction. If you're long, and you raise your take profit, raise your stop loss too. If you're short, and you lower your take profit, lower your stop-loss order as well.

Increasing take-profit targets

You've put together a well-developed trade strategy ahead of your trade, as we've recommended, so now that you're in the trade, why would you change your take-profit objective? That's a very good question, and you'd better make sure you have a very good answer, because we've also touted the virtues of not tampering with a trade plan after the position is opened.

REMEMBER

So what constitutes a very good reason to extend your take-profit objective? Keep an eye out for the following events to consider extending your take-profit targets:

>> **Major new information:** More likely than not, the new information will have to come out of left field. If it was a scheduled event, like a data report or speech, the market speculation surrounding it would have sopped up all the interest and muted its impact. *Major* means it has to come from the very top echelons of decision-making, like the Fed chairman, the European Central

Bank (ECB) president, or other central bank chiefs; the U.S. Treasury secretary; or, increasingly, China. Surprise interest-rate changes or policy shifts are always candidates. The more at odds the information is with current market expectations, the better the chances that it will generate an extensive price move.

>> **Thinner-than-usual liquidity:** Reduced liquidity conditions can provoke more extensive price movements than would otherwise occur, because fewer market participants are involved to absorb the price shocks. Reduced liquidity is most evident during national holidays, seasonal periods (late summer, Christmas/New Year's), end of month, end of quarter, and certain Fridays.

>> **Breaks of major technical levels:** Trend lines dating back several months or years, Fibonacci retracement levels of major recent directional moves, and recent extreme highs and lows are likely to trigger larger-than-normal price movements.

>> **The currency pair:** The more illiquid and volatile the currency pair you're trading, the greater the chances for an extreme move. GBP and JPY are the most common culprits among the majors, and the commodity currencies (AUD, CAD, NZD, and ZAR, or South African rand; see Chapter 9) are also candidates.

WARNING

As you can see, the list is pretty short, and there may be only a dozen or so events in the course of a year that warrant altering your trade plan. Be careful about getting caught up in the day-to-day noise and routinely extending your profit targets — it undermines trading discipline and the basis for your trade strategy.

Tightening stop-loss orders to protect profits

We're generally reluctant to extend our take-profit objectives unless there are significant grounds to do so (see the preceding section) or we're using a trailing stop loss. But when it comes to protecting profits, we're much more comfortable about adjusting stop losses to lock in gains. When you've got a profit in the market, taking steps to protect it is always a smart move.

TIP

When formulating your overall trade plan, always consider what price levels need to be surpassed to justify moving your stop loss. If it happens in the market, you'll be ready and know exactly what to do.

We like to focus on hourly and daily trend-line levels, highs/lows, and breaks of Fibonacci retracement levels (see Chapter 6). When these technical support/resistance points are exceeded, it's an indication that the market has seen fit to move prices into a new level in the overall direction of the trade. When that happens, consider moving your stop-loss order to levels just inside the broken technical level. If the market has second thoughts about sustaining the break, your adjusted stop will then take you out of the trade.

For example, say you're long GBP/USD at 1.5250, your original stop loss is at 1.5180 below, and your take-profit objective is above at 1.5380. Also above is resistance from yesterday's high at 1.5335. If that level is surpassed, consider raising your stop loss to break even (where you entered, at 1.5250) at the minimum. To more aggressively protect profits, you may raise the stop further to 1.5315 or 1.5325, locking in 65 to 75 pips minimum, on the basis that 1.5335 should now act as support.

WARNING

The risk with adjusting stops too aggressively is that the market may come back to test the break level (1.5335, in this example), triggering your adjusted stop loss if it's too close, and then go on to make fresh gains. But the trade-off in that situation is between something and more of something, or potentially nothing and more of nothing. We prefer to have something to show for our efforts.

TIP

Another way to lock in profits in a more dynamic fashion is by using a trailing stop-loss order (see Chapter 4). After a technical level in the direction of your trade is overcome, similar to the preceding example, you may consider instituting a trailing stop to replace your fixed stop-loss order. Set the trailing distance to account for the distance between the current market and the other side of the technical break level, possibly allowing for a margin of error in case the break level is retested.

> » Reporting gains and losses in your taxes
>
> » Getting the scoop on notices, forms, and deductions
>
> » Being aware of specific currency tax details

Chapter **12**

Tax Considerations

After all the research, monitoring, and fancy ins and outs, you finally make a profit with your currency trades (woo-hoo!), but don't celebrate yet. You have one more hurdle before you pop the champagne: taxes (cue the groans and shrieks). Understanding how this tax stuff works is important now since (as you know), it's not what you make, but rather what you keep, that matters. Keeping more of the fruits of your trading labor is the final consideration in your trading process.

REMEMBER

Even though taxes are treated at the "tail end" of the trading process, it's important to discuss your trading goals and activities with your tax consultant *before* you embark on your currency trading activities. You'll be glad you did.

REMEMBER

Keep in mind that this chapter isn't meant to be comprehensive. For a fuller treatment of personal taxes, you should check with your personal tax advisor and get the publications referenced in this chapter by either visiting the Internal Revenue Service (IRS) website at www.irs.gov or calling the IRS publications department at 800-829-3676. Check out the resources at the end of the chapter too.

Determining Whether You Have Trader Tax Status

Are you a serious trader looking at this stuff as a "professional" trader, or are you a "casual" trader doing this as a "side activity" alongside gardening and backgammon? According to the IRS, this matters in the approach you take because each one is distinctly different from a tax perspective.

Most of the folks reading this book probably fall into the category of the casual trader — at least initially. If you're dedicated to your trading success, you may leave this category. In the meanwhile, the pursuit of trading is treated as a sideline or part-time activity.

Trader tax status (TTS) comes with very significant tax benefits, but it's more difficult to qualify for. The IRS looks at several factors to determine whether you qualify for TTS (be sure to discuss the details with your tax advisor if you're serious in your trading pursuits):

» **Frequency:** Are you trading on at least 75 percent of available trading days? In other words, are you an active trader during four of five trading days available in a typical workweek?

» **Substantial volume:** There is now a definable quantity to help determine that you're a professional trader, and that is the volume (or number) of trades you make. According to a tax court case (the Poppe tax case), a professional trader achieved the TTS status because he made an average of 15 trades per week, 60 trades per month, and 720 trades (or more) per year.

» **Average holding period:** Each trade is held open for less than 31 days. This may not be a hard-and-fast rule, but greater trading frequency (that is, shorter holding periods) shows that you're an active trader.

» **Continuity:** The trader shows continuous trading.

» **Formal business evidence:** The trader conducts his activity as a formal business complete with trading equipment (laptop, monitor, and so on) and a dedicated home office.

» **Primary source of income:** The trader intends/attempts to make a living with TTS activity.

If you do qualify for Trader Tax Status (TTS), then take full advantage of it because this status qualifies you for a wide variety of deductions and tax strategies that casual or unprofessional traders cannot take advantage of. Having this status means that the IRS recognizes that your activity is a professional business pursuit.

When you run a business, many expenses may qualify as deductions that aren't allowed if the same transaction is a personal expense. Here is a partial listing of tax benefits:

>> **Home office deduction:** Because TTS can help establish your activity as a business, you have a real opportunity to set up a legitimate home office that is a powerful tax benefit worth potentially thousands of dollars. You can deduct a percentage of rent or mortgage interest, utilities, depreciation, and more. See IRS Publication 587 (www.irs.gov/publications/p587) on how to claim home office deductions.

>> **Equipment:** If you use desktop computers, laptops, monitors, and so forth, you can either use depreciation deductions or use Section 179 to outright expense these assets. (See www.irs.gov/publications/p946 for more information.)

>> **Trading education:** You can write off programs, trading courses, trading software, and so on.

>> **Internet expenses:** You can deduct internet expenses that are tied to your trading activities.

>> **Retirement plan benefits:** As a business, you can qualify for tax-favored small business retirement plans.

TIP

If you're serious about tax-saving strategies in professional trading activities (such as TTS), check out the book *Green's 2021 Trader Tax Guide* by Robert A. Green, CPA (published by Green & Company, Inc.). Find out more at greentradertax.com. Additional resources for tax traders appear later in this chapter.

WARNING

Even though the TTS trader can potentially deduct far more than $3,000 in losses in a given year, keep in mind that it isn't always a great idea. Say that you had a huge net loss in your TTS trading business of $100,000 (gasp!). You could certainly take a deduction of $100,000 in that year, and if you had minimal income in the rest of your tax situation, that loss would likely qualify you to pay no income taxes that year. Sounds good . . . but what if you needed only half of that loss to achieve the same effect of no taxes? Now what? That huge tax loss can't be spread out over multiple years; it would need to be taken in that single given year. Such an event means that the tax loss wasn't optimized to offset other income in subsequent years.

Understanding Ordinary Income, Capital Gains, and Capital Losses

The following sections tell you what you need to know about the tax implications you face when you start currency trading. It's good to know in advance the basics on ordinary income, capital gains, and capital losses because they may affect your investing strategy and your long-term wealth-building plans.

Investigating ordinary income

Your profit can be taxed at the same rate as wages or interest — at your full, regular tax rate. If your tax bracket is 28 percent, for example, that's the rate at which your ordinary income investment profit is taxed. Two types of investment profits get taxed as ordinary income: dividends and short-term capital gains. Check out IRS Publication 550, "Investment Income and Expenses," for more information at www.irs.gov/publications/p550.)

Dividends

For currency traders, dividends aren't a typical source of income. However, you should be diversified and have some of your investable money in other vehicles such as dividend-paying stocks.

Keep in mind that dividends paid from stocks and stock-related exchange-traded funds (ETFs) tend to be qualified dividends, which are taxed at a lower rate than nonqualified dividends. A *qualified dividend* is a dividend that receives preferential tax treatment versus other types of dividends. Qualified dividends are taxed at a lower rate than unqualified dividends or interest.

Short-term capital gains

If you do generate gains with your currency trades, this is the most common form that gain will likely take. Because currency trades are opened and closed within days, weeks, or months, they will likely be short-term gains, and these gains are taxed as ordinary income, which is the highest tax rate.

REMEMBER

The period of time for a short-term capital gain is one year or less. To calculate the time, you use the *trade date* (or *date of execution*). This is the date on which you executed the order, not the settlement date. If the sale date is one year or less after the trade date, it's considered a short-term capital gain. However, if these gains occur in a tax-sheltered plan, such as a 401(k) or an IRA, no tax is triggered. (Find out more about retirement accounts and taxes later in this chapter.)

Looking at long-term capital gains

Long-term capital gains are usually much better for you than ordinary income or short-term gains as far as taxes are concerned. The tax laws reward patient investors and speculators. After you've held the investment vehicle or currency vehicle for at least a year and a day (what a difference a day makes!), your tax rate on that gain is lower. Get more information on capital gains in IRS Publication 550 (www.irs.gov/publications/p550). Fortunately, you can time stock sales, so always consider pushing back the sale date (if possible) to take advantage of the lesser capital gains tax.

REMEMBER

You can control how you manage the tax burden from your trading profits. Gains are taxable only if a sale actually takes place (in other words, only if the gain is "realized"). If, for example, you own a currency ETF called CashBucks ETF that goes from $12 per share to $50, that $38 appreciation isn't subject to taxation unless you actually sell it. Until you sell, that gain is "unrealized." Time your sale carefully and hold on to your investment vehicle for at least a year and a day (to make the gains long-term) to minimize the amount of tax you have to pay on it.

TIP

When you buy your investment vehicle, record the date of purchase and the *cost basis* (the purchase price plus any ancillary charges, such as commissions). This information is very important come tax time should you decide to sell. The date of purchase (also known as the *date of execution*) helps establish the *holding period* (how long you own the vehicle) that determines whether your gains are considered short-term or long-term.

Say you buy 100 shares of CashBucks ETF at $18 and pay a commission of $5. Your cost basis is $1,805 (100 shares times $18 plus $5 commission). If you sell at $55 per share and pay a $9 commission, the total sale amount is $5,491 (100 shares times $55 less $9 commission). If this sale occurs less than a year after the purchase, it's a short-term gain. In the 28 percent tax bracket, the short-term gain of $3,686 ($5,491 − $1,805) is also taxed at 28 percent (the same as ordinary income). As a short-term transaction at the 28 percent tax rate, the tax is $1,032 ($3,686 multiplied by 28 percent). At that moment you say "Gee, my Uncle Sam shouldn't get that much. I think I'll wait a little longer." You hold onto the stock for more than a year to achieve the status of long-term capital gains. How does that change the tax?

REMEMBER

Long-term capital gains are taxed at a more favorable rate than ordinary income. To qualify for long-term capital gains treatment, you must hold the investment for more than one year (in other words, for at least one year and one day).

For anyone in the 28 percent tax bracket or higher, the long-term capital gains rate of 15 percent applies. In this case, the tax is $553 ($3,686 multiplied by 15 percent), resulting in a tax savings to you of $479 ($1,032 less $553). Okay, it's not a fortune, but it's a good chunk of change (and of course you can invest it and make more). Because, at the end of the day, it's about keeping more of your hard-earned money.

Capital gains taxes *can* be lower than the tax on ordinary income, but they aren't higher. If, for example, you're in the 15 percent tax bracket for ordinary income and you have a long-term capital gain that would normally bump you up to the 28 percent tax bracket, the gain is taxed at your lower rate of 15 percent instead of a higher capital gains rate. Check with your tax advisor on a regular basis because this rule could change due to new tax laws.

REMEMBER

Don't automatically sell your investment just because it qualifies for long-term capital gains treatment, even if the sale eases your tax bill. If it is doing well and it continues to achieve your goals, then hold on. The long-term capital gains rate doesn't go down the longer you hold it. Keep it growing if possible.

Coping with capital losses

Ever think that having losses could have a bright side? Perhaps the only real positive regarding losses in your portfolio is that they can reduce your taxes. A *capital loss* means that you lost money on your investments. This amount is generally deductible on your tax return, and you can claim the realized loss on either long-term or short-term investments. This loss can go against your other income and lower your overall tax.

Say you bought a currency ETF called ZeroCash ETF for a total purchase price of $2,800 and sold it later for a total sale amount of $700. Your tax-deductible capital loss would be $2,100.

REMEMBER

For regular, "casual" currency traders, there is a string attached — the string is the same for most speculators and investors. It is that deducting investment losses on your tax return is strictly limited to a maximum loss per taxable year of only $3,000. On the bright side, though, any excess loss isn't really lost — you can carry it forward to the next year. If you have net investment losses on your trades of $5,000 in 2021, you can deduct $3,000 in tax year 2021 and carry the remaining $2,000 loss forward to tax year 2022 and claim that deductible loss of $2,000 on your 2022 tax return. That $2,000 loss can be used to offset any potential gains you may realize in 2022. Using tax software should make this task easy.

Before you can deduct any losses, you must first use them to offset any capital gains. If you realize long-term capital gains of $4,000 in Stock A and long-term capital losses of $3,300 in Stock B, then you have a net long-term capital gain of $700 ($4,000 gain less the offset of $3,300 loss). Whenever possible, see whether losses in your portfolio can be realized to offset any capital gains to reduce potential tax. IRS Publication 550 (www.irs.gov/publications/p550) includes information for investors on capital gains and losses.

TIP

Here's your best strategy: Whenever possible, keep losses on a short-term basis and push your gains into long-term capital gains status. If a transaction can't be tax-free, at the very least try to defer the tax to keep your money working for you. This is loosely based on the general principle of "cut your losers and let your winners run," which, when you look under the hood, is sound tax-wise too.

Evaluating scenarios of gains and losses

Of course, any investor can come up with hundreds of possible gains-and-losses scenarios. For example, you may wonder what happens if you sell part of your holdings now as a short-term capital loss and the remainder later as a long-term capital gain. You must look at each sale (or potential sale) methodically to calculate the gain or loss you would realize from it. Figuring out your gain or loss isn't that complicated. Here are some general rules to help you net out all your gains and losses:

>> **The net result is a short-term gain.** If, after all the plusses and minuses you have a short-term capital gain, it will be taxed as ordinary income (which is the same as other types of income such as W-2 wages and business income).

>> **The net result is a long-term gain.** If, after all the plusses and minuses you have a long-term capital gain, it will be taxed at the lower, more favorable tax rate. If, for example, you are in the 28 percent tax bracket, the gain will be taxed at 15 percent. Check with your tax advisor on changes here that may affect your taxes.

>> **The net result is a loss of $3,000 or less.** This amount is fully deductible against other income. If you're married filing separately, your deduction limit is $1,500.

>> **The net result is a loss that exceeds $3,000.** You can deduct only up to $3,000 in that tax year; the remainder goes forward to future tax years.

WARNING

Some people get the smart idea of "Hey! Why not sell my losing stock by December 31 to grab the short-term loss and just buy back the stock on January 2 so that I can have my cake and eat it, too?" Not so fast. The IRS puts the kibosh on maneuvers like that with something called the *wash-sale rule.* This rule states that if you sell a stock for a loss and buy it back within 30 days, the loss isn't valid because you didn't make any substantial investment change. The wash-sale rule applies only to losses. The way around the rule is simple: Wait at least 31 days before you buy that identical stock back again.

WARNING

Some people try to get around the wash-sale rule by doubling up on their stock position with the intention of selling half. Therefore, the IRS makes the 30-day rule cover both sides of the sale date. That way, an investor can't buy the identical stock within 30 days just before the sale and then realize a short-term loss for tax purposes.

Buckling Down and Paying Taxes to the IRS

Of course, you don't want to pay more taxes than you have to, but as the old cliché goes, "Don't let the tax tail wag the investment dog." You should make currency trades based on your profit-seeking strategy. Doing a trade or buying a particular investment vehicle has to make economic sense before the tax issues. After all, if paying the least amount of taxes is your main driver, then why invest or speculate at all? Seek your profits and build your wealth and prosperity, and you'll have the necessary funds to deal with the resulting tax bill. Just stay informed on tax laws to maximize your gains and minimize your losses. If you're paying a lot in taxes, then the logical inference is that you're successfully profiting in your trading pursuits.

TIP

Try to make tax planning second nature in your day-to-day activities. No, you don't need to bury your head in tax books and tally a blizzard of paperwork and tax projections. We simply mean that when you make a transaction, keep track using investment software or a spreadsheet so you know what to expect come tax time. The more organized your trading transactions are, the easier it will be at tax time and the better shot you'll have at minimizing the tax bite.

The following sections describe the tax forms you need to fill out, as well as some important rules to follow.

Tax notices

Most investors report their investment-related activities on their individual tax returns (Form 1040). The reports that you'll likely receive from brokers and other investment sources include the following:

>> **Brokerage and bank statements:** Monthly statements that you receive

TIP

Carefully review the last statement of the tax year in question (the December statement). It has cumulative "year-to-date" amounts for many key data points such as dividend income for the year and possibly realized gains and losses so that you can match your transactions to any and all 1099s you receive.

>> **Trade confirmations:** Documents to confirm that you bought or sold stock

>> **1099-DIV:** Reporting dividends paid to you

>> **1099-INT:** Reporting interest paid to you

>> **1099-B:** Reporting gross proceeds submitted to you from the sale of investments, such as stocks, options, ETFs, and so on

The 1099B may not necessarily include both the purchase totals and the total proceeds, so make sure to keep your statements and the trade advice or notifications for accuracy in reporting your gains and losses.

>> **Form K-1:** Activity reported for an ETF from the ETF sponsor. You enter this data onto your Form 1040.

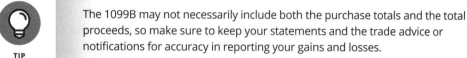

Most brokerage firms provide at their websites the ability to download transactions in a spreadsheet-compatible data file (such as CSV or XLS format) and/or tax software–compatible data files for easy uploading to your software program or to print a hard copy for inclusion with a paper tax return submission.

Tax forms

You'll receive the necessary trading data from the forms in the previous section, and you enter the data into your taxes. The IRS schedules and forms that most investors need to be aware of and/or attach to their Form 1040 include the following:

>> **Schedule B:** To report interest and dividends

>> **Schedule D/Form 8948:** To report capital gains and losses

>> **Form 4952:** Investment Interest Expense Deduction

>> **Form 6781:** To report Section 1256 gains and losses

>> **Publication 17:** Guide to Form 1040

You can get these publications directly from the IRS at 800-829-3676 or you can download them from the website (www.irs.gov). For more information on what records and documentation investors should hang on to, check out IRS Publication 552, "Recordkeeping for Individuals." (See www.irs.gov/pub/irs-pdf/p552.pdf.)

If you plan to do your own taxes, consider using the latest tax software products, which are inexpensive and easy to use. These programs usually have a question-and-answer feature to help you do your taxes step by step, and they include all the necessary forms. Consider getting either TurboTax (www.turbotax.com) or H&R Block at Home (formerly TaxCut; www.hrblock.com/tax-software) at your local software vendor or the company's website. Alternatively, you can get free tax preparation software at www.taxact.com.

TIP

Tax laws can be very hairy and perplexing, and you can easily feel like the mouse going through the maze trying to either find the cheese (tax refund) or just keep more of the hard-earned cheese you took home. Higher (and more complicated) taxes generally aren't good for investors or the economy at large. Fortunately, the recent tax laws do have some good news for most investors. But no matter how friendly or unfriendly the tax environment is, you should stay informed both through your tax advisor, online tax information sources, and through taxpayer advocacy groups like the National Taxpayers Union (www.ntu.org). 'Nuff said.

TIP

An easy place to go to see the tax reform changes is the IRS's site www.taxchanges. us. It shows you the tax changes for 2020, 2021, or subsequent tax years, and it also shows you what changes occurred either by looking at the actual line items on the 1040 or by topic or subtopic. It even shows you how to calculate your paycheck's withholdings so you can more closely match the withholdings to the new potential tax rates so you can avoid under- or overwithholding.

The softer side of the IRS: Tax deductions

In the course of managing your portfolio of currency trades and other investments, you'll probably incur expenses that are tax-deductible. The tax laws allow you to write off certain investment-related expenses as itemized expenses on Schedule A — an attachment to IRS Form 1040. Keep records of your deductions and retain a checklist to remind you which deductions you normally take. IRS Publication 550 ("Investment Income and Expenses") gives you more details. (Check out www.irs.gov/publications/p550.)

The following sections explain two common tax deductions for investors: investment interest and miscellaneous expenses.

TIP

Keep in mind that for 2020, 2021, and going forward, the standard deduction for individuals has increased significantly so you may not need to itemize on Schedule A if the standard deduction gives you a greater tax benefit. For 2020, the standard deduction for those married filing jointly, for example, is $24,800 (in 2019 it was $24,400). Because the 2018 tax act made the standard deduction significantly higher (in 2017 it was only $12,700 for married filing jointly), it made itemizing (using Schedule A) less attractive — total itemized deductions need to be at a higher total than the standard deduction before itemizing makes tax sense. The issue for investors is that many investment-related deductible expenses are claimed as itemized (Schedule A) expenses.

Investment interest

If you pay any interest to a brokerage, such as margin interest or any interest to acquire a taxable financial investment, it's considered investment interest and usually fully deductible as an itemized expense.

WARNING

Keep in mind that not all interest is deductible. Consumer interest or interest paid for any consumer or personal purpose isn't deductible. For more general information, see the section covering interest in IRS Publication 17 (www.irs.gov/pub/irs-pdf/p17.pdf).

Miscellaneous expenses

Most investment-related deductions are reported as miscellaneous expenses. Here are some common deductions:

>> Accounting or bookkeeping fees for keeping records of investment income

>> Any expense related to tax service, tax programs, or tax education

>> Computer expense — you can take a depreciation deduction for your computer if you use it 50 percent of the time or more for managing your investments

>> Investment management or investment advisor's fees (fees paid for advice on tax-exempt investments aren't deductible)

>> Legal fees involving stockholder issues

>> Safe-deposit box rental fee or home safe to hold your securities, unless used to hold personal effects or tax-exempt securities

>> Service charges for collecting interest and dividends

>> Subscription fees for investment advisory services

>> Travel costs to check investments or to confer with advisors regarding income-related investments

REMEMBER

You can deduct only that portion of your miscellaneous expenses that exceeds 2 percent of your adjusted gross income. For more information on deducting miscellaneous expenses, check out IRS Publication 529 at www.irs.gov/pub/irs-pdf/p529.pdf.

Surveying Tax Specifics for Different Types of Currency-Related Activities

The following sections give you details on taxes for various types of currency-related activities.

First things first: Do you use Internal Revenue Code 1256 or 988?

One of the first topics of discussion with your tax advisor will be whether your trading activities will be based on Internal Revenue Code (IRC) 1256 or 988. Each basis involves different rules and different tax rates, and the trader needs to make a determination in the first year:

>> If the trader is trading forex options and futures and is a casual trader, IRC 1256 is most likely to be applied. In this case, the options and futures contracts are subject to 60/40 tax consideration where the gain receives 60 percent long-term capital gain tax treatment and the remaining 40 percent is subject to short-term capital gains taxes. The same split applies in the case of losses. These transactions would then be reported on Form 6781 (see www.irs.gov/pub/irs-pdf/f6781.pdf).

>> Section 988 can be chosen, but the selection must be made during the first year you're trading these currency contracts. Section 988 is more advantageous for professional traders because losses are not subject to the $3,000 tax year limitation (covered earlier in this chapter).

REMEMBER

The discussion on choosing Section 1256 versus Section 988 as your trading basis is a little outside the scope of this chapter and best handled between you and your tax advisor (and the resources at the end of this chapter). But it's important that you know to address it early with your tax advisor.

Taxes on currency ETFs

Currency exchange-traded funds (ETFs), covered in Chapter 13, are usually traded in your stock brokerage account, and they tend to be treated much like any other security in your account such as a stock or other type of ETF.

Most currency ETFs don't pay dividends, but if they do, dividends tend to be treated as "qualified dividends," meaning that they qualify for the more favorable tax rate that usually applies to long-term capital gains. For the usual currency

ETF, the issue is capital gains. If you bought a currency ETF at $25 per share and sold it later at $40 per share, then your gain would be $15 per share. If you had 100 shares in the same example, then your gain would be $1,500 (100 shares times a gain of $15). This would be your taxable gain.

The next thing to check is how long you had these shares. If you held them for less than a year, then the gain is considered short-term and taxed as ordinary income, which is the highest tax rate. If the shares were sold and the time frame for holding them is at least a year and a day, then the gain would be considered long-term, which would be taxed at a more favorable rate and save you a few bucks. Find out more about capital gains earlier in this chapter.

TIP

Keep in mind that this example is about ETF shares in a regular brokerage account. If those shares were in a tax-favored retirement account, such as a 401(k) or an Individual Retirement Account (IRA), then you wouldn't worry about the gain realized inside the retirement account because any taxes would be deferred and not become an issue until later on when distributions are taken.

Taxes on futures and options

Forex and currency futures contracts (see Chapter 14) will be Section 1256 gains and losses. When you receive the brokerage 1099 form, you will report gains and losses on Form 6781 (visit www.irs.gov/pub/irs-pdf/f6781.pdf).

Chapter 15 mentions that options can be used to generate income, and the most common ways to do so are with covered call option writing and writing put options. However, both maneuvers are technically considered capital gains trans-actions and not income (such as dividend or interest income). Options, depending on how long you hold them, will either be short-term capital gains/losses or long-term capital gains/losses. The time frame starts on the date when the option trade is opened, and the clock stops ticking on the date when the trade is closed out.

Taxes on cryptocurrencies

Cryptocurrencies are technically considered assets (even though they are digital). Given that, the normal rules of capital gains apply, as explained earlier in this chapter. If you hold a cryptocurrency for less than a year, you will pay taxes at the full ordinary income tax rate. If you hold it for at least a year and a day, the gain will be treated as a long-term capital gain and will thus be taxed at a lower rate.

WARNING

The issue with cryptocurrencies in recent years is that folks are tempted to not report either their holdings or their gains, and great care needs to be taken here. If tax authorities find out you have assets or gains that you haven't reported, then you invite legal problems. Make sure you treat your cryptocurrency transactions legally and discuss your situation with an informed tax advisor. Find out more about cryptocurrencies in Chapter 16.

Taking Advantage of Tax-Advantaged Retirement Investing

If you're going to invest for the long term (such as your retirement), you may as well maximize your use of tax-sheltered retirement plans. Many different types of plans are available; the following sections touch on only the most popular ones.

TIP

In the realm of retirement planning, the most likely approach is investing and the most likely (suitable) currency vehicles and strategies to consider are currency ETFs (covered in Chapter 13) and covered call option writing (covered in Chapter 15). Additionally, cryptocurrencies (covered in Chapter 16) may become suitable as retirement vehicles as they reach greater acceptance. The most likely cryptocurrency vehicles to reach retirement suitability may be in the form of ETFs.

IRAs

Individual Retirement Accounts (IRAs) are accounts you can open with a financial institution, such as a bank, a brokerage firm, or a mutual fund company. An IRA is available to almost anyone who has earned income, and it allows you to set aside and invest money to help fund your retirement. Opening an IRA is easy, and virtually any bank or mutual fund can guide you through the process. Two basic types of IRAs are traditional and Roth.

Traditional IRA

The traditional Individual Retirement Account (also called the *deductible IRA*) was first popularized in the early 1980s. In a traditional IRA, you can make a tax-deductible contribution of up to $6,000 in 2020 (some restrictions apply). Individuals age 50 and older can make additional "catch-up" investments of $1,000. For 2021 and beyond, the limits will be indexed to inflation.

The money can then grow in the IRA account unfettered by current taxes because the money isn't taxed until you take it out. Because IRAs are designed for retirement purposes, you can start taking money out of your IRA in the year you turn 59½. (That must really disappoint those who want their money in the year they turn 58¾.) The withdrawals at that point are taxed as ordinary income. Fortunately (hopefully?), you'll probably be in a lower tax bracket then, so the tax shouldn't be as burdensome.

REMEMBER

Keep in mind that you're required to start taking distributions from your account when you reach age 70½ (that's gotta be a bummer for those who prefer the age of 71⅞). After that point, you may no longer contribute to a traditional IRA. Again, check with your tax advisor to see how this criterion affects you personally.

WARNING

If you take out money from an IRA too early, the amount is included in your taxable income, and you may be zapped with a 10 percent penalty. You can avoid the penalty if you have a good reason. The IRS provides a list of reasons in Publication 590-B, "Distributions from Individual Retirement Arrangements (IRAs)." (Note the IRS uses the term "Arrangements" rather than "Accounts," but the terms are synonymous.) See www.irs.gov/pub/irs-pdf/p590b.pdf.

To put money into an IRA, you must earn income equal to or greater than the amount you're contributing. *Earned income* is money made either as an employee or a self-employed person. Although traditional IRAs can be great for investors, the toughest part about them is qualifying — they have income limitations and other qualifiers that make them less deductible based on how high your income is. See IRS Publication 590-A, "Contributions to Individual Retirement Arrangements (IRAs)," for more details. Visit www.irs.gov/publications/p590a.

TIP

Wait a minute! If IRAs usually involve mutual funds or bank investments, how does an investor take advantage of them? Here's how: Investors can open a self-directed IRA with a brokerage firm. This means that you can buy and sell stocks in the account with no taxes on dividends or capital gains. The account is tax-deferred, so you don't have to worry about taxes until you start making withdrawals. Also, many dividend reinvestment plans (DRPs) can be set up as IRAs as well.

Roth IRA

The Roth IRA is a great retirement plan that I (coauthor Paul) wish had existed a long time ago. Here are some ways to distinguish the Roth IRA from the traditional IRA:

>> The Roth IRA provides no tax deduction for contributions.

>> Money in the Roth IRA grows tax-free and can be withdrawn tax-free when you turn 59½.

>> The Roth IRA is subject to early distribution penalties (although there are exceptions). Distributions have to be qualified to be penalty- and tax-free; in other words, make sure that any distribution is within the guidelines set by the IRS (see Publication 590-B).

The maximum contribution per year for Roth IRAs is the same as for traditional IRAs. You can open a self-directed account with a broker as well. See IRS Publication 590-A for details on qualifying. Check out www.irs.gov/publications/p590a.

401(k) plans

Company-sponsored 401(k) plans (named after the section in the tax code that allows them) are widely used and very popular. In a 401(k) plan, companies set aside money from their employees' paychecks that employees can use to invest for retirement. Generally, in 2020 you can invest as much as $19,500 of your pre-tax earned income and have it grow tax-deferred. Those over age 50 can contribute up to $6,500 as a "catch-up" contribution.

Usually, the money is put in mutual funds administered through a mutual fund company or an insurance firm. Although most 401(k) plans aren't self-directed, they're in this book for good reason. Because your money is in a mutual fund that may invest in stocks and ETFs, take an active role in finding out the mutual funds in which you're allowed to invest. Most plans offer several types of stock mutual funds. Use your growing knowledge to make more informed choices about your 401(k) plan options. For more information on 401(k) and other retirement plans, check out IRS Publication 560 (www.irs.gov/publications/p560).

If you're an employee, you can also find out more about retirement plans from the Department of Labor at www.dol.gov.

Seeking Some Tax Resources

TIP

Here are some resources to provide further guidance in your tax-saving pursuits:

>> **Green Trader Tax:** Check out www.greentradertax.com.

>> **TraderStatus:** See www.traderstatus.com.

>> **How to Make Any Expense Tax-Deductible:** This course by coauthor Paul helps those who achieve TTS or any home business maximize their tax deductions. More details are at www.ravingcapitalist.com/home/how-to-make-any-expense-tax-deductible/.

4

Forex Alternatives

IN THIS PART . . .

Discover a safer and easier way to trade currencies using currency exchange-traded funds (ETFs).

Find trading opportunities in currency futures.

Use versatile trading vehicles — call and put options.

Check out new opportunities in the world of cryptocurrencies.

IN THIS CHAPTER

» Describing currency ETFs for beginners

» Looking at the advantages of currency ETFs

» Examining ETFs around the world

» Understanding hedged and unhedged ETFs

» Getting more details with ETF resources

Chapter **13**

Currency Exchange-Traded Funds

For those folks whose eyes glaze over when you look at forex and are ready to say "fuggedaboutit!" then this is the chapter for you. I (coauthor Paul — hi!) love this chapter too, especially for beginners, because it dives into a beginner-friendly topic — currency exchange-traded funds (ETFs).

This chapter is distinctive in that it is the only chapter in this book that treats currencies as a longer-term investment — a vehicle that can be held for several years or longer. Meanwhile, other topics that dominate this book (traditional currency trading, currency futures, currency options, and so on) are speculative in nature and the focus is more short-term (days, weeks, and/or months), generally spanning less than a year.

Defining Currency ETFs

REMEMBER

An ETF is defined by what is contained within it. A utilities stock ETF holds a portfolio of utilities stock, for example. A country equity ETF likely holds the top 50 or 100 stocks that are in that country's stock exchange. A currency ETF typically holds either a large deposit of currency (held in a designated financial institution) or futures contracts of the underlying currency. The simplest currency ETFs hold deposits or futures of a single currency. Of course, there are also multi-currency ETFs with a diversified holding in a number of currencies.

Currency ETFs are convenient securities; you can buy them as easily as you can stocks or any ETFs. You can buy one share, 50, 100, or however many you can afford. Table 13-1 lists the main currency ETFs (available at the time of this writing).

TABLE 13-1

Available Currency Exchange-Traded Funds

Symbol	ETF Name	Recent Price Per Share (Aug. 2021)
CEW	WisdomTree Emerging Currency Strategy Fund	$17.91
CROC	ProShares UltraShort Australian Dollar	$47.94
CYB	WisdomTree Chinese Yuan Strategy Fund	$27.82
DBV	Invesco DB G10 Currency Harvest Fund	$24.74
EUFX	ProShares Short Euro	$43.59
EUO	ProShares UltraShort Euro	$24.30
FXA	Invesco CurrencyShares Australian Dollar Trust	$72.90
FXB	Invesco CurrencyShares British Pound Sterling Trust	$133.06
FXC	Invesco CurrencyShares Canadian Dollar Trust	$78.36
FXE	Invesco CurrencyShares Euro Trust	$109.55
FXF	Invesco CurrencyShares Swiss Franc Trust	$97.98
FXY	Invesco CurrencyShares Japanese Yen Trust	$85.21
UDN	Invesco DB US Dollar Index Bearish Fund	$20.92
ULE	ProShares Ultra Euro	$14.37
USDU	WisdomTree Bloomberg U.S. Dollar Bullish Fund	$25.61
UUP	Invesco DB US Dollar Index Bullish Fund	$24.98
YCL	ProShares Ultra Yen	$51.77
YCS	ProShares UltraShort Yen	$76.84

TIP

Keep in mind that Table 13-1 has the most prominent currency ETFs (both bullish and bearish), but don't consider it a comprehensive listing. More ETFs of all stripes are created fairly regularly, and you can do a search at the many ETF sites listed at the end of this chapter. Also keep in mind that as more ETFs come into existence, others may be discontinued. There were currency ETFs on the Russian ruble and the Swedish krona, but those ETFs were recently discontinued.

REMEMBER

The most common purpose of a currency ETF is simple: You're betting on the price directions of currencies on their spot exchange rates. In fact, understanding exposure to spot exchange rates is a very critical concept that should be understood before proceeding with any currency ETF. Given that, check out Chapters 4, 8, and 9.

Picking Out the Pros of Currency ETFs versus Other Currency Vehicles

There is, of course, no such thing as a perfectly good investment or speculative vehicle. However, once in a while you may come across a perfectly bad one. It's important to focus on what is appropriate for you, your investing/speculative style, and the market you're seeking to profit in.

The bottom line in this section is to find out the good, the bad, and the ugly of currency ETFs versus other currency choices.

Currency ETF advantages

Currency options do have some distinct advantages over other currency vehicles, such as the following:

>> **Time frame:** The ability to hold currency ETFs for the short or long term is a plus. If you bought a few shares in a currency ETF and the price went down, no worries! You can either buy some more at the more favorable price, or you can hold your shares until they rise later on — no time frame is necessary.

Meanwhile, other currency vehicles such as forex (currency trading), futures, or options tend to be very short-term in focus, and time can easily go against you in the short term. Currency options, for example, have a finite shelf life and can expire worthless if you aren't careful (options are covered in Chapter 15).

>> **Taxes:** With currency ETFs, you can qualify for more favorable long-term capital gains treatments (see Chapter 12 for details on taxes) if you hold the shares for at least a year and a day. Meanwhile, most other currency vehicles entail short-term moves that tend to have a higher tax rate. Also, taxes on forex and currency futures tend to be more complicated.

>> **More order choices:** Because currency ETFs (much like other ETFs) are transacted in regular brokerage accounts, orders can easily be put on to limit risk (such as trailing stops) or to gain favorable prices (limit orders). Other types of brokerage accounts may or may not have a similar variety to help you in your goals and strategies. Flip to Chapter 4 for an introduction to order types.

>> **Optionable:** Currency ETFs are certainly tradeable, but additionally, many of the major ones are optionable. The currency ETF Invesco DB US Dollar Index Bullish Fund (UUP), for example, has over 200 call and put options of various strike prices and expiration dates available (as of the time of writing) and new ones keep getting issued. More on options is in Chapter 15.

>> **Income potential:** This one could have easily been put in the previous bullet point, but I want to highlight the fact that currency ETFs give you the ability to write covered calls and/or write puts against them so that you can generate income. This means that a currency vehicle could become . . . uh . . . a cash machine! The cool facts are in Chapter 15. Meanwhile, other currency vehicles (like forex and futures) are best suited for short-term gains. The same is true with cryptocurrencies (see Chapter 16).

>> **Marginable:** This one could easily be a negative (if you aren't careful), but done right, it can be another advantage of currency ETFs in your regular brokerage account. If, for example, you have $10,000 worth (market value) of currency ETFs (and/or other stocks and ETFs), they may be marginable (ask your stockbroker), and you could potentially borrow up to 50 percent of the market value. These securities effectively act as collateral, and the interest on the loan tends to be at favorable rates. See Chapter 4 for an introduction to margin.

Other factors when choosing currency ETFs

REMEMBER

Of course, currency ETFs don't act inside a bubble. Other factors do affect their value and performance. Here are some factors to be aware of:

>> Interest rates for the currency

>> Interest rates for the opposing currency (such as for the U.S. dollar)

>> Economic events

>> International trade

>> Political events, decisions, and change of leadership

>> Global conflicts and regional wars

>> Natural disasters such as major earthquakes, tsunamis, and so forth

>> Bailouts and other forms of intervention by central banks

To see the value of investing in a currency ETF, take a look at an obvious example — the performance of the U.S. dollar in recent decades. Check out Figure 13-1.

© John Wiley & Sons, Inc.

FIGURE 13-1:
20-year dollar
index chart.

The chart in Figure 13-1 indicates the movement of the dollar index (futures price) during the last 20 years, and it is telling what happened during two bad moments for both the economy and the financial markets — the tech crash during 2000–2002 and the financial crisis of 2008. In both moments, the dollar gained value as investors sought safe venues for their money. For investors it's a cautionary tale for when bull markets look good and everyone is optimistic, which occurred in the days and months before those crash events. After all, the typical bear market is born at the height of optimism (while bull markets typically start at the depths of pessimism).

How could investors and speculators have played those markets?

>> Investors may play them defensively. As markets go up, caution becomes a greater issue. Stocks typically become overpriced, and prudent investors start to slowly migrate their money to safer vehicles. When stocks are higher, the dollar tends to be lower or trading sideways. At this moment, currency ETFs become a possibility.

>> Speculators may get into bearish positions in anticipation of a market pullback, correction, or crash. They may short the market and also anticipate a rally in the dollar. Another profit opportunity arises with currency ETFs.

Fortunately for you, you can make money when the dollar rises — or crashes — using U.S. dollar ETFs. Keep reading!

Comparing U.S. Dollar Bullish and Bearish ETFs

The U.S. dollar is the world's premier reserve currency, which is what has made it not only a powerful store of value but also a vehicle for those seeking safety in times of economic and political volatility. It's the 800-pound gorilla (or is that the $64,000 question?). The following sections compare bullish and bearish U.S. dollar ETFs.

Feeling bullish

If you are bullish on the U.S. dollar and feel that its value (versus other currencies) will rise in the coming months, then the Invesco DB US Dollar Index Bullish Fund (UUP) is the appropriate choice. Figure 13-2 is a chart of how UUP has performed in recent years (2017–2021).

REMEMBER

The overriding consideration in the value of a currency is its scarcity and acceptance by the market participants (consumers, businesses, and so on). When an economy is perceived as safe, stable, and strong, its currency tends to be strong, and this condition is bullish for the currency's value.

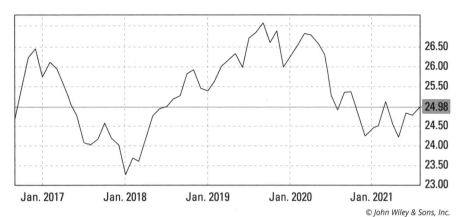

© John Wiley & Sons, Inc.

FIGURE 13-2:
Five-year chart
of UUP.

I (coauthor Paul) am an immigrant (and naturalized citizen), and I came to America in 1963. I watched from a safe distance as my former country (communist Yugoslavia) disintegrated during 1993–94 with civil strife, chaos, and hyperinflation. Yugoslavia's historic inflation occurred as the government vastly overproduced the currency (the dinar), and it ceased to be scarce! The exchange rate was such that hyperinflation shrunk the dinar's value to the point that an excess of 1 million units of it would be the rough equivalent of a single U.S. dollar. That country's society lost confidence in the dinar, and it eventually became worthless (just days before the country ceased to exist).

At the time of writing (summer 2021), the U.S. dollar was being overproduced, which would affect its scarcity, but the currency kept its value because its relative scarcity and acceptance was still greater than the scarcity and acceptance of other currencies. Across the globe, currencies were tumbling in value as they were inflated in countries such as Venezuela and South Africa.

Of course, you can't keep overproducing a currency in perpetuity. The U.S. government and the Federal Reserve are now spending beyond the economy's ability to deal with it during 2022–2024. The federal government for the fiscal year ending October 2021 is on track to have a federal budget deficit of $3 trillion — the single greatest deficit in its history. The Federal Reserve will finance this deficit by issuing debt, and the nation's sovereign debt will soar north of $30 trillion. All of this is mind-boggling, and of course, sooner or later, it means inflation and a U.S. dollar that will ultimately decline.

Given that, how can investors protect themselves? How can speculators profit? Well, I'm glad you asked! Read the next section.

Being bearish

If you are bearish on the U.S. dollar and feel that its value (versus other currencies) will fall in the coming months, then the Invesco DB US Dollar Index Bearish Fund (UDN) is the appropriate choice. Figure 13-3 is a chart of how UDN has performed in recent years (2017–2021).

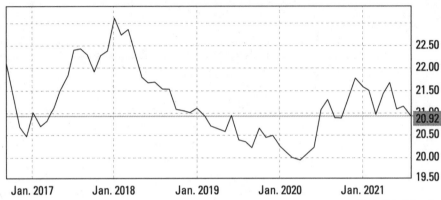

FIGURE 13-3: Five-year chart of UDN.

© John Wiley & Sons, Inc.

REMEMBER

Keep in mind that when you're bearish or bullish on the U.S. dollar, you can get clues from history. As the old saw goes, history may not repeat, but it often rhymes. As long as the U.S. dollar maintains its dominance as the world's premier reserve currency, it will have an advantage versus other currencies during times of economic difficulty and geopolitical problems.

During the 1970s, the U.S. economy was in dreadful shape and inflation was raging. UDN wasn't around as a choice at that time, but very likely it would have done very well. If 2022–2023 mirrors the inflationary times of the 1970s, then you finally have an opportunity with UDN.

REMEMBER

When currencies lose their value, find out what things increase in value so that you can be properly positioned. There is a reason that precious metals such as gold and silver have retained durable value over thousands of years and have a near-perfect record of outliving currencies. Gold, silver, and other hard assets are a diversification against inflation and the overproduction of currencies. For more details on these alternatives (and others), head over to Chapter 21.

Examining Other Currency ETFs

Don't limit your potential trading opportunities to just the U.S. dollar or what affects currencies due to the dynamics of the U.S. economy and financial markets. Frequently there are great profit opportunities with currencies on the other side of the global financial landscape. Read on.

Euro ETFs

Besides the U.S. dollar, the next major trading currency is the euro. It's the U.S. dollar's alter ego — when one rises, the other tends to fall and vice versa. In the short and intermediate term, that generally holds true. It's a major currency pair in Chapter 8.

However, if one — or both — currencies cross the line into overproduction, which has a realistic chance of happening during 2022–2030, then both could severely decline. The same hard assets that are an alternative for the U.S. dollar (gold, silver, and so on; see Chapter 21) will tend to be a suitable alternative for the euro.

In the near term, though, see the euro as another great trading (or investment) vehicle. The following sections cover bullish and bearish options.

A bullish euro ETF

The most active bullish euro currency ETF is the Invesco CurrencyShares Euro Trust (FXE). FXE provides exposure to the euro, the official currency of the Eurozone, relative to the U.S. dollar. FXE increases in value when the euro rises in value and decreases when the U.S. dollar rises.

This fund may be appropriate for investors seeking to hedge exchange rate exposure or bet against the U.S. dollar. For those seeking exposure in their portfolio to the euro/U.S. dollar exchange rate, FXE is the optimal ETF choice. Figure 13-4 is FXE's chart from January 2017 to August 2021.

A bearish euro ETF

TIP

The most active bearish euro ETF is ProShares UltraShort Euro (EUO). EUO is structured to bet against the euro relative to the U.S. dollar. Since this is an aggressively short vehicle, it is not appropriate for investors (not good for long-term investing) but is suitable for those seeking bearish speculative opportunities with the euro. This ETF uses bearish vehicles and/or shorting strategies, making it highly speculative. Figure 13-5 shows the five-year history of EUO from January 2017 to August 2021.

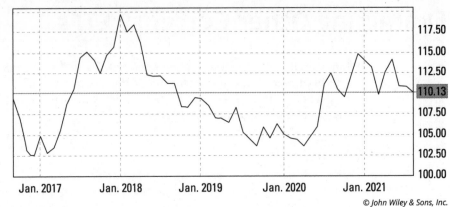

FIGURE 13-4:
Five-year chart
of FXE.

© John Wiley & Sons, Inc.

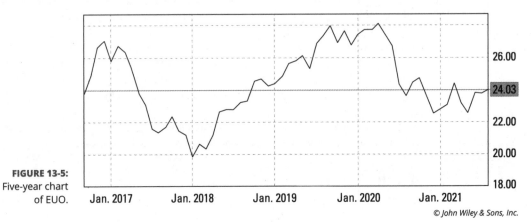

FIGURE 13-5:
Five-year chart
of EUO.

© John Wiley & Sons, Inc.

Yen ETFs

The Japanese yen is another major player on the global currency market. To play the Japanese yen, the most active currency ETF is Invesco CurrencyShares Japanese Yen Trust (FXY).

FXY provides exposure to the Japanese yen relative to the U.S. dollar. It increases in value when the yen rises, and it falls when the U.S. dollar rises. This currency ETF fund can be appropriate for investors seeking to hedge exchange rate exposure or bet against the U.S. dollar.

Figure 13-6 is the FXY chart for the past five years, from January 2017 to August 2021.

TIP

If you're bearish on the yen, then consider the inverse currency ETF ProShares UltraShort Yen (YCS).

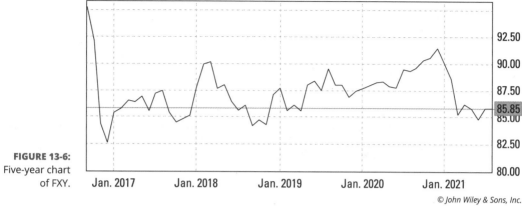

FIGURE 13-6:
Five-year chart
of FXY.

© John Wiley & Sons, Inc.

Choosing Currency ETFs: Hedged or Unhedged?

REMEMBER

Just when you thought you had enough details on your plate when it came to how to choose a currency ETF, here is another wrinkle. Would you like to choose a hedged or unhedged currency ETF? It's not that difficult of a choice:

» *Unhedged* basically means that you're "all in." The portfolio of that particular ETF is structured to be effectively 100 percent committed to that particular asset's prospects, whether the outlook is bearish or bullish. Earlier in this chapter you see two examples of unhedged ETFs on the U.S. dollar: UUP for those unhedged on the bullish side, and UDN, which is committed to the bearish side.

» *Hedged* means that the ETF has vehicles or strategies that may have a countervailing effect to mitigate the approach, thereby including some element of safety.

Think about the following example. Investor A bought 100 shares of stock XYZ. Meanwhile, Investor B bought 90 shares of stock XYZ and used the amount not spent on the other 10 shares on a put option for stock XYZ, which would be profitable only if XYZ stock declined. If XYZ stock were to go up, Investor A would be bullish and would gain a larger profit. Investor B would also gain but a more modest profit. Investor B is hedged in this example. Investor B would look smart if XYZ declined because of the put option, but Investor A is more committed.

Another wrinkle to that example would be if Investor C came along and went short 100 shares of XYZ, which would be an unhedged bearish position. We think you get the point.

TIP

If you want to participate in the world of currency ETFs but want to be more cautious about it, then why not investigate currency hedged ETFs? Table 13-2 is a list to get you started on your research (you can search the chosen ETF in the resources listed at the end of this chapter).

TABLE 13-2   **Hedged Currency ETFs**

Symbol	ETF Name	Recent Price Per Share (Aug. 2021)
ASHX	Xtrackers MSCI China A Inclusion Equity ETF	$29.76
DBAW	Xtrackers MSCI All World ex US Hedged Equity ETF	$33.83
DBEM	Xtrackers MSCI Emerging Markets Hedged Equity ETF	$27.77
DBEU	Xtrackers MSCI Europe Hedged Equity ETF	$35.62
DBEZ	Xtrackers MSCI Eurozone Hedged Equity ETF	$39.47
DBGR	Xtrackers MSCI Germany Hedged Equity ETF	$33.21
DBJP	Xtrackers MSCI Japan Hedged Equity ETF	$48.83
DDLS	WisdomTree Dynamic Currency Hedged Intern'l SmallCap Equity Fund	$35.80
DDWM	WisdomTree Dynamic Currency Hedged International Equity Fund	$31.55
DEFA	iShares Adaptive Currency Hedged MSCI EAFE ETF	$33.68
DXGE	WisdomTree Germany Hedged Equity Fund	$36.63
DXJ	WisdomTree Japan Hedged Equity Fund	$61.47
DXJS	WisdomTree Japan Hedged SmallCap Equity Fund	$44.30
EUSC	WisdomTree Europe Hedged SmallCap Equity Fund	$36.90
FLEH	Franklin FTSE Europe Hedged ETF	$28.73
FLJH	Franklin FTSE Japan Hedged ETF	$30.98
FLQH	Franklin LibertyQ International Equity Hedged ETF	$28.97
HAWX	iShares Currency Hedged MSCI ACWI ex U.S. ETF	$32.79
HDAW	Xtrackers MSCI All World ex US High Dividend Yield Equity ETF	$26.17
HDEF	Xtrackers MSCI EAFE High Dividend Yield Equity ETF	$24.68

Symbol	ETF Name	Recent Price Per Share (Aug. 2021)
HEDJ	WisdomTree Europe Hedged Equity Fund	$80.51
HEFA	iShares Currency Hedged MSCI EAFE ETF	$35.21
HEWC	iShares Currency Hedged MSCI Canada ETF	$32.56
HEWG	iShares Currency Hedged MSCI Germany ETF	$33.67
HEWJ	iShares Currency Hedged MSCI Japan ETF	$38.82
HEWU	iShares Currency Hedged MSCI United Kingdom ETF	$23.22
HEWW	iShares Currency Hedged MSCI Mexico ETF	$17.99
HEZU	iShares Currency Hedged MSCI Eurozone ETF	$37.62
HFXI	IQ 50 Percent Hedged FTSE International ETF	$25.39
HSCZ	iShares Currency Hedged MSCI EAFE Small Cap ETF	$37.40
LVHI	Legg Mason International Low Volatility High Dividend ETF	$26.81
RFAP	First Trust RiverFront Dynamic Asia Pacific ETF	$58.09
RFDI	First Trust RiverFront Dynamic Developed International ETF	$74.32
RFEM	First Trust RiverFront Dynamic Emerging Markets ETF	$71.79
RFEU	First Trust RiverFront Dynamic Europe ETF	$78.73

Studying Some Currency ETF Resources

I (coauthor Paul) think that currency ETFs are a great vehicle for currency-minded investors. The fact that the world of currency ETFs also has both leveraged and inverse ETFs means that speculators have some great profitable opportunities as well.

TIP

Here are some prime resources on ETFs:

>> Currency ETF (www.currencyetf.net)

>> ETF Database (www.etfdb.com)

>> ETF Trends (www.etftrends.com)

» ETF.com (`www.etf.com`)

» ETFguide (`www.etfguide.com`)

» Morningstar ETF ratings (`www.morningstar.com/5-star-etfs`)

» Seeking Alpha on ETFs & Funds (`https://seekingalpha.com/etfs-and-funds`)

Chapter **14**

Currency Futures

You want fast-acting currency price action that could make you a quick fortune or burn a hole in your nest egg? Have we got a market for you! But first fasten your seat belts and put your trays in the upright position. Grab some antacid and have someone put any sharp objects out of reach. The world of futures (currency futures, that is) awaits you!

If you've seen the roller-coaster moves of world markets during 2020–2021, then you have a taste of what's unfolding. Of course, maybe the first question to ask is this: What's the difference between currency trading and currency futures? So glad you asked! This chapter tackles that one first before it gets to the basics of buying contracts, both big and small.

TIP

Understanding futures is great, but when you're ready to trade currency futures, consider currency futures options. Options help you limit risk and may be a better way to trade in the futures market, especially for the novice trader. Options are available not only on futures (both standard contracts and some E-minis) but also on conventional forex vehicles and on currency exchange-traded funds (ETFs; see Chapter 13). For more information on options, check out Chapter 15.

Defining Currency Futures

Obviously, the bulk of this book covers currency trading (forex), which is a spot market, over the counter, and lightly regulated. Currency futures, on the other hand, are traded as contracts that are consummated in the future. Currency futures are traded in an exchange and are regulated.

"Futures" is a reference to futures contracts that are derivatives. This means that the contract being traded doesn't have its own value; it derives value from the underlying asset it's attached to. A (typical) corn futures contract, for example, is a contract that allows the buyer the ability to buy 1,000 bushels of corn at the contracted price stipulated in the contract and at a future delivery date. When they call it "December corn," it refers to the delivery month in the futures contract.

The underlying asset in a currency contract is a set quantity of a given currency. For example, the underlying asset in a standard euro futures contract is 125,000 units of the euro.

Futures for any type of assets are bought and sold by a contract that has an expiration date. There are two parties in the futures contract: the buyer and the seller. One party in the contract agrees to buy a given amount of a given asset and take delivery of it on a predefined date, while the other party agrees to sell it on that date at the agreed-upon price.

Futures contracts are typically scheduled to have expirations four or more times per year. After their initial purchase, the contracts can be further bought and sold on the secondary market until expiration. Upon a contract reaching its expiration, it comes off the board and is no longer listed for trade on the futures market. This is a key difference to be aware of when comparing forex to futures.

TIP

I (coauthor Paul) think that a good way to remember the difference between commodities and futures is that it's somewhat like the difference between a car and a car title. The car is the underlying asset, and the car title is a formal piece of paper that grants a legal claim to the car. In the same way a futures contract precisely describes what it is a claim to (a certain quantity and quality of a commodity), a car title precisely describes what it represents a claim to (a 2021 Honda Accord, its serial number, and so on).

Comparing Currency Trading and Currency Futures

There are some crucial differences between forex and currency futures:

>> **The present versus the future:** The forex is a spot market where transactions are made "on the spot." It's similar to when you buy groceries, for example, in that you make the transaction the same day that you take delivery of (or pick up) the goods in question. Futures, on the other hand, are contracts that result in a future transaction and future delivery. The time element of the present versus the future is an important distinction between currency trading (forex) and currency futures (also referred to as "forex futures").

>> **OTC versus formal exchange:** Forex is transacted on an over-the-counter (OTC) market, and forex brokers are the primary facilitators of the transaction for investors and speculators. This market is lightly regulated. Currency futures are contracts traded on a regulated exchange. The largest exchange for currency futures is the Chicago Mercantile Exchange (CME; www.cmegroup.com), which is overseen by both the governmental regulatory agency Commodity Futures Trading Commission (CFTC) (www.cftc.gov) and the trade association National Futures Association (NFA) (www.nfa.futures.org).

TECHNICAL STUFF

While the CFTC is a governmental entity with full legal power and oversight, the NFA is a private, self-regulatory entity that enforces business ethics among the various exchanges and brokers that fall under their industry-wide oversight.

>> **Transaction specifications:** In forex, the size of the trade is in various lot sizes, and the brokers can also allow for smaller-size transactions. Currency futures are typically in standardized contract sizes, although some of the more popular contracts do come in smaller sizes (as you find out later in this chapter).

Focusing on the Fundamentals of Currency Futures Contracts

At the core of futures trading is the futures contract. There are two types of futures contracts: those with actual products (such as commodities) that are physically delivered (such as 1,000 bushels of corn, 100 ounces of gold, and so forth) and those that have a "cash settlement," meaning that no physical product is delivered but a payment is made according to the contract's terms. Currency futures contracts are of the cash settlement variety, so don't expect anyone to deliver 1,000 bushels of euros to your front lawn when the contract is exercised (but wouldn't that be cool?).

The following sections cover what's in a contract, the concepts of margin and maintenance, widely traded currency futures contracts, and how leverage works.

Basics included in a futures contract

REMEMBER

Like any contract, a futures contract is an agreement. It's a saleable, marketable contract, and it's made on the trading floor of a formal futures exchange — the CME in the case of currency futures. A currency futures contract includes a size, a delivery date, and a price:

>> **A specified size:** Futures contracts get standardized for the same reason that when you go to the store to get a package of bacon, all the packages are 16 ounces (unless otherwise noted). A standard currency futures contract is usually for 100,000 units of that given currency.

>> **A specified delivery date:** Currency futures contracts have finite expiration dates, while forex pairs may be traded into perpetuity.

>> **Market pricing:** Forex spot prices are determined by the interplay of the currency pairs, while currency futures contracts are priced independently by the market.

Margin and maintenance requirements

REMEMBER

A futures contract is an obligation and not an asset; it has no value as collateral for a loan. Because of the potential for a loss as a result of the daily mark-to-market process, however, a margin deposit is required of each party to a security futures contract (including a currency futures contract). This required margin deposit is also referred to as a performance bond. This performance bond or margin is security for the broker.

The basic margin requirement for a currency futures contract is listed at the CME, and your broker will inform you before or at the time of your trade. While many types of futures contracts may have margin requirements of up to 20 percent, currency futures contracts have lower margin requirements. For example, at the time of this writing, the margin requirement on a euro futures contract (125,000 units of the euro) valued at $147,500 (in U.S. dollars) is $2,200. This works out to be margin of approximately 1.5 percent.

Requests for additional margin are known as margin calls. Both the buyer and the seller must individually deposit required margin to their respective accounts.

REMEMBER

Individual brokerage firms can, and in many cases do, require margin that is higher than the exchange requirements. Additionally, margin requirements may vary from brokerage firm to brokerage firm. Furthermore, a brokerage firm can increase its house margin requirements at any time without providing advance notice, and such increases can result in a margin call. For example, some firms may require margin to be positive the business day following the date of the deficiency, or some firms may even require deposit on the same day. Some firms may require margin to be on deposit in the account before they will accept an order for a security futures contract. You should get very familiar with the customer agreement with your brokerage firm before entering into any transactions in security futures contracts.

Brokerage firms generally reserve the right to liquidate a customer's security futures contract positions or sell customer assets to meet a margin call at any time without contacting the customer. Brokerage firms may also enter into equivalent but opposite positions on your account in order to manage the risk created by a margin call. Some customers mistakenly believe that a firm is required to contact them for a margin call and that the firm is not allowed to liquidate securities or other assets in their accounts to meet a margin call unless the firm has contacted them first. This is not the case.

While most firms notify their customers of margin calls and allow some time to deposit additional margin, they aren't required to do so. Even if a firm notifies the customer of a margin call and sets a specified due date for a margin deposit, the firm can still take action as necessary to protect its financial interests, including the immediate liquidation of positions without advance notification to the customer.

TIP

Speculators who want to avoid the problems inherent in the margin of their account may consider options on futures. Generally, options on futures for retail investors and speculators can be bought with cash and without margin. Options on futures have the same basic volatility and can offer great profit potential, but they don't carry the risks of margin. You can lose money in options, but at least the worst-case scenario is that losses are limited to the price of the option and no more. See Chapter 15 for more about options.

Common currency futures contracts

Table 14-1 provides the most widely traded currency futures contracts. They mostly trade on the Chicago Mercantile Exchange (CME).

TABLE 14-1 **Currency Futures Contract Specifications**

Futures Contract	Symbol	Exchange	Size	Minimum Fluctuation	Months Traded*	Screen Schedule
Australian Dollar	6A	CME	A$100,000	.01¢/AD=$10.00	H, M, U, Z	CME Globex 5 p.m.–4 p.m. CT
Brazilian Real	6L	CME	BR100,000	.00005/BR=$5	All 12 months	CME Globex 5 p.m.–4 p.m. CT
British Pound	6B	CME	£62,500	.01¢/£=$6.25	H, M, U, Z	CME Globex 5 p.m.–4 p.m. CT
Canadian Dollar	6C	CME	C$100,000	.01¢/CD=$10.00	H, M, U, Z	CME Globex 5 p.m.–4 p.m. CT
Euro FX	6E	CME	EUR125,000	.01¢/€=$12.50	H, M, U, Z	CME Globex 5 p.m.–4 p.m. CT
Euro FX/JY	RY	CME	EUR125,000	.01€/¥=¥1,250.00	H, M, U, Z	CME Globex 5 p.m.–4 p.m. CT
Japanese Yen	6J	CME	¥12,500,000	$.0000005/¥=$6.25	H, M, U, Z	CME Globex 5 p.m.–4 p.m. CT
Mexican Peso	6M	CME	M.P.500,000	.0025¢/MP=$12.50	All	CME Globex 5 p.m.–4 p.m. CT
New Zealand Dollar	6N	CME	NZ$100,000	.01¢/NZ$=$10.00	H, M, U, Z	CME Globex 5 p.m.–4 p.m. CT
South African Rand	ZAR	CME	SAR500,000	.0025¢/SAR=$12.50	H, M, U, Z	CME Globex 5 p.m.–4 p.m. CT
Swiss Franc	6S	CME	SF125,000	.01¢/SF=$12.50	H, M, U, Z	CME Globex 5 p.m.–4 p.m. CT
U.S. Dollar Index	DX	IFUS	$1,000 x Index	.01=$10.00	H, M, U, Z	8 p.m.–5 p.m.* ET

*For code of months traded, see Table 14-2.

274   PART 4 **Forex Alternatives**

For delivery months, the column reads with letters that the exchange uses to symbolize the delivery month. Table 14-2 gives all the months and their accompanying letter (symbol).

TABLE 14-2   **Delivery Month Codes**

Delivery Month	Symbol Letter
January	F
February	G
March	H
April	J
May	K
June	M
July	N
August	Q
September	U
October	V
November	X
December	Z

Leverage: The double-edged sword

The futures market can offer leverage, which can magnify your gains (or your losses). *Leverage* is the ability to retain control over a valuable asset with a relatively small amount of money. Most people are familiar with leverage in real estate; you gain control of a property valued at $250,000 by making a small down payment of, say, 10 percent ($25,000) and borrow the remaining 90 percent ($225,000). Then if the property goes up to $300,000 in value (a gain of $50,000), your initial invested amount of $25,000 at that point made you 200 percent.

In futures, you get similar leverage. On the plus side, you don't have to use as much money as in real estate and you don't have to wait a long time to see results. On the negative side, the leverage can work against you and you can lose money big-time. There's always a catch!

In futures, the down payment is your initial deposit (not really a down payment; just comparing it with the prior example). As in the previous example, the initial deposit or margin is a small sum that in turn controls a valuable asset as represented by the valuable futures contract.

WARNING

Forex pairs are traded with leverage that can be higher than futures contracts. The appeal (and risk) is that forex has more volatility due to this leverage, which can sometimes be as high as 100 (or more) to 1.

Surveying Basic Futures Trading Strategies

The whole point of speculating in futures contracts is an attempt to figure out what the price will be in the near future and profit from that move (that's the whole enchilada, right?). Your strategies all flow from what your expectation is. Although there are many sophisticated strategies with futures (especially when you combine them with options on futures; see Chapter 15), those are something you can look forward to finding out about after this book. For now, the basics are covered in the following sections — very basic. But some of the best strategies are indeed simple.

TIP

The CME Group published a free report on 25 proven strategies with futures and options, and you can access it here: www.cmegroup.com/education/brochures-and-handbooks/25-proven-strategies.html.

Going long

REMEMBER

In going long, the speculator is making a bullish bet (thinking that the currency will rise in value) on that futures contract. The speculator gets into the contract by agreeing to buy and receive delivery of the underlying asset at a set price. The bet is that the market price will rise above the set price and the profit is the difference. Keep in mind that currency futures contracts are cash-only transactions — there is no delivery of the underlying asset.

Say that Robert the speculator is bullish on the euro. Robert would therefore go long a euro FX futures contract. Typically, the requirement would be an initial margin of 20 percent of the contract's notional value.

Because a standard euro contract would have 125,000 units of the currency and the price is $1.1781 (the recent price of a single euro stated in U.S. dollars), the contract would be worth $147,262.50 at that moment. A margin deposit would be $2,200 (or about 1.5 percent). (For E-mini and E-micro contracts, the margin would be lower since the contracts are smaller, which make them more suitable for novice speculators, as covered later in this chapter.) Robert then buys the

September contract. If the euro were to rise to $1.2281 (5 full cents in U.S. dollars), that contract would be worth $153,512.50 — a total gain of $6,250.

TECHNICAL STUFF

Keep in mind that your outlay was $2,200, so if you were to close out (sell) that contract, you would realize that $6,250 as a gain in a relatively short period of time — likely in a matter of weeks or a month or two. It equates to a 284 percent gain in absolute terms, but if that happened in under two months, then the annualized would actually be a quadruple percentage gain — yeah, baby! Hey, do that a handful of times in a year, and that's a good chunk of change!

But hold on! Before you break open your kid's piggy bank, realize that the position could go against you too. That's the nature of the futures beast. What if the euro went down by that same amount (5 cents in U.S. dollars)?

Step away from the ledge and do the math. If the euro declines to $1.1281 (the original price of $1.1781 less .05 in U.S. dollars), then the contract will have lost value and those 125,000 units will be worth $141,012.50 (125,000 units at $1.1281), and you will have lost $6,250. At that point you can get a call from the futures broker to increase your margin maintenance amount level since this has breached the maintenance level. This is why you must monitor your positions and stay in touch with your broker to avoid margin difficulties.

WARNING

When speculating in futures contracts, *always* be aware of the margin and maintenance levels necessary to be maintained in your account. The broker can help you manage that by telling you what key price levels may trigger a maintenance issue. Brokers and the exchange (CME in this case) regularly publish margin and maintenance requirements for most futures contracts at their website, and you should call the broker if you aren't sure of what the requirements are and how to be compliant.

Other strategies

Yes, you can go "short" on futures contracts, betting that they will go down in value and profiting from that decline. For beginners and "prudent speculators," you can do a *spread,* which is a trade where you can go long one contract and short a different contract in the same currency (or other asset). Spreads are considered by market pros to be the best strategy for beginners because they are generally safer (due to the hedging) yet still give you an attractive profit potential. Of course, going outright "long" or "short" would give you maximum profit potential, but it can generate the most painful losses if you are wrong.

WARNING

Keep in mind that spreads in some rare circumstances may be riskier, such as in the event of market divergence where both positions may go against you — in other words, if your long position goes down and your short position goes up. Again, this is rare but it's a possibility, and you should watch out for it.

TIP

For flexibility and limited risk potential, options on futures contracts are a better consideration for beginners and small speculators. They are covered in Chapter 15.

Reading Currency Futures Quotes

Once you've traded in your futures account and you have your first currency futures contract, you need to watch the price quote. Whether the quote is on a financial smartphone app or at a financial website, reading it won't be that hard. Table 14-3 provides an example (circa August 2021).

TABLE 14-3   **A Sample Currency Futures Quote**

Column #1	2	3	4	5	6	7	8	9
Product	Code	Contract	Last	Change	Open	High	Low	Globex Vol
Euro FX Futures	6EU1	Sep-21	1.1782	0.00005	1.17845	1.17865	1.178	1,579

The quote breaks down as follows:

» Column 1 shows the product name — in this case the contract cited is for the Euro Forex Futures (or currency futures). This contract has 125,000 units of the euro. Given that, at a price of $1.1782 (price per unit in U.S. dollars), the contract would be worth (at that moment) $147,275.

» Column 2 shows you the product or contract code. In this case it is "6EU1." "6E" is for the standard euro contract, the letter "U" is for the expiration month of September, and the number "1" is shorthand for 2021.

» Column 3 shows the contract month and expiration (September 2021). More precisely, this contract would cease trading (expire) as of 9:16 a.m. CT, two business days prior to the third Wednesday of the contract month. Whoa . . . let's hope your clock is working!

» Column 4 indicates the most recent price quoted ($1.1782 per unit).

>> Column 5 is the change of the new price (up or down) from the last price. A move of 0.00005 is equivalent to $6.25 (125,000 × 0.00005).

>> Columns 6, 7, and 8 are the "open," "high," and "low" for that day's price moves.

>> Column 9 is the total contracts traded that day.

TIP

Lastly, some quote dashboards (such as at the CME's site) may include a notice of "OPT," which means that there are options on this particular contract.

REMEMBER

When you're trading a futures contract (currency or otherwise), always check out the "specs" or specifications found on that particular contract that trades at that particular exchange. The currency futures contracts covered in this chapter have their full details — specs and all — at the Chicago Mercantile Exchange (www.cmegroup.com). The specs for the euro contract in Table 14-3 can be found at www.cmegroup.com/markets/fx/g10/euro-fx.contractSpecs.html.

Sizing Up E-Minis and E-Micros

Because futures contracts can be very volatile, risky, and pricey, it behooves small speculators and beginners to consider the world of E-minis and E-micros. They have the same trading opportunities as the larger contracts covered earlier in this chapter, but they are more affordable. They allow you to be more diversified with a wider portfolio of positions (versus having more money tied up in fewer standard contracts) in your futures brokerage account. And yes, there are E-minis and E-micros in the world of currency trading. E-minis and E-micros are powerful vehicles you can add to your currency trading arsenal, and they can open up new trading opportunities.

E-minis 101

E-mini contracts (depending on the underlying asset) may be only half the size of standard contracts. The euro E-mini contract at the CME, for example, has a contract size of 62,500 units of the euro (the standard contract size is 125,000 units). Other contracts may have a different size, so always check out the contract specs at the exchange's site. E-minis have gained a larger share of the trading volume in recent years due to their popularity, liquidity, and tighter bid/ask spreads. Additionally, margin requirements tend to be much less, which makes it easier to trade with less in capital requirements.

TECHNICAL
STUFF

There are many types of E-mini contracts. The most popular have been those on stock indexes such as the S&P 500 and the Nasdaq-100, which are traded each day.

TIP

When a vehicle becomes popular, more research becomes available on it. A good site for E-minis is E-Mini Watch at `emini-watch.com/emini-trading/emini-futures`. The site offers extensive information on the basics of E-minis.

Trading with the E-micro

The E-micro contract is a futures contract traded on the CME that is an even smaller fraction of a standard contract. These contracts are typically one-tenth the size of standard currency contracts. E-micros are a great way for traders to reduce their losses by trading with less, and they have become very popular since being introduced by the CME Group. Euro futures contracts are a good example. A standard contract is 125,000 euros while the E-mini is 62,500 euros (half the standard contract) and the E-micro is 12,500 euros (one-tenth the size of the standard contract).

There are a few types of E-micro contracts. Within the equities markets, there are E-micro futures for the S&P 500, Russell 2000, Nasdaq-100, and Dow Jones Industrial Average. Some of these can be good alternatives to your currency strategies so that you can be diversified and/or hedged in your futures account.

Within the forex market, there are contracts that represent many types of currency pairs, such as the U.S. dollar paired with one of the following:

>> Australian dollar

>> Euro

>> British pound

>> Swiss franc

>> Japanese yen

>> Canadian dollar

>> Chinese renminbi

Common currency E-mini and E-micro contracts

REMEMBER

If you're seeking to speculate in futures, the first step, of course, is doing your research. The second step can be simulated trading, and many brokers and sites have programs and tutorials for that. Finally, you can put up your money and start trading, but the best place to start is with E-minis and E-micros. Earning some small profits is the stepping stone to bigger profits.

The basic difference between the standard currency futures contract and the E-mini is that the E-mini is only traded electronically (the "E"), and the contract size is half the size of the standard contract (the "mini"). This makes it a more affordable trade for smaller speculators. Table 14-4 lists some widely traded currency E-mini and E-micro contracts.

TABLE 14-4 **Common Currency E-Mini and E-Micro Contracts**

Exchange	Product Name	Product Code
CME	E-MINI EURO FX FUTURE	E7
CME	E-MINI J-YEN FUTURE	J7
CME	MICRO AUD/USD FUTURES	M6A
CME	MICRO GBP/USD FUTURES	M6B
CME	MICRO USD/CAD FUTURES	M6C
CME	MICRO EUR/USD FUTURES	M6E
CME	MICRO USD/JPY FUTURES	M6J
CME	MICRO USD/CHF FUTURES	M6S
CME	MICRO CAD/USD FUTURES	MCD
CME	MICRO INR/USD FUTURE	MIR
CME	MICRO JPY/USD	MJY
CME	MICRO USD/CNH FUTURES	MNH

Checking Out Futures Trading Resources and Brokers

TIP

Here are some important sources of guidance and education for your futures trading pursuits:

>> Chicago Mercantile Exchange (www.cmegroup.com)

>> Futures Fundamentals (www.futuresfundamentals.org)

>> FXCM (www.fxcm.com)

>> National Futures Association (www.nfa.futures.org) Get their publication "Opportunity and Risk: An Educational Guide to Trading Futures and Options on Futures" at www.nfa.futures.org/investors/investor-resources/files/opportunity-and-risk-entire.pdf

TIP

Here are some select futures brokers that have extensive guidance and education at their sites:

>> Cannon Trading (www.cannontrading.com)

>> Interactive Brokers (www.interactivebrokers.com)

>> Lasalle Futures Group (www.lasallefutures.com)

>> StoneX Financial (www.danielstrading.com)

>> TradeStation (www.tradestation.com)

>> Van Commodities Inc. (www.vancfo.com)

Chapter **15**

Currency Options

The easiest and least risky way to get involved with currencies is with exchange-traded funds (ETFs), covered in Chapter 13. That is hands down my (coauthor Paul's) favorite way to play currencies (especially for those who are novice investors). However, my favorite way to speculate is with call and put options, and the good news for you is that most currency ETFs (and currency futures, which are covered in Chapter 14) are optionable.

Options can be a low-cost way to speculate, and the risk can be limited to whatever amount you're willing to speculate with. Some options can cost as little as $50 (or less!), which makes this a suitable speculative vehicle for those with limited funds. This chapter gives you the scoop.

Introducing the Basics of Options

Call options and put options (the two speculative vehicles covered in this chapter) are tradeable contracts. They don't have their own intrinsic value; they are vehicles that are referred to as derivatives. A *derivative* is a vehicle that *derives* its value from an underlying asset. In other words, options have no intrinsic value like gold or real estate or even paper assets such as stocks. They are a pure speculative play.

You can use options in many ways:

>> You can use them to make profits when the underlying asset goes up in value (using bullish strategies such as buying a call option).

>> You can use them to make profits when the underlying assets go down in value (using bearish strategies such as buying a put option).

>> You can use options to generate income (selling or writing call/put options).

>> You can use them aggressively for potential gains.

>> You can use them to hedge or to increase safety in your portfolio.

I (coauthor Paul) think that options are excellent and valuable tools in your arsenal whether you're an investor or a speculator. The following sections go over the advantages of options and the assets you can use options with.

TIP

I have been teaching the benefits of call and put options for nearly three decades. My course to help investors and speculators (both novice and experienced) is available at www.ravingcapitalist.com/ultra-investing-with-options.

Why consider options?

Options have many great advantages, such as the following:

>> They can be inexpensive. Depending on what market and/or what asset you're speculating about, a call or put option can be bought for as little as $50 — or less.

>> Whether you're bullish, bearish, or neutral, there are many option strategies that can fit your outlook.

>> They can give you leverage. A single option can have the volatility and firepower of any underlying asset, which could be 100 shares, a currency contract of $100,000 in value, or another pricey vehicle.

>> They can be used for gains or for generating income.

>> You can have a preset, limited risk going in that you can customize.

TIP

The biggest risk with options is that they can expire worthless, which is a big reason I'm an advocate of long-dated options. Most options expire in nine months or less, so check out longer-dated options (called LEAPs), which are a safer way to speculate.

What assets have options on them?

As I note earlier, an option is a derivative, and it derives its value from an underlying asset. Numerous assets are optionable, such as

>> Stocks

>> ETFs

>> Commodities (grains, energy, base metals, precious metals, and so forth)

>> Currencies (that's why you're here!)

>> Bond and interest rate vehicles

>> Alternatives (such as cryptocurrencies, weather futures, and so on)

TIP

When it comes to currencies, these are the most actively traded vehicles with options:

>> Currency ETFs (covered in Chapter 13)

>> Currency futures contracts (covered in Chapter 14)

>> Currency trading, or forex (more limited in choices than the preceding two but still available)

Buying a Call Option for Big Gains

A *call option* is a contract that gives the buyer the right, but not the obligation, to buy a specific asset at a specific price at any time between now and when the option expires. It's essentially a bet on an underlying asset rising in price. If you're bullish on the U.S. dollar, for example, you may consider buying a call option on either a U.S. dollar ETF or on a U.S. dollar currency contract (such as the dollar index, which is traded on the Chicago Mercantile Exchange, or CME).

Call options are marketable securities; they are bought and sold on a regulated exchange. Call options on currency ETFs (or any optionable stock or ETF) are traded on the Chicago Board Options Exchange (the CBOE at www.cboe.com).

REMEMBER

You can have the call option in your trading arsenal for different reasons:

>> **Looking for big gains:** If you're bullish on a given asset or security (and it's optionable), you can buy a call option to speculate seeking large potential profits. Buying a call option is the subject of this section.

>> **Looking for income:** If you're seeking income and have an optionable asset, you can write a call option on the asset. Writing a call option is covered later in this chapter.

>> **Hedging/seeking protection:** Some folks use call options to add safety to a speculative strategy (such as going short). Seeking protection with a call option is covered later in this chapter.

Understanding how buying a call option works

The underlying asset I use here as an example for buying a call option is the PowerShares DB US Dollar Index Bullish ETF (symbol UUP). If you were bullish on the U.S. dollar as an investor, it would be a simple matter of buying however many shares you wanted of this ETF because it's a good way to be bullish and have UUP as a long-term addition to your stock/ETF investment portfolio.

Say that you bought UUP at $20 per share some time ago and you checked the price in mid-August 2021. You see that it's at about $25 per share, giving you a 25 percent gain (a $5 move on a $20 investment is a 25 percent move). Had you bought 100 shares of UUP at $20 per share rather than at $25 per share, your position would be worth $2,500. But what if you had a call option on UUP during the same move?

Say that UUP was at $20 per share and you bought a call option for only $75, and this call option gave you the right, but not the obligation, to buy 100 shares of UUP at $22 per share (the agreed-upon price or "strike" price in the option contract). For the sake of this example, presume that the contract has an expiration date of December 2021. Now what? Say that UUP rises to $25 per share in the weeks and months just prior to the expiration date. Say that UUP hits $25 in September 2021 (three months before expiration). Now you should have a big grin on your face because your call option's value has soared quickly. How is that?

Note that the call option gave you the ability (the right) to buy 100 shares of UUP at $22 per share or a total of $2,200 (100 shares times $22 per share). But now what happens with UUP at $25? Your option will be worth at least $300, or $2,500 minus $2,200. (That's a dollar gain of $225 from your investment of $75, or a percentage gain of 300 percent!) Seriously, those traders at the currency traders forum would envy you if you had a 300 percent gain, and options give you the firepower to do that with limited (and foreseeable) downside risk.

The great thing about your $75 option is that you don't have to shell out $2,200 to buy (and/or then sell) those 100 shares of UUP — you can just sell the option outright for $300 and pocket that $225 profit.

Looking at the features of a call option

REMEMBER

Keep in mind that options are marketable securities and you never need to buy the underlying asset to realize that profit. Given the example in the previous section, here are the main features of call options:

» **Contract:** Remember that an option (in this case a call option) is a contract. It is marketable, and we refer to it as a derivative because it "derives" its value from the underlying asset.

» **Underlying asset:** Options have an underlying asset. In this example, it is 100 shares of a security. The security can be a stock or an ETF (exchange-traded fund). In the previous example, it is 100 shares of UUP. Keep in mind that later in this chapter, we discuss the underlying asset as being a futures contract, which is a different animal but still is an underlying asset.

» **Strike price:** This is the agreed-upon price for the underlying asset in question stipulated in the option contract. In the example, it is $22 per share.

» **Buyer:** One of the two parties in this option (contract) is the buyer of the option.

» **Premium:** The buyer pays money for the option (referred to as the *premium*).

» **Writer (seller of the option):** The buyer pays the premium of the option to the seller, who is technically referred to as the *writer*. Think in terms of "writing a contract" if that helps. When the seller receives the premium, the seller takes on the obligation of the contract, which in this case is that the writer must sell 100 shares of UUP if the contract is exercised (the buyer makes the formal request to receive the underlying asset at the strike price).

» **Expiration date:** This is the contract's expiration date. For option contracts on stocks and ETFs, it is typically on the third Friday of the expiration month.

Distinguishing the "moneyness" of call options

In the world of options, the "moneyness" of the contract is of course a big deal. An option can be "out of the money" (OTM), "at the money" (ATM), or "in the money" (ITM). This refers to the very important relationship between the strike price in the option contract and the market price of the underlying asset.

Table 15-1 breaks down the levels of "moneyness." We use UUP to illustrate this important concept.

TABLE 15-1 ## Being OTM, ATM, or ITM

Call Option	Market Value of UUP	"Moneyness"	Cost to Buy
UUP Call $20 strike price	18	Out of the money	Typically the cheapest
UUP Call $20 strike price	20	At the money	Typically costly
UUP Call $20 strike price	22	In the money	Typically the most expensive

Here are the differences among OTM, ATM, and ITM:

>> **Out of the money (OTM):** As you can see in Table 15-1, if the strike price for the UUP call option is $20, any price of UUP below $20 is out of the money (OTM). In other words, why would anyone exercise the option to buy it at $20 if you can buy it at a cheaper market price? If UUP were at $18, then you could buy 100 shares at $1,800 — there's no point using an option with a $20 strike price to buy UUP for a total of $2,000 — hence, this would be an "out of the money" option.

OTM options are the cheapest ones to buy. The more out of the money they are, the cheaper they are.

>> **At the money (ATM):** "At the money" is likely the simplest one to understand and explain. This is when the underlying asset's price is at parity or generally equal to the option's strike price. In Table 15-1, if UUP is at about $20 and the strike price is at $20, then this option is at the money (ATM).

This option is, of course, more expensive than the OTM option.

>> **In the money (ITM):** This is the most expensive option, and every options trader's dream is to buy an OTM or ATM option and see it become ITM — as soon as possible! In other words, you generally wouldn't buy this option because it is too pricey and much of the gain has already materialized. This becomes a good time to cash out the option (before the market suddenly turns against you and ITM profits vanish).

REMEMBER

When you buy an option, you pay for it (the premium). But what exactly are you buying? You are buying a combination of intrinsic value and time value.

Writing a Call Option to Generate Income

Earlier in this chapter, we cover the call option from the buyer's perspective. The buyer is seeking gains, and options done well can deliver some great gains. But as we point out, options can be versatile and can fill a different need from speculating for gains — how about generating an income?

Using the same trade features from the previous sections, now take a look at the writer's (option seller's) perspective. Say that you own 100 shares of the same security, UUP. Owning 100 shares of an optionable security gives you the ability to write a covered call option and generate an income. If you own, say, 200 shares, you can write two covered calls, as follows.

You own 200 shares of UUP and you would like to generate income from this security. The share price is $20, and you see that you can write a call option for $75 per contract. If you have 200 shares, you have enough underlying assets to write two contracts (giving you income of 2 × $75 or a total of $150).

REMEMBER

When you write a call option, you create an obligation to sell a given asset. But since you own the asset already (in this case, shares of UUP as the underlying asset), your obligation is said to be "covered," so we actually say you wrote a *covered* call option. Now, can you write a call that is "uncovered"? Yes, it can be done. It's referred to as an "uncovered" or "naked" call, which can be a dangerous speculation. More on that appears later in this chapter.

Anyway, in our example, you write two covered calls (since you have 200 shares of UUP). This would give you income of $150 (2 call options times the premium of $75 per contract). This $150 of income equates in this instance to an equivalent dividend yield of 3.75 percent, which isn't bad. We say "equivalent yield" since the 200 shares are valued at $4,000 (200 shares × $20 per share) and $150 of option income equates to 3.75 percent of $4,000.

Now in exchange for this, you would have to sell your stock at $22 per share if and when the option is exercised between now and when that option expires. The following sections look at all the possible scenarios if you did do (write) this covered call.

REMEMBER

When you write a covered call option, look at all the scenarios to price out the good, the bad, and the ugly so you know exactly what will happen and you aren't stuck with a losing trade.

What if the security goes to the strike price or higher?

When you write a covered call at the strike price of $22, you have to sell your security at $22 per share. In this example, the two contracts would obligate you to see 200 shares at $22 and your proceeds would be $4,400 (200 times $22 per share). But what if UUP goes to $25 per share? Or $30? Or more?

You're stuck at $22 per share since that is the strike price — the agreed-upon price — in the call option contract. Note that this was the trade-off in the covered call that you wrote. Sure, you wouldn't lose money on the deal, but you would limit your potential gain due to the limiting strike price of $22. Of course, you wouldn't do too badly — your cost basis was $4,000 (200 shares × $20 per share) and you ultimately received a total of $4,550 ($4,400 proceeds of the sale plus $150 from the premium of the covered call) for a net gain of $550, or a net percentage gain of 13.75 percent.

TIP

With a cash balance of $4,550 in your account, you're ready to deploy that. There are, of course, a variety of things you could do with that, but in the spirit of this chapter, why not consider selling a put option to generate even more cash from UUP? Find out more (with a thought-provoking example) later in this chapter.

What if you don't want to sell at the strike price?

WARNING

Hold on a moment here . . . what happens if UUP rises and goes to $22 or higher, but you have a change of heart in the middle of doing your covered call and say, "But I don't want to sell my UUP!" Fortunately, you can keep your UUP stock, but it can be a tad ugly to do so. You can do it by buying back the covered call option you wrote. That sounds simple — and it is — but you'll lose money on the deal. Here's how it works.

Say UUP goes to $23 per share — a dollar per share above the strike price of $22. Buying back the covered call options removes the obligation of selling your UUP at $22, but it results in a loss. Say the $22 strike price call option you wrote rose in price (which it would if UUP's market price went up) to $125 per call option contract. Buying back both would cost you $250 total (2 contracts × $125). Your net loss will be $100. You received $150 when you originally wrote those two calls, and since you paid $250 to buy them back (and remove the obligation), your net loss is then $100. However, is it really so horrible?

Sure, you realized a net loss of $100, but keep in mind that you still have UUP. Its price went from $20 per share to $23, so on 200 shares of UUP you are up a total of $600 (200 shares × $3 per share unrealized gain) on that end, so you're not hurting that badly.

What if the security's price stays flat or moves sideways?

TIP

Say that UUP goes sideways between now and when it expires (December 2021). What if UUP goes from $20 to $21, then back to $20, then back to $21, then down to $19, and then back to $20? In that case, you would probably keep UUP and the $22 option would likely expire worthless in December. You keep the 200 shares and also the premium of $150. And then what? Well, why not do another covered call and earn more premium income? Why not turn UUP (or whatever stock or ETF you have) into a cash cow?

What if the security's price goes down?

What if UUP does down to $19 . . . or $18 . . . or $17 or lower? Your covered call would sharply go down in price since the price of calls generally loses value as the underlying asset goes down. This development can offer opportunities. If you were still bullish on UUP, you could buy back the covered call at a profit and remove that $22 "price ceiling" on the shares. Say that UUP is at $17, for example. The odds are good that the $22 covered call lost plenty of value. Say that the call's value went from $75 per contract to $30. That means that you could buy back both of those contracts for a total of $60 (2 × $30) and realize a profit of $90 ($150 − $60).

Meanwhile, if you're still bullish on UUP, this pullback in the share price can offer a buying opportunity. Some may seize that moment and buy 100 shares at $17, giving them an opportunity to expand total shares to 300 shares and to write up to three covered calls, offering the chance to increase cash flow by doing more covered calls.

How often can you write a covered call?

Earlier in this chapter, we mention that 200 shares of UUP would provide the opportunity to write two covered calls for a total premium income of $150 and that this amount was equivalent to an effective yield of 3.75 percent. That's not bad, but here's the kicker. What if, during the course of a calendar year, you had the opportunity to write two or three or more covered calls? What if you wrote a covered call on 100 shares of your currency ETF in January for $75 and that option expired in, say, April, and you did the same covered call trade two more times during the remainder of that calendar year? Assume for this example's sake that in each of those trades, you realized premium income of $75.

If you did at least three covered calls, you'd receive a total of $225 on the same lot of 100 shares and your effective yield would be north of 10 percent. Earning $225 on $2,000 worth of shares (100 × $20 per share) equates to an 11.25 percent yield. For speculators that may sound okay, but to those who want income, that is a great amount. What income-oriented investor wouldn't want a double-digit yield at a time when interest rates are in the very low single digits? (Mic drop moment.)

Using a Call Option for Safety or Hedging

"Going short" is a speculative strategy betting on the fall of a given asset. Many speculators have gone short on all sorts of assets such as stocks, ETFs, commodities, and of course, currencies. Very few things that are traded are immune from downward movements of their market prices, so it makes sense that you can speculate by seeking a profit with a bet on something going down.

Of course, in this chapter, the optimal way to make a bet on something falling in price would be to buy a put option since it's a less risky way of making a bearish bet (see the next section). But many folks prefer the act of "going short," which is the act of selling that given asset at today's (presumably) higher price with the objective of making a profit by buying back that same asset at a lower price later and booking the difference as a profit.

Say the asset's market price is $2,000 (like, for example, 100 shares of a $20 stock or currency ETF), but you think it will go down to $1,200. You can sell it today at $2,000 (it is done in your brokerage account where the broker borrows the asset and sells it instantly). If you're correct in your expectations that the asset will plummet to $1,200, then you will buy it back at that price and the asset will be returned to the broker. If you sold it at $2,000 and then bought it back at $1,200, you would book a profit of $800 when the trade was closed out. Nice trades if you can make them!

But what if you're wrong? In this case, what happens if the asset doesn't go down but actually goes up? Note that you're on the hook for buying it back regardless of the price. What if it goes to $3,000? In that case you would lose $1,000. But what if it continued to rise to $3,200, then $3,500, and so on? Your losses could be unlimited, and it would be a financial bloodbath for you.

But what if in this case you bought some "protection" against a price rise that could hurt you? This is one of those rare moments that a call option could be used as a "hedge" or "protective" call option. The call option could cost, for example, $75. It would be cheap protection, but it would give you some offset in the case of the asset's price going against you. Now, if you were ultimately correct and the asset did go down to $1,200, that $75 call option would become worthless, but look at the favorable math. You would have made an $800 profit less a $75 loss, giving you a net profit of $725 (not too shabby!).

Picking Apart Put Options

REMEMBER

A put option is a contract that gives the buyer the right, but not the obligation, to sell a specific asset at a specific price between now and when the option expires. Keep in mind that the price action reverses versus the call option. In other words, the lower the market price goes, the more valuable your put option is.

In the same way that call options have three basic uses (as explained earlier in this chapter), we can flip it and apply the same concepts for put options.

Use #1: Bearish speculation

If you believe that the underlying asset will soon be declining or crashing and you want to make the big bucks when that bearish move occurs, then you would consider buying a put option. Again using UUP as an example, say that it is at $20 per share and you think or expect that it will fall to, say, $17, then you may consider buying a put option at a strike price of $19. If this option will expire December 2021, for example, you could buy this $19 put option for, say, $70.

TIP

If UUP stays flat, moves sideways, or goes up, the put option will lose value. If the stock doesn't trend your way, consider cashing it out at a loss a month or two before expiration so you can recoup some value. Otherwise, the option will be in danger of becoming totally worthless.

Use#2: Generating income

If your goal is to generate income, you're fine if the put option loses value or becomes worthless because you didn't buy the option — you sold (wrote) it. Think about the earlier income example but with you on the other side of the trade. You wrote a put option at the $19 strike price that expires December 2021, and you received the premium of $70 as option income.

Remember that there are trade-offs here. You received income, but in exchange you have an obligation. In this case, you must buy UUP at $19 during the life of the option. If UUP doesn't go down to $19, the option will ultimately expire worthless, but that means that you keep the $70.

In writing the put option, keep in mind that it does need to be "covered," so to speak. The covered call writer needs to secure their obligation by having in the account 100 shares of that particular security in the event that the option is exercised and the call buyer wants the security. In the put option, you don't need to have 100 shares of the underlying stock or ETF, but you must have enough cash or buying power to cover the potential purchase.

When you have enough cash in the account to cover the purchase, the put is referred to as a *cash-secured put.* So if the strike price is $19, you must have at least $1,900 in cash in the account. A second way to secure or cover the potential purchase is by having enough qualified stock in your account that can act as "collateral" to secure the purchase. This is called a *portfolio-secured put.*

Keep in mind that if UUP does go down and hits $19 or lower, the put writer must buy at $19, but when you factor in the $70 premium received, the net price is actually lower. Those shares do indeed cost $1,900 (100 shares times $19), but the actual amount paid is $1,830 ($1,900 minus the $70 option income received), meaning that the actual price per share is $18.30.

What if UUP falls to $18 or $17 or lower? It doesn't matter; you're still obligated to buy it at $19. Even though cash-secured put writing can be relatively safe to do, it's still a form of speculating!

Use#3: For hedging and protection

Say that you bought UUP long ago at $10 per share and now it's at $20. Presume you're still bullish and you plan to hold on to it longer, but you're getting skittish and you think that a pullback in the price is a looming possibility. You don't want to sell — maybe you aren't ready to turn that large capital gain into a taxable, realized gain. Regardless of your reason, you're concerned about a potential, yet temporary (hopefully!), near-term decline. What can you do?

You may consider buying a put option on your own security. This strategy is referred to as a *protective put.* If the decline doesn't materialize, the put will likely lose value and ultimately become worthless. You're not that concerned because you bought that put option as a form of insurance. What if you're correct in your concern and UUP does decline in the near term?

As UUP declines, the put option you bought rises in value. At some point you can cash out the put at a profit. Hopefully, the profit from the put will offset some or possibly most of the decline in UUP. Some folks may use their put option profits to purchase more shares of UUP, taking advantage of the near-term decline as a buying opportunity.

Considering Some Combination Trades

Earlier in this chapter, we cover "single use" option strategies — buy a call (or a put) and write/sell a call (or a put). This section covers a few popular option combination strategies that many successful traders use in the currency markets and other markets. We can't get comprehensive, but keep in mind that the resources at the end of the chapter have sites that cover virtually all the available option combination strategies, their use, setup, and so on.

Debit spreads and credit spreads

Debit spreads and *credit spreads* refer to the combination trade cost after you price out all the components. If you buy a call option for $100 and you write (sell) a call for $75, then the net debit spread is $25, meaning that the net cost you're paying for this combination trade is only $25.

If you're doing an options trade where you're paying $50 for an option and you're also writing an option for $60, this is called a *net credit spread* since the net amount is $10 of income or gain put into your account.

Diagonal and vertical calendar spreads

In the world of option combination trades, when you have two or more legs, it's possible for those options to expire in the same month or on the same date (referred to as a *vertical calendar spread*) or in different months or on different dates (referred to as a *diagonal calendar spread*).

Say that you bought both a call and a put option on the same asset (a neutral combination strategy such as the "long strangle" or the "long straddle"). A purely neutral strategy might mean that both options expire on the same date. But what if you're a little more bullish than bearish? In that case you may buy a call option with a longer shelf life while the put option has a shorter shelf life. Maybe the call option expires June 2022 while the put expires March 2022. This would be an example of a *diagonal option spread.*

The bull call spread

We have used our friend the U.S. dollar ETF (symbol UUP) and have extracted the following example straight from the CBOE's quote data. Table 15-2 illustrates a popular combination trade called the *bull call spread* and the benefits of using it.

Each of the options involved is referred to as a "leg," and it may also be referred to as a "long leg" or a "short leg" depending on the outlook. The "long leg" may be the bullish component of the trade while the "short leg" may be the bearish component. Both options in the spread are out of the money (explained earlier in this chapter), but one is more so than the other and the difference in strike prices is the profit differential for the trader.

TECHNICAL STUFF

One question may pop up if you have a short leg: How is it being secured? In a spread, you don't necessarily need 100 shares of a given stock or ETF to secure the call option that you wrote because the long call option you bought acts as the collateral, so to speak, and secures it. Keep in mind that when you buy a put, that gives you the right, but not the obligation, to acquire 100 shares. This position, in turn, secures your obligation when you need to sell 100 shares. Because of this, a spread can be a stand-alone trade.

In Table 15-2, presume that UUP is at $20.

TABLE 15-2 **The Bull Call Spread**

The Leg	Strike Price	Cost/Price	Expiration
Buy call option (long leg)	$21 (OTM)	Pay $65	March 2022
Sell/write call option (short leg)	$22 (farther OTM)	Receive $45	March 2022
(A debit spread)	**Cost of spread =**	**$20**	**(A vertical spread)**

If you had bought the $21 call option expiring in March 2022, it would have cost $65 — a 100 percent bullish play with unlimited profit potential. However, the spread is not as bullish and is a safer bet as well as costing less money. The bull call spread is said to be a moderate bullish strategy, but besides limiting the risk, it also limits the profit potential to the difference in the strike prices.

In this combination, you see two call options on UUP. They have the same expiration but two different strike prices:

>> The primary leg is the long call at 21, which is closer to the original market price of UUP ($20), so it is almost ATM.

>> The second leg is the call option that you wrote, which is farther away at $22, so it is OTM. The purpose of this second leg is to hedge the position, and the money received ($45) helps to pay for the trade. In other words, if this combination is a total loser, you're out only $20.

Here are the basic scenarios that could unfold with this bull call spread:

>> **UUP goes down or sideways:** In the event that the price of UUP (or whatever optionable asset you're moderately bullish on) does not rise but instead goes down, or the price stays flat or moves sideways (and never reaches $21), both legs of the bull call spread lose value. If you do nothing and UUP's price does not reach the closest price of $21, then ultimately all the options in the trade expire worthless.

TIP

If the asset's price movement doesn't budge upward within a reasonable time, close out the trade and recoup some value so it isn't a complete loss. Even the best traders have losing trades, but they do what they can to minimize losses. If the spread's expiration date is, for example, March 2022 and the price isn't moving your way, consider closing the trade a few months before the expiration to reclaim some of the money deployed. Then do your research to find your next trade and hopefully have better luck.

>> **UUP reaches the spread's range:** Say that in this example UUP does go up and hits $21. This means that the leg you are long on went from being out of the money to in the money, and that leg is likely profitable. Meanwhile, the short leg (the option you wrote which is a liability) is still out of the money, so this may be an opportune time to close out (sell) the entire spread and gain a profit.

>> **UUP goes up past the spread's range:** What happens if UUP goes north of the $21–$22 price range? It doesn't matter how high UUP's price rises since the profit is locked at the $21–$22 price range. Imagine, for a minute, that UUP hits $30 per share. Well, the $21 call option you bought is offset by the $22 call you wrote, and no matter how high UUP rises, your profit is the price differential of $100, or the difference between 100 shares at $21 per share and 100 shares at $22 per share.

TIP

This example keeps it simple with a one-dollar price spread ($21–$22). That limits the potential gain to $100. But what if you did a two-dollar spread, such as a $21–$23 spread? In that case you'd widen the potential profit to $200. Just keep in mind that the cost would be a little more — do the calculations.

TIP

In the preceding example, the cost of the spread was $20 and the potential gain was $100. That is a 5-to-1 profit-to-cost ratio in that you're risking $20 to make $100. In that case, the ratio is worthwhile. Any time a spread gives you a 4-to-1 or better ratio, it can be a good consideration.

The bear put spread

The bull call spread is for bullish speculators, but bearish combinations await you too. What if you're moderately bearish on UUP? If you wanted to be purely bearish, you could just buy a put option. But if you're not that bearish — if you want to hedge or be more moderate in your approach — then a bear put spread is worth considering.

Say UUP is at $20 and you expect it to decline in the near future to $17 or lower. In the bear put spread, you buy a put (the primary leg, which is the long put) with the strike price near the stock's price while writing a put (the second leg, which is the short put) at a strike price that is farther away (out of the money, or OTM). Table 15-3 has the basic setup.

TABLE 15-3

The Bear Put Spread

The Leg	Strike Price	Cost/Price	Expiration
Long put	$19	Pay $50	March 2022
Short put	$18	Receive $35	March 2022
(A debit spread)	**Cost of spread =**	**$15**	**(A vertical spread)**

Here are the basic scenarios that could unfold with this bear put spread:

>> **UUP's price either goes up or moves sideways:** A bear put spread is a moderate bearish strategy. You're betting the price goes down — but what if it doesn't? If UUP, in our example, does not approach the $19 price level, then the bear put spread won't be profitable. If UUP moves sideways, stays flat, or goes up, this trade will lose value quickly.

REMEMBER

Give yourself an exit strategy not only in this type of option combination but also in most option strategies in case they don't work in your favor. Try to exit before the position becomes worthless or nearly worthless. Reclaim some value if possible so you can redeploy the funds in a new and hopefully more successful trade.

>> **UUP goes down to the spread's range:** If UUP does go down to the first level of $19, then start getting ready to cash out with a profit. If the $19 option goes profitable (which is what you want), then don't be shy about closing out the trade and locking in a profit. Of course, you can stay in the trade to see whether a greater profit materializes, and that's fine if ample time is left in the spread and other factors look positive (such as the "technicals" that are covered in Chapter 6). Just keep in mind that profits can be fleeting, so monitor carefully and stick to your exit strategy.

>> **UUP declines past the spread's range:** This is the same scenario we describe in the bull call spread in the previous section, when the underlying asset shoots past the spread's range (except this is the mirror opposite).

If UUP plummets past the range (goes below $19–$18), then cash out quickly because your profit is limited to the differential before the $19 put and the $18 put ($100 max profit potential).

Breaking Down the Mechanics of Making Options Trades

Every brokerage is a little different, but most of what it takes to make your trades is generally the same, as you find out in the following sections.

Choosing a brokerage firm and gaining approval for options

If you're doing options trades on stocks, regular ETFs, and currency ETFs (covered in Chapter 13), then a regular stock brokerage account will suffice. If you're doing options trades on currency futures (covered in Chapter 14), then consider an account with a commodities futures brokerage firm. Chapter 14 provides a selected listing.

Once you have selected your brokerage firm, contact them or visit their site for details on gaining options trading approval. In the world of stock brokerage accounts, there are several levels of options approval. You will be asked questions about your trading objectives (growth, speculation, income, and so on) and your profile (such as your experience level) and how often you seek to trade. Here are typical approval levels:

>> **Level 1:** You will only be allowed to do covered call writing. This is considered the safest way to trade options, and many brokerage firms even allow this in retirement/IRA accounts. This level is usually very easy to be approved for.

>> **Level 2:** Each successive level gives you all the power of the prior level plus more approved trades. Level 2 allows you the ability to do covered calls (Level 1) and also buy options.

>> **Next levels:** Every brokerage gives you further ability at various levels, such as doing spreads and other combinations.

>> **Highest level:** This is "full trading," which allows you virtually all the options trading strategies except probably naked call writing, which is risky and typically not allowed for most retail investors.

WARNING

The bottom line is to ask questions before you open your account. I (coauthor Paul) recall finding a futures brokerage for my client that offered every type of trade and asset available *except* the one asset I wanted to help my client with — ugh! I assumed too much, and I needed to ask before all the hassles of opening an account.

Placing an order

When you're ready to place a trade, either on the phone with a live broker or online at the broker's website, keep in mind the orders in Table 15-4 for your guidance.

TABLE 15-4   ## Orders for Options Trades

If you want to . . .	Then you would . . .	Comment
Buy a call or put option	"BUY TO OPEN"	You're going long.
Cash in that put or call	"SELL TO CLOSE"	You're closing a long position.
Write a covered call or sell a put	"SELL TO OPEN"	You're going short.
Close out (buy back) a covered call or a put you sold	"BUY TO CLOSE"	You're closing a short position before expiration.
Allow the option to expire	DO NOTHING*	An option can expire with no action by you.

Check with your broker in advance about policy on expiration. If you bought a call/put option and it is at the money or in the money, some brokers will automatically exercise it at the strike price.

TIP

Here are a few tips and guidelines for placing options trades:

>> Know the terminology. In general, if you're buying calls and options, you're "buying to open" because option contracts are referred to as "being open" and "being closed" to enter and then to exit.

>> Determine how many contracts you want. At the site you will enter a number for how many contracts you will be trading.

>> Review bid and ask prices to figure how much you will pay for your options trade(s) and/or how much you will receive when you cash them out. See the next section for more on bid and ask prices.

>> Understand limit orders versus market orders. Use limit orders to control how much you're willing to pay (or how much you're willing to receive) when you make a trade.

Reading an options table

Table 15-5 is an example of an options table, which provides the latest options price quotes. The following sections break down the columns in the table. The security in this example has the symbol UUP, which is PowerShares DB US Dollar Index Bullish (a currency ETF).

TABLE 15-5   **A Sample Options Table**

Column 1	2	3	4	5	6	7	8
Option symbol/ Option type	Last	Net Change	Bid	Ask	Vol.	Open Interest	Implied Volatility (IV)
UUP220318C00020000	1.75	0.25	1.50	1.80	58	400	.114

TECHNICAL STUFF

Many options quote tables will give you the "greeks," meaning they include data linked to volatility such as delta, gamma, and so on. I (coauthor Paul) personally don't use the greeks, but they are covered in depth in the resources listed at the end of this chapter.

Column 1

This column shows you the name in code for the security. The name breaks down as follows:

>> UUP is the symbol

>> 220318 indicates the expiration as the year (22)

>> C = Call, the type of option

>> 20000 is the strike price, which is $20 followed by three zeros.

REMEMBER

Most options tend to have a shelf life of nine months or less. An option issued in August 2021, for example, will likely expire in May 2022. Of course, new options are issued constantly, so you'll see a variety of expirations from which you can choose your time frame for an option's expiration. I (coauthor Paul) personally prefer (especially for beginners) options that have a long shelf life such as LEAPs, which stands for Long-term Equity Anticipation Securities. It sounds fancy but they are essentially like all the other options except for one crucial difference: They have a time span of one year or more.

For example, as I look at UUP options quotes table at www.cboe.com (at the time of writing in August 2021), I see call and put options with an expiration of January 2023 — a shelf life of over 16 months. I see other securities with expirations for September 2023 — a time frame exceeding two full years! Yes, you'll pay more for these options due to the extended time frame, but when it comes time to sell them, you'll get more too.

TIP

If you're tracking a particular security (such as a currency ETF, covered in Chapter 13), don't be shy about contacting the Chicago Board Options Exchange and asking them when the next round of options will be activated for trading. That way you can time your trade for maximum time value if you like.

Column 2

"Last" indicates the price of the most recent order. In this case, it indicates 1.75, which is $175. The reason for this is that since an option contract is 100 shares, you use 100 as the multiplier to know how much you're paying for the contract (not including commissions and transaction fees).

Column 3

"Net change" is how much the price has changed today (so far) from the closing price at the end of the prior day's trading session.

Columns 4 and 5

The "Bid" and the "Ask" are important prices that act as exit points and entry points for your trade if you place a market order. In this table you see the bid of $1.50 and the ask of $1.80. This means that if you place a market order to buy this option, it will cost you $180. If the market is volatile, you may pay a little more or a little less. If you're cashing out or writing your option, the amount you will receive is $150.

WARNING

Placing market orders puts your trade's price at the mercy of market volatility, and you can easily pay too much getting into a trade or not earn as much as you think when you exit a trade. It's better to use limit orders so you have greater control over how much you pay for a given trade. In this example, consider putting in a limit order somewhere between the bid and the ask. In effect, it is "negotiating" with the market and not budging on your desired price.

TIP

For this example, put in a limit order for $1.65 (this is midway between bid and ask) and then "submit" your order. If it fills, great! If not, you can change your order and move up the limit price to $1.70 if you're intent on getting it placed. Keep in mind that a limit order essentially states "fill it at my chosen price *or better*." In other words, you may get in at a more favorable price than your stated limit order price.

Columns 6 and 7

"Volume" (Column 6) is a reference to how many contracts have traded so far in that trading session (58, in this example). "Open interest" (Column 7) gives you a total tally of how many total contracts are in the marketplace. The open interest can give you an idea of how bullish or bearish the market is on a given option contract.

TIP

In this case, the open interest for this call option is 400. What would you think if you looked at the $20 put option and you noticed that the open interest was, say, 100 total contracts? The inference here is that the market is more bullish than bearish by a 4-to-1 ratio. You can look at the open interest to see whether it gives you clues to help you decide on a trade (especially if you're a contrarian).

Column 8

"Implied volatility" is essentially the market's expectation about this option's potential price movement. The higher the number, the more the market implies that this option has the power to move quickly upward or downward. In general, options that have higher implied volatility tend to have higher prices.

Getting a Few Golden Rules for Options Beginners

REMEMBER

Of course, we want you to maximize your profits and minimize your losses, so here are some golden rules to keep in mind as you wade into the exciting world of options:

>> You don't have to be an expert in options to make money with them, but you should become as proficient as possible about the underlying asset. That's the secret sauce. Because options derive their value from the underlying asset,

you should spend most of your time understanding this particular asset, the intricacies of its particular market, supply and demand fundamentals, and so on.

>> Get the longest time frame you can afford. Because the market in the short term can be very unpredictable and often seemingly irrational, the longer the time frame the better, and the longer the time frame, the greater the chance of a winning trade. For example, I (coauthor Paul) like LEAPs, which have a time frame or "shelf life" of one year, two years, or longer. (See the earlier section "Column 1" for more information.)

>> An option is a wasting asset since it can lose value over time if the underlying asset is not moving in the direction of the strike price during the shelf life of the option. (In other words, time is not on your side.) While time is usually an asset in the world of investing, options have an expiration date, so decide what you will do with them months before the expiration. Of course, if you wrote options, then the expiration date is a friendlier event for you.

>> When you have the good fortune of having profitable trades, always be sure to move a portion of your profits to a safer venue, such as a savings account, or to your investment portfolio to reinvest these profits in vehicles such as dividend-paying stocks and ETFs.

>> Never speculate with more money than you can afford to lose. Limit your exposure to a relatively small percentage of your investable portfolio, such as 5 percent or less. One of my favorite ways to "fund" the purchases of call and put options is by using money that comes in from writing call and put options. If, for example, I wrote a covered call and received $1,000, that would be my limit for purchasing options. That way if I lose every dime of that $1,000, I know it came from options and I didn't harm the principal.

>> Focus on underlying assets that you understand and can specialize in. Too many folks do options in a wide, scattered variety of vehicles, making it unwieldy to track and monitor every market.

>> When you're timing a purchase for a call option, it's optimal to make that trade on a down day since call options will be cheaper and you can get in at a favorable price (if possible). A second choice is a placid or calm market day. On days that you're timing a purchase for a put option, it's optimal to buy on up days since put options will generally be cheaper (if possible).

>> If you're going to write a covered call option or sell/cash one out, it's optimal to do it on an up day to maximize the price. Also, if you're going to write a put option or sell/cash one out, then consider doing so on a down day to optimize the price.

>> Be a contrarian. If everyone is bullish on a given asset, that means that call options are more valuable and may be a good consideration to cash out (if you own a call option). Another consideration can be to write a covered call. Being a contrarian on the bearish side is fine, but make sure the asset in question that has plummeted has good fundamentals and has the potential for a rebound.

Trying Options Tutorials and Resources

For those who trade options, there are plenty of resources and guidance. Here are some:

TIP

>> **Chicago Board Options Exchange** (www.cboe.com): The CBOE has extensive educational materials and programs at their site for both beginners and experienced options traders.

Go to the CBOE site and sign up for their free options newsletters to get lots of great tips and news about the options market. In addition, you will get mailings from them when they do free live option seminars in your local area.

>> **Options Industry Council** (www.optionseducation.org): This is the industry trade group for all exchanges that trade options. They have plenty of educational materials and programs at their site. In addition, anyone can call them and ask general questions about options at 888-OPTIONS.

>> *High-Level Investing For Dummies* by Paul Mladjenvoic (Wiley): This guide has an extensive section on options and options combination trades.

>> *Trading Options For Dummies,* 3rd edition, by Joe Duarte (Wiley): This book provides A-to-Z coverage on trading options.

>> **The Options Guide** (www.theoptionsguide.com): This is an extensive resource of options trading tutorials.

>> **Option Trading-Pedia** (www.optiontradingpedia.com/): Check out an encyclopedia of options trading articles and tutorials.

>> *Ultra-Investing with Options* (online course): Coauthor Paul's course for beginners is at www.ravingcapitalist.com/home/ultra-investing-with-options/.

>> **Chicago Mercantile Group** (www.cmegroup.com): If you're interested in options on futures contracts, go to this extensive site for general information and education.

» *A Guide to Investing with Options* by Virginia B. Morris (Lightbulb Press): This neat little book nicely explains options and lays out useful illustrations and visuals.

» **I Love Theta** (https://ilovetheta.com/the-option-greeks): This site has a great explanation of the option "greeks."

IN THIS CHAPTER

» Defining cryptocurrencies, their pros, and their cons

» Making the most of methods for participating in cryptos

» Listing the biggest cryptocurrencies and taking steps to get them

» Considering cryptocurrency exchange-traded funds

» Getting the scoop on important rules and resources

Chapter **16**

Trading Cryptocurrencies

How could you do a book on currency trading without covering the new kid on the block: cryptocurrencies? How can you talk about trading opportunities in vehicles such as the U.S. dollar or the euro and ignore the monster moves that have occurred in recent years with Bitcoin, Ethereum, and other cryptocurrencies? Wonder no more: This chapter introduces you to the world of cryptocurrencies.

Cryptocurrencies are a great complement to your currency trading universe because they have advantages that traditional currencies don't have. Cryptocurrencies, especially the long-standing vehicles of Bitcoin and Ethereum, have been pure supply-and-demand plays versus the politics and governmental machinations and management (oversupply!) of traditional currencies (run by central banking officials). Since traditional currencies can be produced in greater quantities — which, in turn, reduce the subsequent value of each unit of currency — cryptocurrencies gain value since their supply is greatly limited (while demand has been rising). This central feature makes cryptocurrencies an attractive hedge and alternative vehicle.

Describing Cryptocurrencies

REMEMBER

Cryptocurrencies (such as Bitcoin and Ethereum) went from obscurity (circa 2012) to the hot speculative vehicle to chase during 2019–2021. Cryptocurrencies are private, digital currencies that became popular in recent years as alternatives to mainstream currencies. They became currencies through innovative, new technologies (such as blockchain technology) that made these currencies very difficult to hack or to copy. In this way, they can maintain a strict quantity and ensure a quality necessary for currencies: scarcity.

Currencies that are overproduced subsequently lose their value (inflation!) — a condition all-too-common throughout history. As cryptocurrencies gained notoriety, and their usage as a store of value and as a means of exchange increased, they reached acceptance on the investing and speculative landscapes.

WARNING

It's important to highlight an important point: Cryptocurrencies are a speculative vehicle, and as such, interested parties should tread carefully. They can be very volatile, so the safest way to participate is with relatively small amounts. Cryptocurrencies have also gained acceptance as a means of exchange in business transactions (to buy/sell goods and services), and this is the safest way to participate. More importantly, it's best to do your research before you make your first purchase. The rest of this chapter can help you get started.

Considering the Main Benefits and Issues of Cryptocurrencies

Here are the primary reasons one should consider cryptocurrencies (more are included in the resources listed at the end of this chapter):

>> **Diversification:** Because mainstream currencies (such as the U.S. dollar and the euro) have no limits to being created by their respective government central banks, over-creation can lead to a currency collapse. This type of collapse has happened numerous times throughout history. In recent years, countries such as Venezuela and Zimbabwe have seen their currencies crash through rampant overproduction. Cryptocurrencies provide diversification by exhibiting qualities that mainstream currencies do not have, such as limited supply and growing demand.

>> **Store of value:** Due to rising demand and limited supply, cryptocurrencies have experienced rising (yet volatile) price rises, which can be a good counterplay to the inflationary problems with traditional currencies. In the event that you may need "regular" money, cryptocurrencies can be sold (or "cashed out"), giving you the cash you need (and hopefully more than when you initially got into cryptocurrencies).

>> **Means of exchange:** Cryptocurrencies can be used to make purchases as more and more vendors and purchasing venues allow for the use of cryptocurrencies as a transactional medium.

>> **Privacy:** While your cash and credit transactions are (more and more) visible and trackable by watchful governments and financial institutions, cryptocurrencies have exhibited more privacy and security.

WARNING

But watch out! Cryptocurrencies have some disadvantages:

>> **Volatility:** Cryptocurrencies have exhibited a great degree of volatility. It may be great for the speculative trader, but the risks for loss are certainly there if you bought at a high price and then need your money when the cryptocurrency prices are down.

>> **Taxes:** Most taxing authorities (including the IRS) do see cryptocurrencies as assets that may have taxable capital gains, so you must do proper recording and reporting.

>> **Political risks:** Many governmental authorities may perceive cryptocurrencies as a competitive threat and possibly as an unacceptable alternative to their own currencies. Given that, the possibility exists that governments may enact laws that greatly limit or threaten cryptocurrencies with either restrictions or even possible banning, which would harm your cryptocurrency value and ownership.

It's Your Choice: Participating in the Cryptocurrency World in Three Ways

For beginners and small investors/speculators, there are three ways to participate in the world of "cryptos": having a cryptocurrency wallet, using a brokerage account, or conducting business transactions.

The greatest control: A cryptocurrency wallet

For many folks, this is the preferred way to participate. A cryptocurrency wallet is a software program that allows you to safely store, receive, and pay with cryptocurrencies. Obviously, cryptocurrencies are digital — they're not like physical paper money and coins you can keep in your pocket or wallet. The wallet can come as an app on your laptop or smartphone, or it can come as a physical flash drive. Find out more in the later section "Selecting storage."

The simplest approach: A brokerage account

Probably the simplest way to participate in cryptocurrencies is through a broker that makes buying and selling cryptocurrencies as easy as buying and selling stocks or exchange-traded funds (ETFs) inside your typical brokerage account. My (coauthor Paul's) first cryptocurrency transaction happened when I bought $75 worth of Bitcoin in my stock brokerage account. Of course, a single unit of Bitcoin is a huge sum (about $49,000 as I write this), but I prefer to use a dollar-cost averaging approach (covered later in this chapter).

TIP

Given how expensive Bitcoin was then (and still is!), my brokerage account made it easy to buy a small, fractional piece of Bitcoin, and at any given time, I can make a fractional purchase and accumulate my holdings. When the time comes, I can sell all or a portion of my Bitcoin holdings just as easily. Find out more about brokers and trading platforms later in this chapter.

WARNING

Some folks like to trade cryptocurrencies through their accounts to actively buy and sell using the same conventions (such as technical analysis, covered in Chapter 6, and other trading approaches) used in forex and other markets. That's fine, but the risk of loss and transaction costs increases.

The safest approach: Business transactions

Business transactions are the safest (least risky?) way to participate in cryptocurrencies. You can offer them as a payment option in your business, even if your business is a part-time enterprise from home and you're a sole entrepreneur or freelancer. You can sell goods and services and receive payment in a cryptocurrency and store this money in your app or flash-drive wallet. Because you don't buy the cryptocurrency with your own money, you reduce your exposure to potential loss.

Once you have cryptocurrencies, you can use them to buy goods and services. Because cryptocurrencies can rise or fall in value, this could offer both risks and rewards. Say that you received payments in Bitcoin when it was at $40,000 per unit and the transaction was for $400. In that case, you would receive a fractional amount of .01 Bitcoin. Suppose that time passed and Bitcoin was now $80,000 per unit. Your fractional amount of .01 Bitcoin is now worth $800 (.01 of $80,000) and your "buying power" has doubled. Of course, this could be a double-edged sword. That $400 of Bitcoin would shrink if Bitcoin fell to, say, $30,000 per unit, and your .01 fractional ownership would be worth only $300.

Looking at Leading Cryptocurrencies

In this section we focus on the main cryptocurrencies. Table 16-1 lists them in order from highest market value to lowest at the time of writing.

TABLE 16-1

Leading Cryptocurrencies

Name	Symbol	Price (USD)	Market Cap	Vol (24H)
Bitcoin	BTC	45,785.50	$861.28B	$34.69B
Ethereum	ETH	3,101.78	$363.86B	$25.70B
Cardano	ADA	2.1409	$69.32B	$4.99B
Binance Coin	BNB	408.22	$68.82B	$2.53B
Tether	USDT	1.0003	$64.08B	$87.75B
XRP	XRP	1.17763	$54.75B	$8.06B
Dogecoin	DOGE	0.313526	$41.99B	$6.71B
USD Coin	USDC	0.99957	$27.56B	$3.67B
Polkadot	DOT	24.832	$24.62B	$2.71B
Solana	SOL	78.463	$22.11B	$5.01B
Uniswap	UNI	27.098	$15.99B	$838.53M
Terra	LUNA	29.603	$12.27B	$2.41B
Bitcoin Cash	BCH	647.57	$12.22B	$2.86B
Chainlink	LINK	26.6	$11.91B	$1.79B
Binance USD	BUSD	0.9997	$11.89B	$6.56B

In Table 16-1, you have the following information:

>> **Column 1:** Cryptocurrency name. These are the most familiar and established cryptocurrencies.

>> **Column 2:** Symbol. When you are ready to buy/sell, mainstream cryptocurrencies have symbols just as stocks and ETFs do.

>> **Column 3:** Price for one unit, or what one unit of this cryptocurrency costs.

>> **Column 4:** Market cap. This column indicates the total market value of this issued cryptocurrency. This is the same concept as the market cap ("market capitalization" or total market value) of stocks.

>> **Column 5:** Daily volume (24H column). This indicates how much of that currency has traded that day.

The following sections go into more detail on the some of the biggest names in the world of cryptocurrencies.

WARNING

There are literally thousands of cryptocurrencies, and some of them will not be sustainable. The opportunities for loss are just as real as the opportunities for gain. All currencies are subject to the confidence and acceptance of the public. The moment that the public loses confidence in a given currency, it ceases to accept it as a store of value and a means of exchange. Throughout history, when a particular currency is subject to rampant overproduction, it's the underlying cause of hyperinflation and the collapse of the currency. This risk has been true of regular currencies throughout history, and no doubt this risk will be present in the proliferating cryptocurrency space. For newbies to cryptocurrencies, it's best to stick to those cryptocurrencies that are established and have gained wide acceptance in the marketplace. Use cryptocurrencies that have exhibited acceptance through greater participation and usage by both the public and financial institutions so you can avoid the risk that can occur in the world of currencies (crypto and otherwise).

TIP

Of course, the following sections discuss only a few examples of the more than 2,000 cryptocurrency choices. To scour this world and find all the serious cryptocurrency choices, consider heading to Investing.com. If a cryptocurrency ends up at Investing.com, it's a major achievement since this site is a major hub for serious investors and speculators in the financial world. Go specifically to the section on cryptocurrencies to start your research: www.investing.com/crypto/.

Bitcoin (The mother of all cryptos)

Born circa 2012, Bitcoin is the 800-pound gorilla of the crypto world. It is stunning to think that in the early years, you could have bought a single unit of it for under $100. The world ignored it — until it made its move. Supply and demand took over.

As more money from investors and speculators moved in, very limited supply met rising demand. Bitcoin's first bubble hit in 2018 (see Figure 16-1).

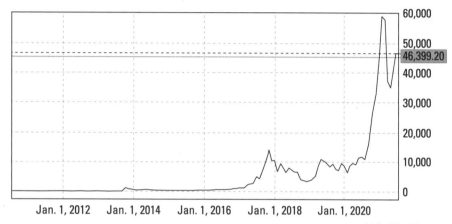

FIGURE 16-1: Bitcoin's lifetime chart.

© John Wiley & Sons, Inc.

In Figure 16-2, you can view the most recent five years of Bitcoin; it was at the height of its move during early 2021 before falling back.

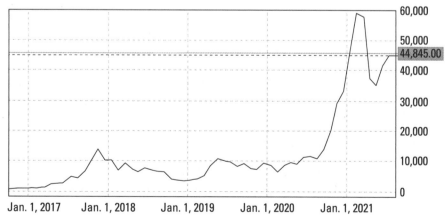

FIGURE 16-2: Bitcoin's five-year chart.

© John Wiley & Sons, Inc.

TIP

As Bitcoin visibly became the "top dog" in the global cryptocurrency world during late 2020–2021, it should be a cautionary tale for traders. Bitcoin has become a rising and falling vehicle much like other assets, so it will experience bullish and bearish conditions. This is where your "contrarian" side should kick in. Be more cautious when everyone is ebullient (it doesn't hurt to take some profits off the table and sell a portion in bullish times), and consider buying when everyone is bearish and pessimistic.

Ethereum

Ethereum is the crypto world's second banana, and it's a worthy alternative to Bitcoin. It's obviously less pricey, but you can realize the same roller-coaster ride, as you see in Figure 16-3.

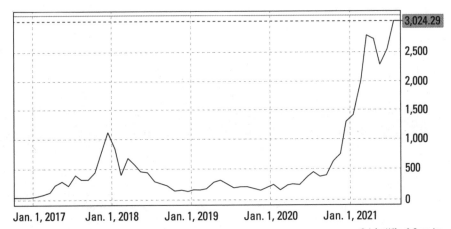

FIGURE 16-3:
Ethereum's five-year chart.

© John Wiley & Sons, Inc.

Launched in early 2014, Ethereum became a competing cryptocurrency on the then-newly launched blockchain technology, and it quickly became popular with developers and tech capitalists. As of September 2021, it is the second most popular cryptocurrency (as measured by market capitalization), and part of its popularity is that its cost per unit is less than a tenth of Bitcoin's unit price.

Dogecoin

Don't worry; I won't cover every cryptocurrency (who's got the time?), but I will spotlight one crypto that is relatively low-priced and has attracted many speculators: Dogecoin (see Figure 16-4).

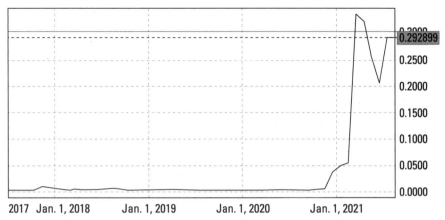

0.292899

0.2500

0.2000

0.1500

0.1000

0.0500

0.0000

2017   Jan. 1, 2018   Jan. 1, 2019   Jan. 1, 2020   Jan. 1, 2021

FIGURE 16-4:
Dogecoin's
five-year chart.

© John Wiley & Sons, Inc.

Dogecoin is highlighted here primarily as an example of a popular and yet very low-cost cryptocurrency. It actually started as a joke by some developers but quickly became a serious vehicle for transactions and trading.

Taking the First Steps to Buying Cryptocurrencies

REMEMBER

Actually getting into cryptocurrencies isn't as difficult as you may think. Here are the first things to address before you head over to an exchange or broker for your first transactions:

>> **A reliable internet connection:** Whether it's your laptop or smartphone (or whatever the next gadget is), a reliable connection comes first. Cryptos are digital and using/buying/selling them is dependent on internet technology — and electricity!

>> **A payment method:** Buying cryptos means using a payment method. Depending on the platform, broker, and so on, it can mean using services (such as PayPal), credit/debit cards (such as Visa/ Mastercard), or ACH services to debit your bank account for the funds.

>> **KYC documentation:** Because of the risks of money laundering and a batch of other criminal concerns, most financial institutions adopt the "Know Your Customer" approach. You will need legitimate proof of both your identity (driver's license or other acceptable government-issued ID) and proof of your address (such as a recent utility bill, bank statement, or other proof).

Every broker, platform, or financial institution can be different, so check with their customer service department. Speaking of which, the following sections help you choose a broker or platform and select your cryptocurrency storage.

Choosing a platform or broker

Full-service trading platforms basically are to cryptocurrencies what stock exchanges are to stocks. One basic difference is that cryptocurrency platforms allow you to participate directly without a broker if you choose. Although there are about 300 trading platforms in this global market, the following two are likely the best choices for beginners:

>> Coinbase (www.coinbase.com) is a cryptocurrency exchange with extensive information, news, and views. It has been around since the dawn of cryptos (circa 2012), and it trades most of the cryptocurrencies available. It has over 68 million users.

>> Binance (www.binance.com) has a robust selection of cryptocurrencies to trade and has become a popular trading platform with guidance for beginners and traders.

Given that, why use a broker? Many brokers offer convenience and the ability to do non-cryptocurrency transactions (such as buy stocks, ETFs, and so on), so the choice will partly depend on your individual goals and needs.

TIP

Not all brokerage firms can make cryptocurrency transactions in your account (not yet, anyway), but some have been trailblazers and have immediately implemented the trading ability for account holders. If you want to buy and sell cryptos tomorrow, find a suitable broker today. Here is a list to get you rolling:

>> Block Fi (www.blockfi.com)

>> eToro (www.etoro.com)

>> Gemini (www.gemini.com)

>> Interactive Brokers (www.interactivebrokers.com)

>> TradeStation (www.tradestation.com)

>> Voyager (www.investvoyager.com)

>> Webull (www.webull.com)

Every broker is a little different, so make sure you ask about issues that are important to your personal investing and trading goals. Here are some questions to ask brokers (and yourself!):

>> What is the minimum to invest?

>> What types of cryptocurrencies can I trade?

>> What are the commissions and/or transaction charges?

>> What regulatory agencies oversee your firm?

>> Besides cryptocurrencies, what other vehicles (stocks and so on) can be traded with your firm?

>> Is your firm covered by SIPC (Securities Investor Protection Corporation; www.sipc.org)?

TIP

Research financial sites about brokers and platforms and read all the posts and reviews before you proceed. There are some great sites that compare brokers, and these same sites have started to compare and analyze the growing popularity of brokers that may specialize in cryptocurrencies. There are two great sites that regularly compare and analyze brokers, and they have recently tackled the world of cryptocurrency brokers (and regular brokers that allow for crypto investing and trading):

>> Head over to the site Compare Brokers (www.comparebrokers.co). They recently did their 2021 survey found at comparebrokers.co/compare/cryptocurrency-brokers.

>> Another great site to check out for this new breed of brokers is Bankrate (www.bankrate.com).

Selecting storage

Here is a very important consideration: How will you store your cryptocurrencies? Obviously, when you buy stocks, they are effectively "stored" in your stock brokerage account (regular or retirement). If you're trading them at a broker, then they will be present there, of course.

Cryptocurrencies (unlike stocks and ETFs) can be like a medium of exchange in addition to being a store of value. In the same way you may carry your paper money in a conventional wallet, a digital wallet now comes into play.

You need safe storage for your cryptocurrencies because folks would love to access your funds regardless of what kind of wallet you ultimately use. Yesterday's pickpocket is today's hacker, so safe storage is a concern. Here are the basic wallet choices:

>> **Hot wallet:** A "hot" wallet is an online wallet. This can be accessed only when you're online since it's connected (or stored) on the internet. These may be easy to use, but the risk of hacking will always be present.

>> **Cold wallet:** A "cold" wallet is an offline wallet such as a flash-drive type of storage device. These can typically be connected to the internet through a USB-accessible port. This can be a very secure device, but you ultimately have the same concern as you would with a physical, conventional wallet. In other words, what happens when you lose it or it is physically stolen? If it's gone, so are your cryptocurrency funds.

Examining Cryptocurrency ETFs

Like my uncle from Bratislava would say, "You show me a popular product, and I will show you an exchange–traded fund covering it in 1 . . . 2 . . . 3 . . ." For those of you too skittish about direct involvement with cryptocurrencies (or any new, hot, shiny investment vehicle), it won't take too long for derivatives like ETFs and mutual funds to come along.

Here are the top choices so far at the time of writing (the symbol follows the name in parentheses) with a brief description:

>> **The Bitwise 10 Crypto Index Fund (symbol BITW):** BITW is the first crypto-currency index fund (launched in 2017). It holds the ten largest cryptocurrencies.

>> **Bitwise Crypto Industry Innovators ETF (BITQ):** This ETF invests primarily in cryptocurrency-related companies such as blockchain, trading platforms, and so forth.

>> **BTC etc Physical Bitcoin ETC (BTCE):** BTCE invests in Bitcoin and was originally launched in Germany. It currently has over $1 billion in assets. Ask your broker whether this is available yet for U.S. investors.

>> **Purpose Bitcoin ETF (BTCC):** This ETF was launched in Canada in March 2021.

>> **Evolve Bitcoin ETF (EBIT):** This ETF was launched on the Toronto Stock Exchange in early 2021.

>> **CI Galaxy Bitcoin ETF (BTCX):** BTCX was the third Bitcoin ETF to launch in Canada on the Toronto Stock Exchange.

WARNING

The preceding ETFs were launched outside the United States (primarily Canada), so discuss them with your financial advisor to see whether they are suitable for you. Cryptocurrency ETFs can be purchased through regular stock brokerage accounts and may be acquired in individual retirement accounts (IRAs) and other retirement accounts. The bottom line is to double-check with your financial advisor.

TIP

As I write this in the summer of 2021, major U.S.-listed ETFs for cryptocurrencies are in the works and will likely be available in late 2021 or early 2022 so keep monitoring. Their availability will likely be news events in the financial media, the sites listed at the end of this chapter, and through sites such as ETF Database (www.etfdb.com) and ETF Trends (www.etftrends.com).

Getting a Few Golden Rules about Cryptocurrencies

Once you've waded through all the information on cryptocurrencies, you can check out some simple "golden rules" to hopefully keep you on the right track for crypto-success:

>> **Do your homework.** In the world of investing and speculating, these vehicles have only been here for a very short time. Do plenty of research and stick to a path with not only the most established cryptocurrencies but also well-established brokers. (The next section can help.)

WARNING

>> **Don't borrow or get into margin.** When Bitcoin soared in its first bubble, many folks got excited and rushed in. Some borrowed money, and then Bitcoin crashed. Until more time passes so that we see which cryptos stand the test of time, understand that these vehicles are 100 percent speculation, even if you take an investing approach.

>> **Start with a transactional approach.** Years ago, when folks asked me (coauthor Paul) about getting involved in cryptocurrencies, my recommendation was to take the safe route: Use them as payment for services in your business (even if it's a sideline business from home) because this is the safest way to get involved. As you get more comfortable, you can move on to the next golden rule.

TIP

>> **Buy incrementally.** Don't put thousands of dollars into a given cryptocurrency all at once looking for homerun profits. It's safer to dollar-cost-average your way, putting in a small amount at regular intervals so you can take advantage of market fluctuations.

REMEMBER

» **Keep your other assets.** No matter how much you're willing to buy with cryptos, stay diversified. Keep some money in the bank, keep some money in stocks, keep some money in mutual funds, and so on. Having the bulk of your money in a given asset makes you look like a genius when that asset is soaring, but it impoverishes you when it's crashing.

» **Remember that investing is better than trading.** Trading basically means you are jumping in and jumping out, trying to take advantage of market swings. That can be difficult. Patient investing is less risky than trading.

» **Watch politicians and bankers.** Our portfolios are subject to how well the economy and financial markets are doing. These things are, in turn, subject to the systemic policies pushed by politicians and the macro-policies of central bankers. These groups are not generally friendly to vehicles that compete with their currencies. Some government policies have the power to cause your cryptocurrencies to decline in value, so always be vigilant about what policies may be coming in the near future.

TIP

» **Be a contrarian.** Buy when it is down; sell when it is up. No, you don't need a crystal ball to see where today's investments will go tomorrow. What you need is the discipline to see what you can do today given what the market is doing in front of you at the moment. When Bitcoin and other cryptocurrencies crashed in 2018, did you see it as a buying opportunity and buy when it was wallowing in a bear market? When these same vehicles were soaring to the moon, did you have the discipline to take some profits "off the table"?

» **Have a goal amount.** If you're patiently investing in cryptocurrencies, do you have an exit strategy? When these vehicles are climbing to new heights and they hit a number that meets your needs — such as having enough money to buy a new home, or reaching an amount where you can cash out and buy income-producing assets for retirement — what amount is it?

REMEMBER

» **Ask yourself why you're in cryptocurrencies.** Keep asking yourself: Why am I speculating in these volatile vehicles? Is it for current income or long-term appreciation? If you don't know why you are in a given asset, the risk will rise. Risk isn't just something tied to the asset; risk is also within the person involved. Don't just strive to understand cryptocurrencies; strive to understand yourself and your financial goals.

ARE BITCOIN FUTURES IN YOUR PRESENT?

If you're seeking speculative trading opportunities in cryptocurrencies, then consider Bitcoin futures, which are currently available as futures contracts and traded at the Chicago Mercantile Exchange run by the CME Group (www.cmegroup.com). At the time of writing, the only cryptocurrency being traded as a futures contract is Bitcoin. A single futures contract has five Bitcoins as its underlying asset. If one Bitcoin was, for example, worth $40,000 (market price), then a contract would be worth $200,000 (5 × $40,000). Options on these contracts may become available later.

The latest wrinkle for futures traders are micro Bitcoin futures, which are one-tenth the size of a single Bitcoin. If one Bitcoin was $40,000, then a micro Bitcoin futures contract would be $4,000. This makes Bitcoin futures trading more affordable for small speculators.

For more information on standard Bitcoin futures, go to www.cmegroup.com/markets/cryptocurrencies/bitcoin/bitcoin.contractSpecs.html. For more information on micro-bitcoin futures, go to www.cmegroup.com/trading/micro-bitcoin-futures.html. Chapter 14 introduces currency futures.

Digging into Cryptocurrency Resources

TIP

Here's a laundry list of resources you can use to research the world of cryptocurrencies:

>> *Cryptocurrency Investing For Dummies* by Kiana Danial and published by Wiley. This is an excellent intro as Danial breaks down cryptos for beginners and offers guidance on all the basics.

>> Investopedia (www.Investopedia.com) is a popular financial site, and if you do a search for "cryptocurrencies," you'll find a tutorial and extensive information on what they are and how to buy/sell them.

>> Coin Gecko (www.coingecko.com) has a blog with comprehensive information on the cryptocurrency market.

>> Coin Desk (www.coindesk.com) provides market data and crypto news and views.

» Bitcoin magazine (thebitcoinmagazine.org)

» Coin Market Cap (www.coinmarketcap.com)

» Cryptalker (www.cryptalker.com)

» Find a listing of the top cryptocurrency blogs and websites at blog. feedspot.com/cryptocurrency_blogs.

» Check out LinkedIn (www.linkedin.com) since there is a growing number of cryptocurrency-related groups involved in areas ranging from trading news and views to forums of investors and traders sharing tips, strategies, and ideas.

5

The Part of Tens

Discover the positive habits of the most successful traders.

Manage risk effectively as you trade currencies.

Find resources for more forex information.

Review important rules for currency beginners.

Look at vehicles and strategies to diversify away from currencies.

Chapter **17**

Ten Habits of Successful Currency Traders

Here are ten rules we think define the best currency traders we've ever seen. Many of these rules apply to traders in any market, but some of them are unique to the currency market.

REMEMBER

The important idea to keep in mind: No one is born with all these habits. The only way to acquire them is the way other successful currency traders have — through patience, discipline, and experience.

Trading with a Plan

No successful trader will last very long without a well-conceived game plan for each trade. Sure, you may have some short-run success winging it, but the day of reckoning will surely come. Successful currency traders have a specific plan of attack for each position, including position size, entry point, stop-loss exit, and take-profit exit.

They stay flexible with their take profits, sometimes settling for less if they judge that that's all they can take out of the market at the moment, other times extending their profit targets if market developments are shifting in their favor. But they never move their stop-loss orders from the original setting unless it's in favor of the position to lock in profits. Flip to Part 3 for details on carrying out a trading plan.

Anticipating Event Outcomes

Trading is very similar to chess, in which the best players are thinking several moves ahead of their opponents. Successful forex traders look ahead to future events and consider how much the market has (or has not) priced in an expected outcome. They also consider the likely reactions if the event matches, or fails to match, those expectations. Then they construct trading strategies based on those alternative outcomes. While the rest of the market is trying to figure out what to make of the event, checking charts and redrawing trend lines, the forward-looking trader has a game plan already in place and is ready to trade.

Staying Flexible

Successful currency traders resist getting emotionally attached to positions. They recognize that it's not about being right or wrong — it's about making money. They adapt to incoming news and information, and quickly abandon an open position if events run counter to it instead of waiting for price action to take them out of their trade. At the same time, they're alert to fresh opportunities that may develop in the market and are prepared to react. To be prepared, they must keep sufficient margin available for additional positions. Also, they need an ongoing mental model of other major pairs so they can factor in fresh news and events. They may not be actively trading AUD/USD, but they still know the lay of the land for Aussie.

Being Prepared for Trading

Successful currency traders are always prepared, at least as much as possible in a market that's open 24 hours a day and subject to random events from half a world away. To stay on top of their game, successful currency traders are prepared for the following:

>> **Upcoming economic data releases in the next week to two weeks:** Know what the prior report indicated and what's expected in the upcoming report.

- **Scheduled speakers:** Find out who's speaking (central bankers or finance officials), what they've said in the past, and what they're likely to say this time.

- **Central bank interest-rate-setting meetings and announcement times:** Know when they're scheduled and what decision the market is expecting.

- **Important gatherings of financial leaders, such as G20 meetings or monthly get-togethers of Eurozone finance ministers:** Get a sense of whether currencies are on the agenda and what actions are expected.

- **Liquidity conditions:** Stay aware of time periods — such as end of month, market closings or holidays, and time of day (for example, European close, option expirations, or daily fixings) — when market liquidity may be affected.

- **Unexpected events:** Use rate alerts to stay on top of price movements outside expected ranges. Follow up on alerts to check for significant news and to assess potential trading opportunities.

Keeping Technically Alert

Even if they're not pursuing a technical-based trading strategy themselves, successful currency traders are still aware of important technical levels in the currency pairs they're trading. For instance, they know the key Fibonacci retracement levels, where various moving averages are, important short- and long-term trend lines, and major recent highs and lows (see Chapter 6).

TIP

You may be trading based on price behavior or momentum analysis, but be sure to keep abreast of key technical levels as part of your overall strategy.

Going with the Flow (Trading the Range)

Successful currency traders are able to assess whether the market is trending or likely to remain confined to ranges. If they think the market is trending, they aim to go with the flow more often than against it. When the short-term trend is higher, they're looking for levels to get long at, and vice versa when the direction is down. At the same time, they're aware that trends pause and frequently correct, so they're also actively taking profit at key technical points as the larger trend unfolds.

If the environment favors range trading, successful currency traders are able to switch gears and become contrarians, selling near the top of the range when everyone else is buying, or buying near the bottom of the range when everyone else is selling. Just as important, when they're in range-trading mode, they've defined an ultimate point when the range is broken. If that point is hit, they throw in the towel without any remorse, possibly even reversing direction and jumping on the breakout.

Focusing on a Few Pairs

Many successful forex traders focus on only one or two currency pairs for most of their trading. Doing so enables them to get a better feel for those markets in terms of price levels and price behavior. It also narrows the amount of information and data they need to monitor. Above all, they recognize that different currency pairs have different trading characteristics, and they're able to adjust their tactics from one pair to the next.

TIP

Focus on gaining experience and success in just one or two major pairs before trying to broaden your scope and take on the whole market. Look at other pairs only when they're trending or trading at key levels. Chapter 8 has details on major currency pairs; Chapter 9 covers minor currency pairs.

Protecting Profits

There are numerous market aphorisms on the benefits of taking profits, such as "You can't go broke taking profit." One of our favorites is "Bulls and bears each get a seat at the table, but pigs get slaughtered."

Successful traders take profit regularly, whether it's a partial take profit (reducing the size of a winning position) or squaring up completely and stepping back after a profitable market movement. Above all, when a trade is in the money, successful traders focus on keeping what they've made and not giving it up for the chance to make a little more.

REMEMBER

If you don't take some money off the table from time to time, the market will do it for you.

Trading with Stop Losses

All successful traders lose money from time to time. What makes them successful in the long run is that their losses are relatively small compared to their average winning trades. The absolute key is to have a stop loss in place at all times to prevent an everyday losing trade from becoming an account killer. (See Chapter 4 for more about stop losses.)

TIP

No one likes to lose money, but the best traders are able to accept it as part of the cost of doing business. And the only way they can regularly accept losses is by keeping them small in the first place. Master this habit, and you're halfway there.

Watching Other Markets

Currencies don't trade in a vacuum, and smart traders keep an eye on other major financial markets as a matter of routine. The primary markets they focus on are benchmark bond yields of the major currencies (U.S., German, UK, and Japanese ten-year government notes), oil, gold, and major global stock indexes.

On an intraday basis, they look to these other markets for confirmation of short-term U.S. dollar directional bias. For example, if the dollar is moving higher, U.S. ten-year yields are rising, and gold is falling, it's confirmation from other markets in favor of the dollar's move higher. If yields are flat or down, and gold is higher, the dollar's move up may be only short lived. On a longer-term basis, currency traders analyze those other markets for significant technical levels and overall directional trends, just as they do the currencies.

TIP

Spend the extra money for charting services that include live rate feeds for those other markets.

IN THIS CHAPTER

» **Limiting the financial downside**

» **Getting a handle on human nature**

» **Managing your market exposure**

Chapter **18**

Ten Rules of Risk Management

When people think about risk management in the context of currency trading, the natural tendency is to zero in on the risk of losing money. No two ways about it, that's the ultimate risk. But traders can head down many different streets before they get to their final realized profit or loss address.

Throughout this book, we stress that risk management is a multifaceted process that ends only with the final trading tally. Because risk is always present, focus on the main points in this chapter to minimize losses and (hopefully) maximize gains. Sometimes, what you don't know *can* hurt you.

How you navigate the avenues of risk has as much to with trading outcomes as it does with whether you ever reach the final destination. In this chapter, we group ten practical rules of risk management to guide you in your forex trading.

Trade with Stop-Loss Orders

Stop-loss orders are the ultimate risk-limiting tools. (The exception is data/events where stop-loss order executions may be subject to substantial slippage. Avoid that risk by not carrying positions into news releases.) If you trade without stop-loss orders, you're exposed to virtually unlimited risk. Always have a stop-loss order in place for every open position, and don't move the stop-loss order except to protect profits. Do your analysis and risk calculations before you enter the trade, and then stick to your trading plan. Chapter 11 has more about stop-loss orders.

Leverage to a Minimum

Position size ultimately determines how much financial risk you're exposed to — the larger the position, the greater the risk. Don't be seduced by high leverage ratios and take too large a position. Trading too large a position relative to your available margin reduces your cushion against routine, adverse price movements. Keep your use of leverage to the minimum needed to trade your strategy.

TIP

You can request a lower leverage ratio from most forex brokerages to systemically limit your leverage utilization. Just because they offer 50:1 or 100:1 leverage doesn't mean you have to use it all.

Trade with a Plan

REMEMBER

The best way to limit the inevitable emotional reactions that come with trading is to develop a complete trading plan from entry to exit (stop loss and take profit) before you ever open a position. (We devote most of Part 3 to the merits of trading with a plan.) Committing yourself to having a trade plan for every strategy will also keep you from speculating on a whim or *overtrading* (always having an open position). Of course, no trading plan will work if you don't follow it, which brings us back to the human risks in trading. You stand a much better chance of sticking to a trading plan if you've drawn one up in the first place.

Stay on Top of the Market

Make sure you have a firm grasp of what's happening in the market and the currency pair you're trading. Know what data and events are scheduled in the days and weeks ahead. Consider liquidity conditions during your trade plan's time horizon. What has the market priced in and priced out? Anticipating market events and conditions won't guarantee a winning trade, but it will alert you to potentially disruptive circumstances that you can factor into your trading plan to limit overall risk.

Look for the Right Opportunities

The currency market trades around the clock, but that doesn't mean you have to be in it all the time. Pick your spots and choose your timing; don't get pulled in by the noise. Keep your ammunition dry, and look for trade setups with a clearly defined risk/reward scenario. Be opportunistic, and spend your time and efforts looking for trading opportunities still to come instead of getting caught up in the market move of the moment. Other opportunities will surely develop, and you'll be ready for them.

Step Back from the Market

REMEMBER

When you're not involved in the market, a funny thing happens: Your perspective is clearer, and your objectivity is at its peak because you're not emotionally invested in a market position. Make it a point to square up and step back from the market on a regular basis. Use the downtime to catch up on your charting (see Chapter 6) and fundamental analysis (see Chapter 7). Take time off completely and just forget about the markets for a while. When you return, you'll be refreshed and thinking more clearly, ready for new trading opportunities.

Take Profit Regularly

Taking profit regularly is the surest way to limit risk. By definition, if you take profit — even partial profit — you're reducing your exposure to market risk. Your trade plan may have a more aggressive profit target, but if market events play out in your favor, it pays to protect what you've gained by taking partial profit or adjusting your stop-loss orders to lock in some of the gains. It may be a fluke that the market jumped 40 pips in your favor on a data release, or it may be a fluke that the market dropped back by 50 pips ten minutes later. The only way to be sure is to take some profit. You can't go broke taking profit.

REMEMBER

Currency trading through futures, options, and other speculative vehicles may be a great way to build wealth, but it is *not* a great way to preserve wealth. Given that, make it a habit to migrate some of your profits to safer venues, such as bank savings or more stable and reliable investments such as conservative, dividend-paying stocks and conservative exchange-traded funds (ETFs) and mutual funds. Flip to Part 4 for details.

Understand Currency-Pair Selection

Market risk varies significantly from one currency pair to the next, based on volatility, liquidity, data sensitivity, and many other factors. Each currency pair brings its own idiosyncrasies to the table, requiring different analytical tools or strategic approaches. Different currency pairs also carry higher or lower margin utilizations and pip values. Make sure that you understand what currency pair you're trading and that your trading plan reflects that pair's characteristics. (Chapters 8 and 9 look at the trading behavior and drivers of the most heavily traded currency pairs and crosses. Not all currency pairs are the same.)

Double-Check for Accuracy

WARNING

Currency trading is a fast-paced environment made even faster by electronic trading. The risk of human error in inputting trades and orders is ever present, and diligence is required on your part to avoid costly errors. A stop-loss order won't help if it's entered for the wrong currency pair or the wrong amount. Make it part of your routine to double-check every trade and order entry you make, ideally before you submit it but at least immediately after you make it. Mistakes happen to everyone, but only careless traders let minor errors slip through and become big disasters.

Take Money Out of Your Trading Account

Here's one you won't see in many trading books: If you've made some money in the market, make periodic withdrawals from your trading account. We call it *taking money off the table.* If your profit stays in your margin account, it's subject to future trading decisions, which represents an unknown risk. Keep your margin balance at a level that allows you to trade in sizes you're comfortable with. Also, remember why you're trading — it's not just about the money, but what you can do with it. Withdraw your profits, and spend or invest them the way you always said you would.

TIP

Limit your trading and speculating to no more than 5 or 10 percent of your total investable assets. Yes, we hope your currency trading gives you life-changing profits, but the hope is that you won't experience the opposite, which is life-changing *losses.* This is why part of limiting your risk going in is to limit how much of your money is at risk from the start.

Chapter **19**

Ten Great Resources for Currency Trading

This book gives you a solid foundation for understanding the ins and outs of currency trading, but it can't cover all the subdisciplines of trading, such as technical analysis, market psychology, and strategy development. Those subjects are deep enough and rich enough to warrant further study on their own as you develop your own trading style and favorite techniques. We think you'll find the following suggested additional resources very helpful in gaining a deeper understanding of the technical tools, economic data reports, and practical applications of strategy and psychology.

TIP

When all else falls short, here are some "best of" lists so that a trader with any experience level can find appropriate trading and forex sites with news, views, and guidance. These two sites give you a cornucopia of trading and/or forex trading resources:

» Top 100 Forex Blogs and Websites to Follow in 2021 (blog.feedspot.com/ forex_blogs/)

» Best of the Web subdirectory of forex sites (botw.org/top/Business/ Investing/Commodities_and_Futures/Forex/)

Technical Analysis of the Financial Markets

Technical Analysis of the Financial Markets: A Comprehensive Guide to Trading Methods and Applications, by John J. Murphy (New York Institute of Finance), is *the* encyclopedia of technical analysis, written by perhaps the most prominent technical practitioner in the market. Murphy covers all the tools and all the rules in depth, from both a theoretical and a practical standpoint. Murphy also lays out one of the most comprehensive reviews of chart patterns you'll find anywhere. If you're going to have only one book on technical analysis in your library, make it this one.

Japanese Candlestick Charting Techniques

We're huge proponents of candlestick charting, and for our money, *Japanese Candlestick Charting Techniques: A Contemporary Guide to the Ancient Investment Techniques of the Far East,* 2nd Edition, by Steve Nison (Prentice Hall), is the best book on candlesticks out there. Nison takes you inside the linguistic and cultural meanings behind the myriad candle patterns, which leaves you with a more intuitive understanding of the patterns. With that greater understanding, you're more likely to spot viable candlestick patterns and understand what they're telling you. We keep this book handy and refer to it frequently in our own candlestick observations. (We look at several key candlestick patterns in Chapter 6.)

Elliott Wave Principle

Elliott Wave Principle: Key to Market Behavior, by A. J. Frost and Robert R. Prechter, Jr. (Wiley), is the go-to guide if you're interested in finding out more about the Elliott wave principle. Elliott wave patterns are an important part of currency price movements, especially if you intend to trade from a medium- to longer-term perspective. This book explains the philosophy behind Ralph Nelson Elliott's theories of price patterns and provides practical examples of how to apply those theories to all financial markets.

Technical Analysis For Dummies

Technical Analysis For Dummies, 4th Edition, by Barbara Rockefeller (Wiley), is an excellent introduction to the many and varied tools and methods of technical analysis, all delivered in the easy-to-read *For Dummies* style. Rockefeller takes you through all the important tools and approaches, and provides plenty of real-life do's and don'ts that you can apply to your own trading.

The Book of Five Rings

The Book of Five Rings, by Miyamoto Musashi and translated by William Scott Wilson (Shambhala), is known as *Go Rin No Sho* in Japanese. This relatively short book (about 150 pages) is a fascinating exposition on the philosophy of strategy and rules of tactical warfare. Musashi was the greatest samurai ever to live, and this book is his end-of-life distillation of all the rules of strategy and swordsmanship gained in his lifetime.

Musashi's exhortations on timing and staying calm in the midst of chaos are as applicable to successful trading today as they were to martial artists in the mid-17th century, when the book first appeared. This book is not for a single reading only. Pull it out and reread it often. Not only does it contain advice on strategy and mental discipline, but it also offers lessons on personal fulfillment and finding a spiritual, focused, and balanced existence.

Market Wizards: Interviews with Top Traders

In *Market Wizards: Interviews with Top Traders* (Wiley), Jack D. Schwager, a veteran trader himself, interviews the legends of the trading world for their insights and philosophies of trading. *Wizards* is not confined strictly to the forex market; it offers a wider-ranging discussion of stocks, futures, and currency trading. In it, you discover how the likes of Richard Dennis, Bruce Kovener, and Paul Tudor Jones, to name just a few, approach trading. These traders are living legends today, but they all started out relatively modestly and succeeded through discipline, strategy, and diligence while managing intense psychological pressures. If you're in search of a trading style, these guys have plenty to offer.

FOREX.com

What better resource for forex than one of the premier forex sites? Would you author a *For Dummies* book on elephant-foot umbrella stands without a site with the same name? Seriously, the site (www.forex.com) has much to offer. Free analysis, news, and insights along with free education for beginners earns this site a place in this chapter. I (coauthor Paul) like that novice traders can open a demo account so you can learn before you risk any money. Besides forex, the site also covers futures, gold, and options.

Zero Hedge

Zero Hedge (www.zerohedge.com) is a news website and content aggregator that reports on economics and the goings-on of Wall Street. This is one of the first websites we check each day due to its contrarian analysis. It often takes the opposite side of what the market thinks, which can be a refreshing and much-needed change in perspective. The blog also posts the most interesting and relevant research from some of the world's most prominent analysts. The posts are signed under a pseudonym, Tyler Durden, a character from the film *Fight Club.* There is a lot of speculation over who Tyler Durden actually is; at the time of writing, it is still unconfirmed. Be sure to check our Zero Hedge on Twitter at @zerohedge.

BabyPips.com

BabyPips.com (www.babypips.com) says it's a "beginner's guide to forex trading," but some of the posts are fairly sophisticated, so we recommend it for beginner to intermediate traders who are trying to up their game. One of the best things about this site is that some of the contributors talk you through their trades. They go through the reason for their trades, the setup, and the execution. They often post after the trades are closed out to let you know what went well and what didn't, and why. This site is a good place to find out more about market dynamics and market discipline.

Forex Factory

Forex Factory (`www.forexfactory.com`) may not be as pretty as some other sites, but it's an extremely useful resource. Here's why:

>> It has one of the most-trusted economic calendars out there, which is extremely useful if your broker doesn't provide you with one.

>> It includes market news and has a trade feed with its members' latest positions; the feed is updated in real time.

>> Perhaps the most useful thing about Forex Factory is its trader forums. These forums have different threads of conversation that offer you the chance to join a community of retail traders and talk through your ideas, problems, and so on.

>> It's free!

Chapter **20**

Ten (Or So) Golden Rules for Currency Trading Beginners

urrency trading can be a great pursuit, but it pays to learn from all those who came before you as they went through the school of hard knocks. Beginners, more than any other group, need solid, proven parameters to help minimize losses and maximize gains. What better way to end this book than with a batch of ideas and strategies to help beginners start off their currency trading the right way.

Read, Read, Read

There are many great posts, tutorials, online courses, and video programs on the basics of currency trading. Many beginners' resources are listed throughout this book and in Chapter 19. Additionally, whatever brokerage platform you trade on will have educational tools and resources to get you ready for your trades.

Simulate Trading First

Unlike years ago, today's internet-driven world gives you the opportunity to do simulated trading, allowing you to get comfortable with currency trading (or any trading) without risking a dime. This is the place to start with forex and other forms of currency trading. Many forex brokers make simulated trading available for website visitors (even if you aren't a client). Go to your favorite search engine and enter "simulated currency trading" or a similar term, and you can get going today.

TIP

Of course, many of the sites referenced within these pages either have simulated trading programs or are linked to some. When you generate your simulated gains (or losses), be sure to ask yourself questions about why they occurred. Simulated trading activity is meant to prepare you for the real deal, so ask yourself the hard questions over why you made or lost money. Your real trades will be that much sweeter to your wallet.

Start Small

Once you get the hang of trading, it's time to dip your toe in the water. No, don't empty your 401(k) plan or break open your kid's piggy bank for your forex trading account — forex trading can be done initially for under $100. Just check out the forex brokers' minimum balance requirements. The point here is that whether you lose or make money on an initial trade, you will learn. Generating a loss of $57 on your first forex trade is a cheap lesson — and the amount of the loss is not life-changing, which is a good lesson in and of itself.

Keep a Ceiling on Your Total Speculating

When me and the missus are on vacation, once in a while we head to the local casino just for the fun of it. But we are very strict on one simple rule: "Total betting limit is $40. Period." The same holds true for speculative ventures such as currency trading.

TIP

The bottom line here is that you need to set a total limit for your speculative activities, perhaps no more than 2–5 percent of your investable portfolio. If your total investable portfolio is $100,000, then your maximum limit is $5,000.

Be Diversified

And while you're at it, don't bet the full amount on a single trade. Be diversified and have a batch of bets on multiple trades. Diversification isn't only useful in the world of investing; it's equally appropriate in the world of currency trading. Too many beginners want to "bag the elephant," have that homerun trade, and then plan their luxury cruise. Yes, it's possible, but 99 percent of the time that huge, "all-in" bet becomes a loser — and a potentially huge one at that.

Have a Rule on Profits (and Losses!)

If you do enough trading, you'll have some profitable trades. Why not shift a portion of those profits away from your pot of "trading money" and transfer it to your pot of "investment money"? Trading, be it currencies or commodities or lottery tickets, can be a way to build wealth, but it isn't a way to preserve wealth. You want your trading profits to build your wealth. Wealth includes vehicles where time is on your side, as with long-term positions in appreciating assets such as stocks, hard assets (real estate, precious metals, and the like), exchange-traded funds (ETFs), and mutual funds.

REMEMBER

I (coauthor Paul) have seen it all too often: traders riding high with profitable trades that have unrealized profits only to see those unrealized profits shrink and disappear (into realized losses). Have something to show for your hard-earned trading activities. Take money off the table and into tangible assets of enduring value.

Analyze the Trade That Went Bad

All too often, we make a profitable trade and we feel confident and are raring to go with the next trade. But when we lose money, we can forget that we paid for a lesson. The question has to be asked: Why did this trade go wrong? What can we do next time to avoid repeating our mistake(s)?

Trading knowledge and experience are really designed to help you with subsequent trades until you understand how it works. Use every trade (especially the losing ones!) to learn and get better.

Learn from Others

You don't need to re-invent the wheel and trade blind or throw trades on the wall and see what sticks. Thousands of traders have come before you, and many of them have documented their trading successes and failures in the form of books and educational programs. Many courses are low-cost and even free. You can find some valuable courses on popular video platforms such as YouTube, Vimeo, and Rumble or on educational platforms such as Udemy. Head down to the library and borrow some trading books.

REMEMBER

You aren't the first to make mistakes, and you won't be the last. Get insights from the good and bad that others more experienced than you have experienced.

Recognize That History May Not Repeat, but It Does Rhyme

Currency markets, like many markets, tend to zigzag up and down much like a roller coaster. Understanding that the market risk varies significantly from one currency pair to the next — based on the volatility, liquidity, and data ebbs and flows of the currency you are eyeing — will help you with timing trades. When I (coauthor Paul) see a currency that's down but fundamentally strong, I see an entry point for a bullish trade. If that currency is riding high and looking "toppy," then a bearish trade is a good bet.

Watching for peaks and troughs in the currency's chart (see Chapter 6) can be useful for beginners to help determine entry and exit points for their trades. The macro point here is that being a contrarian is a time-tested approach that can give you an edge.

TIP

Become a contrarian with the ebbs and flows of the market. If everybody, for example, is bullish on the euro and its chart is showing that its price is sky high, it's probably not a bad idea to take a small contrarian position. No currency rises forever, and no sound currency (in the short term, anyway) falls forever. Given that, consider being the contrarian. It may be the best trading opportunity facing you.

Specialize If Possible (In Other Words, Focus!)

Some of the most successful students that I (coauthor Paul) have had in my trading and speculating courses tend to specialize in a given category or type of trade. Trying to understand the ebbs and flows of a wide variety of currencies requires spreading yourself too much to the point that the old saying kicks in: "He's a jack of all trades, but a master of none."

I keep thinking of that guy in the talent show who keeps 37 plates spinning simultaneously on those long sticks — that's something you don't want to do. Hey, who needs a nervous breakdown, am I right? Now, I realize that earlier in this chapter, I mention being diversified in your positions, and that holds true. Having three to five (give or take) positions and watching them like a hawk is better than having 37 different positions that are all over the place.

Know That Successful Trading Isn't Just What You Do but How You Do It

Too many folks focus on the "what" (making profitable trades) but forget to add the "how," which means adding discipline to those trades to enhance the chances of winning and diminish the chances of losing.

Your brokerage account has tools within it — brokerage orders such as stop-loss orders, limit orders, trade triggers, and trailing stops that you can employ easily from day one (see Chapter 4). Use brokerage trading technology to your advantage to make successful trading easier, especially in tough and uncertain markets.

Of course, most markets are uncertain to some degree, so adding discipline essentially means adding some degree of certainty. It helps to create predictability in entry and exit points. Ultimately, it means a better night's sleep and less of the "coulda, woulda, shoulda" syndrome that accompanies many trades gone bad.

Finally, Don't Stop Educating Yourself

REMEMBER

As the author of *Stock Investing For Dummies* (Wiley) and as a fellow who has been involved in stock investing (and teaching about it) since the 1980s (right after the Pleistocene Era), I (coauthor Paul) am still learning about stock investing — and I don't foresee a time that I will stop learning. I start off this chapter with recommending education before you get involved in currency trading, and I end this chapter with emphasis on continuing that education. The primary point is this: How badly do you want to be successful (and profitable!) in the world of currencies? Ongoing education means that you are committed to your own success, and it is the key to your ongoing profitability and financial goals.

Chapter **21**

Ten Alternatives to Currencies

This entire book has focused on understanding and hopefully profiting from currency trading (and related currency vehicles and strategies), but it's equally important to understand opposing vehicles (or "anti-currencies," so to speak) to be diversified in your total investing and speculative wealth-building pursuits. As I (coauthor Paul) emphasize in earlier chapters, currency speculating and trading should occupy only a small portion of your total investable portfolio. Be mindful of other vehicles that can be great accompaniments to currency strategies and vehicles.

In that spirit, I present the top ten alternatives to currencies here. Check out Part 4 for more on forex alternatives.

Gold

"And in this corner, the reigning champion since the days of Noah — gold!" Yes, gold has outlasted every currency since the dawn of civilization. I would even be comfortable making the forecast that gold will still be standing as the top store of value long after today's currencies hit history's dustbin.

Of course I can't do justice to gold in this snippet of a relatively short chapter. You should seriously consider gold (and the topic of the next section, silver) as an important component in your portfolio.

TIP

Take a closer look at gold (and silver) as a diversification not only for your currency trades but for the rest of your portfolio (stocks, mutual funds, and so on) with the book *Investing in Gold and Silver For Dummies* (published by Wiley and written by your humble coauthor Paul). These precious metals are the ultimate alternative and counterplay to currencies and all paper assets. Gold breached the $2,000 level in 2020, and economic and monetary conditions during 2021–2022 are bullish for new potential highs for gold. During 2000–2021, gold has risen over 500 percent as it has generally outperformed most currencies and many other major investment vehicles.

Silver

Silver is another alternative to currency trading, and it's also a cheaper alternative to gold (see the previous section). Silver has dual properties of being both a precious metal and also an industrial metal:

>> As a precious metal, it has been used as a means of exchange and a store of value for literally thousands of years.

>> The great news for investors and speculators is that silver has seen new uses in recent decades for a myriad of industrial applications and uses in healthcare, consumer electronics, solar energy, smartphones, and much more. These new uses have increased demand tremendously, but supply has been more constrained in recent years. These market conditions make silver an attractive investment vehicle in the coming years.

During 2000–2021, silver has soared nearly 400 percent, and conditions for 2021–2025 look bullish for gold's sidekick.

Cryptocurrencies

Although many cryptocurrencies have come into being in recent years, they do play a part for those in the world of currency and forex speculating. Cryptocurrencies such as Bitcoin are very limited in quantity, which maintains an element of scarcity that is not there with mainstream currencies, which can be potentially limitless in their quantity. Holding a scarce currency as a diversification against a currency that is plentiful (meaning that its value per unit can drop over time) is an important hedge against the overproduction (inflation!) of mainstream currencies.

TIP Precious metals and cryptocurrencies the utility and online approach with the backing of hard assets. This one-two combination makes them a potent alternative to mainstream currencies and currency-related strategies.

TIP For more information and resources on cryptocurrencies, check out Chapter 16. You can also read *Cryptocurrency Investing For Dummies* by Kiana Danial (Wiley).

Common Stocks

Stocks belong in most portfolios for a variety of solid investing and speculative reasons (appreciation, income potential, and so on). Very often stocks are a good diversification from your currency positions. There are many categories and types of stocks to choose from, but my preference for currency traders is stocks that are dividend payers and are in the area of "human need" such as food, water, beverages, utilities, and the like. These types of stocks are most commonly found in the consumer staples and utilities sectors.

Why? When currencies are overproduced, resulting in inflation, the consumer prices of necessities are pushed upward and this, in turn, has a positive effect on the desirability of the stocks of companies that produce these necessities. Additionally, these companies tend to pay dividends, and dividends of the leading companies in these sectors tend to meet (or exceed) the rate of inflation.

TIP For more detailed information and guidance on stock investing, check out the latest edition of *Stock Investing For Dummies* (written by coauthor Paul and published by Wiley).

The "I" Bond

All sorts of bonds are available for investors, ranging from high-quality, "triple A" rated, low-interest corporate (or municipal or treasury) bonds to low-quality, low-rated, and relatively high-interest "junk bonds" (typically low-rated corporate or municipal bonds). Most of these types of bonds tend to be fixed interest, which means the bond issuer (a corporate or governmental entity) pays a fixed amount of interest annually for the life of the bond, which can be up to 25 or 30 years or more.

TIP

But as inflation rises, these types of bonds tend to fall in market value as investors switch from low-yielding bonds to higher-yielding issues. What's an investor to do? A good alternative is a U.S. Treasury–issued savings bond referred to as an "I" bond ("I" standing for inflation). To find out more about the I bond, head over to www.savingsbonds.gov.

Commodities

Commodities are the stuff of life — the stuff we use and need on a daily basis ranging from food (corn, soybeans, and so on) to what turns our lights on and runs our vehicles (oil or natural gas, for example) to what builds our homes and factories (such as copper, iron, and lumber). When currencies drop in value, commodities are among those things that experience price increases. Given this, commodities have a place in a diversified portfolio.

TIP

How can you participate in commodities? There are a variety of ways ranging from investing in the stocks of companies that participate in the commodities sector to exchange-traded funds (ETFs) that mirror a variety of commodities. You can search for commodities ETFs via websites such as ETF Database (www.etfdb.com) to gain more details on these vehicles.

Mutual Funds

Mutual funds have been a perennial favorite of investors for decades, and they can be good alternative accompaniments to your currency investments and speculations. A mutual fund is a conduit; it helps you conveniently invest in a portfolio that contains a variety of vehicles (stocks, bonds, commodities, and so on). It is actively managed by a portfolio manager who buys, sells, and holds a portfolio of investments according to the mission and goals of the mutual fund.

With over 10,000 different mutual funds, you can find one that augments your currency strategies. If, for example, you feel that interest rates will rise, which can often strengthen a currency's value, a money market fund may be a good choice. If you believe that a currency's prospects are bearish, then you may consider mutual funds with portfolios that can benefit from a weaker currency, such as a large-cap stock mutual fund or a precious metals mining mutual fund.

TIP

You can do your research in the world of mutual funds at sites such as the following:

>> MutualFunds.com (www.mutualfunds.com)

>> Investment Management Education Alliance (imealliance.com)

>> Investment Company Institute (www.ici.org)

Country Exchange-Traded Funds

Because currencies are typically tied to the fortunes of a given country, country exchange-traded funds can provide a great way to augment your currency strategies. If you feel that the Japanese yen will do well in the coming year, then of course you would consider the Yen ETF, but you may also consider the ETF on Japanese securities for bearish or bullish plays against the yen.

Frequently, when the currency is having difficulty in a given country, that country's stock market tends to act in a contrary move. When Venezuela, for example, had a currency crisis during 2016–2020 (hyperinflation), the stock market had risen sharply.

TIP

For more information on country ETFs, check out Chapter 13 and find them in these venues (along with details):

>> ETF Database (www.etfdb.com)

>> ETFguide (www.etfguide.com)

>> ETF Channel (www.etfchannel.com)

Collectibles

Collectibles are definitely a little offbeat, but they represent a legitimate way to play currencies from a totally different angle. In periods of currency instability or inflation, hard assets tend to do well. I cover other hard assets in this chapter (such as gold, silver, and real estate), but collectibles can also do very well in similar conditions.

What are examples of collectibles? Numismatic coins (also known as collectible coins), investment-grade stamps (called philatelics), autographs, antique furniture, old comics (pre-1980), and fine art are among the major subcategories of collectibles.

WARNING

Keep in mind that this category does require extensive experience and research to understand what you're buying. Too many people have either overpaid or been outright defrauded, so it pays to find out as much as possible from as many reliable sources as you can to understand how this market works and how to do well.

Find out more about collectibles at sites including these:

>> Coin Collecting (www.coincollecting.com): Since many collectible coins also have gold and silver content, they can have great value. This site covers the hobby and provides coin resources and value guidance.

>> Collectors Weekly (www.collectorsweekly.com): Find lots of guidance here on categories ranging from baseball cards to world coins.

>> Fun.com (www.fun.com): If you have collectibles tied to movies, toys, and other entertainment-related memorabilia, this is a great site.

Real Estate Investment Trusts

Real estate is considered a hard asset, and it generally does well in inflationary times (when currencies decline in their purchasing power and value). The easiest way to play real estate is through real estate investment trusts (REITs), which can be purchased as easily as a stock or ETF through your brokerage account.

TIP

To find out more about REITs, head over to www.reit.com.

IN THIS APPENDIX

» **Finding out what type of trader you are**

» **Developing a strategy based on your trader type**

Appendix

Trading Strategies

The forex market is the largest financial market in the world. A market with more than $6 trillion a day in turnover presents plenty of opportunities for the retail trader, but those opportunities won't be handed to you on a silver platter — you have to work hard to ensure you're successful in the forex market. In this appendix, we set you up to do exactly that by helping you choose the right trading strategy for you and giving you tips on implementing that strategy.

What's Your Sign? Determining Your Trader Type

REMEMBER

There are thousands of forex strategies, but you need to choose the one that works best for *you*. At FOREX.com, we've grouped traders based on personality types and developed specific strategies for each. We've identified three trader types:

» **The scalper:** A scalper is a trader who looks for short, minimally profitable opportunities in the market that can add up over time. If you're a scalper, you don't have the patience to hold a position for a lengthy period, and you grow bored easily when keeping trades active for too long. You're motivated by the excitement of seeing fast-moving markets, sometimes trading around major news events to realize the vast potential of a large move in a very short period of time. You aren't happy about placing a losing trade, but you're typically less impacted both financially and emotionally due to the small nature and frequency of the trades that you place.

>> **The swing trader:** A swing trader is someone who typically enjoys staying in a trade for as little as a few hours to potentially days. If you're a swing trader, you like the analysis aspect of trading — finding patterns that develop and exploiting them like a cunning strategist. Because you place fewer trades on a daily and weekly basis, losing trades can have more of an impact on your psyche, so keeping your longer-term goals in mind and sticking to the plan are imperative.

>> **The position trader:** A position trader has a much longer time frame in mind than most other traders. If you're a position trader, you may be in a trade for months or even years if your conviction is strong enough. Usually based on a fundamental perspective of political, sentimental, or supply/demand reasoning, you brush off the fear of short-term movements. You're much more tolerant of drawdowns and can take losses for a very long time before finally admitting defeat.

TIP

To more precisely determine what type of trader you are, take the quiz at www. dummies.com/personal-finance/investing/currency-day-trading/ what-kind-of-trader-are-you/. *Note:* You can move between trader types. At the start, you may feel more comfortable as a scalper, but as you become more confident, you may prefer to be a swing trader and hold trades for a slightly longer period of time.

REMEMBER

There's no "right" or "wrong" trader type — you just need to identify the type of trader *you* are and trade accordingly.

Looking at Trading Strategies Based on Trader Type

In this section, we offer some actionable trade ideas for each trader type. These strategies have been developed by FOREX.com's research team. We're grateful for input from Matt Weller, Neal Gilbert, Fawad Razaqzada, Chris Tedder, and our former colleague Chris Tevere.

For the scalper: The Red Zone strategy

News trading (buying and selling around high-impact economic data) is notoriously difficult, to the point that many traders intentionally close all their trades ahead of major news reports like non-farm payrolls (NFP) or central bank meetings. To be successful with this style of trading, you need to have a predetermined, disciplined structure — you don't want to haphazardly place emotional trades.

TIP

One potentially effective strategy is to take advantage of markets' tendency to gravitate toward round numbers, like 1.3200 in a currency pair like EUR/USD. These levels are significant for two primary reasons:

» Newer traders often set stop losses at or around these levels.

» Option strike prices are overwhelmingly set at round handles.

With a large swath of traders focusing on these areas, it's no wonder that they exert a strong influence on the market. The difficulty is determining how to design a trading strategy to take advantage of this tendency.

To describe the Red Zone strategy, we like to evoke the analogy of a football game. The final 20 yards before the end zone, where good teams have historically scored a touchdown 50 percent to 70 percent of the time, is referred to as the "red zone." For our non-American friends, this area is analogous to the penalty area in your version of football (which Americans call soccer), where a team is more likely to score a goal on any open shot.

Note that in both of these examples (football and soccer, er, football), a score isn't guaranteed — it's just more likely.

The same idea can be applied to trading. When an instrument comes within 20 points of a round number (the "red zone"), a continuation to that round number becomes more likely, particularly following a supportive news event.

How it works

Here are the Red Zone strategy buy rules:

» Wait for a news-driven move.

» Set a buy-stop order at 0.*xx*80 ($*xx*8.00 for gold, $*xx*.80 for oil).

» Set a target at 0.*xx*98 ($*xx*9.80 for gold, $*xx*.98 for oil).

» Set a stop loss at 0.*xx*60 ($*xx*6.00 for gold, $*xx*.60 for oil).

Here are the Red Zone strategy sell rules:

» Wait for a news-driven move.

» Set a sell-stop order at 0.*xx*20 ($*xx*2.00 for gold, $*xx*.20 for oil).

>> Set a target at 0.*xx*02 ($*xx*0.20 for gold, $*xx*.02 for oil).

>> Set a stop loss at 0.*xx*40 ($*xx*4.00 for gold, $*xx*.40 for oil).

TIP

Because this is a short-term trading strategy, you want to trade heavily traded markets, such as major currency pairs, gold, oil, and widely followed indices, with low bid and ask spreads. You may also want to focus on trading only during times of *high liquidity* (when many different traders are buying and selling) to improve the speed of entries and exits.

The Red Zone strategy in action

Example 1: EUR/USD Buy

This first example (see Figure A-1) shows the ideal execution of the strategy. Following the release of weak U.S. housing data, the EUR/USD rallied strongly toward 1.2700. In anticipation of a continuation to that level, the strategy suggested placing a buy-stop order at 1.2680 with a stop loss at 1.2660 and a target at 1.2698. When the buy order was triggered, the EUR/USD went on to hit the target within 15 minutes for a winning trade. Although the EUR/USD eventually rallied another 20 pips, the highest-probability trade was the initial run to 1.2700.

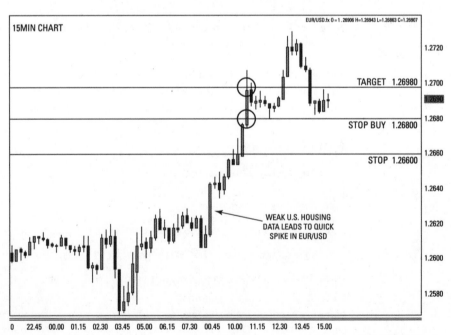

FIGURE A-1:
EUR/USD
short-term chart,
Example 1.

© John Wiley & Sons, Inc.

Example 2: EUR/USD Buy

A few weeks later, the EUR/USD was making another run for the 1.2700 handle after the announcement of a new European Stability Mechanism (ESM) for supporting the European banking sector. As in the preceding example, a buy-stop order was set at 1.2680 with a stop loss at 1.2660 and a target at 1.2698. In this case, though, rates lost momentum before reaching 1.2700 and hit the stop about an hour after entry for a 20-pip loss. As Figure A-2 shows, the failure to continue up to 1.2700 foreshadowed further consolidation, and prices eventually rolled over. When the currency pair reverses 20 pips from the entry, the probability of a move up to the round number decreases.

FIGURE A-2: EUR/USD short-term chart, Example 2.

© John Wiley & Sons, Inc.

Example 3: AUD/USD Sell

Our final example (see Figure A-3) is a sell scalp on the AUD/USD. After dovish Reserve Bank of Australia (RBA) minutes, rates were approaching the 0.9300 level from the topside, and the strategy suggested setting a sell-stop order at 0.9320 with a stop loss at 0.9340 and a target at 0.9302. Following entry, the pair sold off to hit the target for an 18-pip gain within an hour. Although the AUD/USD did continue to drop from there, the Red Zone strategy is only concerned with taking a small, higher-probability slice out of news-driven moves.

© John Wiley & Sons, Inc.

FIGURE A-3:
AUD/USD
short-term chart,
Example 3.

For the scalper: The Opening Range Breakout strategy

Let's face it: The whole purpose of doing any form of analysis — whether it's technical, fundamental, or statistical — is to try to identify higher-probability trading opportunities. One such strategy is to use a European opening range. This strategy typically focuses on EUR/USD, but it can be applied to any of the European majors.

REMEMBER

The forex market is open 24 hours a day (Sunday evening through Friday evening Eastern time), but market activity in a given pair is not necessarily consistent throughout. The forex market is typically divided into three major sessions:

>> **London:** Open 3 a.m. Eastern time, close 12 p.m. (noon) Eastern time

>> **New York:** Open 8 a.m. local time, close 5 p.m. local time

>> **Tokyo:** Open 6 p.m. Eastern time, close 3 a.m. Eastern time during the winter months; open 5 p.m. Eastern time, close 2 a.m. Eastern time during the summer months

How it works

Here are the basics of the Opening Range Breakout strategy:

» Identify the high and low during the half-hour just prior to the London open (2:30 a.m. to 3 a.m. Eastern time), and then look for a breakout of this range +/–10 pips or 1/10 of the daily Average True Range (ATR) and maintain above/below this level for 10 to 15 minutes. You're trying to detect a direction of the "flow" for the remainder of the day.

» From there, look to manage this bullish or bearish bias by focusing on one-, two-, or five-minute charts and using a combination of moving averages (13-SMA, 144-EMA, and 169-EMA) and oscillators (RSI, stochastics, and CCI).

» Other factors to include are major news announcements (usually in efforts of avoidance) and the time of day (when major markets open/close, option expirations, fixings, and so on).

Noteworthy times to be aware of include the following:

» **Major option expirations:**

- New York expiry: 10 a.m. local time

- Japan expiry: 3 p.m. local time

» **Currency fixings:**

- London fix: 4 p.m. local time

- Tokyo fix: 8:55 a.m. local time

» **Currency futures:** International Monetary Market (IMM) starts trading 6 p.m. Eastern time Sunday and closes 5 p.m. Eastern time Friday. During this time, the IMM trades electronically for 23 hours on a typical trading day and closes during the 5 p.m. to 6 p.m. hour Eastern time.

» **U.S. equity markets:** Open 9:30 a.m. Eastern time, close 4 p.m. Eastern time

TIP

Ideally, if price is struggling near these events (typically spotted by a bullish/bearish divergence with an oscillator), it could be prudent to reduce the position size ahead of time. Additionally, this type of approach may help to minimize the emotional aspect to trading, because there's an identifiable area to know where you're wrong (the opposite side of the breakout's high/low).

The Opening Range Breakout strategy in action

In this example, EUR/USD made an important low during the 2:30 a.m. to 3 a.m. Eastern time time frame (which was preceded by an RSI bullish divergence with price) and shot higher shortly thereafter (as shown in Figure A-4). EUR/USD appeared comfortable above the two-minute 144/169-EMAs, while the 13-period simple moving average (SMA) remained above the EMAs, and RSI continued to find support into the key 40/45 zone. Consequently, there was no reason to divert from the intraday bullish bias.

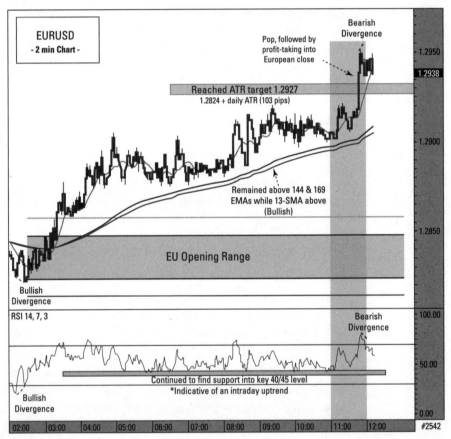

FIGURE A-4: EUR/USD two-minute chart.

© John Wiley & Sons, Inc.

Plus, as highlighted earlier, another factor to keep in mind is the time of day. In the forex market, most London traders tend to close their positioning between 11 a.m. and noon Eastern time, while traders in New York close between 4 p.m. and 5 p.m. Eastern time. Accordingly, price often sees a final end-of-day push, followed by profit taking (typically spotted by a bullish/bearish divergence with an oscillator) near these times of the day.

Sure enough, just after 11 a.m. Eastern time in our example, EUR/USD pushed higher once again to finally reach the intraday ATR target of 1.2927, which was then followed by a bearish divergence with RSI just ahead of noon Eastern time.

Here are some general observations regarding potential opening range scenarios per week (these are just overall findings — they should *not* be expected):

>> **Two days of the week:** Won't do much (finish roughly flat)

>> **Once a week:** False break and potential reversal

>> **One day a week:** Respectable movement (50 to 70 pips from highs/lows)

>> **One day a week:** Reaches ATR target (pip amount generally equal to Average True Range using a 14-day period)

Note: If the ATR is achieved earlier in the week, the likelihood of it occurring twice in the same week is dramatically reduced. If it does occur, it's typically in the opposing direction.

REMEMBER

As a forex trader, when volatility begins to pick up, you usually want to be trading currencies, not sitting on the sidelines. As a result, if this strategy has yet to achieve the ATR target on Monday, Tuesday, or Wednesday of a particular week, it may be sensible to pay close attention to this tactic on Thursday and Friday. Conversely, if the ATR is reached earlier in the week, it may be prudent to be on the lookout for potential market failures in the latter half of the week because they could be the marking of a false break and/or possible outright reversal.

TIP

Most important, the goal is not for you to think, "Wow, I need to implement this strategy right away." Rather, the goal is to analyze the way that you approach the market on a day-to-day or week-to-week basis and think about whether you're adequately taking into account time — because time may actually be more significant to a trader than price!

For the swing trader: The Favorite Fib strategy

The Favorite Fib is a Fibonacci-based strategy that takes advantage of momentum. It can be used on various time frames and markets, including forex majors, stock indices, and commodities, providing the trader with endless opportunities. The strategy may be used, for example, after some major economic news — ideally, at the earlier stages of the move following the news. But if the news merely causes a corrective rally or sell-off inside an established trend, then this strategy won't work as well. It's best suited for markets that are in a clear strong trend — for example, when the price is making fresh all-time, multiyear, or multi-month highs or lows.

A FIBONACCI REFRESHER

In the 13th century, Leonardo Fibonacci developed a sequence of numbers called the *Fibonacci sequence,* where each number in the series is the equivalent of the sum of the two numbers previous to it. (We could get really mathematical here, but we'll spare you the algebraic details.) This is the Fibonacci sequence: 0, 1, 1, 2, 3, 5, 8, 13, 21, 34, 55, 89, 144, and so on, out to infinity.

From this number sequence, we get Fibonacci ratios, which are important for traders. The math involved behind the Fibonacci ratios is pretty simple. All you have to do is take certain numbers from the Fibonacci sequence and follow a pattern of division throughout it. As an example, take a number in the sequence and divide it by the number that follows it:

$0 \div 1 = 0$

$1 \div 1 = 1$

$1 \div 2 = 0.5$

$2 \div 3 = 0.667$

$3 \div 5 = 0.6$

$5 \div 8 = 0.625$

$8 \div 13 = 0.615$

$13 \div 21 = 0.619$

$21 \div 34 = 0.618$

$34 \div 55 = 0.618$

$55 \div 89 = 0.618$

Notice a pattern developing here? Starting at $21 \div 34$ going out to infinity, you will *always* get 0.618! Other important ratios derived from Fibonacci numbers include 38.2 percent and 23.6 percent. (***Note:*** 50 percent isn't a Fibonacci ratio, but it's often used when looking at Fibonacci ratios.)

So, how do we use Fibonacci for trading? The relationship between these numbers gives us the common Fibonacci retracements pattern that is used in technical analysis. During a trend, currencies will often pull back or retrace a certain percentage of a previous move, before continuing in the previous trend. We use Fibonacci ratios to determine key support and resistance levels during this retracement process. You can also use Fibonacci extensions to see where prices may go in the future, based on the same Fibonacci ratios. (Chapter 6 has more information on technical analysis.)

The longer the time frame, the more effective the Favorite Fib strategy works. It's typically used on one- or four-hour time frames, although sometimes it can be applied to the daily time frame, too. The shortest time frame on which you can use this strategy is about 15 minutes.

TIP

If the trade is based on a longer time frame, it's a good idea to zoom in to a five-minute chart in order to refine entry.

How it works

The Favorite Fib strategy is based on some Fibonacci retracement and extension levels: the 38.2 percent and 50 percent retracement levels (the latter is not technically a Fibonacci level; see the nearby sidebar for more information), and the 127.2 percent, 161.8 percent, and 261.8 percent Fibonacci extension levels.

To understand how the strategy works, say that following a strong upward move (for example, from point A to point B), the market retraces a little (to point C) because of profit taking and/or top picking, before continuing in the original direction (beyond point B). The strategy requires three price swings — the move from point A to point B, from point B to point C (correction), and from point C to point D (extension). Figure A-5 shows what a Favorite Fib buy strategy would typically look like.

In the Favorite Fib strategy, you're interested in some part of the CD leg of the move — the bit beyond point B, where entry is based. The profit target would be determined by a Fibonacci extension level of the BC move (more on this later).

One condition for this strategy to work well is that you need momentum. By definition, this implies that point C should represent a shallow retracement of AB, and then a continuation in the original direction, beyond point B. So, if price retraces more than 50 percent, or too much time elapses before it breaks point B, then the entry signal would not be valid.

REMEMBER

In other words, for optimal entry signal, you need a strong move from point A to point B; a relatively quick and shallow retracement of less than 50 percent to point C; and then a continuation toward point D.

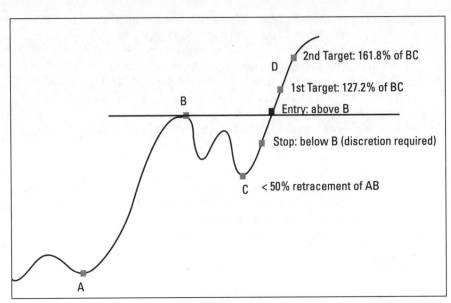

2nd Target: 161.8% of BC

D

1st Target: 127.2% of BC

B

Entry: above B

Stop: below B (discretion required)

C < 50% retracement of AB

A

© John Wiley & Sons, Inc.

FIGURE A-5:
An example of a
Fibonacci buy
strategy.

When point C is established, all the strategy's parameters can be determined.

Entry

The entry would be based on break of point B, and the objective is to ride the move toward point D, which would be a Fibonacci level, determined by the BC swing.

For a buy (sell) trade, the entry can be via a buy-stop (sell-stop) order a few pips/points above (below) point B, or it can be via a market/limit buy order after point B is broken.

Entry via a stop order ensures the trade will be triggered. However, in the case of a false breakout, it can mean buying (selling) right at the high (low). What's more, if the market gaps, the entry may not be at the same level as the one the trader had chosen.

Entry via a market or limit order allows the trader some time to determine whether the breakout above (below) point B is genuine or false. If price holds above (below) point B for, say, a few minutes, then the trader may want to buy (sell) at the best available price. However, the risk is that the market moves quickly toward the target without a pullback, and the trader misses the opportunity.

If the entry is based on a longer time frame — like the four-hour chart — the trader may want to hold fire and zoom into a five- or ten-minute chart and wait until price closes above (below) point B on the shorter time frame before buying (selling).

Targets

The Favorite Fib strategy has two targets:

» The 127.2 percent level of BC, at which point the stop loss would be adjusted to break even to eliminate risk

» The 161.8 percent extension level of BC (or sometimes the 261.8 percent), at which point the position should be closed

One way to estimate which level price will most likely extend to is by looking at the retracement of the AB swing (that is, point C). If the retracement is around 38.2 percent or lower, point D may be at the 161.8 percent or sometimes 261.8 percent extension of BC. However, if price achieves a deeper retracement — say, to the 61.8 percent or 78.6 percent Fibonacci level of AB, then you should expect point D to complete around the 127.2 percent extension of BC. Of course, this would *not* be a valid Favorite Fib entry, because the retracement is greater than 50 percent.

Stop loss

For a buy (sell) trade, the stop loss will be some distance below (above) point B, ideally below (above) a small fractal within the larger swing. The maximum distance between the stop loss and entry should be less than the distance between entry and the profit target. In other words, the risk-to-reward ratio should be better than 1:1 (ideally, 1:2 or better).

Final notes

Here are some final takeaways on the Favorite Fib strategy:

» For a higher probability trade, the entry should be in the direction of the underlying long- or medium-term trend.

» The speculator should be aware of other, longer-term technical levels when trading the Favorite Fib strategy. For example, if the 200-day moving average is at 1.8560 and the target for the long position is at 1.8580, this trade should not be taken. In this situation, it may be better to take profit at around the 200-day average rather than hope for price to reach the 161.8 percent extension (the original profit target that was based on a shorter time frame).

The minute you notice yourself *hoping* for something to happen is when you know the trade is in trouble — get out as soon as possible.

WARNING

» The trader should avoid taking on opposing simultaneous trades in similar markets (for example, going long on NZD/USD and short on AUD/USD). A trader who is feeling bearish about the AUD and at the same time bullish about NZD should look for a short trade on the AUD/NZD pair instead.

>> If price breaks point B, triggers the entry order, and then loses momentum prior to reaching the first target (127.2 percent), the trader should close the trade at the best available price (even if it's worse than the entry price — why wait until being stopped out?). After all, the whole objective of the entry was based on expectation of a generous continuation move, which hasn't happened.

REMEMBER

You can't force the market to give you what you desire. Never blame the market for getting it wrong — it all comes down to your own ability (or lack thereof) to respond to changing dynamics or conditions of the market.

The Favorite Fib strategy in action

Example 1: Buy NZD/USD

Figure A-6 shows you what NZD/USD looks like before it has reached its Favorite Fib target.

FIGURE A-6: NZD/USD hourly chart.

© John Wiley & Sons, Inc.

Figure A-7 shows you how NZD/USD managed to reach its target Fibonacci resistance level. Fibonacci can seem a bit like magic — the support and resistance levels really do work!

FIGURE A-7:
NZD/USD hit the target.

© John Wiley & Sons, Inc.

Example 2: Buy GBP/USD ahead of a key economic release

As you can see in Figure A-8, GBP/USD was trading higher ahead of a key economic release.

After the economic data release, the pound reached its target (see Figure A-9). This is another example of how Fibonacci extensions can work in practice.

FIGURE A-8:
GBP/USD
hourly chart.

For the swing trader: The Moving Average Crossover strategy

Moving averages are one of the most commonly used technical indicators across a wide range of markets. They have become a staple part of many trading strategies because they're simple to use and apply. Although moving averages have been around for a long time, their capability to be easily measured, tested, and applied makes them an ideal foundation for modern trading strategies, which can incorporate both technical and fundamental analyses.

The two main types of moving averages are simple moving averages and exponential moving averages; both are averages of a particular amount of data over a predetermined period of time. While simple moving averages aren't weighted toward any particular point in time, exponential moving averages put greater emphasis on more recent data. In this trading strategy, we focus on simple moving averages; the goal is to help determine entry and exit signals, as well as support and resistance levels.

GBP/USD 1HR

1.60874 _____ 261.8%

1.6073

1.6050

1.60099 _____ Target 161.8%

1.6000

1.59831 _____ 127.2%

1.59620 \ 1.59609

Bought 1.59640

1.5950

1.58887 _____ Target ↓ 38.2%

1.5900

1.58845 1.58840

1.5850

1.5800

1.57719

22:00   12th   20:00   13th   20:00   16th   16:00   17th   14:00   18th   12:00   23:00   19th

© John Wiley & Sons, Inc.

FIGURE A-9:
GBP/USD hourly
chart after the
economic data.

How it works

Most trading platforms plot simple moving averages for you, but it's important to understand how they're calculated so you can better comprehend what's happening with price action. For example, a ten-day SMA is calculated by getting the closing price over the last ten days and dividing it by ten. When plotted on a chart, the SMA appears as a line that approximately follows price action — the shorter the time period of the SMA, the closer it will follow price action.

A favorite trading strategy of ours involves 4-period, 9-period, and 18-period moving averages, helping to ascertain which direction the market is trending. The use of these three moving averages has been a favorite of many investors and gained notoriety in the futures market for stocks. We retain the basic concepts of this strategy but put our own spin on them and apply them to numerous markets.

REMEMBER

First, it's important to remember that shorter moving averages will hug price action more closely than longer ones because they're focused more on recent prices. From this, we can deduce that shorter moving averages will be the first to react to a movement in price action. In this case, we look at simple moving averages crossing over, which may signal a buy or sell opportunity, as well as when to exit the position (we use simple moving averages because they provide clearer signals in this case). It's important to note that this strategy should be used in conjunction with the overall trend of the market.

Entry

A buy/sell signal is given when the 4-period SMA crosses over the 9-period SMA *and* they both then cross over the 18-period SMA. Generally, the sharper the push from all moving averages, the stronger the buy/sell signal is, unless it's following a substantial move higher or lower. So, if price action is wandering sideways and the 4-period and 8-period SMAs just drift over the 18-period, then the buy/sell signal is weak, in which case we keep an eye on price to ensure it remains below/above the 18-period SMA. Whereas if the first two moving averages shoot above/below the 18-period SMA with a purpose, then the buy/sell signal is stronger. (In this case, a confirmation of a strong upward/downward trend can come from an aggressive push higher/lower from the 18-period SMA.)

Aggressive traders can enter the position if they see a strong crossover of the 4-period and the 9-period SMAs in anticipation of both crossing the 18-period SMA. In this case, we recommend ensuring that all moving averages are running in the direction of the break and that you keep a close eye on momentum. If momentum starts to dwindle early, it can be an indication of a weak trend.

REMEMBER

Keep an eye on the overall trend by using medium-term and long-term time frames. If the market is trending in either direction, then investors have to be watchful of retracements in the opposite direction. Sometimes price action can retrace sharply, which causes the 4-period and 9-period SMAs to cross over the 18-period quickly, but because it's a retracement and not part of the overall trend, price action can run out of steam fairly quickly. A trend that's losing momentum will become evident sooner in the short-term SMAs.

Exit

This is where the strategy becomes more subjective. Our favored path of attack from here is to judge the strength of the trend and proceed accordingly. You can wait for the aforementioned moving averages to recross each other, or you can use your own judgment to determine when to exit the position. In a strong trend, it's sometimes worth exiting the trend when it starts to head in the wrong direction over a few time periods, because sharp pushes in either direction can be subject to retracements. In weak trends, we tend to favor trailing stops. In any case, a big warning sign is when the 4-period and 9-period SMAs cross back over the 18-period SMA, especially if the trade isn't working out as planned (that is, it's a good time to get out to prevent possible further losses).

Stop

Ideally, a stop should be placed far enough away that it isn't triggered prematurely but close enough to minimize losses. It's basically there in case of a sharp spike in the wrong direction. In many cases, the 4-period and 8-period SMAs will cross over the 18-period SMA before a stop is triggered, which should be a signal to cut your losses.

Final notes

TIP

Here are some final takeaways on the Moving Average Crossover strategy:

» We highly recommend using stop orders for all trades; however, placing such orders will not necessarily limit your losses.

» Look at short and multiple time frames; for instance, look at both the 10- and 15-minute charts simultaneously.

» Center your trading strategy on an effective risk-reward ratio.

» Keep an eye on the overall trend. Cautious traders should avoid going against the grain.

» Have an exit strategy before you enter the trade and wait for the signals. Don't let emotions cloud your judgment as the market starts to move.

Investors may improve their odds of identifying trading by using this strategy in conjunction with other analysis, which can help to determine the overall trend of price action and why the market is reacting the way it is. Did price action just break a key resistance/support zone? Was there an event that caused price action to spike in either direction?

The Moving Average Crossover strategy in action

Buy example: USD/JPY ten-minute chart

Notice that there is a strong push higher in price action after the crossover, and then there are a few opportunities to exit the trade (see Figure A-10). It's also interesting to note that when the 4-period and 8-period SMAs cross back under the 18-period SMA, it's a very uninteresting crossover (price action and the SMAs are very flat), so it wouldn't entice us to get short.

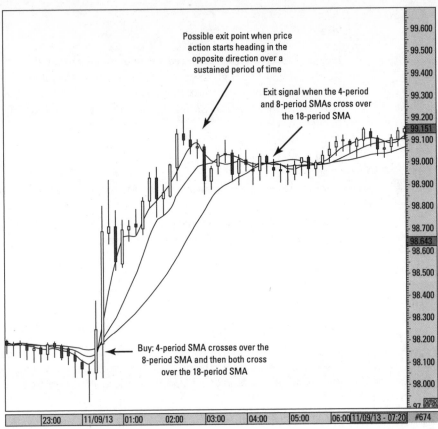

Possible exit point when price action starts heading in the opposite direction over a sustained period of time

Exit signal when the 4-period and 8-period SMAs cross over the 18-period SMA

Buy: 4-period SMA crosses over the 8-period SMA and then both cross over the 18-period SMA

© John Wiley & Sons, Inc.

FIGURE A-10:
Using moving averages to make a trade.

Sell example: NZD/USD 15-minute chart

Here, there isn't a strong sell signal, but the overall trend of the pair is lower, so we're comfortable getting short (see Figure A-11). We would obviously set a stop, which is largely discretionary, just in case price action suddenly shoots higher.

For the position trader: Trading the Ichimoku cloud

In this section, we provide a strategy for the position trader. We call it trading the Ichimoku cloud.

Sell: 4-period SMA crosses over the 8-period SMA and then both cross over the 18-period SMA

Two exit signals: price is starting to retrace and the 4-period and 8-period SMAs crossover the 18-period SMA

FIGURE A-11:
NZD/USD
short-term chart.

© John Wiley & Sons, Inc.

How it works

You may hear people talk about trading the cloud. They're referring to Ichimoku clouds (short for Ichimoku Kinko Hyo, which translates to "one-glance equilibrium chart"). It's a moving average–based trend identification system composed of five different lines, two of which form the system's main component, the cloud. Ichimoku analysis is primarily longer term and best utilized on daily or weekly charts. In addition to assisting in detecting trends, the components of the system are also very useful in identifying key levels of support and resistance. A unique feature of the cloud is that it factors in time as well as price, because the cloud is projected several periods outs.

The Ichimoku approach was developed in the 1930s in Japan by Goichi Hosoda, a Japanese journalist. Hosoda spent 30 years developing his idea before releasing his findings to the public in the 1960s. Despite the numerous components of the system, the approach is easy to understand and follow (there is a reason why it's named the "one-glance" chart). Furthermore, Ichimoku can be used for all liquid financial markets. In this section, we cover the components and derivations of the Ichimoku system and explain how signals of varying degrees of strength are formed.

The Ichimoku chart contains five different lines with both a Japanese name and an English name that can be used interchangeably. The lines are modified moving averages because they're calculated by using highs and lows rather than closing prices. These lines are overlaid on a price chart so that prices can be viewed in relation to the Ichimoku chart, allowing you to quickly and easily identify a trend, as well as key support and resistance levels.

The five lines of the Ichimoku chart and derivations are as follows:

» **Conversion (tenkan) line:** (Highest high + lowest low)/2 from prior 9 days

» **Base (kijun) line:** (Highest high + lowest low)/2 from prior 26 days

» **Leading span 1 (senkou span A):** Average of tenkan/kijun lines from prior 26 days projected 26 days ahead

» **Leading span 2 (senkou span B):** Daily average from prior 52 days projected 26 days ahead

» **Lagging span (chikou):** Today's close projected 26 days backward

TECHNICAL STUFF

The numbers 9, 26, and 52 are used in the traditional approach. In the past, a trading week in Japan was six days (one week minus Saturday). So, 9 represents a week and a half, 26 is the typical number of trading days in a month (30 days minus 4 Saturdays), and 52 is used to represent two months of trading days.

Ichimoku's most prominent feature, the cloud (kumo), is formed by leading spans 1 and 2. The space between the two lines creates the Ichimoku cloud.

There are a number of ways that signals can be formed using an Ichimoku chart. The most common method is to look at the price position relative to the cloud, also referred to as the *simple form.* A break above the cloud is viewed as a bullish signal, and a break below is seen as bearish. Price movement that is contained within the cloud shows a consolidation and, therefore, no clear trend.

Crossovers of the conversion (tenkan) and base (kijun) lines generate what are referred to as *main form signals.* This is similar to the typical moving average crossover where a faster moving average (the conversion line) crosses a slower moving average (the base line). When the faster moving average rises above the slower moving average, a bullish signal is generated. Likewise, when the faster moving average crosses below the slower one, a bearish signal is formed. The difference with the Ichimoku chart is that not all signals are equal. Signal strength depends on the location of prices relative to the cloud:

>> **Strong signal:** Price above/below the cloud in the direction of the crossover

>> **Medium signal:** Price inside the cloud

>> **Weak signal:** Price above the cloud when a bearish crossover occurs, or price below the cloud when a bullish crossover is made

The strategy in action

Figure A-12 shows you how to trade EUR/USD using Ichimoku clouds. As you can see, this is a slightly longer-term chart — it's a daily chart, because this strategy can favor traders who prefer a slightly longer time frame.

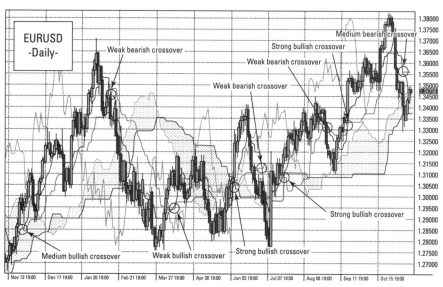

FIGURE A-12:
EUR/USD
daily chart.

© John Wiley & Sons, Inc.

Index

A

B

Bitcoin magazine (website), 322

Bitwise 10 crypto Index Fund (BITW), 318

Bitwise Crypto Industry Innovators ETF (BITQ), 318

black box funds, 46

Block Fi (website), 316

Bloomberg, 84, 91, 140

bonds, 33

The Book of Five Rings (Musashi), 339

breakouts, 215–220, 233

British pound, 29

British Retail Consortium (BRC) retail sales monitor and shop price index, 161

brokerage account, for cryptocurrency, 310

brokerage firms, choosing, 299–300

brokerage statements, 244

brokers

  choosing for cryptocurrency, 316–317

  for currency futures, 282

BTC etc Physical Bitcoin ETC (BTCE), 318

buck, 30

budget deficits, 158–159

building permits, 152

bull call spread, 296–297

bull flag, 121

bullish divergence, 132

bullish engulfing line, 127

bullish ETFs, 260–262

bullish Euro ETFs, 263–264

Bureau of Economic Analysis (website), 140

Bureau of Labor Statistics (website), 140, 141

business sector, 143

business transactions, cryptocurrency for, 310–311

business-level data reports, 152–155

buying

  call options, 285–288

  cryptocurrencies, 315–318

  at current market, 210

  online, 220–222

  simultaneously with selling, 53–59

by-elections, 105

C

calculating

  credit risk, 102–104

  markets with price bars, 115–116

  risk sentiment, 105, 106

calculating profit and loss with pips, 61–62

call options

  buying, 285–288

  writing, 289–292

Canada

  Canadian dollar, 29

  data reports, 162

  USD/CAD, 190–194, 196–198

Canadian dollar, 29. *See also* USD/CAD

canceling orders, 223

Candlestick Charting For Dummies (Rhoads), 116

candlestick patterns

  about, 115–117, 123–124

  doji, 124–125

  engulfing lines, 127

  hammers, 125–126

  shooting stars, 125–126

  spinning tops, 126–127

  tweezer bottoms, 127–128

  tweezer tops, 127–128

Cannon Trading (website), 282

capacity utilization, 154

capital expenditures, 143

capital gains

  evaluating scenarios of, 243–244

  long-term, 241–242

  short-term, 240

capital losses, 242–244

cash market, 38–41

CBI distributive trade survey, 161

central bankers, 90–91, 92

central banks

  about, 48–51

  effect of credibility on liquidity of EUR/USD, 168

Chancellor of the Exchequer, 97–98

changing interest rates incrementally, 88

M

main form signals, 377

maintenance requirements, in futures contracts, 272–273

manufacturing payrolls, in monthly employment report, 148

margin calls, 60

margin of error, allowing for a, 174

marginable, as a pro of currency ETFs, 258

margins
  balancing, 59–60
  factoring profit and loss into calculations, 62
  requirements of, in futures contracts, 272–273

market holidays, 65

market interest
  AUD/USD, 196–197
  defined, 22
  NZD/USD, 196–197
  USD/CAD, 196–197

Market Wizards: Interviews with Top Traders (Schwager), 339

markets
  buying at current, 210
  interbank, 38–41
  measuring with price bars, 115–116
  monitoring, 226–230, 333
  pricing in futures contracts, 272
  selling at current, 210
  stepping back from, 333
  watching other, 329

MarketWatch, 84, 91, 140

mark-to-market, 60

means of exchange, cryptocurrencies and, 309

measured move objective, 121

mechanics
  buying and selling simultaneously, 53–59
  currency prices, 67–68
  executing trades, 68–77
  interest rates, 62–67
  profit and loss, 59–62
  rollovers, 62–67

mergers & acquisitions (M&A), 44

minimum leveraging, 332

Ministry of Finance (MOF), 97, 177

minor currency pairs, 190–198

miscellaneous expenses, 247

Mladjenovic, Paul (author)
  High-Level Investing For Dummies, 305
  Investing in Gold and Silver For Dummies, 350
  Stock Investing For Dummies, 351

models, 46

momentum and trend analysis, 111

momentum oscillators, 130–133

momentum studies, 132

monetary policy
  about, 86–87
  benchmark interest rates, 87
  central bankers, 90–91, 92
  changing interest rates incrementally, 88
  expansionary, 87–88
  interpreting communications, 91–93
  restrictive, 88
  unconventional easing, 89

Monetary Policy Committees (MPCs), 92

money, taking out of trading accounts, 335

"moneyness" of call options, 287–288

monitoring
  markets, 226–230, 333
  other financial markets, 228–230
  trend lines, 231–233

Morningstar ETF ratings (website), 268

Morris, Virginia B. (author)
  A Guide to Investing with Options, 306

Moving Average Convergence/Divergence (MACD), 133

Moving Average Crossover strategy, 370–374

moving averages, 135–136

multilateral intervention, 100

Murphy, John J. (author)
  Technical Analysis of the Financial Markets: A Comprehensive Guide to Trading Methods and Applications, 338

unemployment rate, in monthly employment report, 147

unhedged currency ETFs, 265–267

unilateral intervention, 99

United Kingdom
  data reports, 161
  responsibility for currency in, 97–98

United States. *See also* U.S. dollar
  interest rates, 175–176
  market-moving economic data reports in, 146–159
  monthly employment report, 147–148
  responsibility for currency in, 96
  U.S. Treasury yields, 228–229

University of Michigan consumer sentiment index, 150

unrealized profit and loss, 60–61

updating
  order levels, 234–236
  trade plan, 230–234

U.S. dollar
  central role in forex markets, 54
  currency pairs, 55

U.S. dollar index, 28–30

USD/CAD currency pair
  tactical trading considerations in, 196–198
  trading fundamentals of, 190–194

USD/CHF, as leading indicator, 171

USD/JPY currency pair
  about, 174
  price action behavior, 179–181
  tactical trading considerations, 181–182
  trading fundamentals, 174–178

V

value dates, 64–65, 309

Van Commodities Inc. (website), 282

verbal intervention, 99

vertical calendar spreads, 295

VIX Index, 106

voice brokers, 40

volatility
  cryptocurrencies and, 309
  defined, 180
  of trades, 212

Volcker Rule, 40

Voyager (website), 316

W

waiting for confirmation, 114–115

wallet, cryptocurrency, 310

Warning icon, 4

wash-sale rule, 243

wealth effect, 151

websites
  ADP national employment report, 148
  BabyPips.com, 340
  Bankrate, 317
  Binance, 316
  Bitcoin magazine, 322
  Block Fi, 316
  Bloomberg, 84, 91, 140
  Bureau of Economic Analysis, 140
  Bureau of Labor Statistics, 140, 141
  Cannon Trading, 282
  Cheat Sheet, 5, 34
  Chicago Board Options Exchange (CBOE), 285, 305
  Chicago Mercantile Exchange (CME), 271, 282
  Chicago Mercantile Group, 305
  Coin Collecting, 354
  Coin Desk, 321
  Coin Gecko, 321
  Coin Market Cap, 322
  Coinbase, 316
  Collectors Weekly, 354
  Commerce Department, 140
  Commodity Futures Trading Commission (CFTC), 271
  Compare Brokers, 317
  Conference Board, 149
  Corporate Finance Institute, 154
  Cryptalker, 322

About the Authors

Paul Mladjenovic is the CEO of www.RavingCapitalist.com and was a Certified Financial Planner (CFP) from 1985 to 2021. He is the author of *Stock Investing For Dummies, Investing in Gold and Silver For Dummies, High-Level Investing For Dummies,* and other *For Dummies* titles. He joins Kathleen Brooks and Brian Dolan for the fourth edition of *Currency Trading For Dummies.* Paul has been a financial, business, and economics educator for nearly four decades, and his online courses can be found at his main site as well as on Udemy.com, Skillshare.com, and other educational platforms. He is frequently cited and/or interviewed by the financial media on current financial and economic issues. For continued guidance on currency trading, check out his dedicated reader page at www.RavingCapitalist.com/forex.

Kathleen Brooks is the research director at FOREX.com and has many years of experience in financial markets. FX is her specialty. She has worked in the institutional and retail side of forex trading, starting out as a trading analyst with BP. Kathleen produces research on G10 and emerging-market currencies using both fundamental and technical analysis methods. She focuses on providing FOREX.com clients with actionable trading ideas on a daily basis, alongside producing longer-term strategic pieces of research.

Kathleen has spearheaded FOREX.com's award-winning research offering since she joined GAIN Capital in 2010. She also led the development of its social media presence; the @FOREXcom Twitter account that she contributes to has more than 193,000 followers.

Her views on financial markets, economics, and politics are regularly quoted in the global financial press. She is a familiar face to many as a regular on business TV, including Bloomberg, BBC, Sky News, and Fox Business, both in the United Kingdom and farther afield. She also presents weekly webinars for FOREX.com and FXStreet and has spoken at forex and finance conferences around the world, including in London, the Middle East, and Australia.

Kathleen is also a published author, having penned *Kathleen Brooks on Forex* (Harriman House). Kathleen and her team at FOREX.com won Best Analysis at the 2014 FXStreet Forex Best Awards. She is a graduate of both Trinity College Dublin and Columbia University.

Brian Dolan is a 20-plus-year veteran of the currency market. He has analyzed the G10 currency markets with a blend of fundamental and technical analysis to provide actionable trading strategies.

Brian has also been a frequent commentator on currency-market developments for major news media, including the *Wall Street Journal*, Reuters, Bloomberg, Dow Jones, CNN Money, and MarketWatch. Prior to his time at GAIN Capital, Brian was a vice president at Bank Julius Bär, where he advised hedge funds and high-net-worth individuals on currencies. He spent the first 12 years of his forex career trading major currency pairs in the interbank market in New York at some of the world's largest banks, including Credit Suisse, Dai-Ichi Kangyo Bank, and American Express Bank, as well as two years in Bermuda as a proprietary trader at Butterfield Bank. Brian is a graduate of Dartmouth College.

Dedication

Paul Mladjenovic: I dedicate this fourth edition to the works of Kathleen Brooks and Brian Dolan in providing their forex guidance in the first three editions. I also dedicate this to the appreciated readers in the *For Dummies* universe . . . I wish all of you continued success and my gratitude for joining this author team.

Authors' Acknowledgments

Kathleen Brooks and Brian Dolan: Readers of this book will benefit from the experience we've gained from our time at GAIN Capital. From the trading team to marketing and client services, there are so many people who have helped guide the research team and make it what it is today. A special mention to Samantha Roady for setting the whole process in motion and encouraging us to go the full distance. How could we forget the rest of FOREX.com's award-wining research team: Chris Tedder, Matt Weller, Fawad Razaqzada, and Neal Gilbert. You can thank them for contributing their superb forex-trading strategies to the appendix of this book. Finally, thanks to all the editors and staff at John Wiley & Sons, Inc., who have helped with this edition.

Publisher's Acknowledgments

Associate Acquisitions Editor: Kelsey Baird

Senior Managing Editor: Kristie Pyles

Project Manager and Development Editor: Georgette Beatty

Copy Editor: Christine Pingleton

Technical Editor: Tod McElhaney

Production Editor: Tamilmani Varadharaj

Cover Image: © bbostjan/Getty Images

Take dummies with you everywhere you go!

Whether you are excited about e-books, want more from the web, must have your mobile apps, or are swept up in social media, dummies makes everything easier.

Find us online!

f y ▶ g+ in p

dummies.com

dummies
A Wiley Brand

Leverage the power

Dummies is the global leader in the reference category and one of the most trusted and highly regarded brands in the world. No longer just focused on books, customers now have access to the dummies content they need in the format they want. Together we'll craft a solution that engages your customers, stands out from the competition, and helps you meet your goals.

Advertising & Sponsorships

Connect with an engaged audience on a powerful multimedia site, and position your message alongside expert how-to content. Dummies.com is a one-stop shop for free, online information and know-how curated by a team of experts.

- Targeted ads
- Video
- Email Marketing
- Microsites
- Sweepstakes sponsorship

20 MILLION PAGE VIEWS EVERY SINGLE MONTH

15 MILLION UNIQUE VISITORS PER MONTH

43% OF ALL VISITORS ACCESS THE SITE VIA THEIR MOBILE DEVICES

700,000 NEWSLETTER SUBSCRIPTIONS TO THE INBOXES OF

300,000 UNIQUE INDIVIDUALS EVERY WEEK

# of dummies

Custom Publishing

Reach a global audience in any language by creating a solution that will differentiate you from competitors, amplify your message, and encourage customers to make a buying decision.

- Apps
- Books
- eBooks
- Video
- Audio
- Webinars

Brand Licensing & Content

Leverage the strength of the world's most popular reference brand to reach new audiences and channels of distribution.

For more information, visit dummies.com/biz

PERSONAL ENRICHMENT

Staying Sharp
9781119187790
USA $26.00
CAN $31.99
UK £19.99

Facebook
9781119179030
USA $21.99
CAN $25.99
UK £16.99

Guitar
9781119293354
USA $24.99
CAN $29.99
UK £17.99

Investing
9781119293347
USA $22.99
CAN $27.99
UK £16.99

Beekeeping
9781119310068
USA $22.99
CAN $27.99
UK £16.99

Digital Photography
9781119235606
USA $24.99
CAN $29.99
UK £17.99

Meditation
9781119251163
USA $24.99
CAN $29.99
UK £17.99

Pregnancy
9781119235491
USA $26.99
CAN $31.99
UK £19.99

Samsung Galaxy S7
9781119279952
USA $24.99
CAN $29.99
UK £17.99

iPhone
9781119283133
USA $24.99
CAN $29.99
UK £17.99

Crocheting
9781119287117
USA $24.99
CAN $29.99
UK £16.99

Nutrition
9781119130246
USA $22.99
CAN $27.99
UK £16.99

PROFESSIONAL DEVELOPMENT

Windows 10
9781119311041
USA $24.99
CAN $29.99
UK £17.99

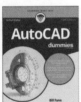

AutoCAD
9781119255796
USA $39.99
CAN $47.99
UK £27.99

Excel 2016
9781119293439
USA $26.99
CAN $31.99
UK £19.99

QuickBooks 2017
9781119281467
USA $26.99
CAN $31.99
UK £19.99

macOS Sierra
9781119280651
USA $29.99
CAN $35.99
UK £21.99

LinkedIn
9781119251132
USA $24.99
CAN $29.99
UK £17.99

Windows 10 All-in-One
9781119310563
USA $34.00
CAN $41.99
UK £24.99

SharePoint 2016
9781119181705
USA $29.99
CAN $35.99
UK £21.99

Fundamental Analysis
9781119263593
USA $26.99
CAN $31.99
UK £19.99

Networking
9781119257769
USA $29.99
CAN $35.99
UK £21.99

Office 2016
9781119293477
USA $26.99
CAN $31.99
UK £19.99

Office 365
9781119265313
USA $24.99
CAN $29.99
UK £17.99

Salesforce.com
9781119239314
USA $29.99
CAN $35.99
UK £21.99

Coding
9781119293323
USA $29.99
CAN $35.99
UK £21.99

dummies.com

dummies
A Wiley Brand